7

KISS HIM, NOT ME!

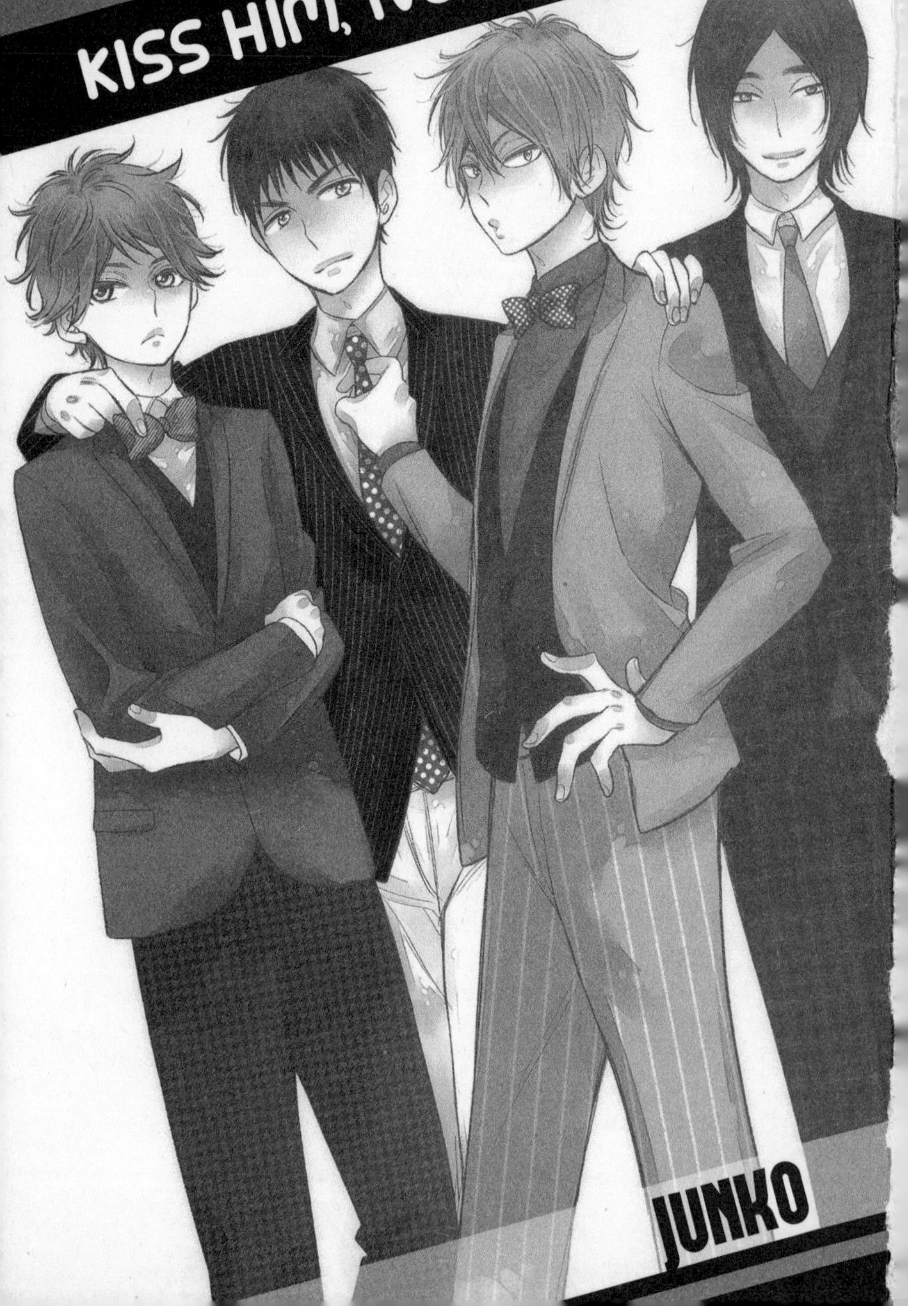

JUNKO

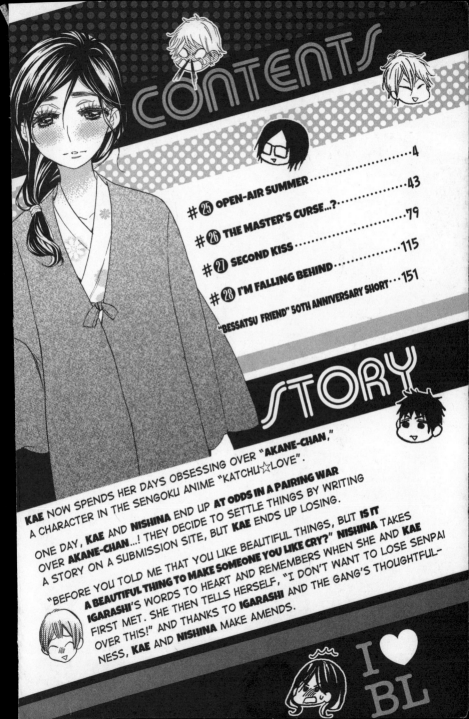

CONTENTS

STORY

KAE NOW SPENDS HER DAYS OBSESSING OVER "AKANE-CHAN," A CHARACTER IN THE SENGOKU ANIME "KATCHU☆LOVE".

ONE DAY, KAE AND NISHINA END UP AT ODDS IN A PAIRING WAR OVER AKANE-CHAN...! THEY DECIDE TO SETTLE THINGS BY WRITING A STORY ON A SUBMISSION SITE, BUT KAE ENDS UP LOSING.

"BEFORE YOU TOLD ME THAT YOU LIKE BEAUTIFUL THINGS, BUT IS IT A BEAUTIFUL THING TO MAKE SOMEONE YOU LIKE CRY?" NISHINA TAKES IGARASHI'S WORDS TO HEART AND REMEMBERS WHEN SHE AND KAE FIRST MET. SHE THEN TELLS HERSELF, "I DON'T WANT TO LOSE SENPAI OVER THIS!" AND THANKS TO IGARASHI AND THE GANG'S THOUGHTFUL-NESS, KAE AND NISHINA MAKE AMENDS.

I♥BL

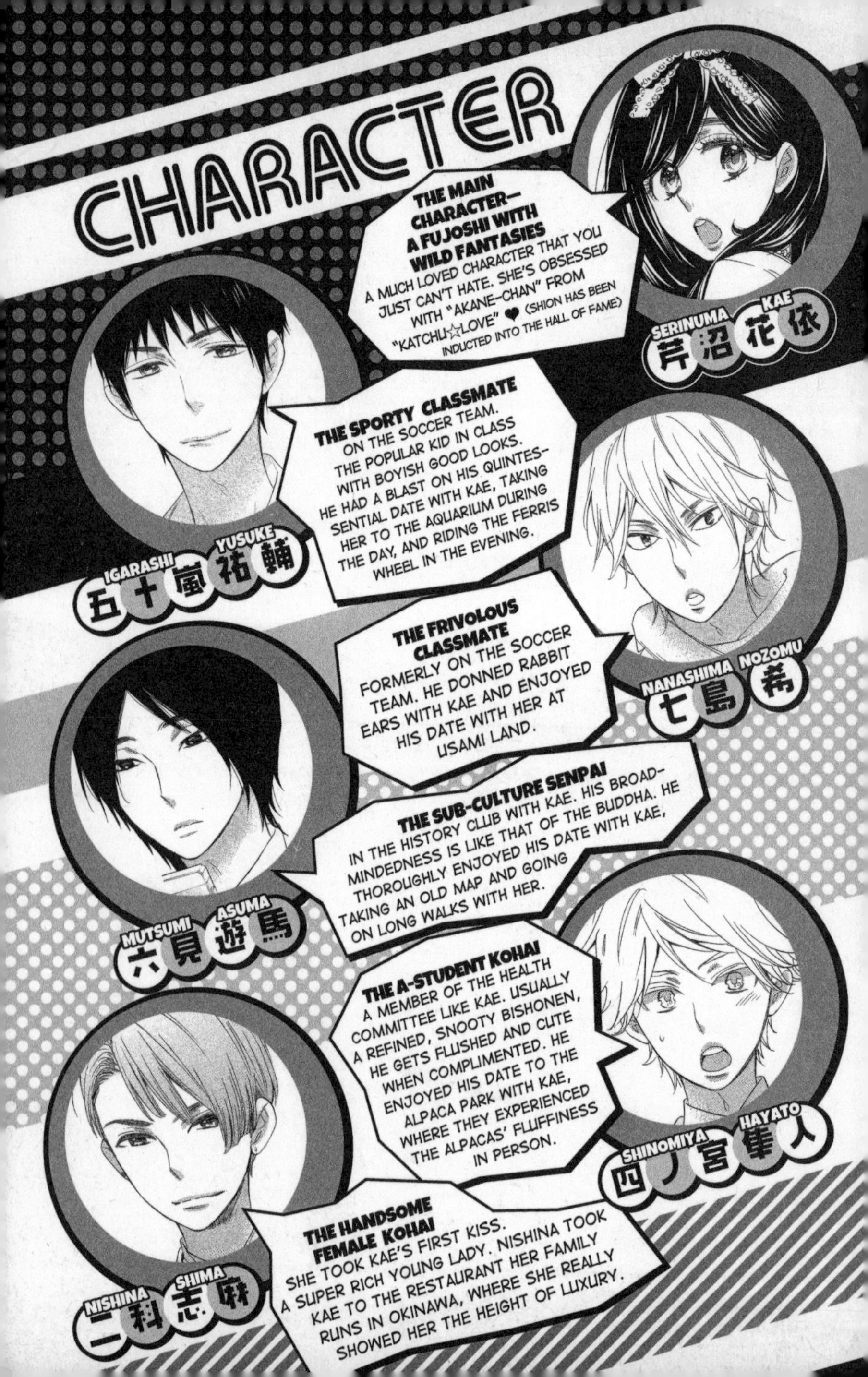
CHARACTER
THE MAIN CHARACTER—A FUJOSHI WITH WILD FANTASIES
A MUCH LOVED CHARACTER THAT YOU JUST CAN'T HATE. SHE'S OBSESSED WITH "AKANE-CHAN" FROM "KATCHU☆LOVE" ❤ (SHION HAS BEEN INDUCTED INTO THE HALL OF FAME)
SERINUMA KAE
芹沼花依
THE SPORTY CLASSMATE
ON THE SOCCER TEAM. THE POPULAR KID IN CLASS WITH BOYISH GOOD LOOKS. HE HAD A BLAST ON HIS QUINTES-SENTIAL DATE WITH KAE, TAKING HER TO THE AQUARIUM DURING THE DAY, AND RIDING THE FERRIS WHEEL IN THE EVENING.
IGARASHI YUSUKE
五十嵐祐輔
THE FRIVOLOUS CLASSMATE
FORMERLY ON THE SOCCER TEAM. HE DONNED RABBIT EARS WITH KAE AND ENJOYED HIS DATE WITH HER AT USAMI LAND.
NANASHIMA NOZOMU
七島希
THE SUB-CULTURE SENPAI
IN THE HISTORY CLUB WITH KAE. HIS BROAD-MINDEDNESS IS LIKE THAT OF THE BUDDHA. HE THOROUGHLY ENJOYED HIS DATE WITH KAE, TAKING AN OLD MAP AND GOING ON LONG WALKS WITH HER.
MUTSUMI ASUMA
六見遊馬
THE A-STUDENT KOHAI
A MEMBER OF THE HEALTH COMMITTEE LIKE KAE. USUALLY A REFINED, SNOOTY BISHONEN, HE GETS FLUSHED AND CUTE WHEN COMPLIMENTED. HE ENJOYED HIS DATE TO THE ALPACA PARK WITH KAE, WHERE THEY EXPERIENCED THE ALPACAS' FLUFFINESS IN PERSON.
SHINOMIYA HAYATO
四ノ宮隼人
THE HANDSOME FEMALE KOHAI
SHE TOOK KAE'S FIRST KISS. A SUPER RICH YOUNG LADY. NISHINA TOOK KAE TO THE RESTAURANT HER FAMILY RUNS IN OKINAWA, WHERE SHE REALLY SHOWED HER THE HEIGHT OF LUXURY.
NISHINA SHIMA
二科志麻

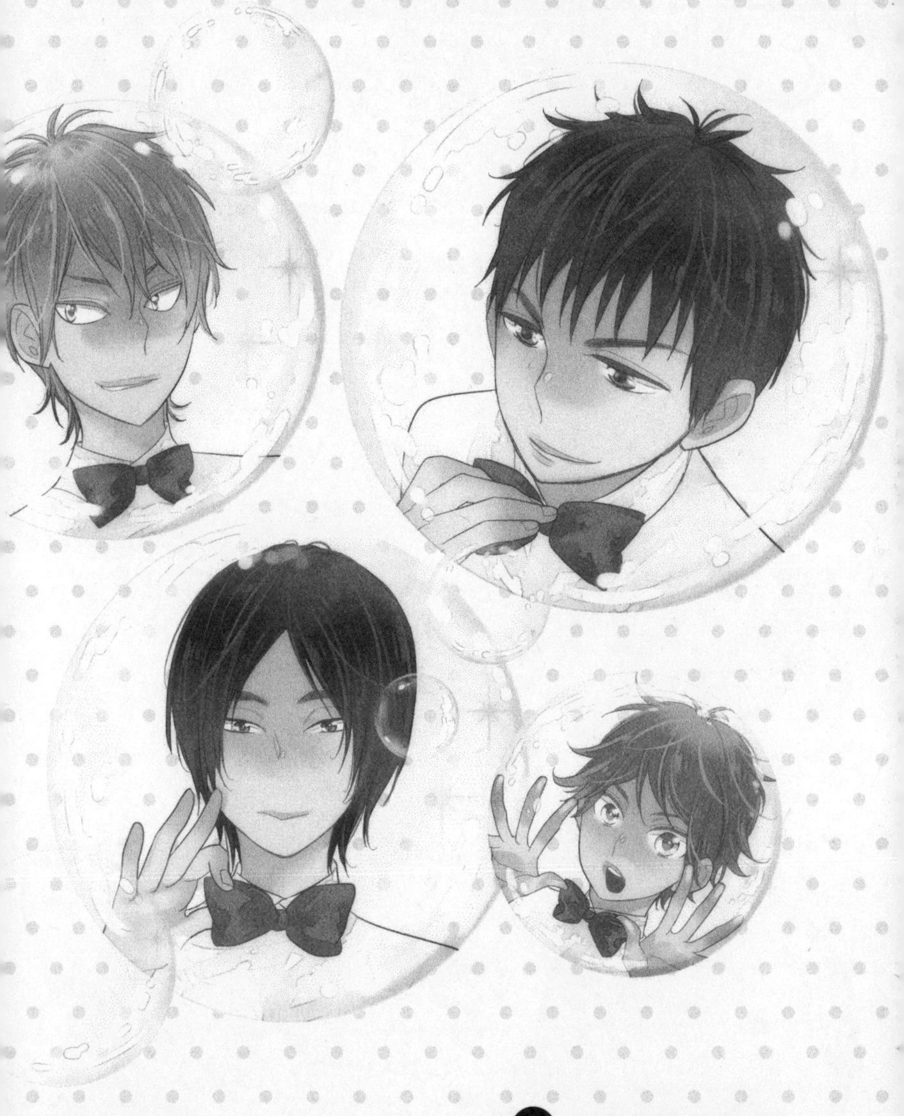

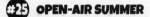

#25 OPEN-AIR SUMMER

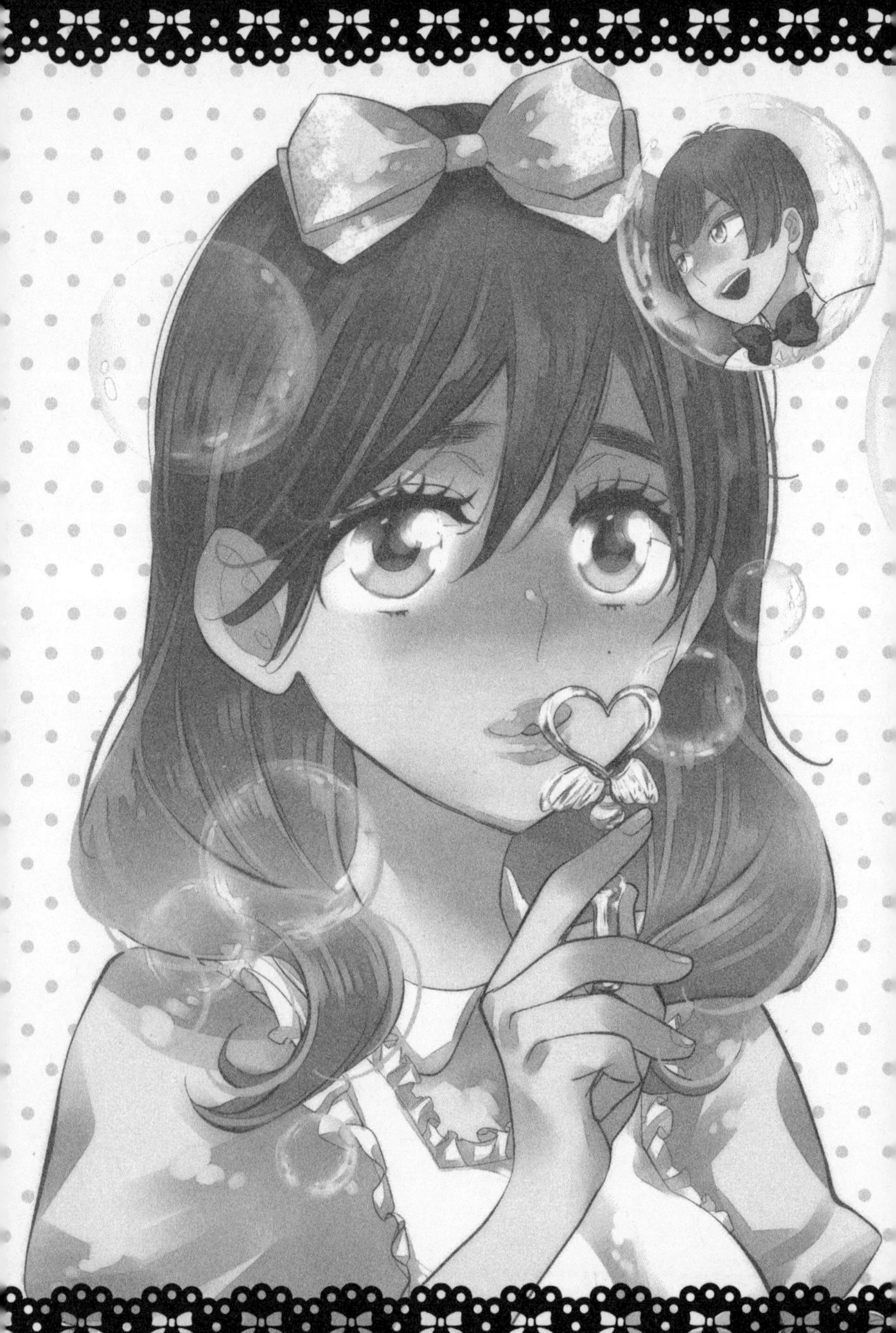

KISS HIM, NOT ME!

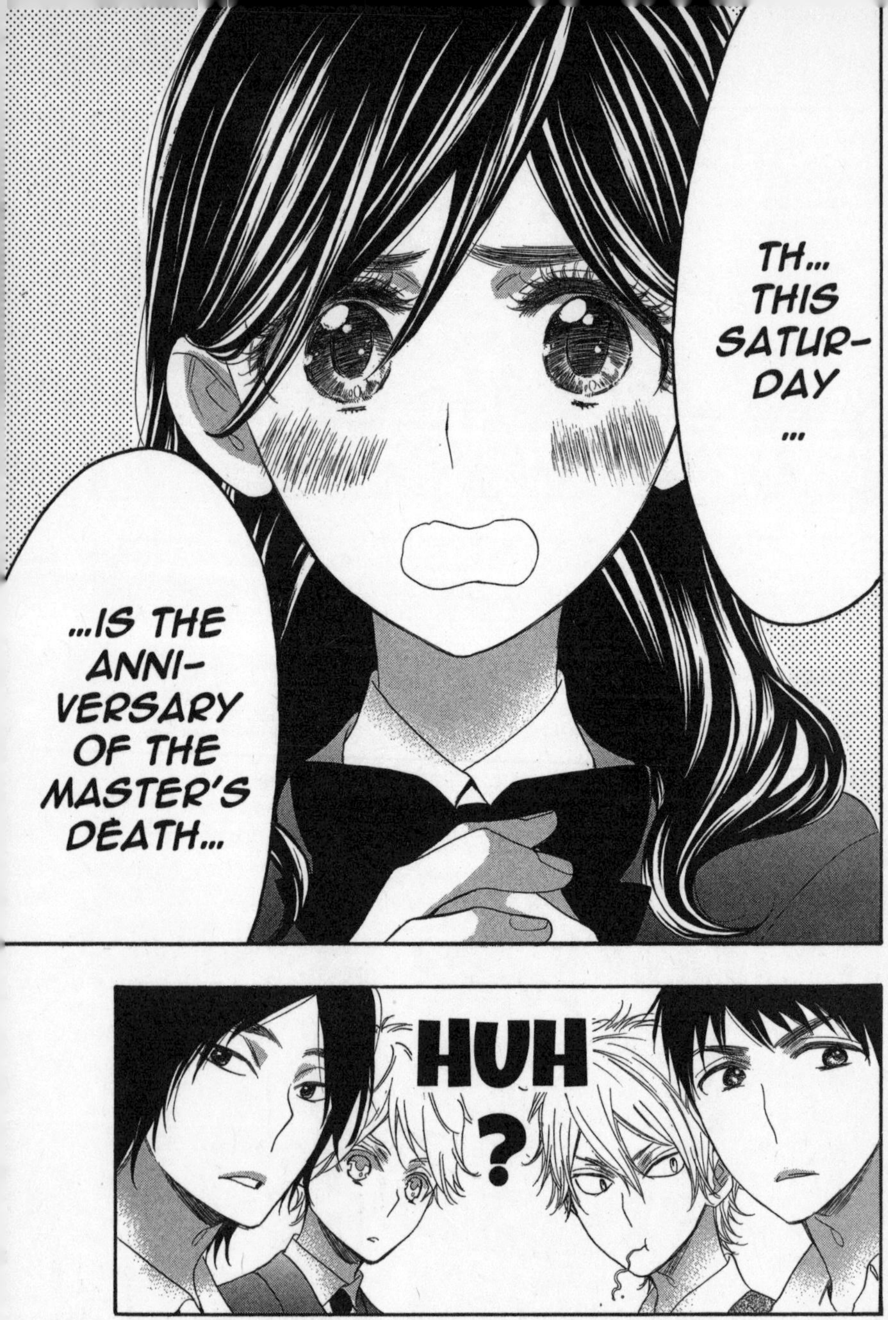
TH... THIS SATUR-DAY ...
...IS THE ANNI-VERSARY OF THE MASTER'S DEATH...
HUH ?

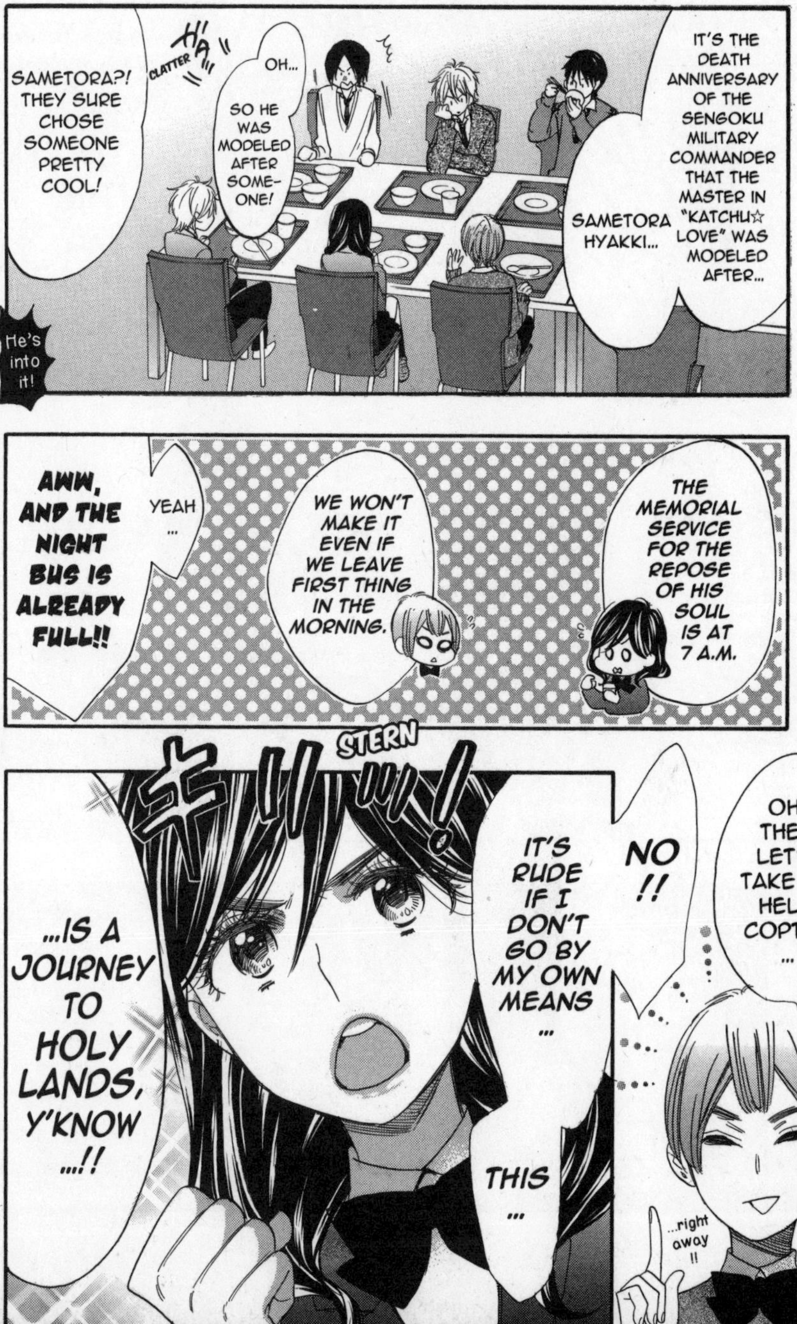
IT'S THE DEATH ANNIVERSARY OF THE SENGOKU MILITARY COMMANDER THAT THE MASTER IN "KATCHU☆LOVE" WAS MODELED AFTER...
SAMETORA HYAKKI...
OH... SO HE WAS MODELED AFTER SOME-ONE!
HA
CLATTER
SAMETORA?! THEY SURE CHOSE SOMEONE PRETTY COOL!
He's into it!
THE MEMORIAL SERVICE FOR THE REPOSE OF HIS SOUL IS AT 7 A.M.
WE WON'T MAKE IT EVEN IF WE LEAVE FIRST THING IN THE MORNING.
YEAH ...
AWW, AND THE NIGHT BUS IS ALREADY FULL!!
STERN
OH! THEN LET'S TAKE MY HELI-COPTER ...
We'll get there ...
...right away !!
NO !!
IT'S RUDE IF I DON'T GO BY MY OWN MEANS ...
THIS ...
...IS A JOURNEY TO HOLY LANDS, Y'KNOW ...!!

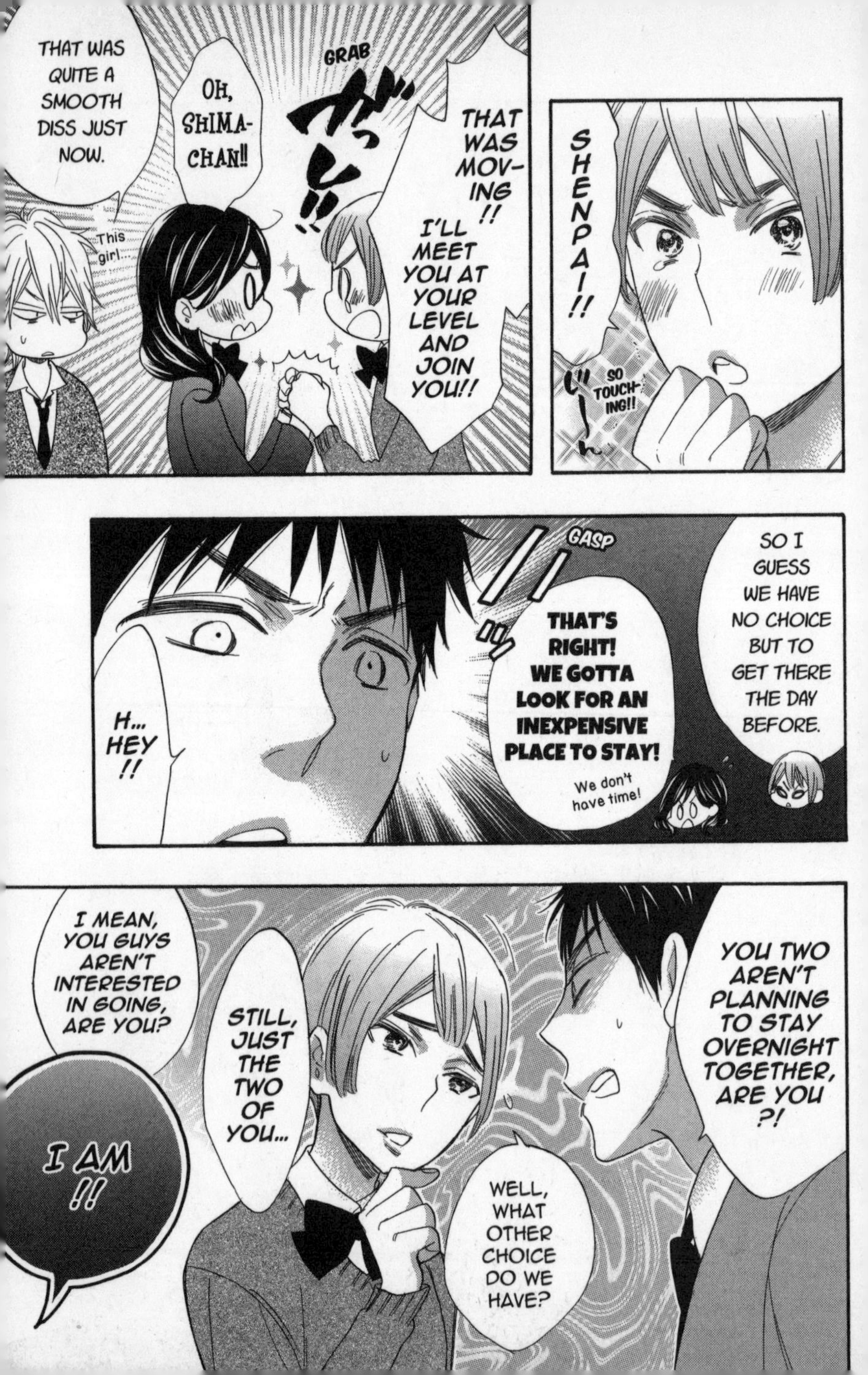
SHENPAI!!
SO TOUCHING!!
THAT WAS MOVING!! I'LL MEET YOU AT YOUR LEVEL AND JOIN YOU!!
GRAB
OH, SHIMA-CHAN!!
THAT WAS QUITE A SMOOTH DISS JUST NOW.
This girl...
SO I GUESS WE HAVE NO CHOICE BUT TO GET THERE THE DAY BEFORE.
GASP
THAT'S RIGHT! WE GOTTA LOOK FOR AN INEXPENSIVE PLACE TO STAY!
We don't have time!
H... HEY!!
YOU TWO AREN'T PLANNING TO STAY OVERNIGHT TOGETHER, ARE YOU?!
WELL, WHAT OTHER CHOICE DO WE HAVE?
STILL, JUST THE TWO OF YOU...
I MEAN, YOU GUYS AREN'T INTERESTED IN GOING, ARE YOU?
I AM!!

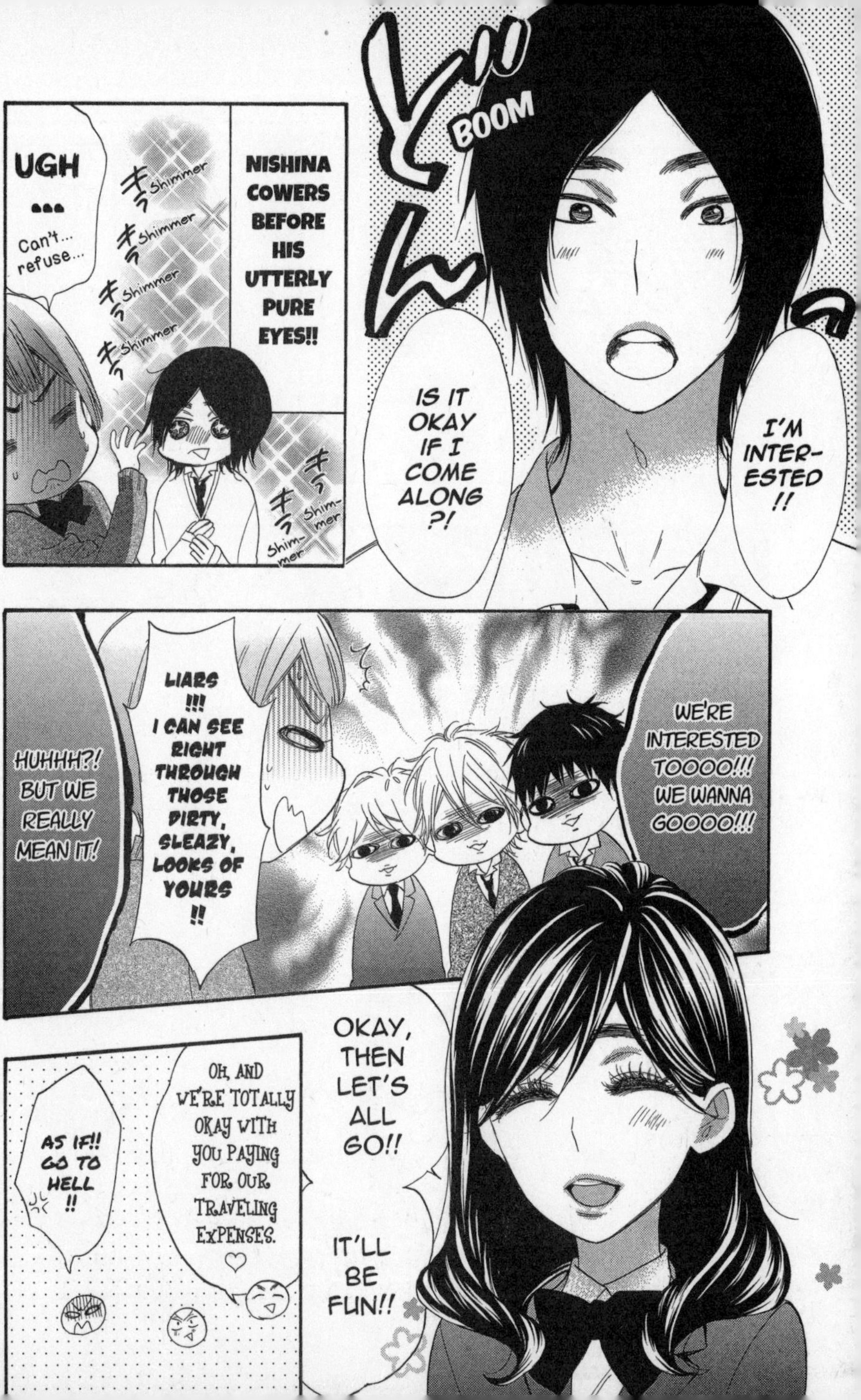
BOOM
I'M INTERESTED!!
IS IT OKAY IF I COME ALONG?!
NISHINA COWERS BEFORE HIS UTTERLY PURE EYES!!
Shimmer
Shimmer
Shimmer
Shimmer
Shimmer
Shimmer
UGH...
Can't... refuse...
WE'RE INTERESTED TOOOO!!! WE WANNA GOOOO!!!
LIARS!!! I CAN SEE RIGHT THROUGH THOSE DIRTY, SLEAZY, LOOKS OF YOURS!!
HUHHH?! BUT WE REALLY MEAN IT!
OKAY, THEN LET'S ALL GO!!
IT'LL BE FUN!!
OH, AND WE'RE TOTALLY OKAY WITH YOU PAYING FOR OUR TRAVELING EXPENSES. ♡
AS IF!! GO TO HELL!!

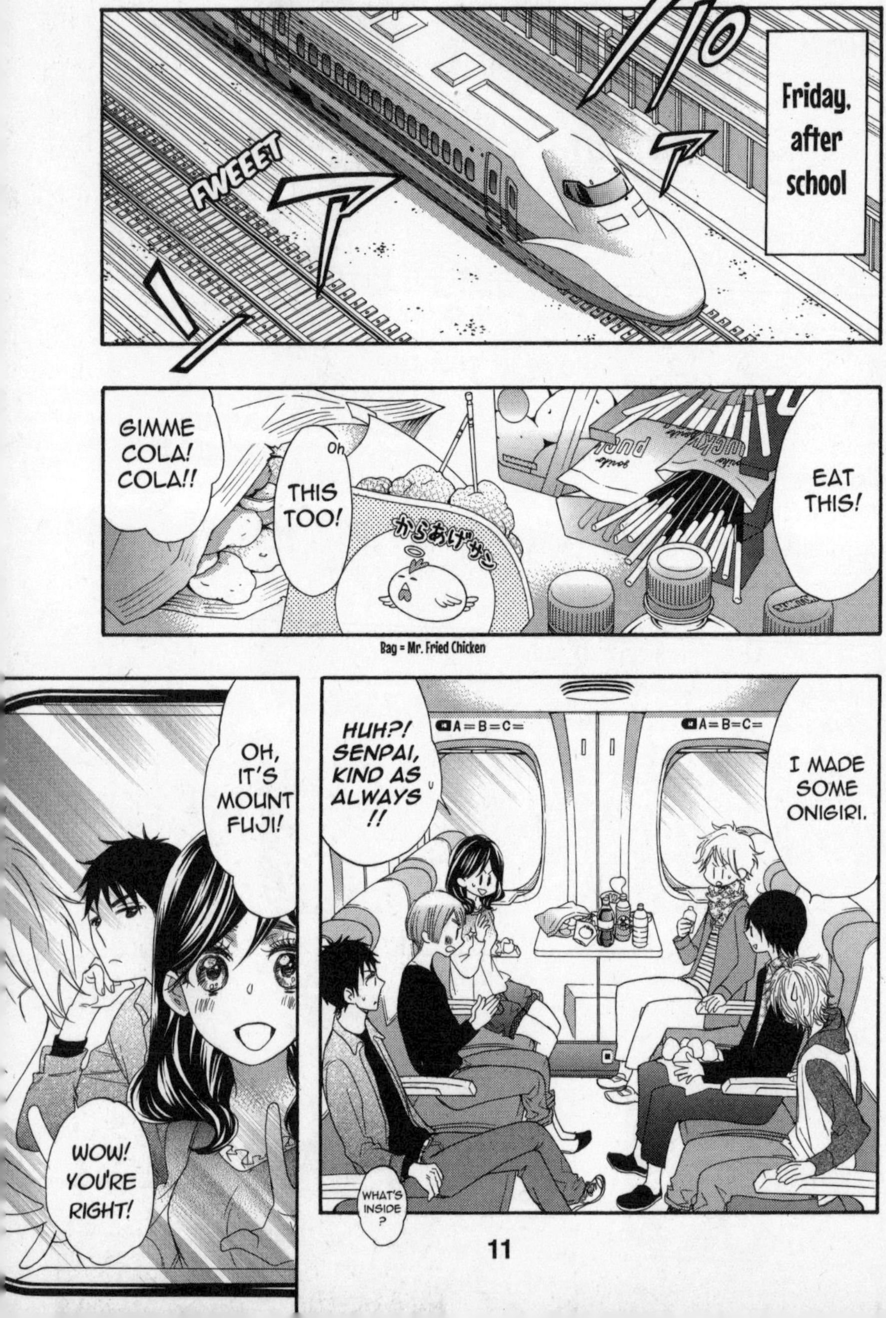
Friday, after school
FWEEET
EAT THIS!
Oh
THIS TOO!
GIMME COLA! COLA!!
からあげサン
I MADE SOME ONIGIRI.
A=B=C=
A=B=C=
HUH?! SENPAI, KIND AS ALWAYS!!
WHAT'S INSIDE?
OH, IT'S MOUNT FUJI!
WOW! YOU'RE RIGHT!
Bag = Mr. Fried Chicken

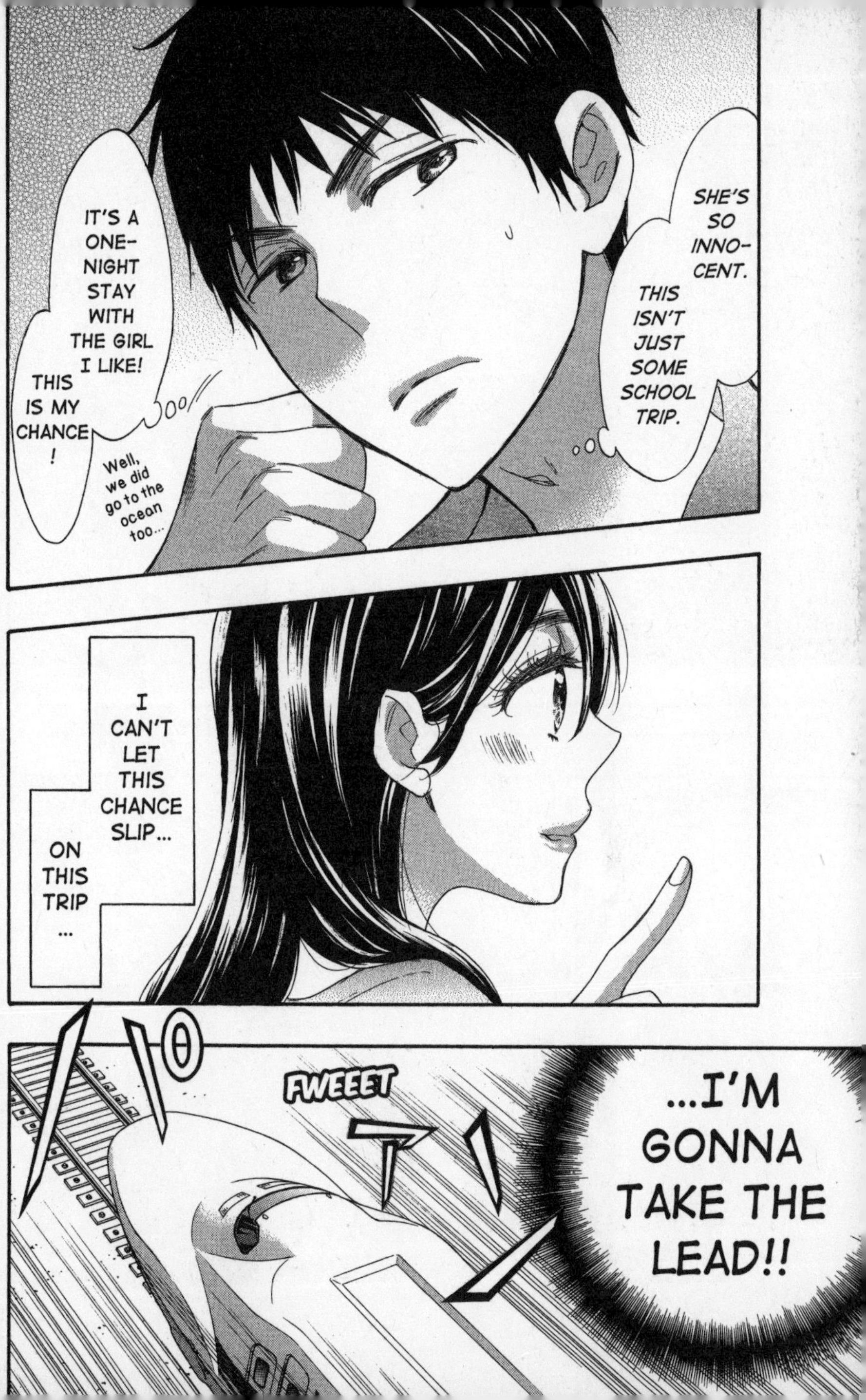
SHE'S SO INNO-CENT.
THIS ISN'T JUST SOME SCHOOL TRIP.
IT'S A ONE-NIGHT STAY WITH THE GIRL I LIKE!
THIS IS MY CHANCE!
Well, we did go to the ocean too...
I CAN'T LET THIS CHANCE SLIP...
ON THIS TRIP...
...I'M GONNA TAKE THE LEAD!!
FWEEET

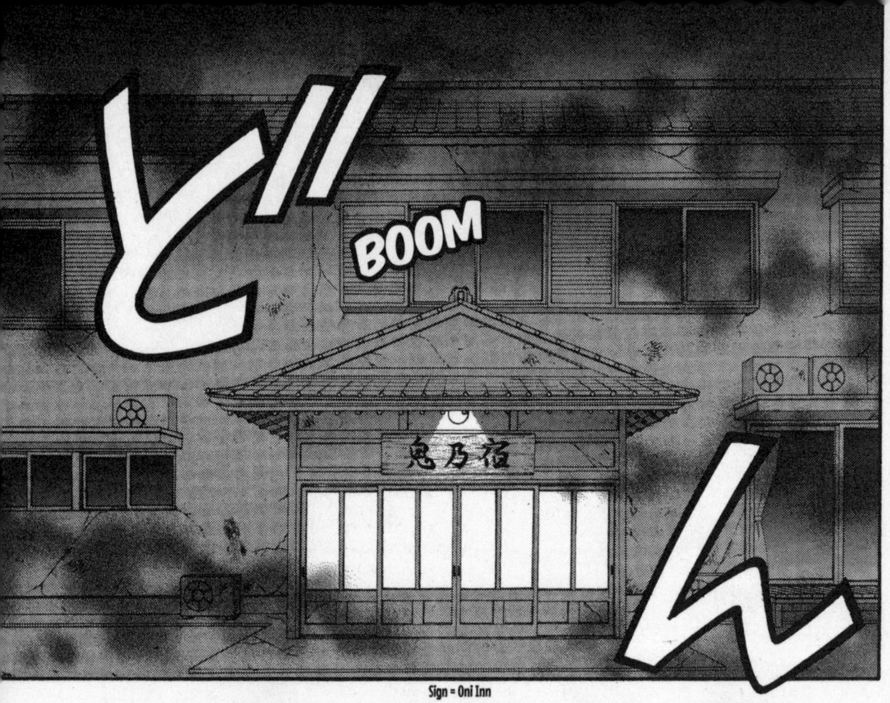
BOOM
鬼乃宿

Sign = Oni Inn

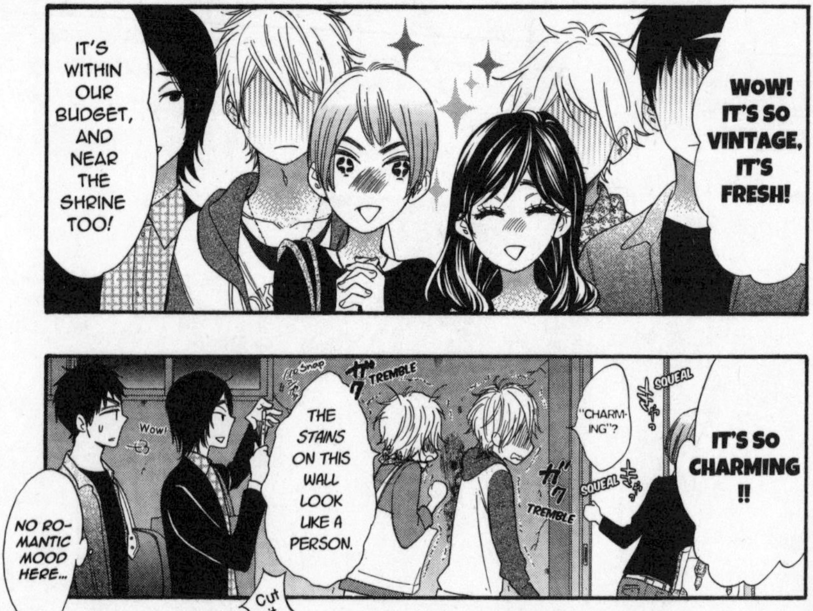
WOW! IT'S SO VINTAGE, IT'S FRESH!
IT'S WITHIN OUR BUDGET, AND NEAR THE SHRINE TOO!
IT'S SO CHARMING!!
SQUEAL
SQUEAL
"CHARM-ING"?
TREMBLE
TREMBLE
Snap
THE STAINS ON THIS WALL LOOK LIKE A PERSON.
Cut it out!
Wow!
NO RO-MANTIC MOOD HERE...

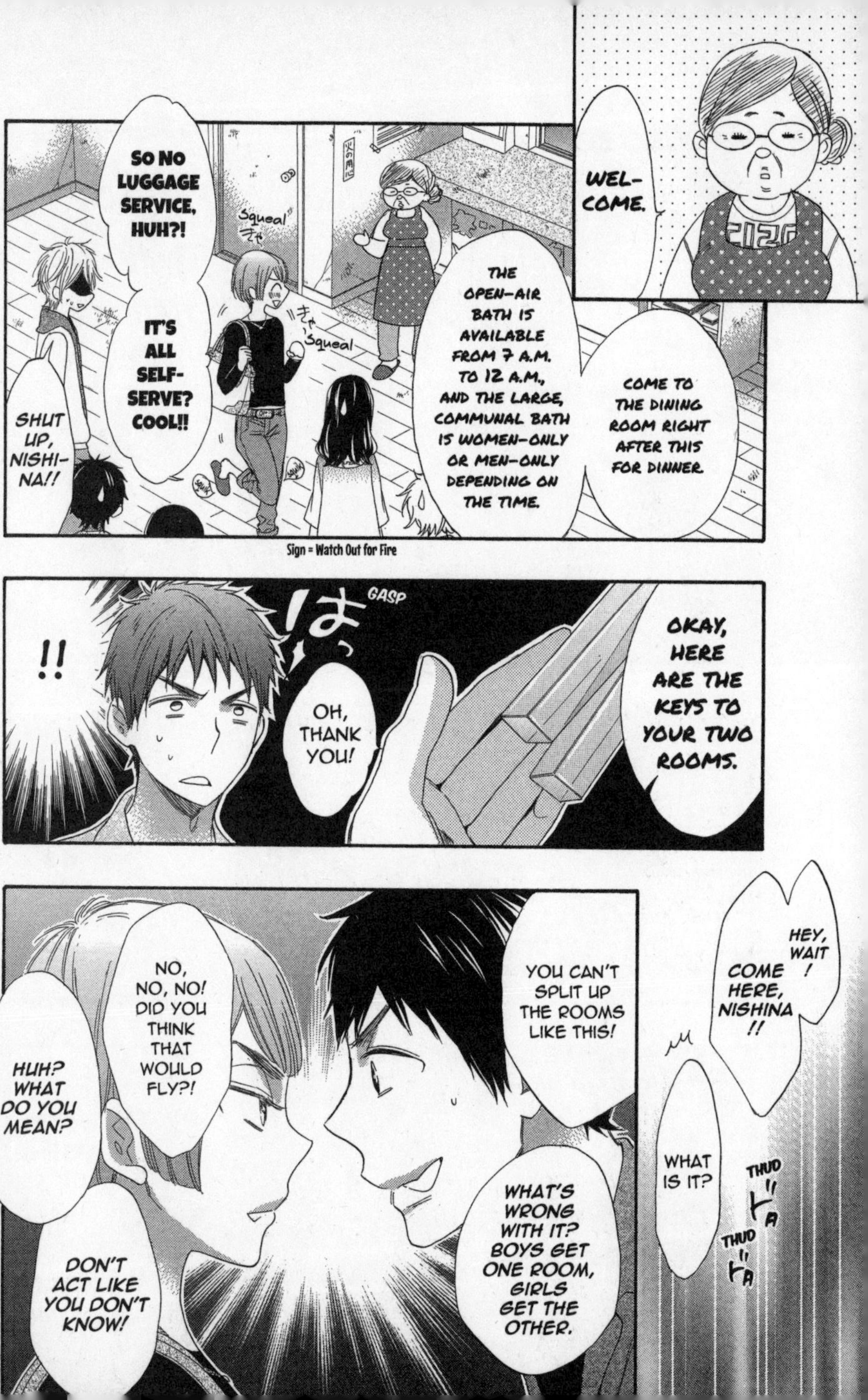
WEL- COME.
COME TO THE DINING ROOM RIGHT AFTER THIS FOR DINNER.
THE OPEN-AIR BATH IS AVAILABLE FROM 7 A.M. TO 12 A.M., AND THE LARGE, COMMUNAL BATH IS WOMEN-ONLY OR MEN-ONLY DEPENDING ON THE TIME.
Squeal きゃ
Squeal きゃ
SO NO LUGGAGE SERVICE, HUH?!
IT'S ALL SELF-SERVE? COOL!!
SHUT UP, NISHINA!!
OKAY, HERE ARE THE KEYS TO YOUR TWO ROOMS.
GASP はっ
OH, THANK YOU!
!!
HEY, WAIT!
COME HERE, NISHINA!!
WHAT IS IT?
THUD ドッ
THUD ドッ
YOU CAN'T SPLIT UP THE ROOMS LIKE THIS!
WHAT'S WRONG WITH IT? BOYS GET ONE ROOM, GIRLS GET THE OTHER.
NO, NO, NO! DID YOU THINK THAT WOULD FLY?!
HUH? WHAT DO YOU MEAN?
DON'T ACT LIKE YOU DON'T KNOW!

Sign = Watch Out for Fire

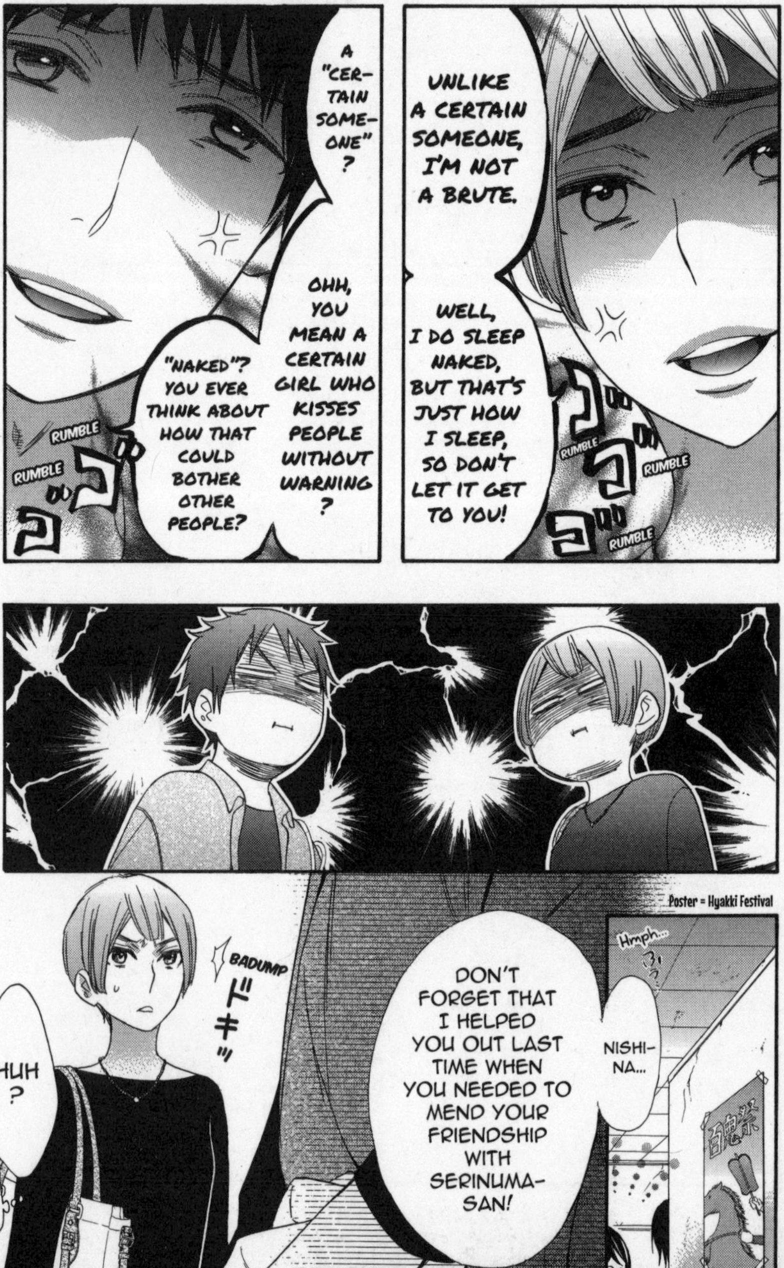
UNLIKE A CERTAIN SOMEONE, I'M NOT A BRUTE.
A "CERTAIN SOMEONE"?
WELL, I DO SLEEP NAKED, BUT THAT'S JUST HOW I SLEEP, SO DON'T LET IT GET TO YOU!
RUMBLE RUMBLE RUMBLE
OHH, YOU MEAN A CERTAIN GIRL WHO KISSES PEOPLE WITHOUT WARNING?
"NAKED"? YOU EVER THINK ABOUT HOW THAT COULD BOTHER OTHER PEOPLE?
RUMBLE RUMBLE
Poster = Hyakki Festival
Hmph...
NISHINA...
DON'T FORGET THAT I HELPED YOU OUT LAST TIME WHEN YOU NEEDED TO MEND YOUR FRIENDSHIP WITH SERINUMA-SAN!
BADUMP
HUH?
So he wants me to return the favor...?

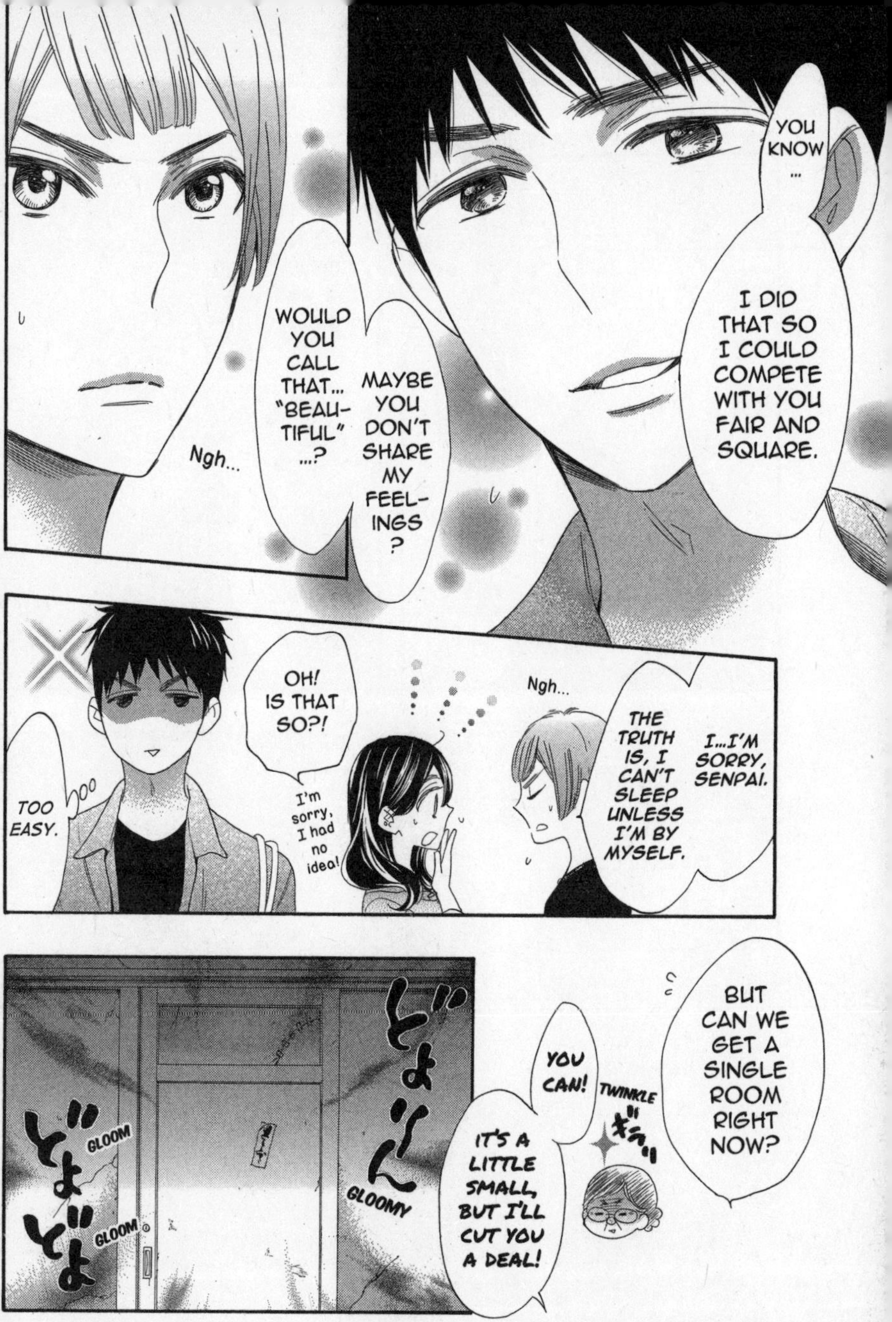
YOU KNOW ...
I DID THAT SO I COULD COMPETE WITH YOU FAIR AND SQUARE.
MAYBE YOU DON'T SHARE MY FEELINGS?
WOULD YOU CALL THAT... "BEAUTIFUL" ...?
Ngh...
I...I'M SORRY, SENPAI.
THE TRUTH IS, I CAN'T SLEEP UNLESS I'M BY MYSELF.
Ngh...
OH! IS THAT SO?!
I'm sorry, I had no idea!
TOO EASY.
BUT CAN WE GET A SINGLE ROOM RIGHT NOW?
YOU CAN!
TWINKLE
IT'S A LITTLE SMALL, BUT I'LL CUT YOU A DEAL!
どよ〜ん
GLOOMY
どよどよ
GLOOM
GLOOM

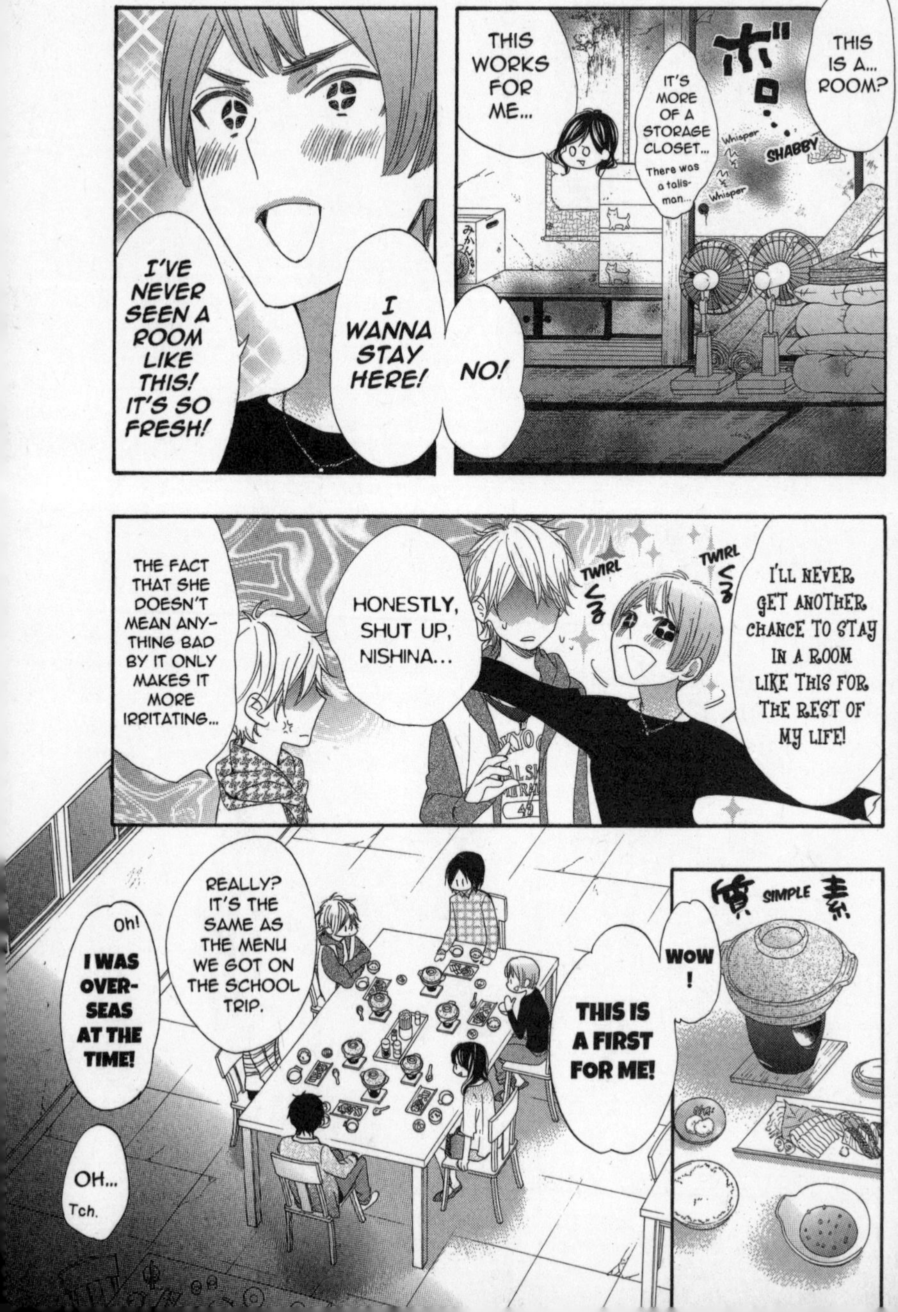
THIS IS A... ROOM?
ボロ
SHABBY
Whisper
IT'S MORE OF A STORAGE CLOSET...
There was a talisman...
Whisper
THIS WORKS FOR ME...
NO!
I WANNA STAY HERE!
I'VE NEVER SEEN A ROOM LIKE THIS! IT'S SO FRESH!
I'LL NEVER GET ANOTHER CHANCE TO STAY IN A ROOM LIKE THIS FOR THE REST OF MY LIFE!
TWIRL
TWIRL
HONESTLY, SHUT UP, NISHINA...
THE FACT THAT SHE DOESN'T MEAN ANY-THING BAD BY IT ONLY MAKES IT MORE IRRITATING...
質
SIMPLE
素
WOW!
THIS IS A FIRST FOR ME!
REALLY? IT'S THE SAME AS THE MENU WE GOT ON THE SCHOOL TRIP.
Oh!
I WAS OVER-SEAS AT THE TIME!
OH...
Tch.

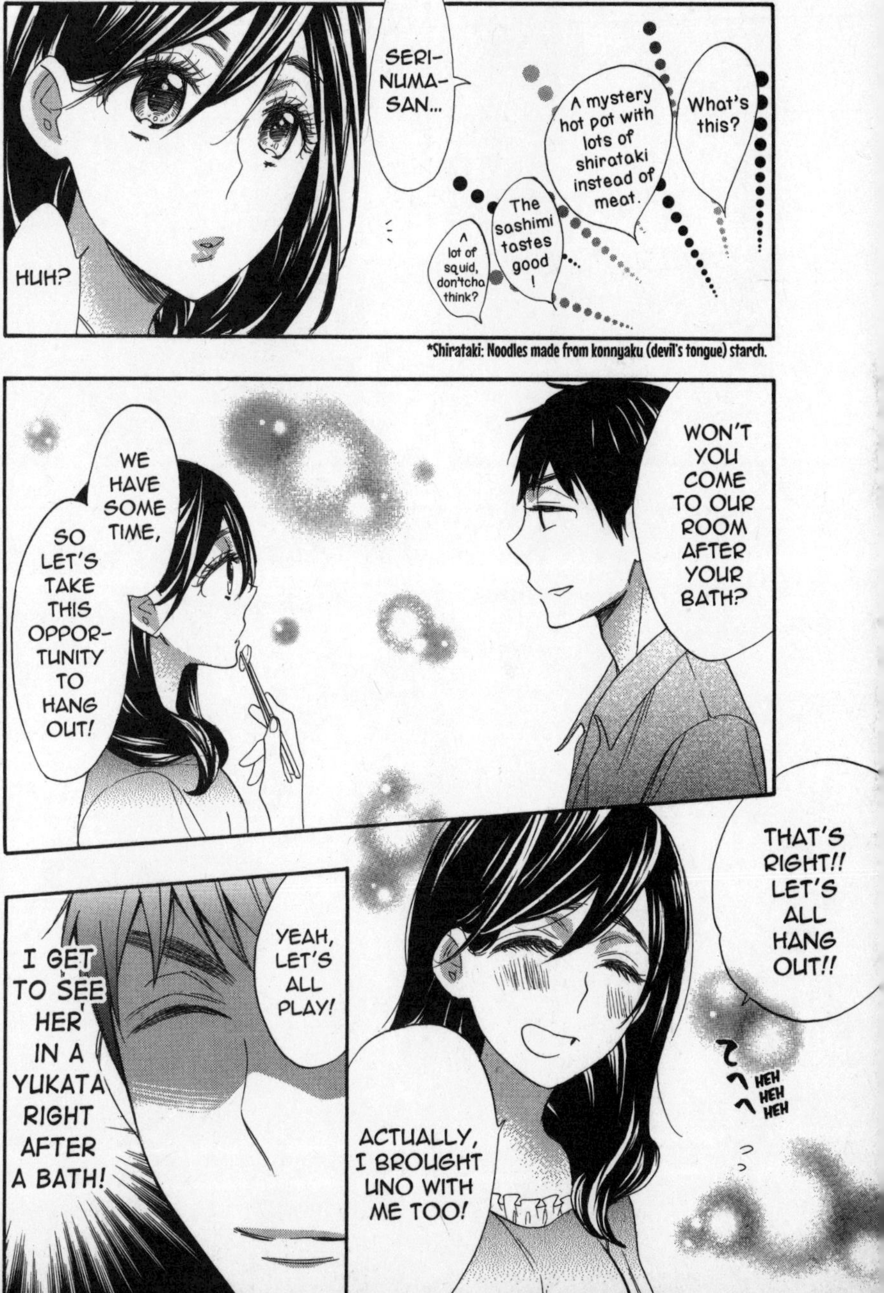
What's this?
A mystery hot pot with lots of shirataki instead of meat.
The sashimi tastes good!
A lot of squid, don'tcha think?
SERI-NUMA-SAN...
HUH?
*Shirataki: Noodles made from konnyaku (devil's tongue) starch.
WON'T YOU COME TO OUR ROOM AFTER YOUR BATH?
WE HAVE SOME TIME, SO LET'S TAKE THIS OPPORTUNITY TO HANG OUT!
THAT'S RIGHT!! LET'S ALL HANG OUT!!
HEH HEH HEH
ACTUALLY, I BROUGHT UNO WITH ME TOO!
YEAH, LET'S ALL PLAY!
I GET TO SEE HER IN A YUKATA RIGHT AFTER A BATH!

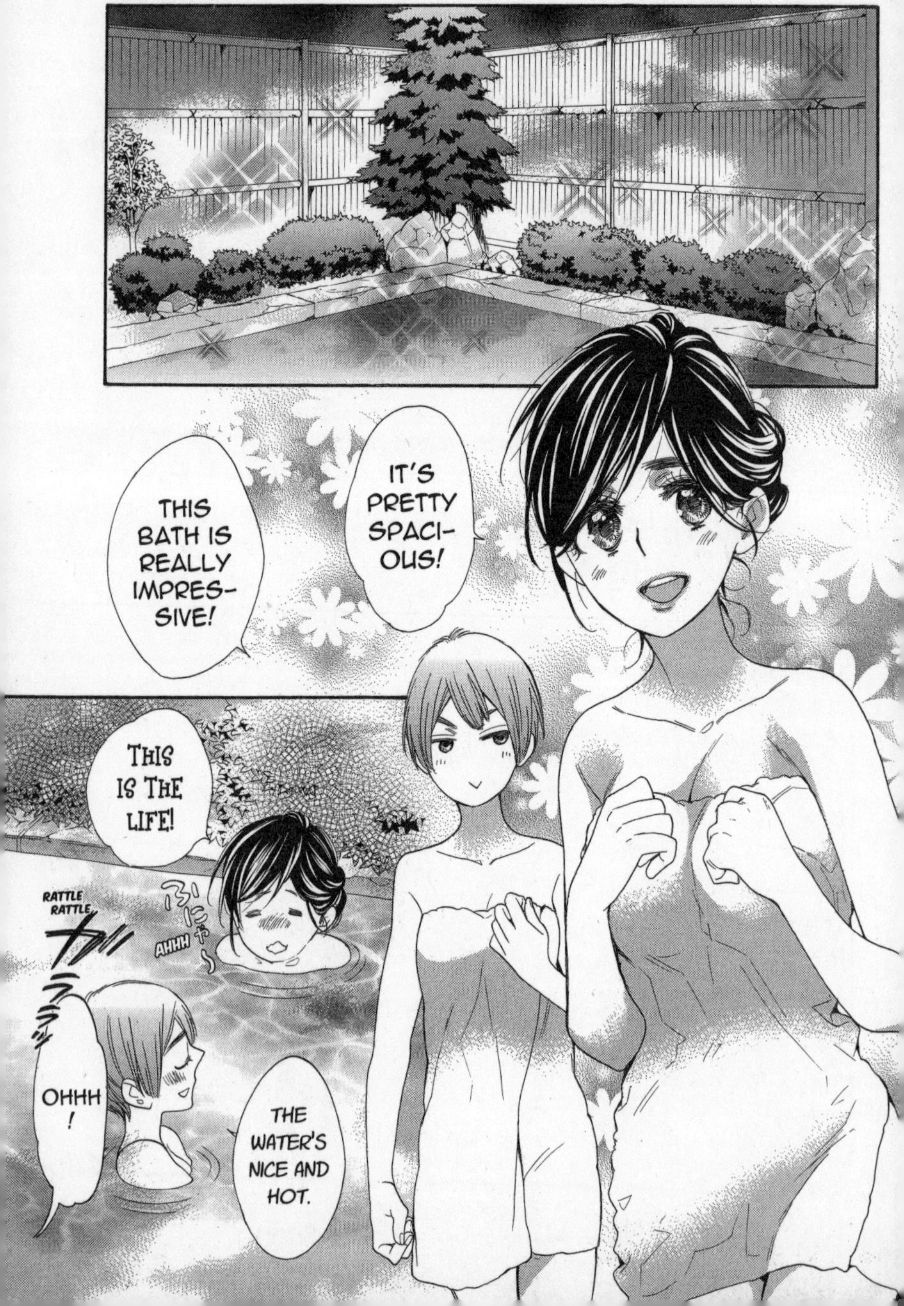

IT'S PRETTY SPACIOUS!
THIS BATH IS REALLY IMPRESSIVE!
THIS IS THE LIFE!
ふにゃ~
AHHH
THE WATER'S NICE AND HOT.
ガラララッ
RATTLE RATTLE
OHHH!

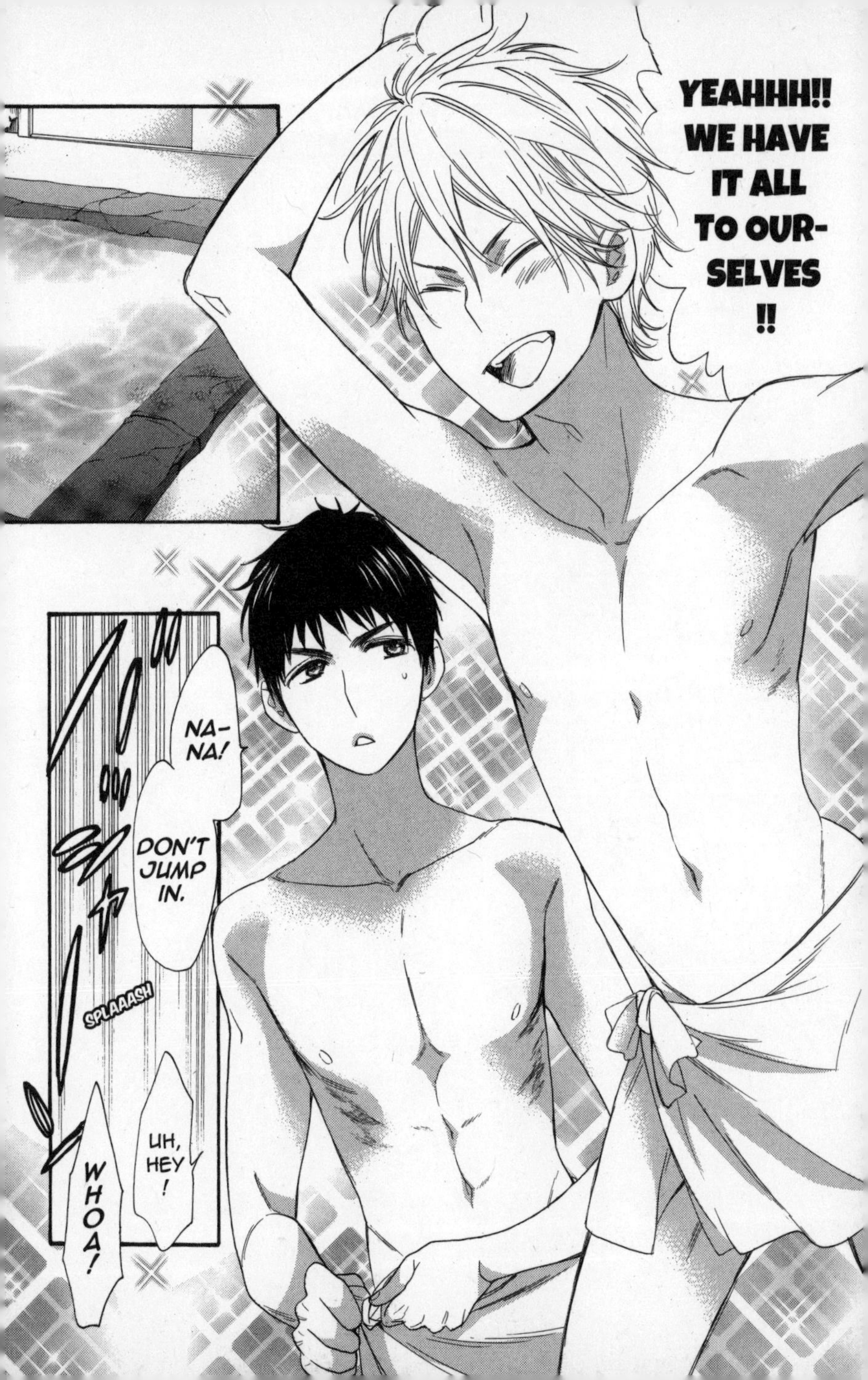
YEAHHH!! WE HAVE IT ALL TO OURSELVES!!
NA-NA!
DON'T JUMP IN.
SPLAAASH
UH, HEY!
WHOA!

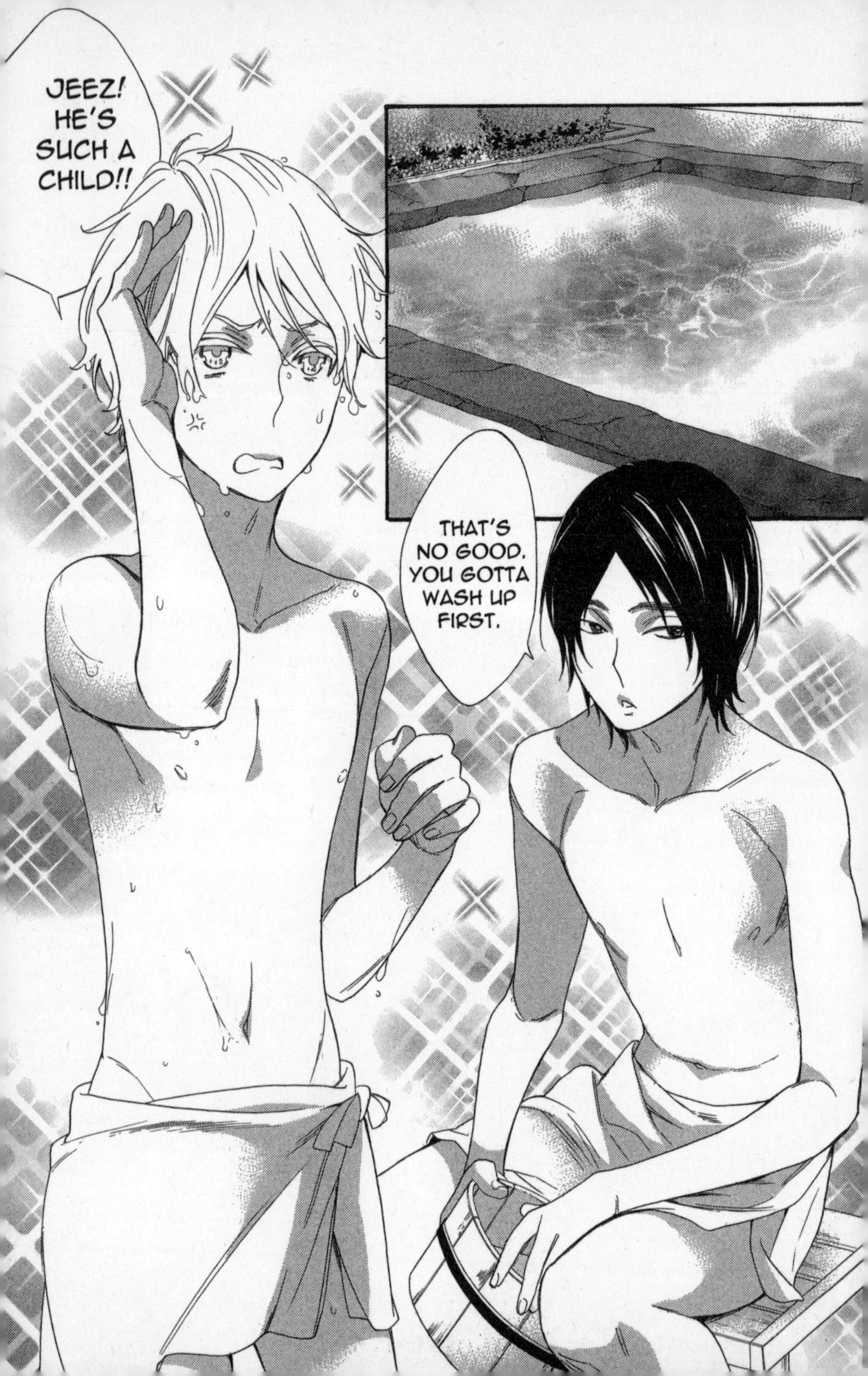
THAT'S NO GOOD. YOU GOTTA WASH UP FIRST.
JEEZ! HE'S SUCH A CHILD!!

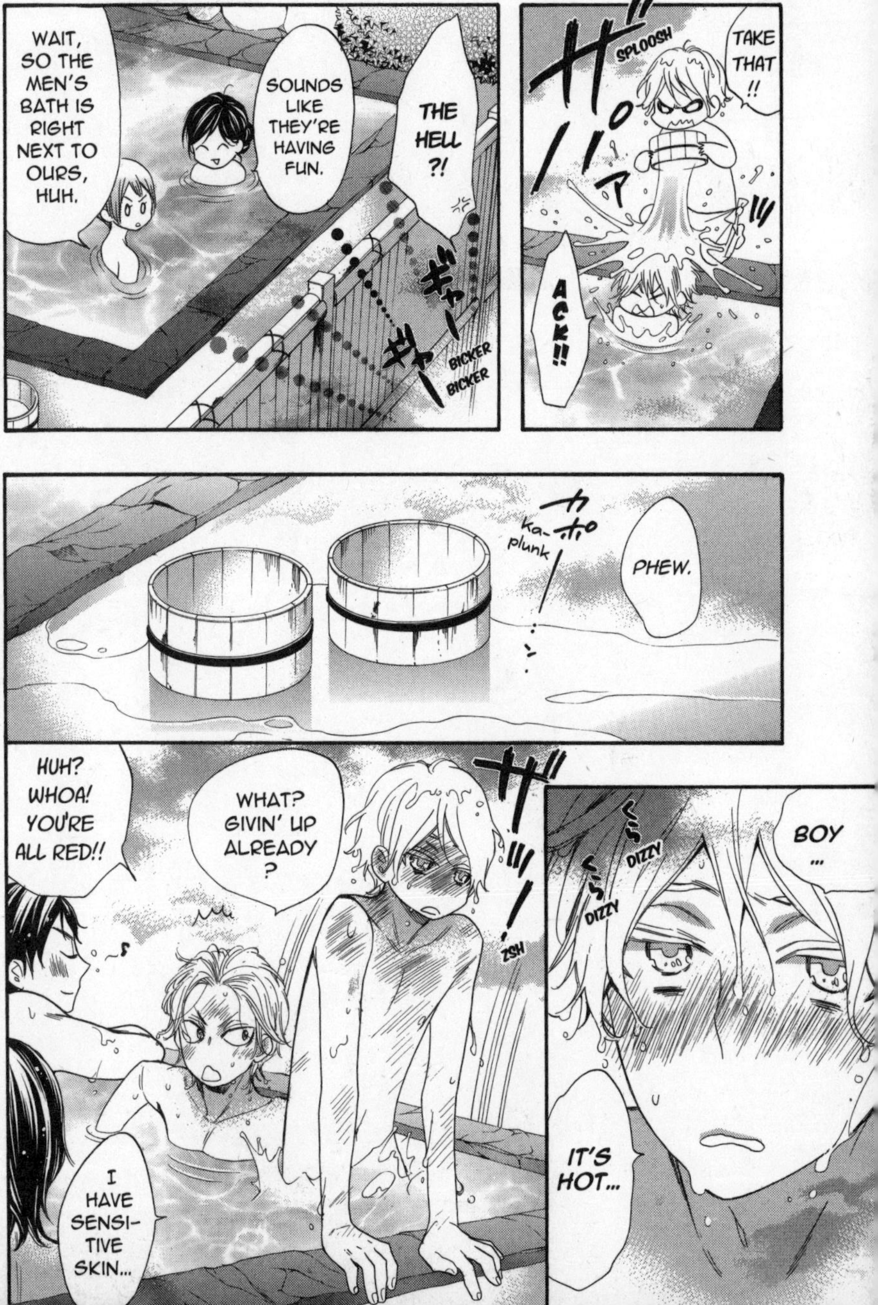
SPLOOSH
TAKE THAT!!
ACK!!
THE HELL?!
SOUNDS LIKE THEY'RE HAVING FUN.
WAIT, SO THE MEN'S BATH IS RIGHT NEXT TO OURS, HUH.
BICKER BICKER
PHEW.
ka-plunk
BOY...
DIZZY DIZZY
IT'S HOT...
ZSH
WHAT? GIVIN' UP ALREADY?
HUH? WHOA! YOU'RE ALL RED!!
I HAVE SENSI-TIVE SKIN...

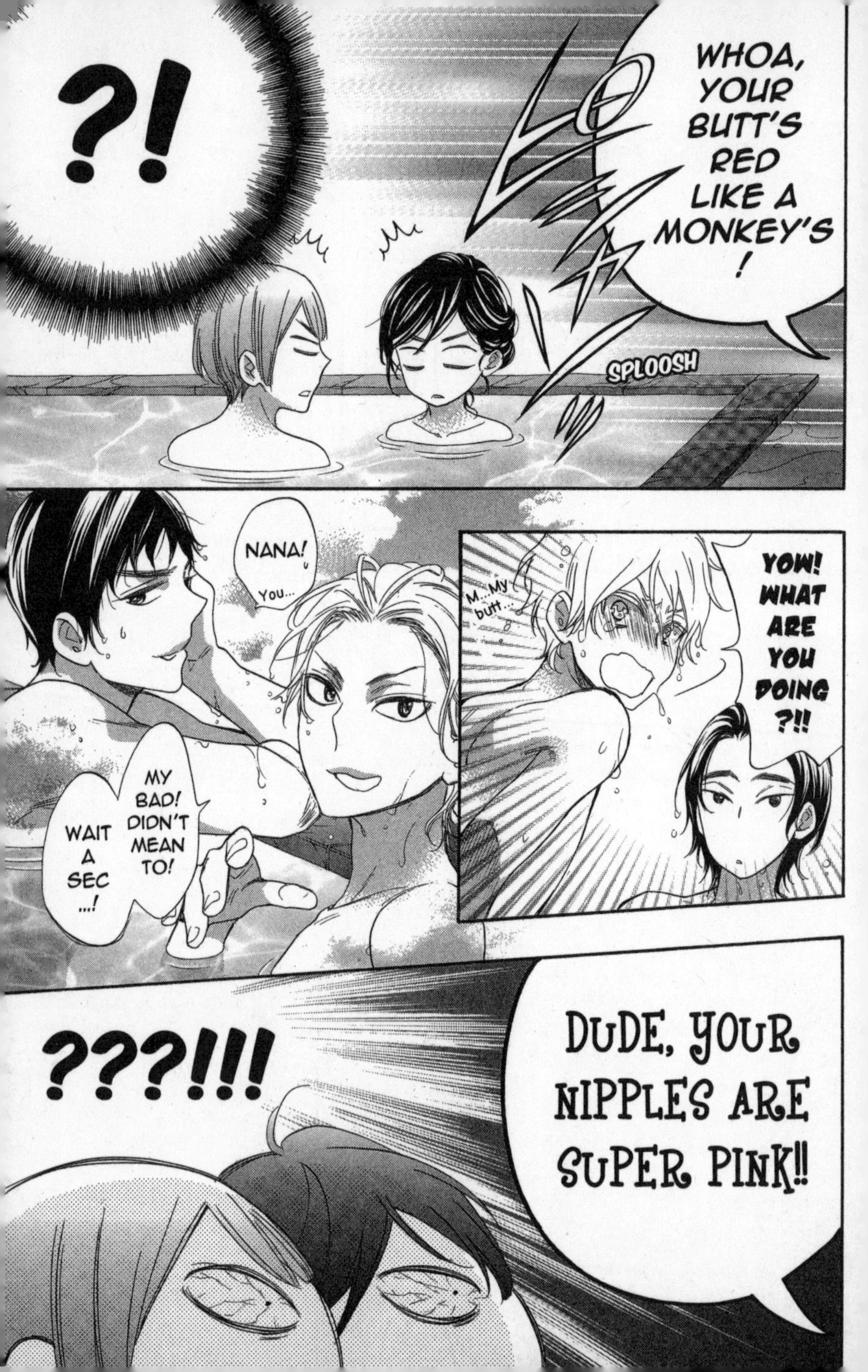
WHOA, YOUR BUTT'S RED LIKE A MONKEY'S!
SPLOOSH
?!
YOW! WHAT ARE YOU DOING?!!
M...My butt...
NANA!
You...
MY BAD! DIDN'T MEAN TO!
WAIT A SEC...!
DUDE, YOUR NIPPLES ARE SUPER PINK!!
???!!!

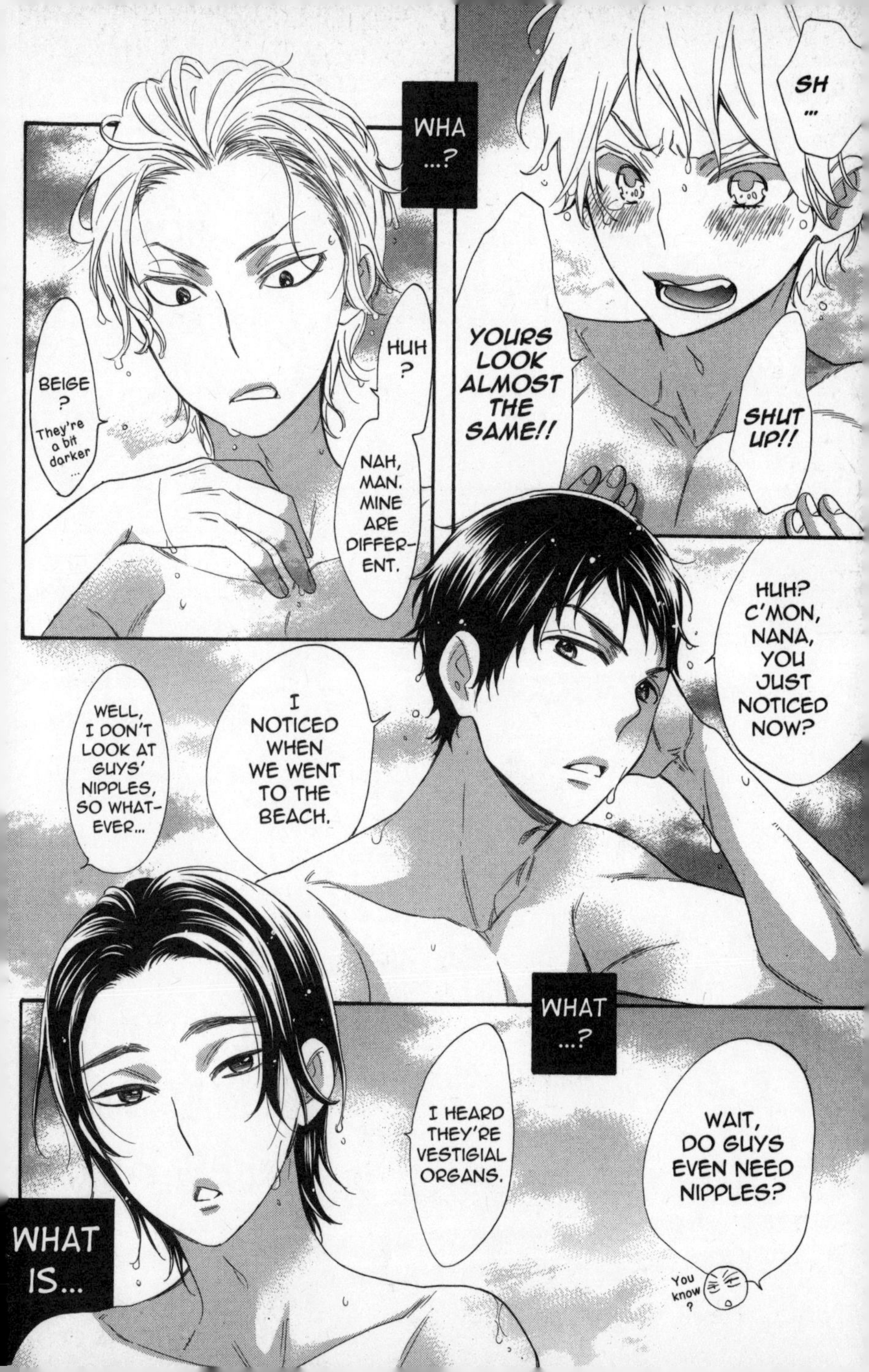
SH ...
SHUT UP!!
YOURS LOOK ALMOST THE SAME!!
WHA ...?
HUH ?
NAH, MAN. MINE ARE DIFFER-ENT.
BEIGE ? They're a bit darker ...
HUH? C'MON, NANA, YOU JUST NOTICED NOW?
I NOTICED WHEN WE WENT TO THE BEACH.
WELL, I DON'T LOOK AT GUYS' NIPPLES, SO WHAT-EVER...
WHAT ...?
WAIT, DO GUYS EVEN NEED NIPPLES?
You know ?
I HEARD THEY'RE VESTIGIAL ORGANS.
WHAT IS...

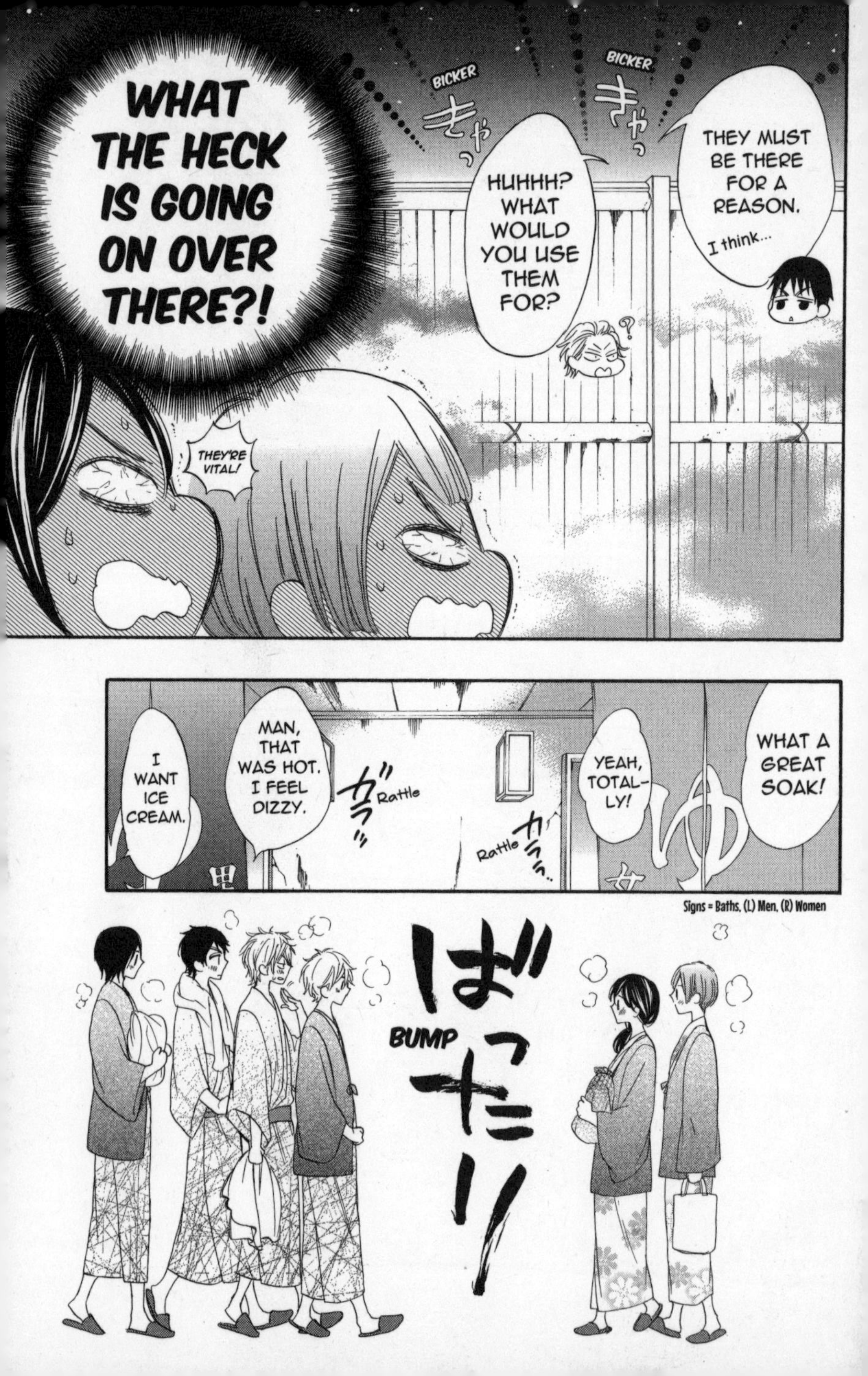
BICKER
THEY MUST BE THERE FOR A REASON.
I think...
BICKER
HUHHH? WHAT WOULD YOU USE THEM FOR?
WHAT THE HECK IS GOING ON OVER THERE?!
THEY'RE VITAL!
WHAT A GREAT SOAK!
YEAH, TOTALLY!
Rattle
Rattle
MAN, THAT WAS HOT. I FEEL DIZZY.
I WANT ICE CREAM.
ばったり
BUMP
Signs = Baths, (L) Men, (R) Women

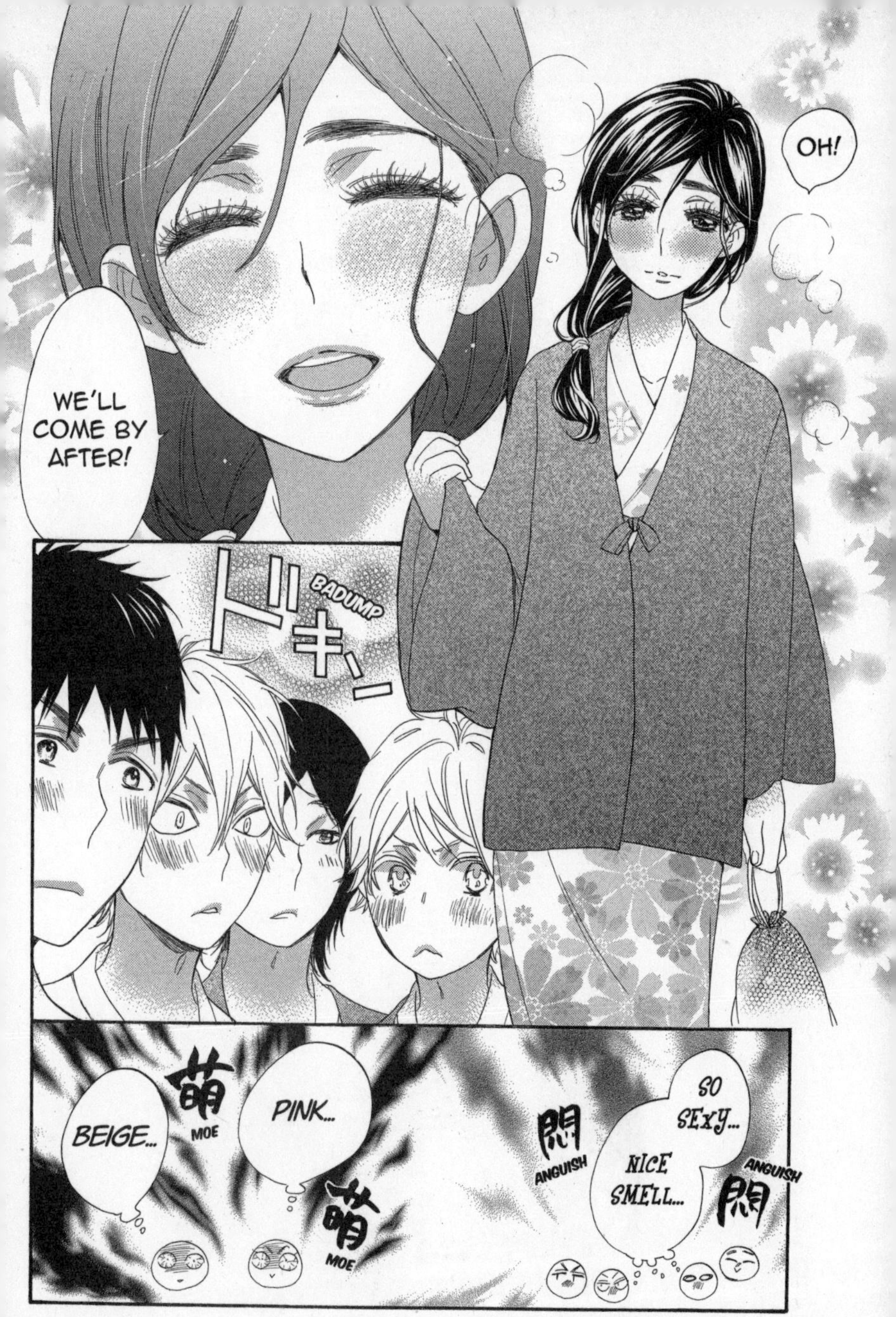
OH!
WE'LL COME BY AFTER!
ドキッ
BADUMP
SO SEXY...
NICE SMELL...
悶
ANGUISH
悶
ANGUISH
PINK...
萌
MOE
萌
MOE
BEIGE...

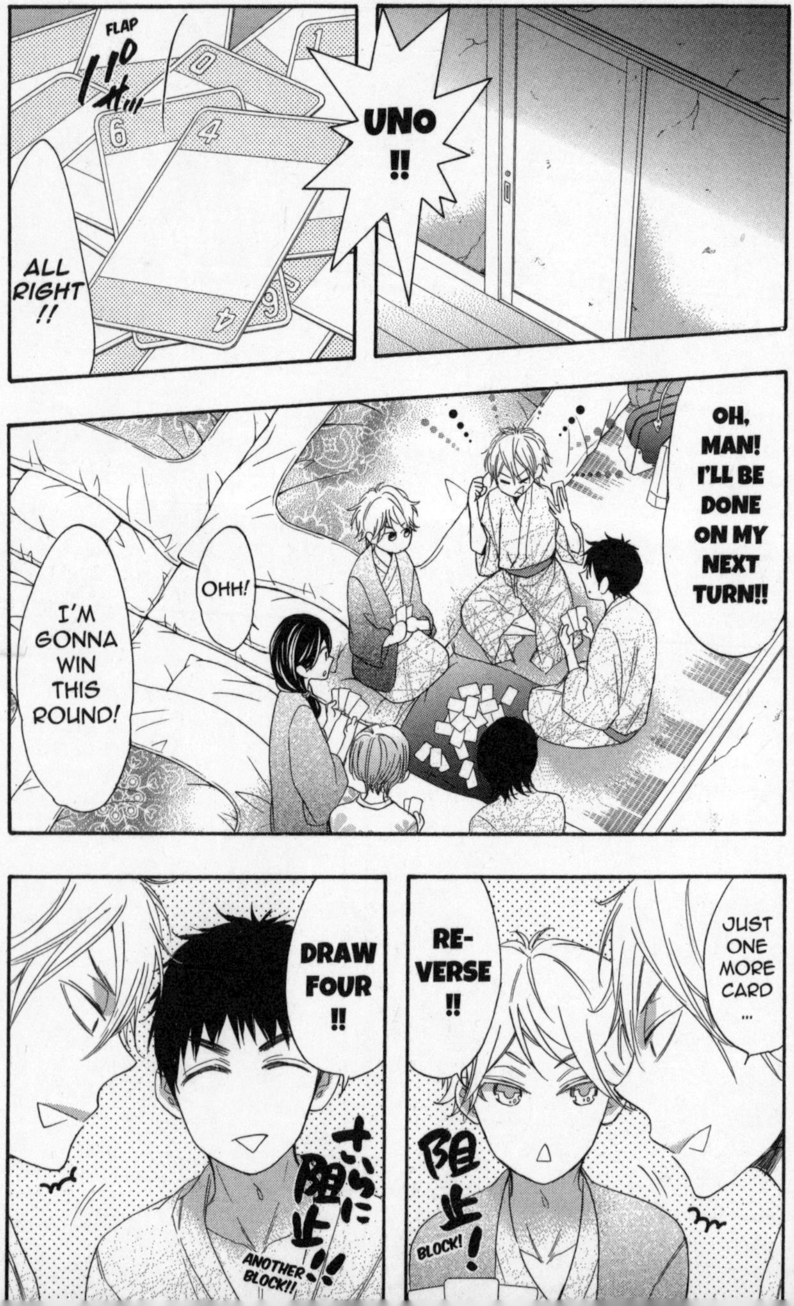
UNO!!
FLAP
ALL RIGHT!!
OH, MAN! I'LL BE DONE ON MY NEXT TURN!!
OHH!
I'M GONNA WIN THIS ROUND!
JUST ONE MORE CARD...
RE-VERSE!!
BLOCK!
DRAW FOUR!!
ANOTHER BLOCK!!

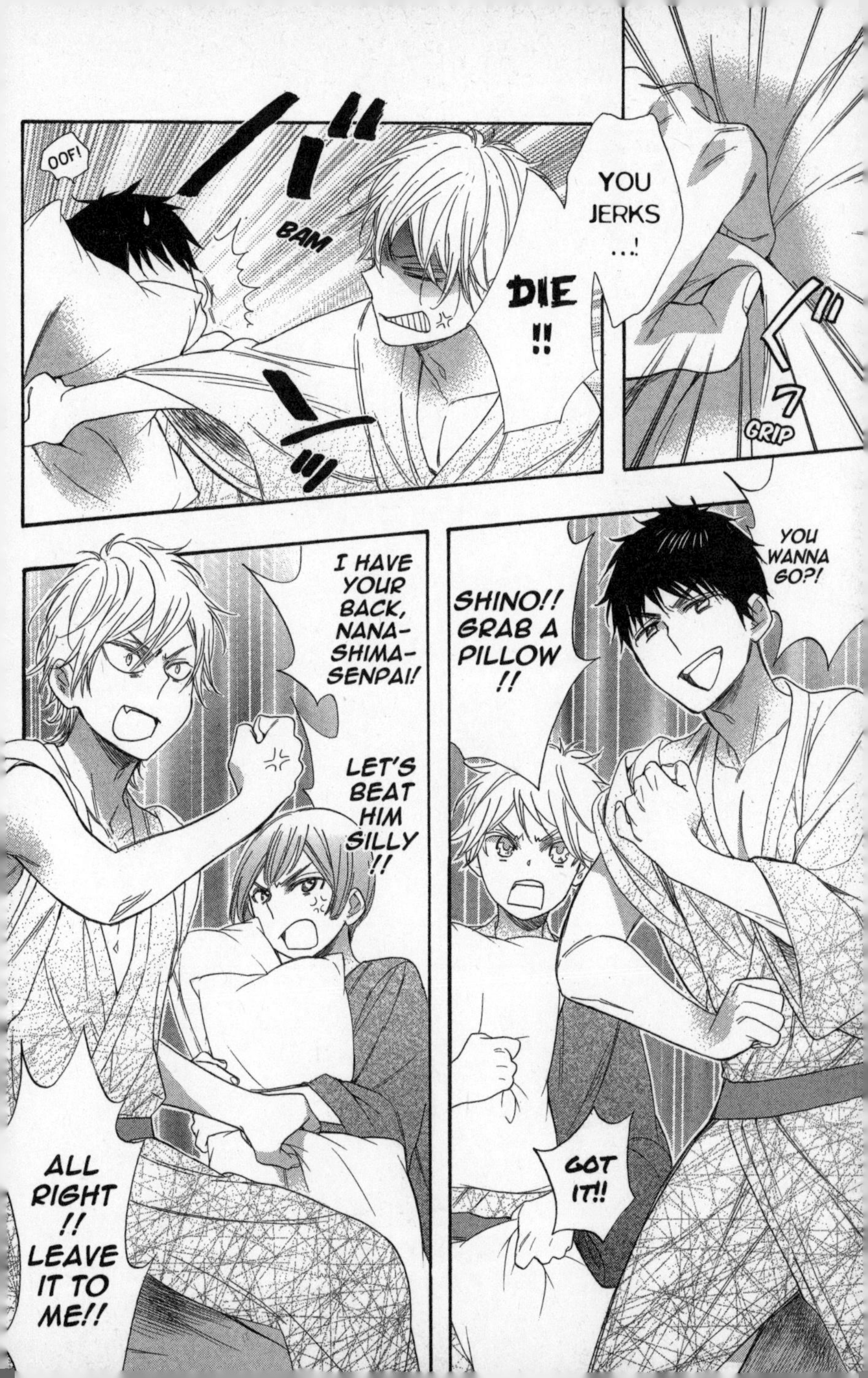
YOU JERKS ...!
GRIP
DIE !!
BAM
OOF!
YOU WANNA GO?!
SHINO!! GRAB A PILLOW !!
GOT IT!!
I HAVE YOUR BACK, NANA-SHIMA-SENPAI!
LET'S BEAT HIM SILLY !!
ALL RIGHT !! LEAVE IT TO ME!!

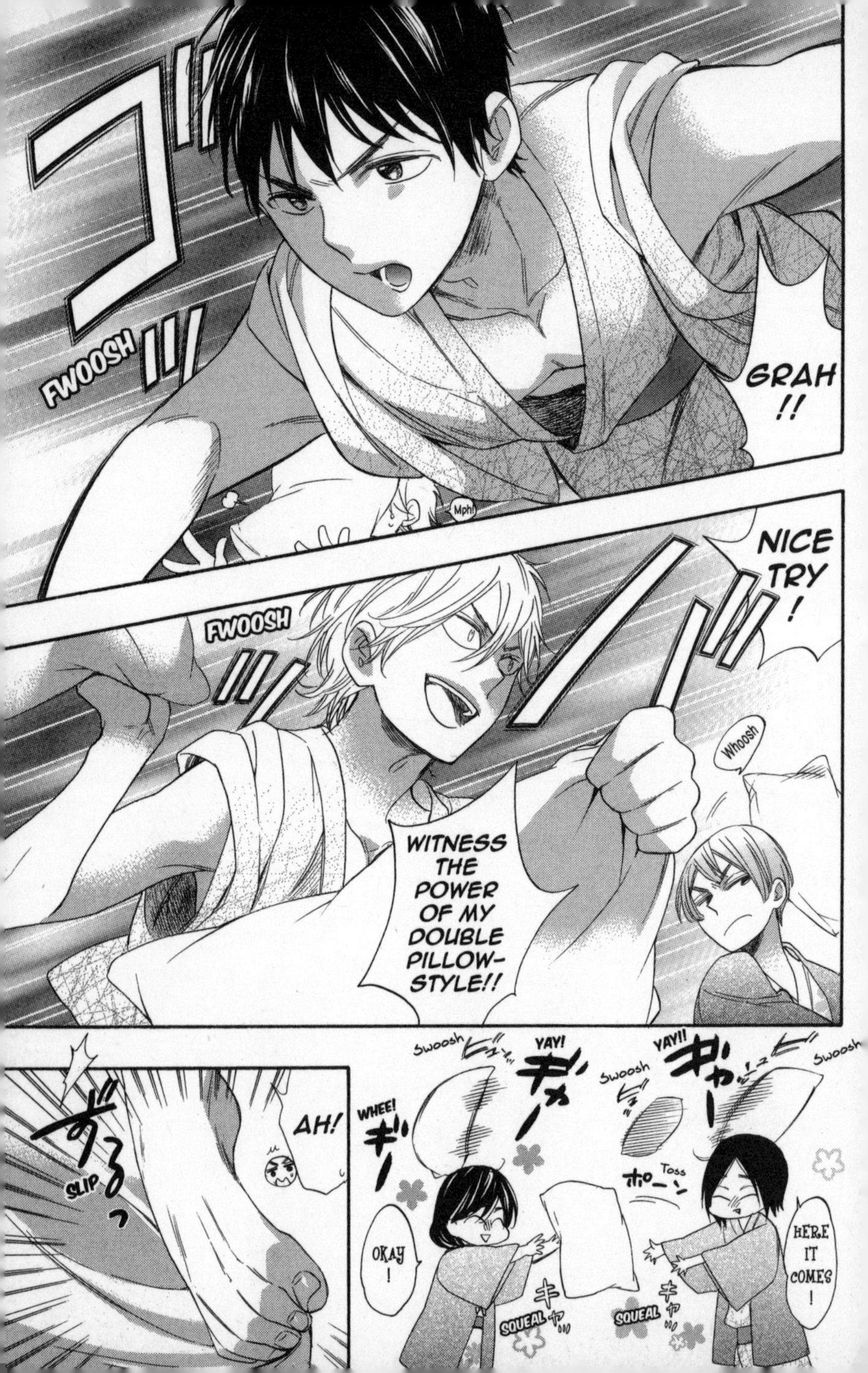
GRAH!!
FWOOSH
Mph!
NICE TRY!
FWOOSH
Whoosh
WITNESS THE POWER OF MY DOUBLE PILLOW-STYLE!!
Swoosh
YAY!!
Swoosh
Toss
HERE IT COMES!
SQUEAL
YAY!
Swoosh
WHEE!
OKAY!
SQUEAL
AH!
SLIP

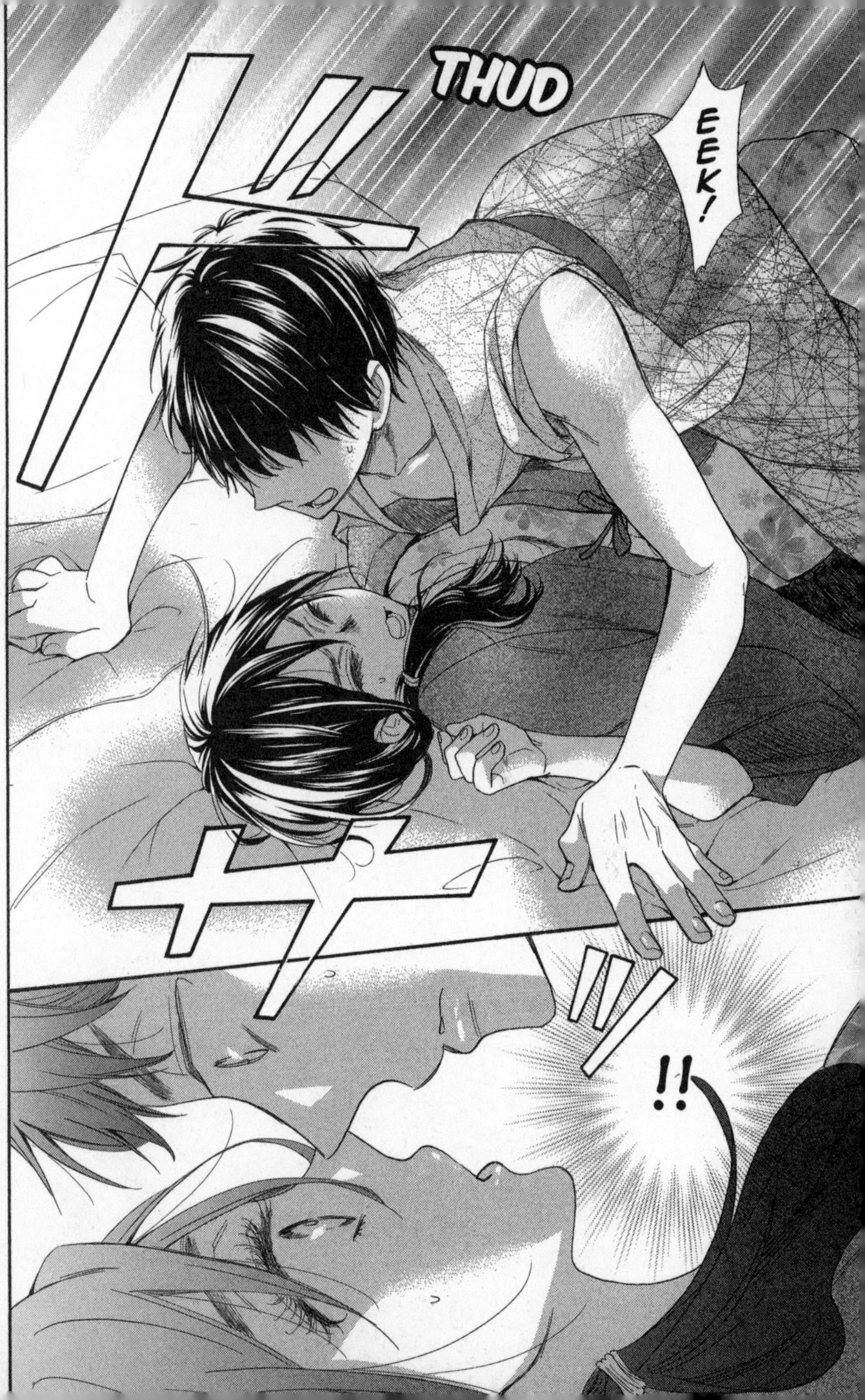
EEK!
THUD
!!

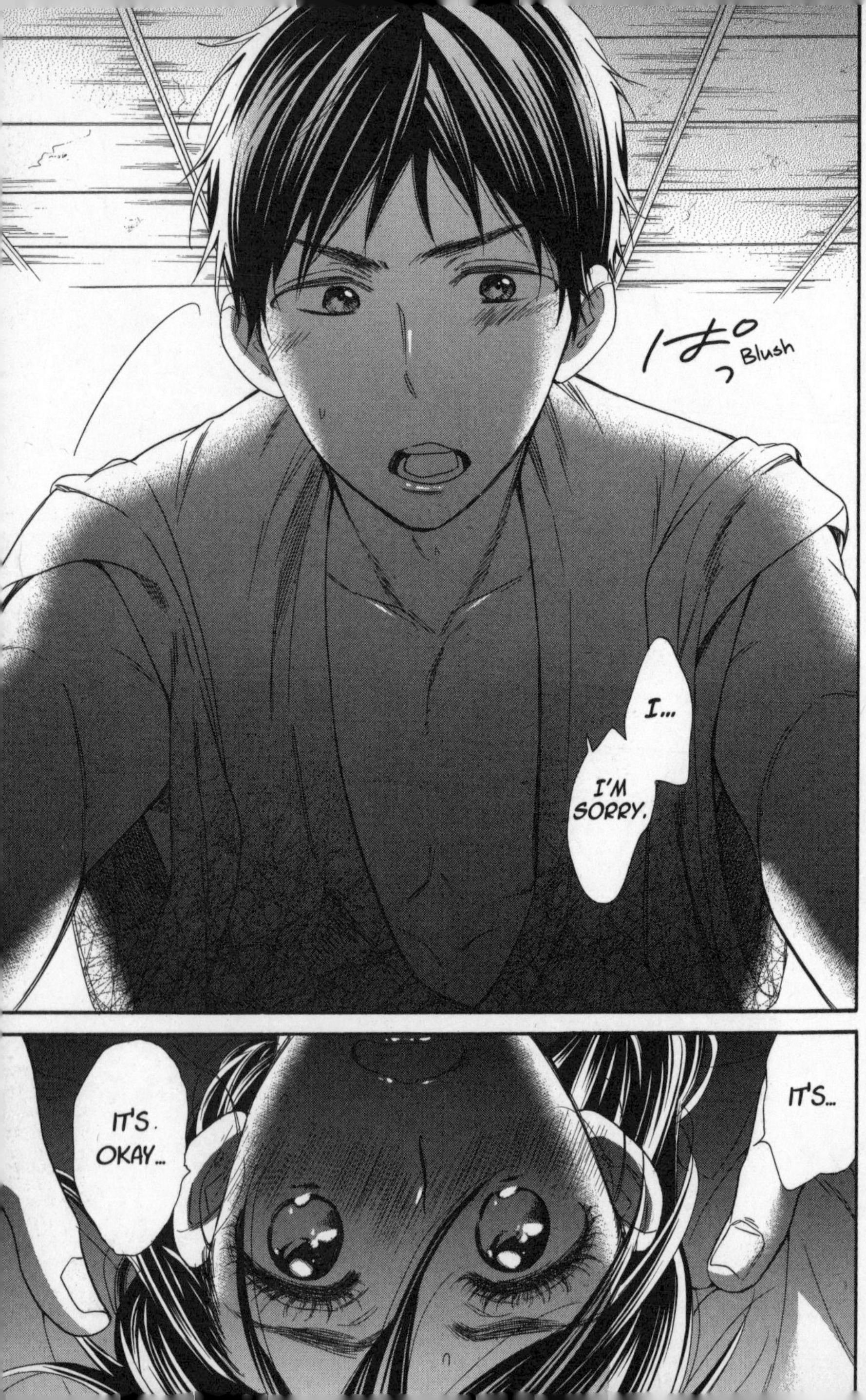
ぱっ Blush
I...
I'M SORRY.
IT'S...
IT'S OKAY...

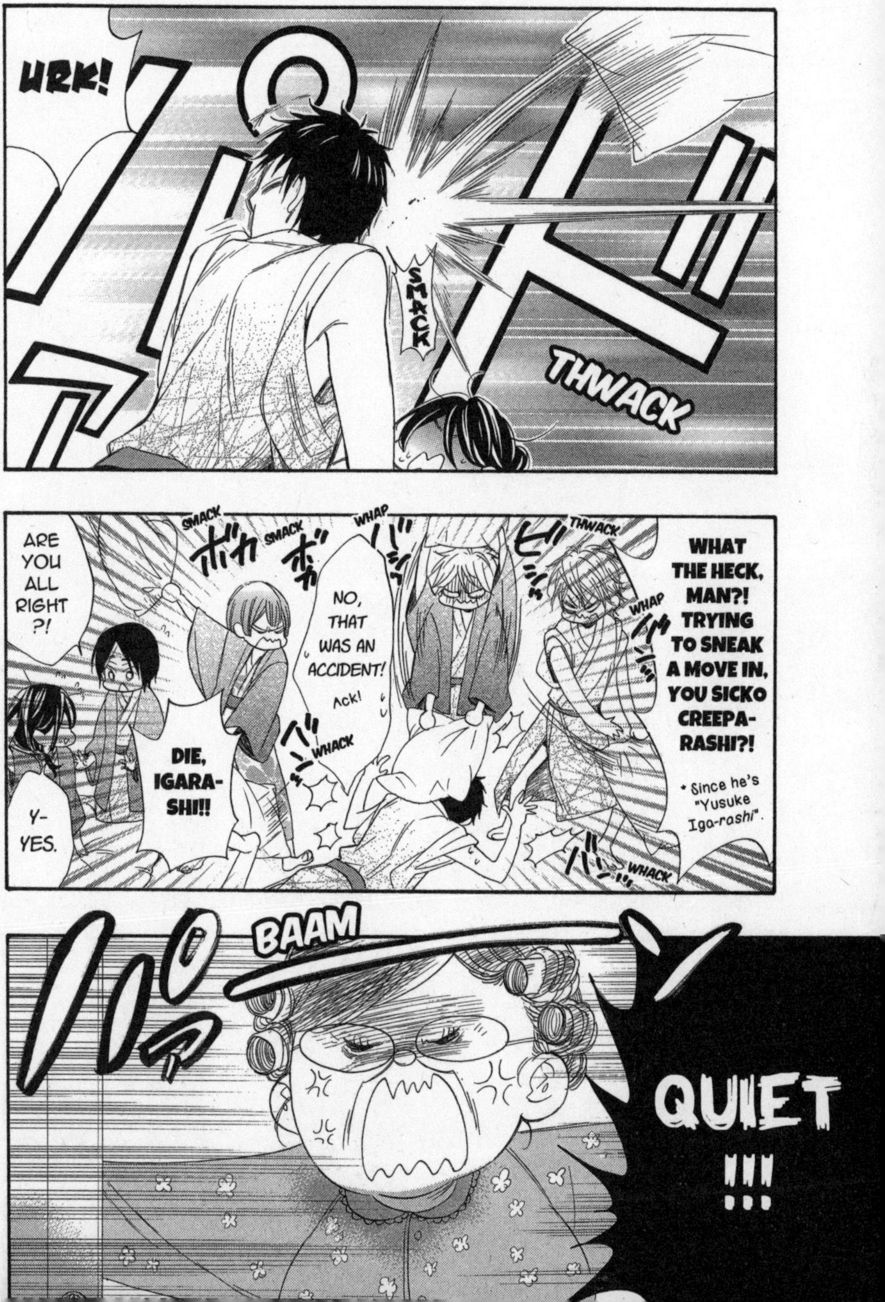
THWACK
SMACK
URK!
WHAT THE HECK, MAN?! TRYING TO SNEAK A MOVE IN, YOU SICKO CREEPA-RASHI?!
* Since he's "Yusuke Iga-rashi".
THWACK
WHAP
WHAP
WHACK
NO, THAT WAS AN ACCIDENT!
Ack!
SMACK
SMACK
WHACK
DIE, IGARA-SHI!!
ARE YOU ALL RIGHT?!
Y-YES.
QUIET!!!
BAAM

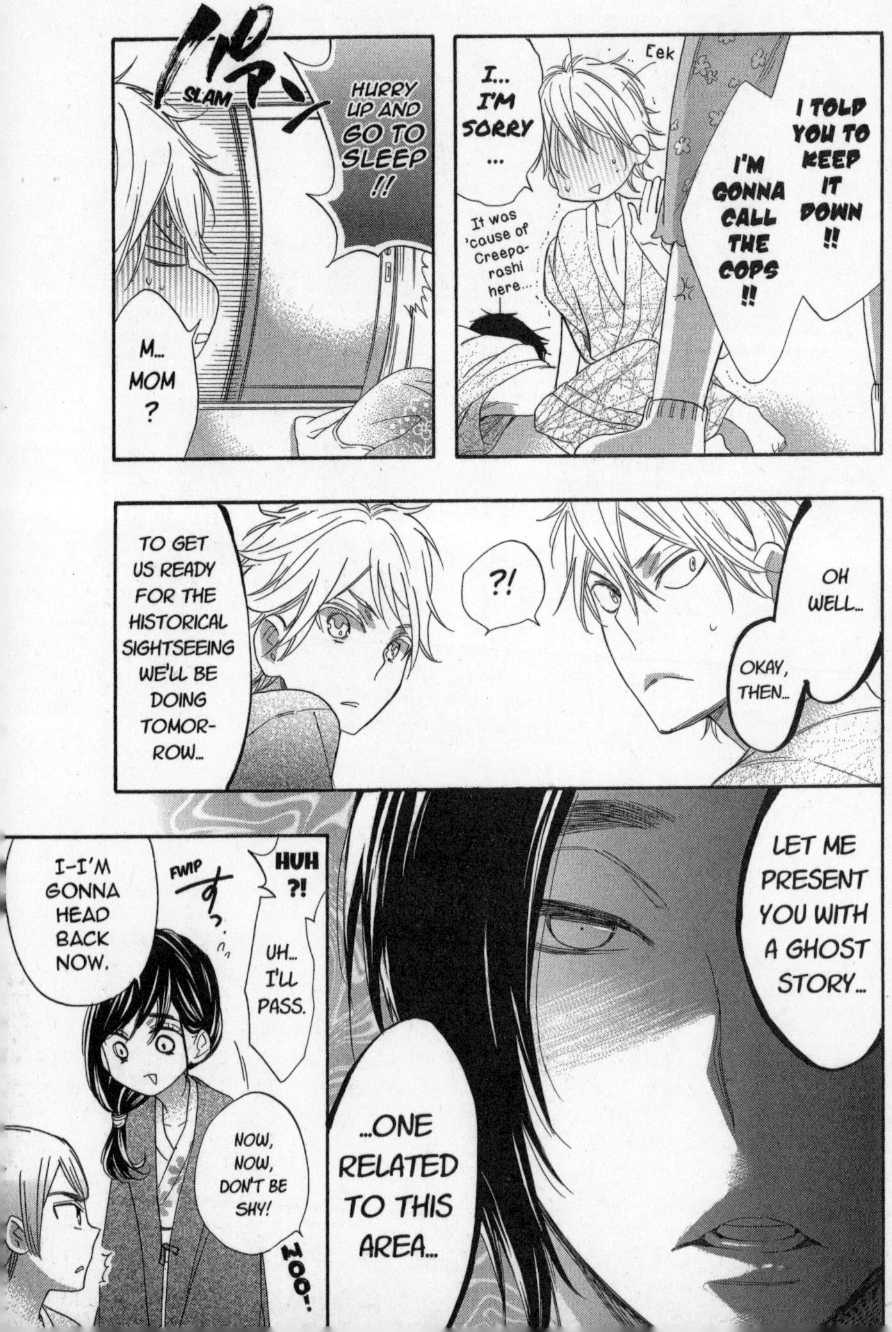
I TOLD YOU TO KEEP IT DOWN!!
I'M GONNA CALL THE COPS!!
Eek
I... I'M SORRY...
It was 'cause of Creepa-rashi here...
SLAM
HURRY UP AND GO TO SLEEP!!
M... MOM?
OH WELL...
OKAY, THEN...
?!
TO GET US READY FOR THE HISTORICAL SIGHTSEEING WE'LL BE DOING TOMORROW...
LET ME PRESENT YOU WITH A GHOST STORY...
...ONE RELATED TO THIS AREA...
HUH?!
UH... I'LL PASS.
FWIP
I-I'M GONNA HEAD BACK NOW.
NOW, NOW, DON'T BE SHY!
WOO!

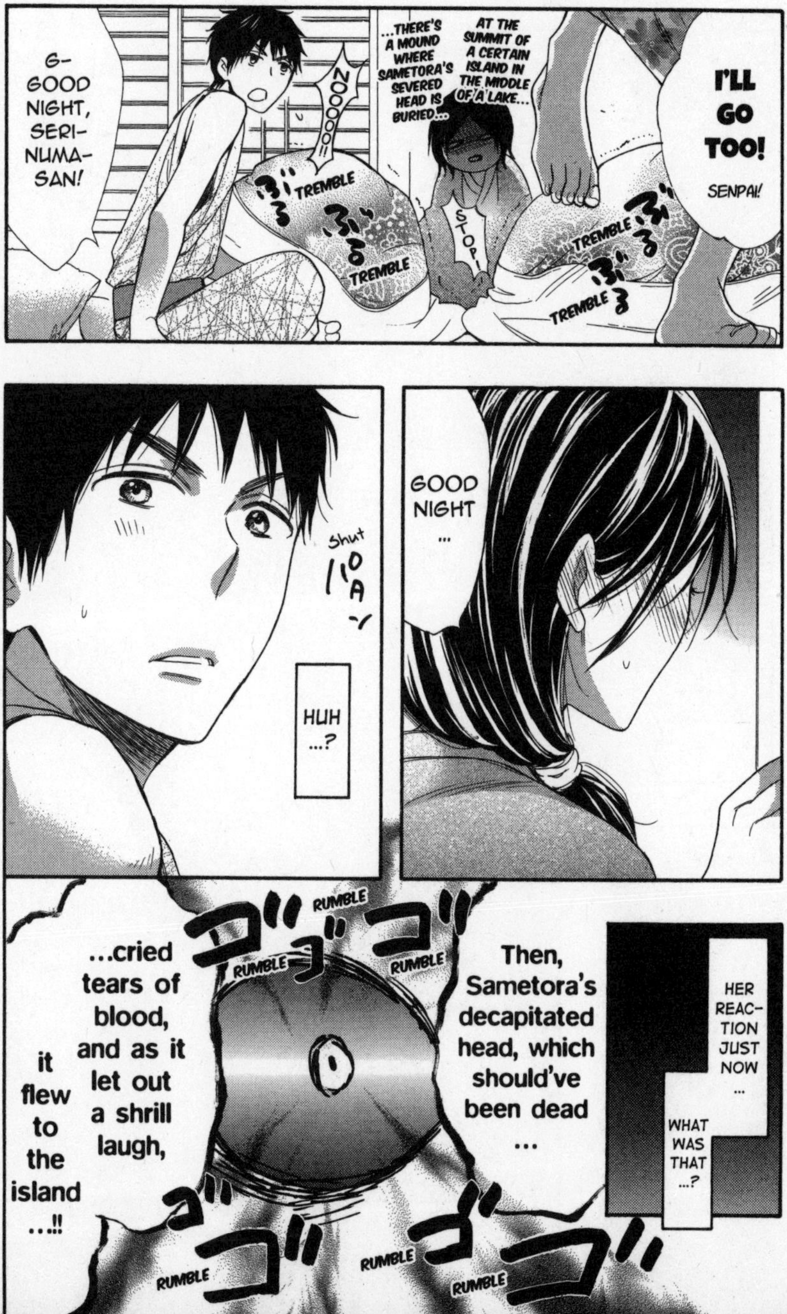
I'LL GO TOO!
SENPAI!
AT THE SUMMIT OF A CERTAIN ISLAND IN THE MIDDLE OF A LAKE...
...THERE'S A MOUND WHERE SAMETORA'S SEVERED HEAD IS BURIED...
ぶるぶる TREMBLE TREMBLE
ぶるぶる TREMBLE TREMBLE
STOP!
NOOOOOO!!
ぶるぶる TREMBLE TREMBLE
G-GOOD NIGHT, SERI-NUMA-SAN!
GOOD NIGHT ...
Shut パタン
HUH ...?
HER REAC-TION JUST NOW ...
WHAT WAS THAT ...?
Then, Sametora's decapitated head, which should've been dead ...
ゴゴゴ RUMBLE RUMBLE RUMBLE
...cried tears of blood, and as it let out a shrill laugh,
it flew to the island ...!!
ゴゴゴゴ RUMBLE RUMBLE RUMBLE

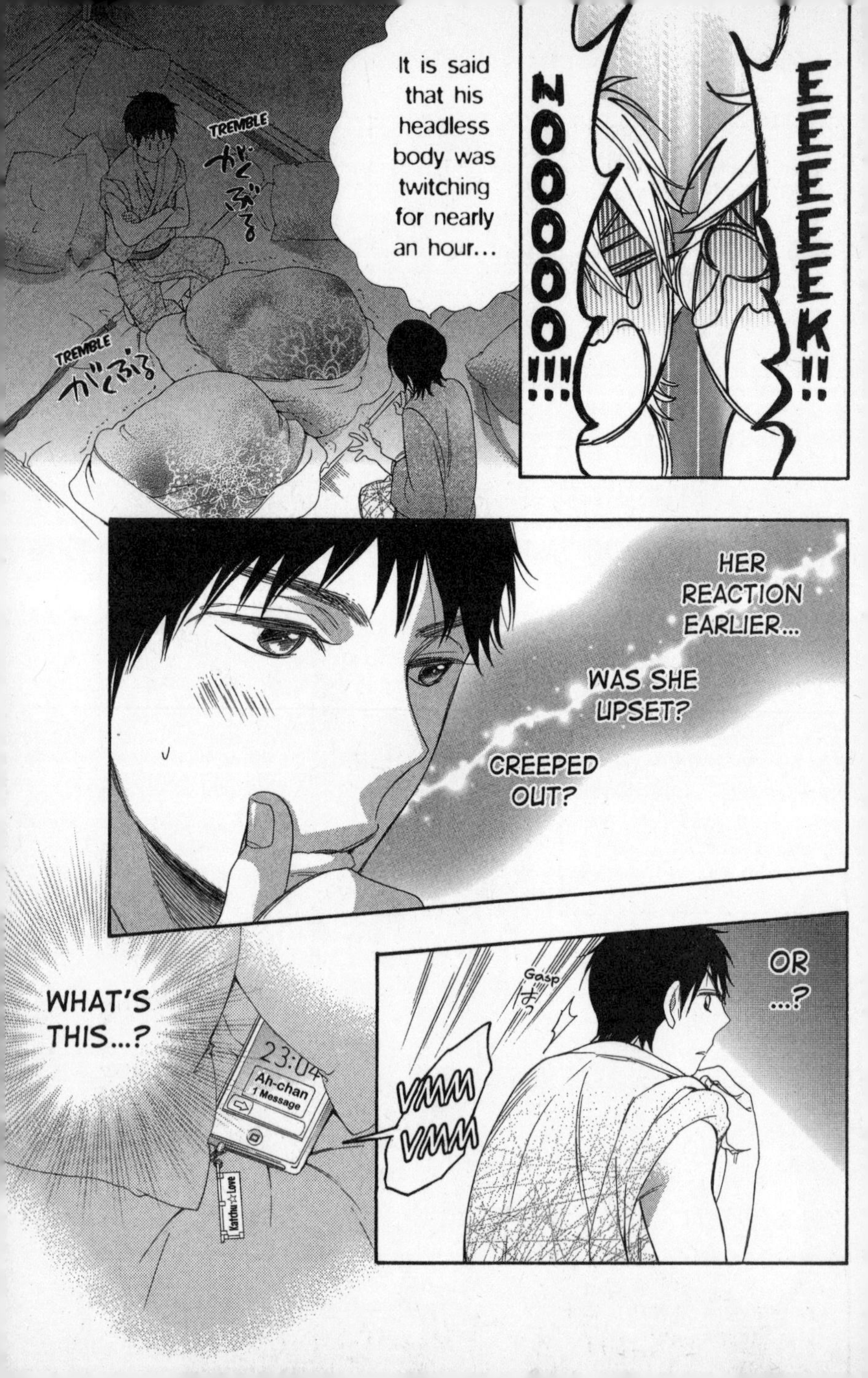
EEEEEEK!!
NOOOOO!!!
It is said that his headless body was twitching for nearly an hour...
TREMBLE
がくぶる
TREMBLE
がくぶる
HER REACTION EARLIER...
WAS SHE UPSET?
CREEPED OUT?
OR ...?
Gasp
VMM VMM
WHAT'S THIS...?
23:04
Ah-chan
1 Message
Katchu☆Love

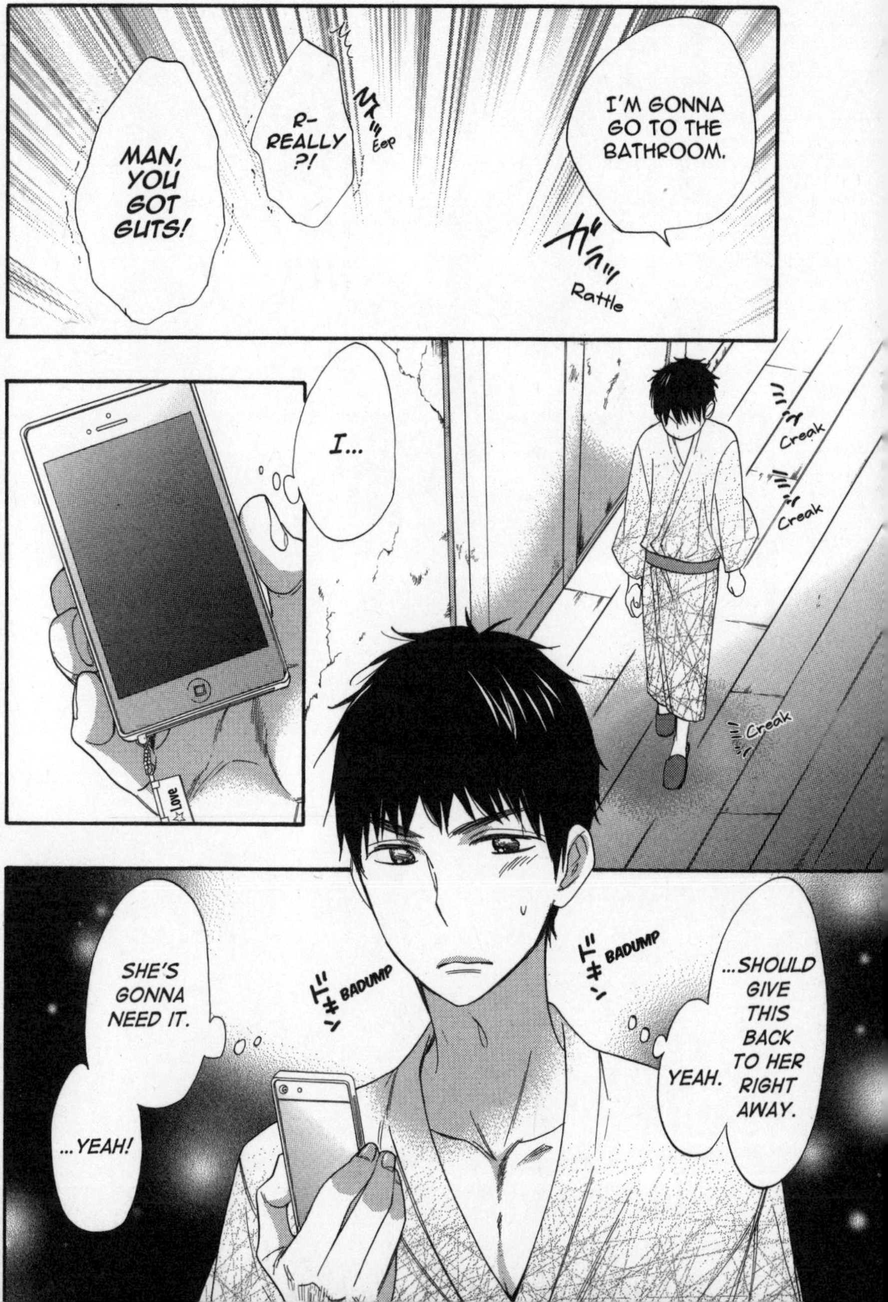
I'M GONNA GO TO THE BATHROOM.
Rattle
R-REALLY?!
Eep
MAN, YOU GOT GUTS!
Creak
Creak
Creak
I...
Love
...SHOULD GIVE THIS BACK TO HER RIGHT AWAY.
YEAH.
BADUMP
BADUMP
SHE'S GONNA NEED IT.
...YEAH!

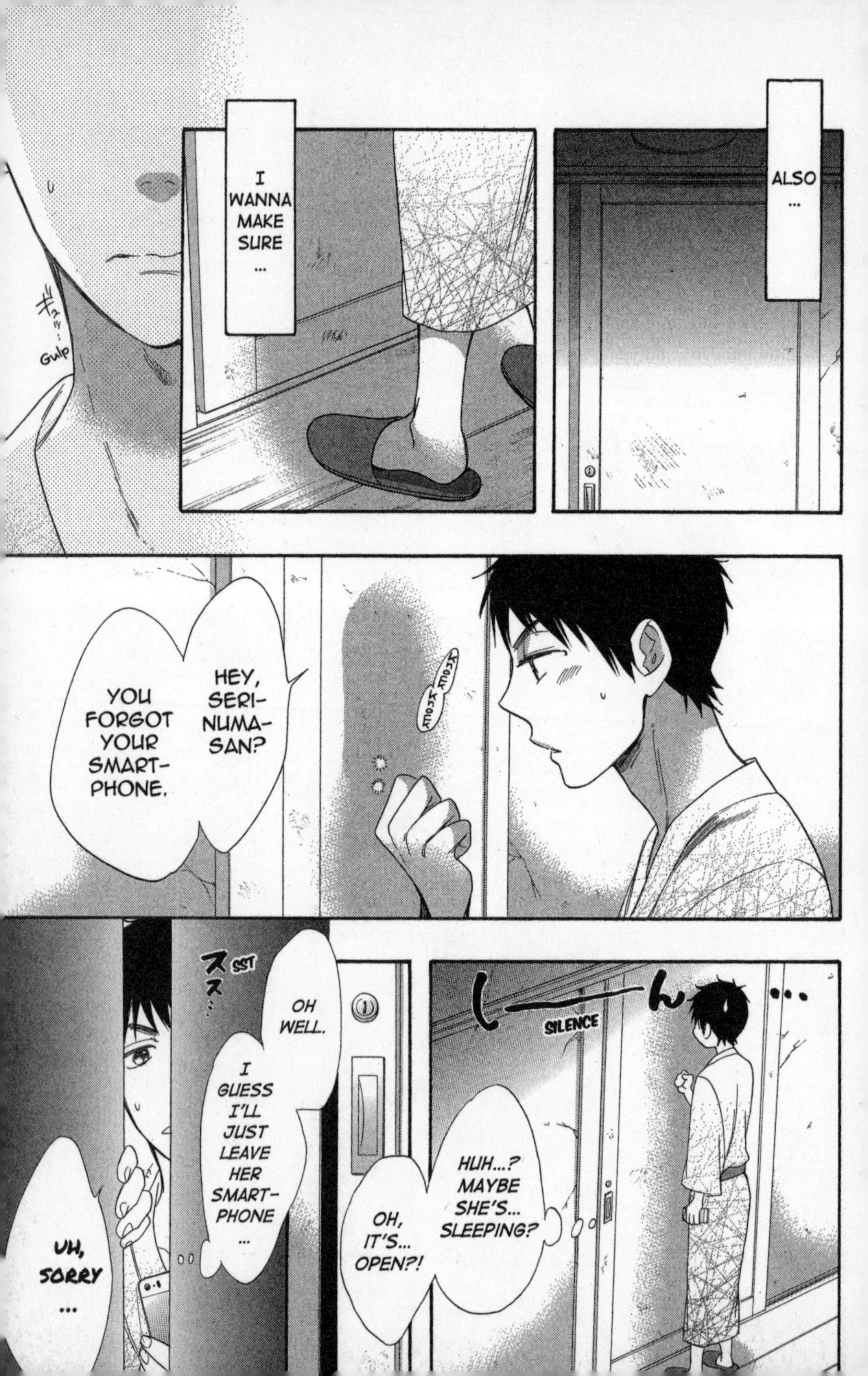
ALSO ...
I WANNA MAKE SURE ...
Gulp
KNOCK KNOCK
HEY, SERI-NUMA-SAN?
YOU FORGOT YOUR SMART-PHONE.
SILENCE
HUH...? MAYBE SHE'S... SLEEPING?
OH, IT'S... OPEN?!
SST
OH WELL.
I GUESS I'LL JUST LEAVE HER SMART-PHONE ...
UH, SORRY ...

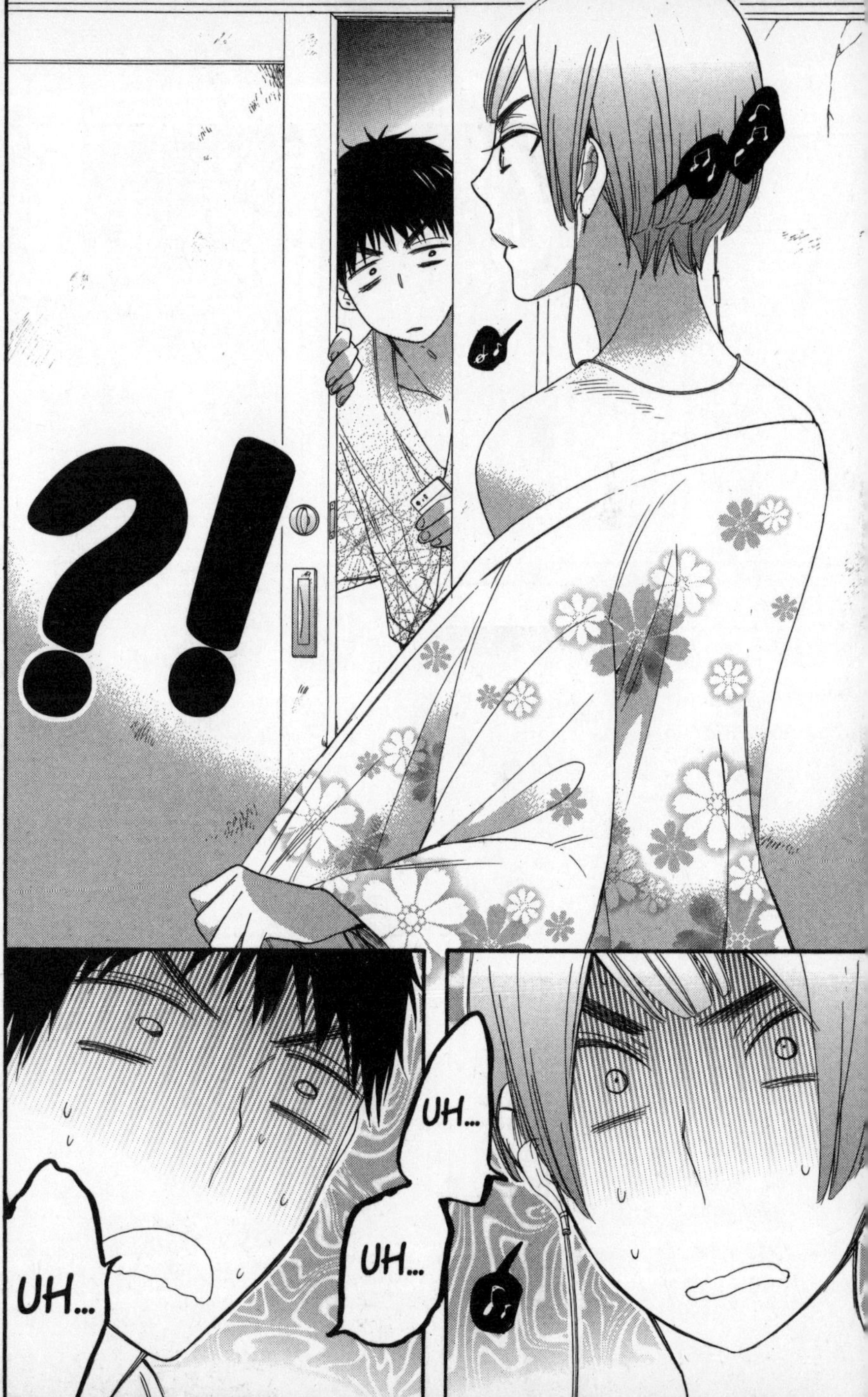
?!
UH...
UH...
UH...

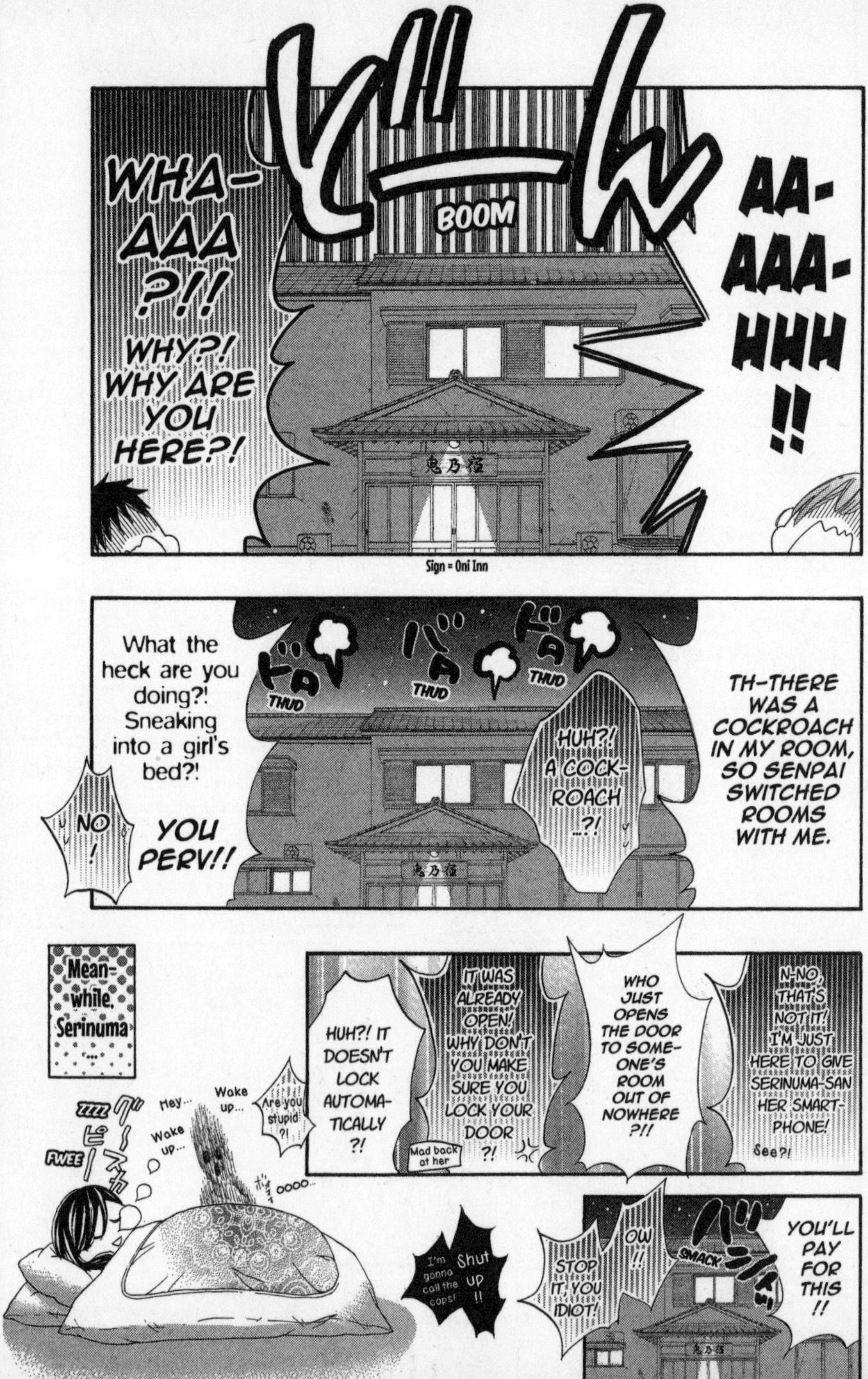
AA-AAA-HHH!!
BOOM
WHA-AAA?!!
WHY?! WHY ARE YOU HERE?!
Sign = Oni Inn
TH-THERE WAS A COCKROACH IN MY ROOM, SO SENPAI SWITCHED ROOMS WITH ME.
HUH?! A COCKROACH...?!
THUD
THUD
THUD
What the heck are you doing?! Sneaking into a girl's bed?!
YOU PERV!!
NO!
N-NO, THAT'S NOT IT! I'M JUST HERE TO GIVE SERINUMA-SAN HER SMARTPHONE!
See?!
WHO JUST OPENS THE DOOR TO SOMEONE'S ROOM OUT OF NOWHERE?!!
IT WAS ALREADY OPEN! WHY DON'T YOU MAKE SURE YOU LOCK YOUR DOOR?!
Mad back at her
HUH?! IT DOESN'T LOCK AUTOMATICALLY?!
YOU'LL PAY FOR THIS!!
SMACK
OW!!
STOP IT, YOU IDIOT!
Shut up!!
I'm gonna call the cops!
Meanwhile, Serinuma...
Are you stupid?!
Wake up...
Hey...
Wake up...
oooo...
zzzz
FWEE

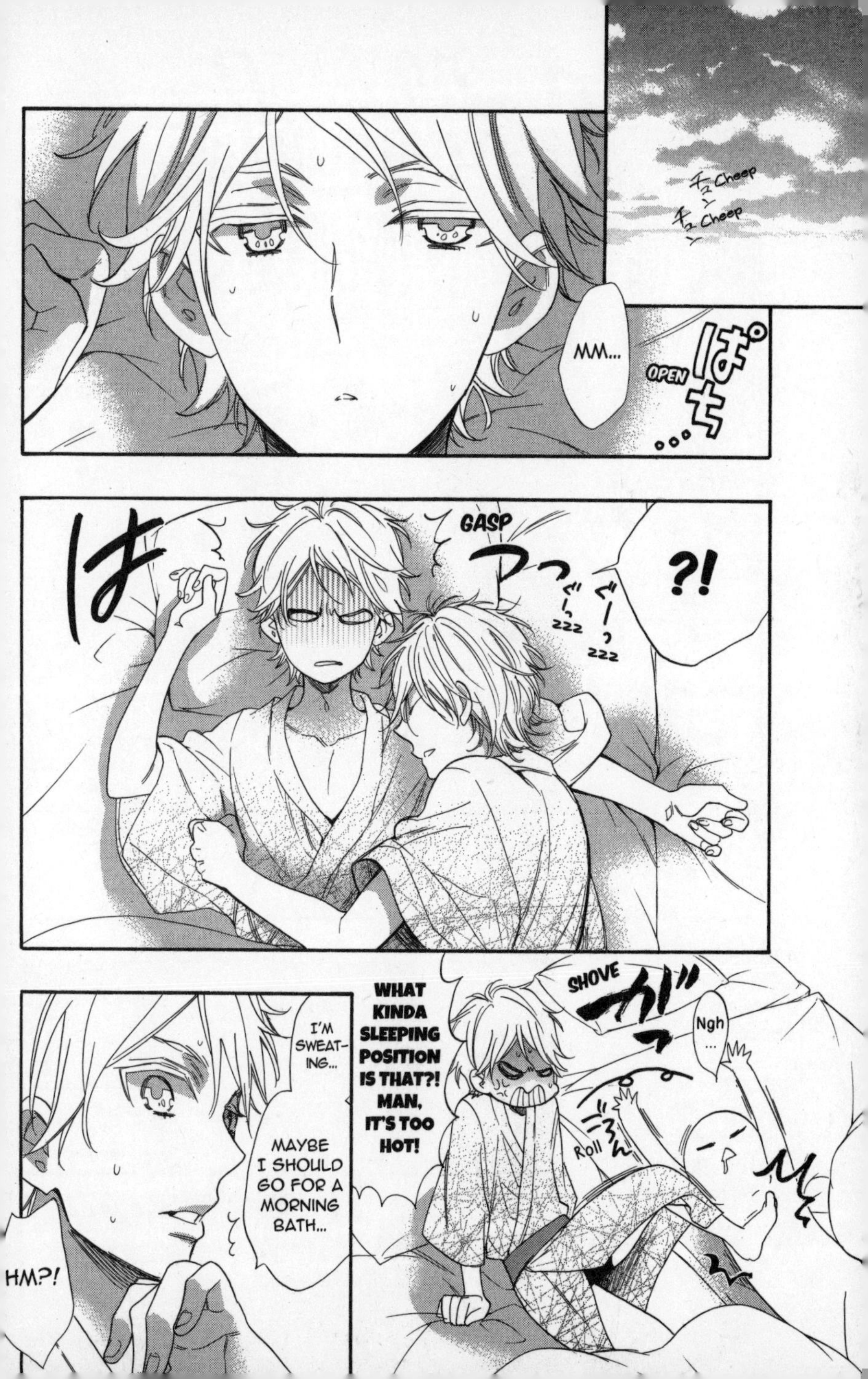

Cheep
Cheep
MM...
OPEN
ぱち...
?!
GASP
はっ
zzz
zzz
SHOVE
Ngh...
WHAT KINDA SLEEPING POSITION IS THAT?! MAN, IT'S TOO HOT!
Roll
I'M SWEAT-ING...
MAYBE I SHOULD GO FOR A MORNING BATH...
HM?!

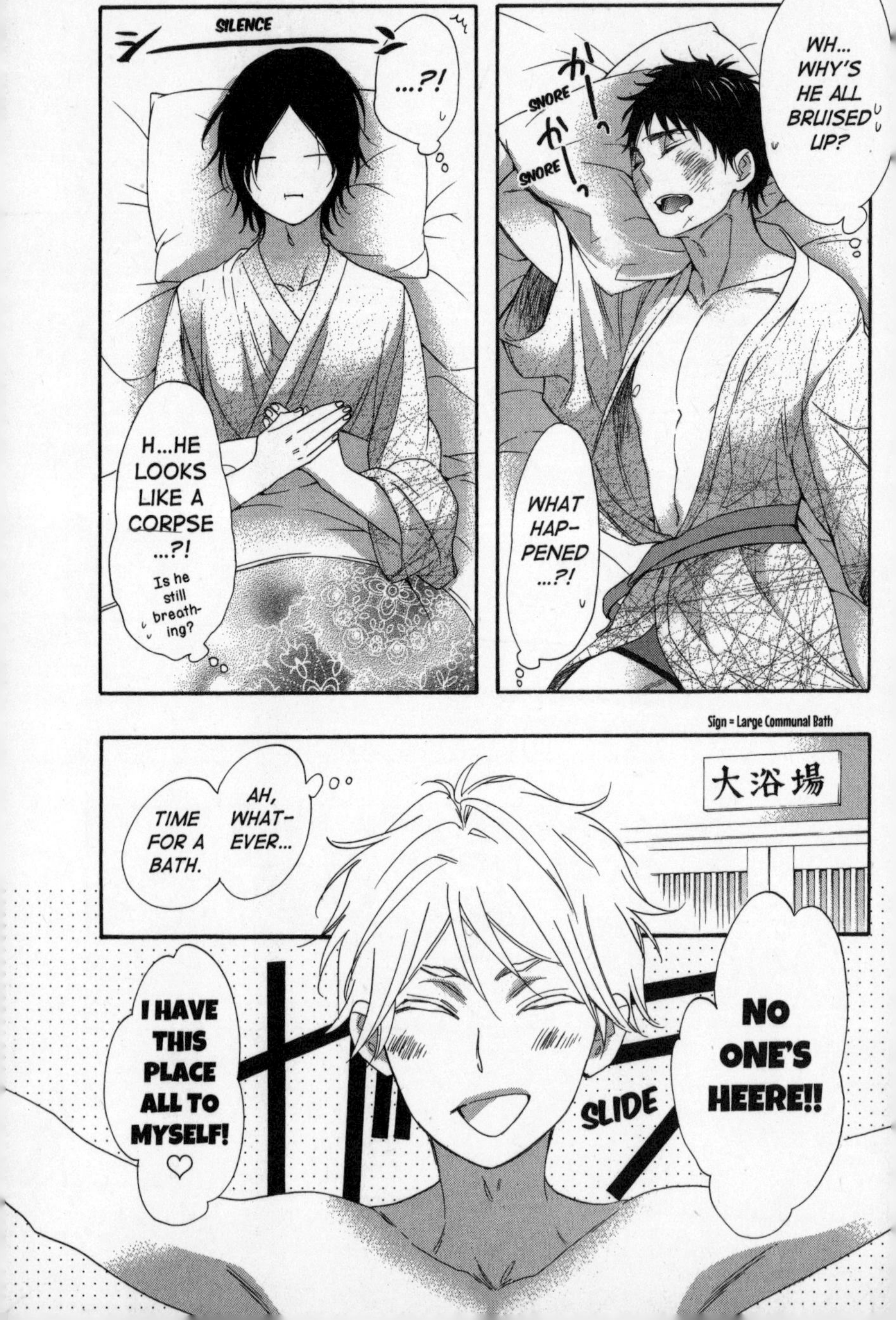
WH... WHY'S HE ALL BRUISED UP?
かーっ
SNORE
かーっ
SNORE
WHAT HAP-PENED ...?!
SILENCE
...?!
H...HE LOOKS LIKE A CORPSE ...?!
Is he still breath-ing?
Sign = Large Communal Bath
大浴場
AH, WHAT-EVER...
TIME FOR A BATH.
NO ONE'S HEERE!!
SLIDE
I HAVE THIS PLACE ALL TO MYSELF! ♡

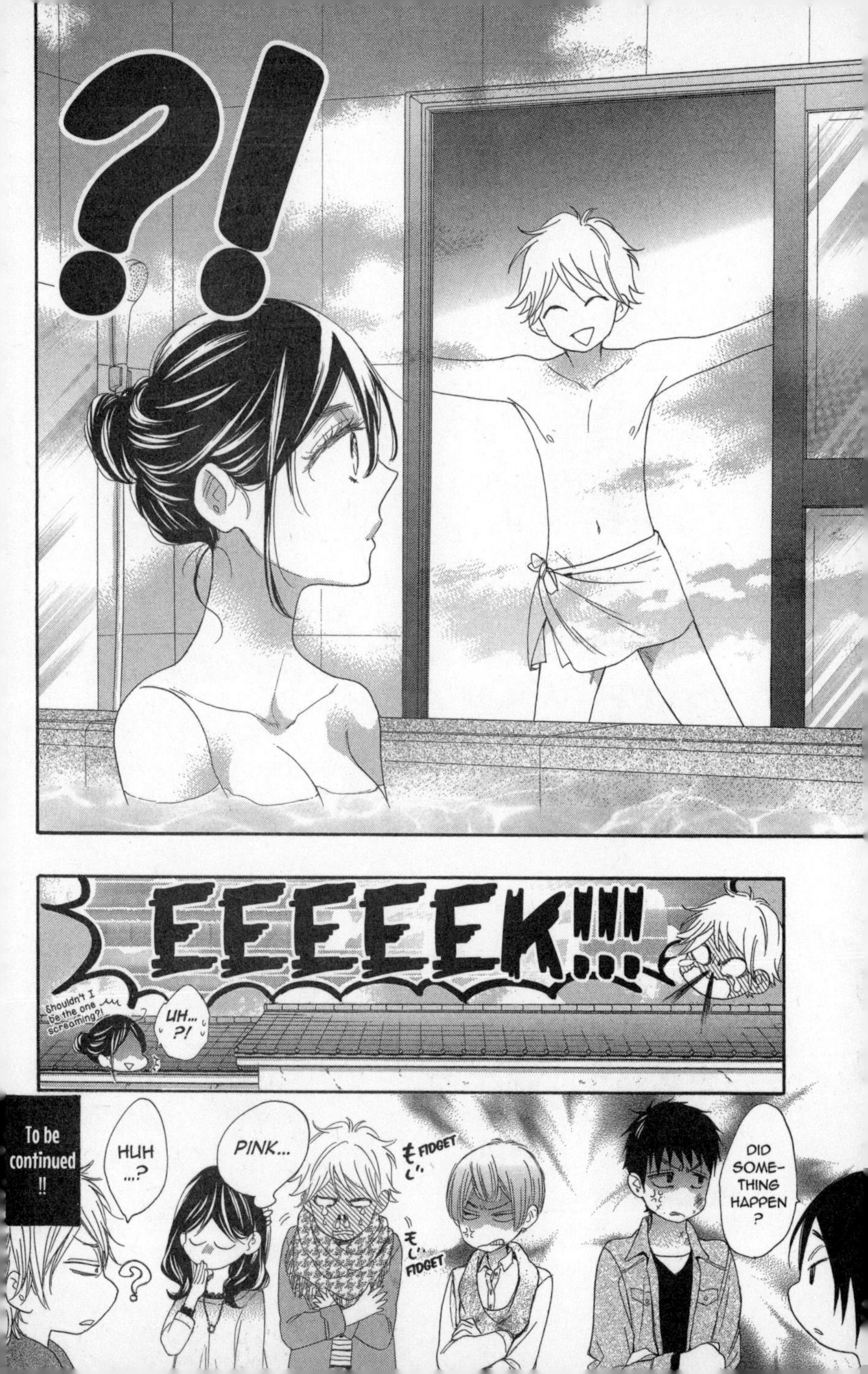
?!
EEEEEK!!!
UH... ?!
Shouldn't I be the one screaming?!
DID SOME-THING HAPPEN ?
FIDGET
FIDGET
PINK...
HUH ...?
To be continued !!

#28 THE MASTER'S CURSE...?

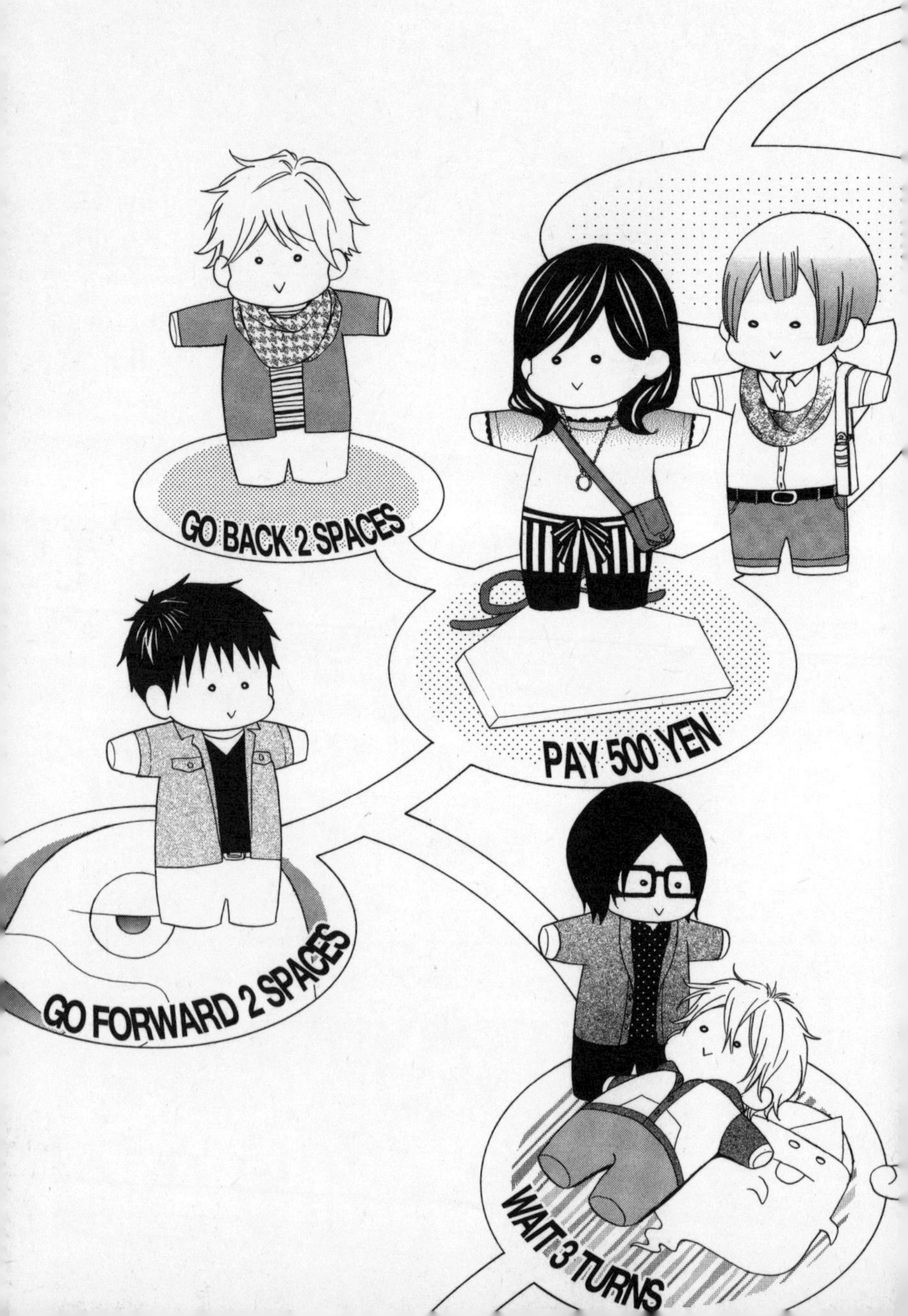
PAY 500 YEN
GO BACK 2 SPACES
WAIT 3 TURNS
GO FORWARD 2 SPACES

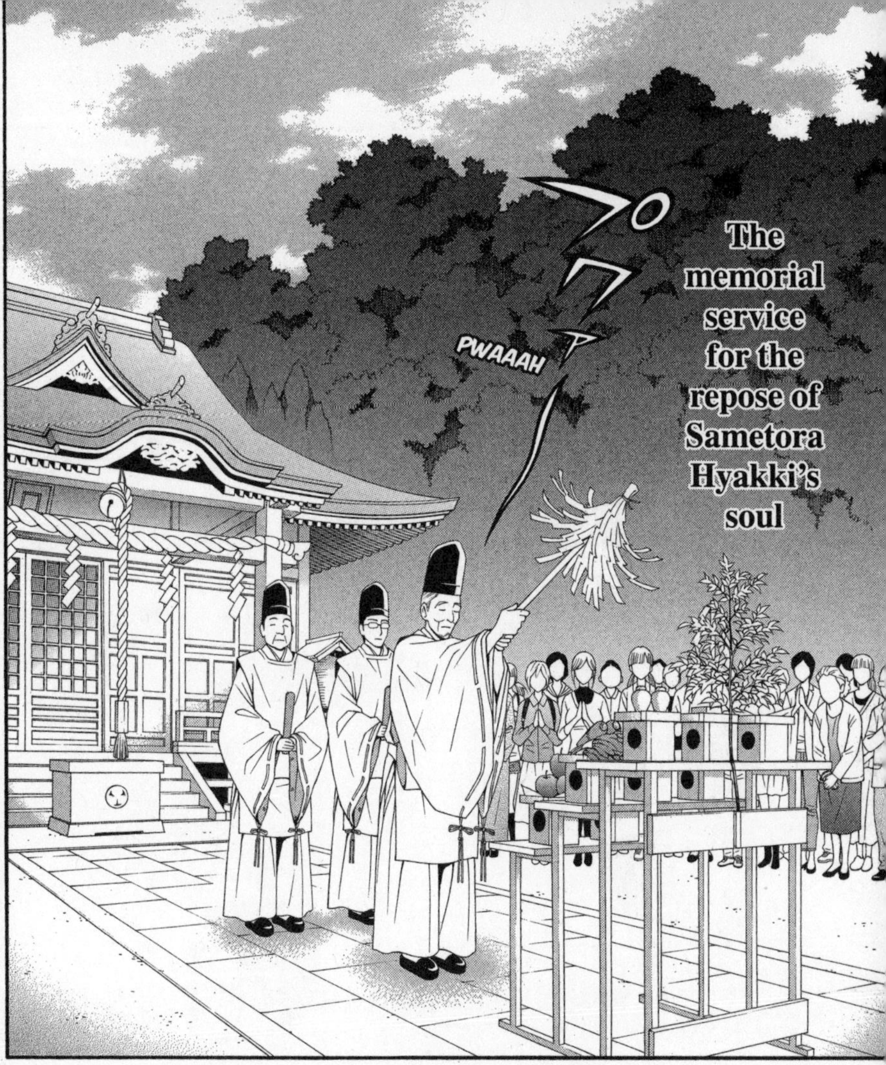
The memorial service for the repose of Sametora Hyakki's soul
PWAAAH

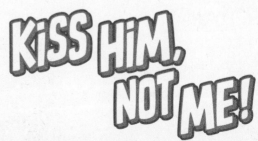

KiSS HiM, NOT ME!

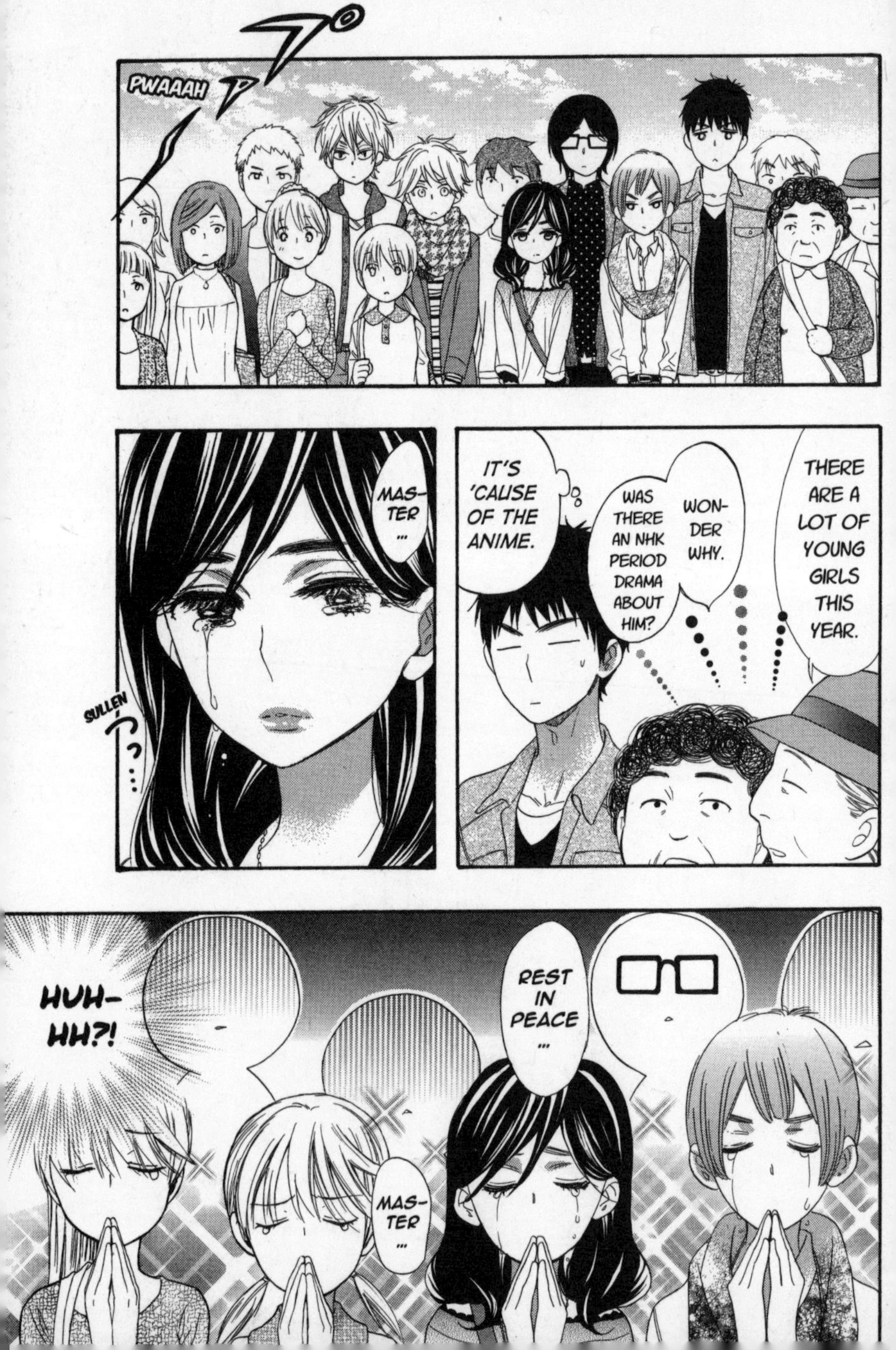
PWAAAH
THERE ARE A LOT OF YOUNG GIRLS THIS YEAR.
WONDER WHY.
WAS THERE AN NHK PERIOD DRAMA ABOUT HIM?
IT'S 'CAUSE OF THE ANIME.
MASTER...
SULLEN
REST IN PEACE...
HUH-HH?!
MASTER...

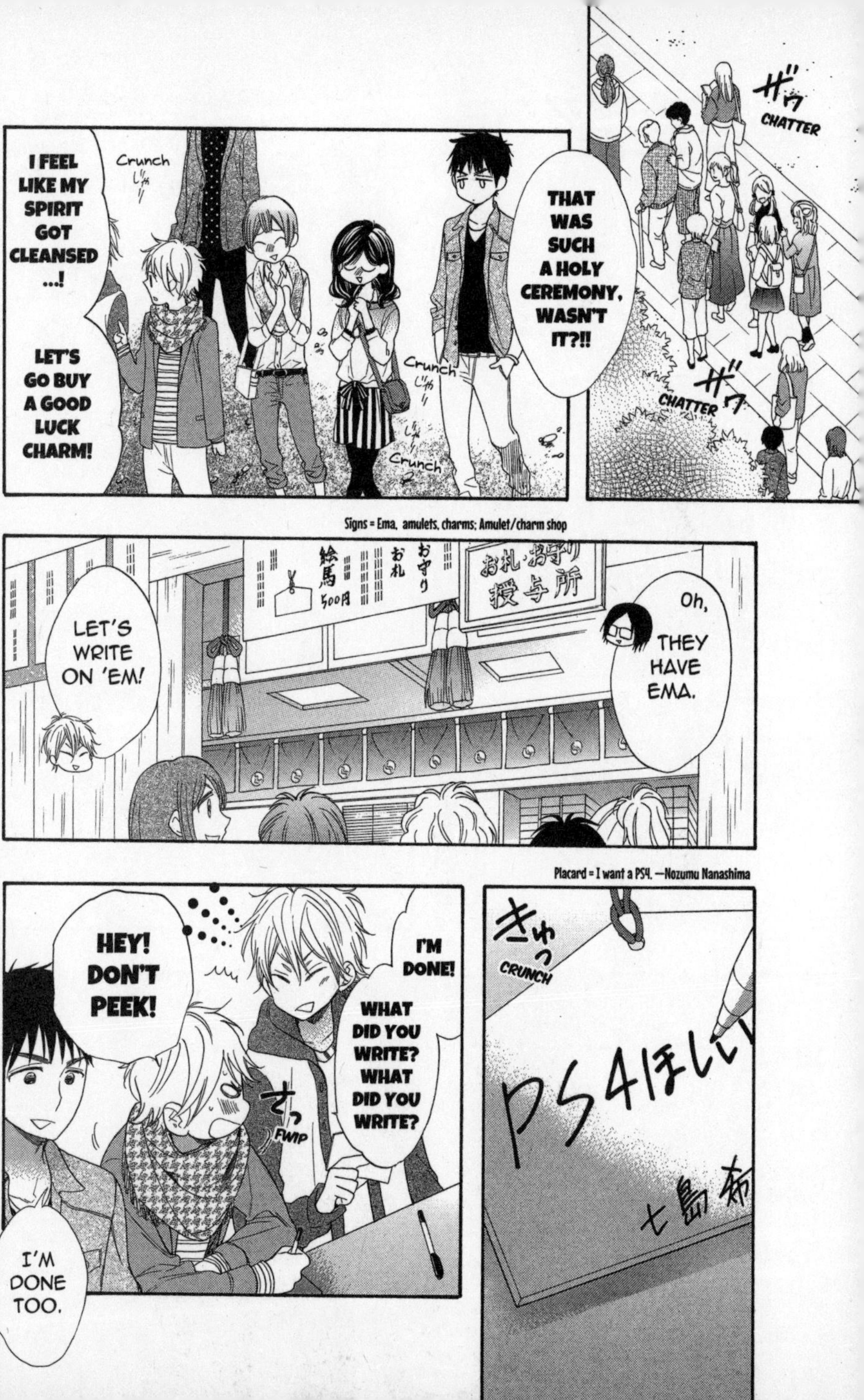
ザワ
CHATTER
ザワ
CHATTER
THAT WAS SUCH A HOLY CEREMONY, WASN'T IT?!!
I FEEL LIKE MY SPIRIT GOT CLEANSED ...!
Crunch
Crunch
Crunch
LET'S GO BUY A GOOD LUCK CHARM!
お札 お守り 授与所
お守り
お札
絵馬 500円
Oh, THEY HAVE EMA.
LET'S WRITE ON 'EM!
きゅっ
CRUNCH
PS4ほしい
七島希
I'M DONE!
WHAT DID YOU WRITE? WHAT DID YOU WRITE?
HEY! DON'T PEEK!
さっ
FWIP
I'M DONE TOO.

Signs = Ema, amulets, charms; Amulet/charm shop

Placard = I want a PS4. —Nozumu Nanashima

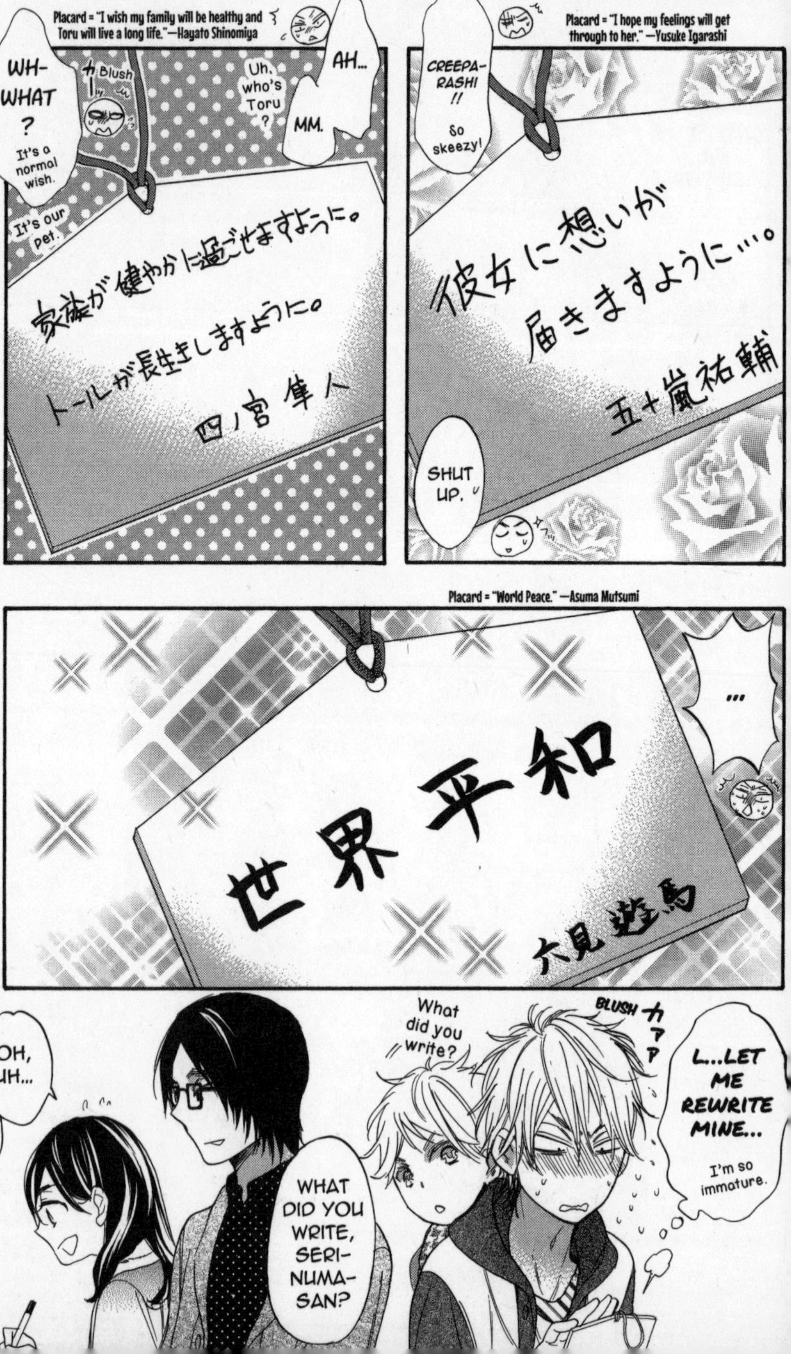
Placard = "I hope my feelings will get through to her." —Yusuke Igarashi
彼女に想いが届きますように…。
五十嵐祐輔
CREEPARASHI!!
So skeezy!
SHUT UP.
Placard = "I wish my family will be healthy and Toru will live a long life." —Hayato Shinomiya
AH... MM.
Uh, who's Toru?
WH-WHAT?
Blush
It's a normal wish.
It's our pet.
家族が健やかに過ごせますように。
トールが長生きしますように。
四ノ宮隼人
Placard = "World Peace." —Asuma Mutsumi
...
世界平和
六見遊馬
BLUSH
L...LET ME REWRITE MINE...
I'm so immature.
What did you write?
WHAT DID YOU WRITE, SERINUMA-SAN?
OH, UH...
ALL DONE!

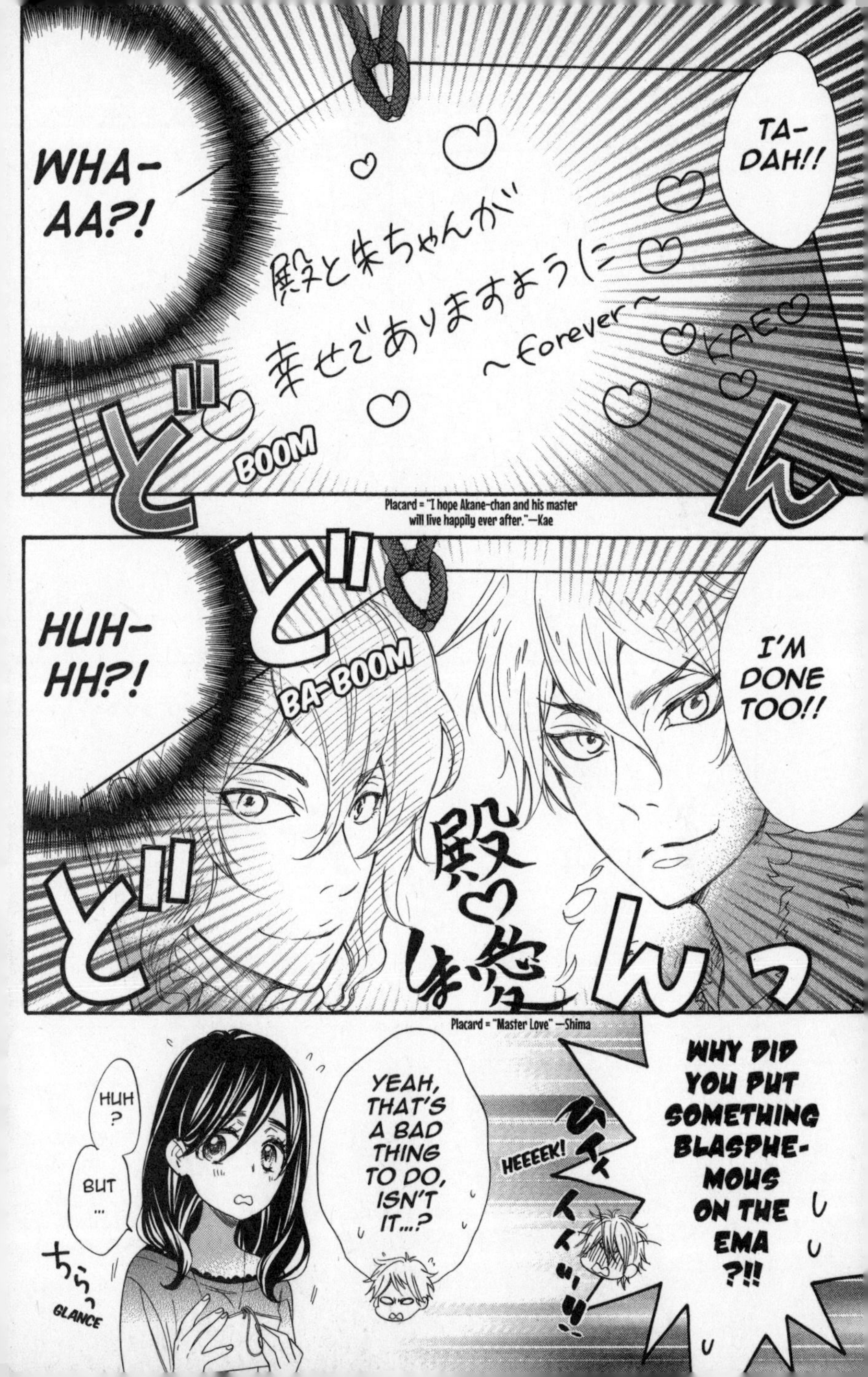
TA-DAH!!
殿と朱ちゃんが幸せでありますように
～Forever～
KAE
WHA-AA?!
どどん
BOOM
Placard = "I hope Akane-chan and his master will live happily ever after."—Kae
I'M DONE TOO!!
殿♡しま命
HUH-HH?!
どどんっ
BA-BOOM
Placard = "Master Love" —Shima
WHY DID YOU PUT SOMETHING BLASPHEMOUS ON THE EMA?!!
ひイイイッ!!
HEEEEK!
YEAH, THAT'S A BAD THING TO DO, ISN'T IT...?
HUH?
BUT...
ちらっ
GLANCE

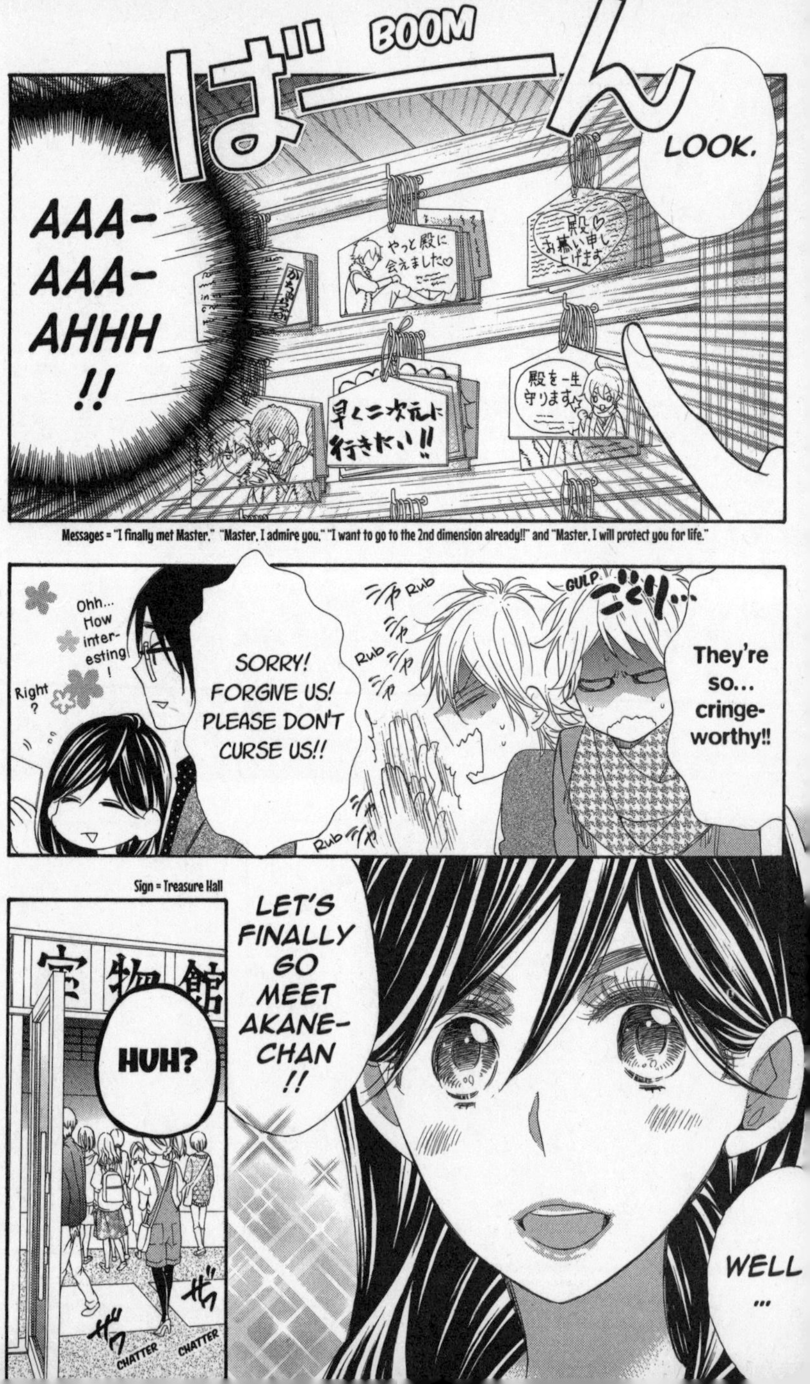

BOOM
ばーん
LOOK.
AAA-AAA-AHHH!!
殿♡ お慕い申し上げます
やっと殿に会えました♡
殿を一生守ります☆
早く二次元に行きたい!!
Messages = "I finally met Master." "Master, I admire you." "I want to go to the 2nd dimension already!!" and "Master, I will protect you for life."
They're so... cringe-worthy!!
GULP ごくり…
Rub
Rub
Rub
SORRY! FORGIVE US! PLEASE DON'T CURSE US!!
Ohh... How interesting!
Right?
WELL...
LET'S FINALLY GO MEET AKANE-CHAN!!
Sign = Treasure Hall
宝物館
HUH?
CHATTER CHATTER

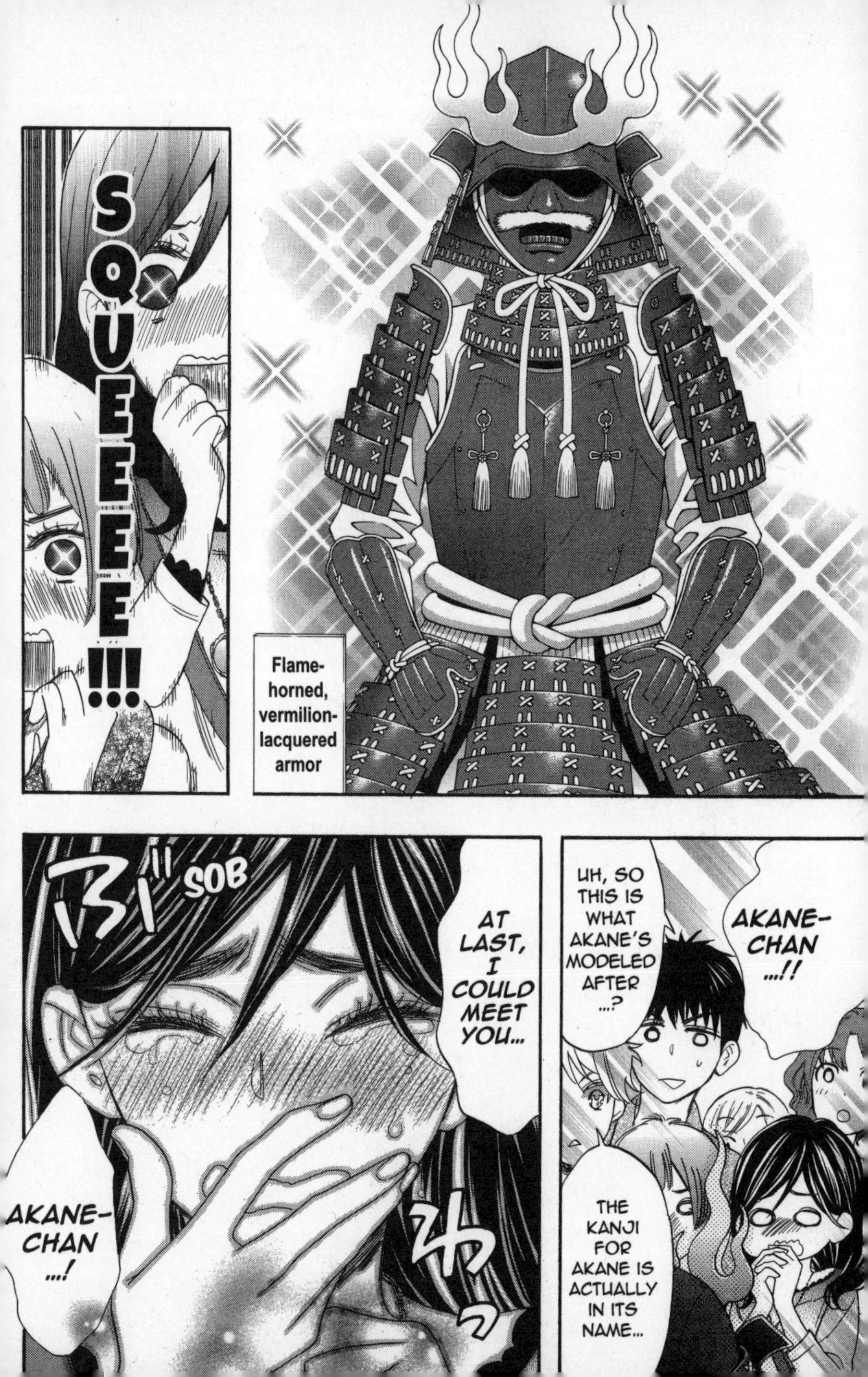
Flame-horned, vermilion-lacquered armor
SQUEEEEE!!!
AKANE-CHAN...!!
UH, SO THIS IS WHAT AKANE'S MODELED AFTER...?
THE KANJI FOR AKANE IS ACTUALLY IN ITS NAME...
SOB
AT LAST, I COULD MEET YOU...
AKANE-CHAN...!

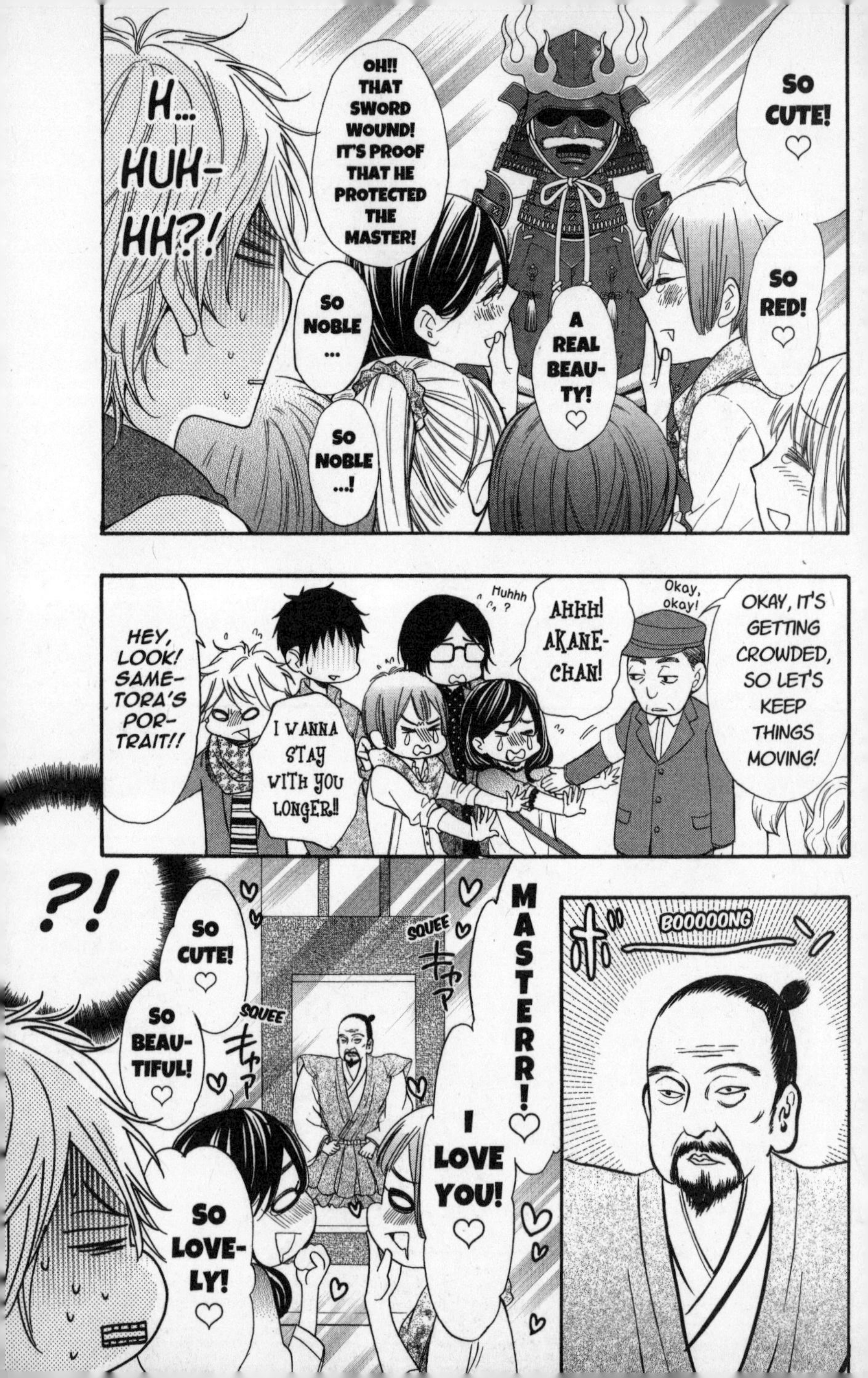
SO CUTE! ♡
SO RED! ♡
A REAL BEAU-TY! ♡
OH!! THAT SWORD WOUND! IT'S PROOF THAT HE PROTECTED THE MASTER!
SO NOBLE ...
SO NOBLE ...!
H... HUH-HH?!
OKAY, IT'S GETTING CROWDED, SO LET'S KEEP THINGS MOVING!
Okay, okay!
AHHH! AKANE-CHAN!
Muhhh ?
I WANNA STAY WITH YOU LONGER!!
HEY, LOOK! SAME-TORA'S POR-TRAIT!!
BOOOOONG
MASTERR! ♡
I LOVE YOU! ♡
SQUEE
SO CUTE! ♡
SQUEE
SO BEAU-TIFUL! ♡
SO LOVE-LY! ♡
?!

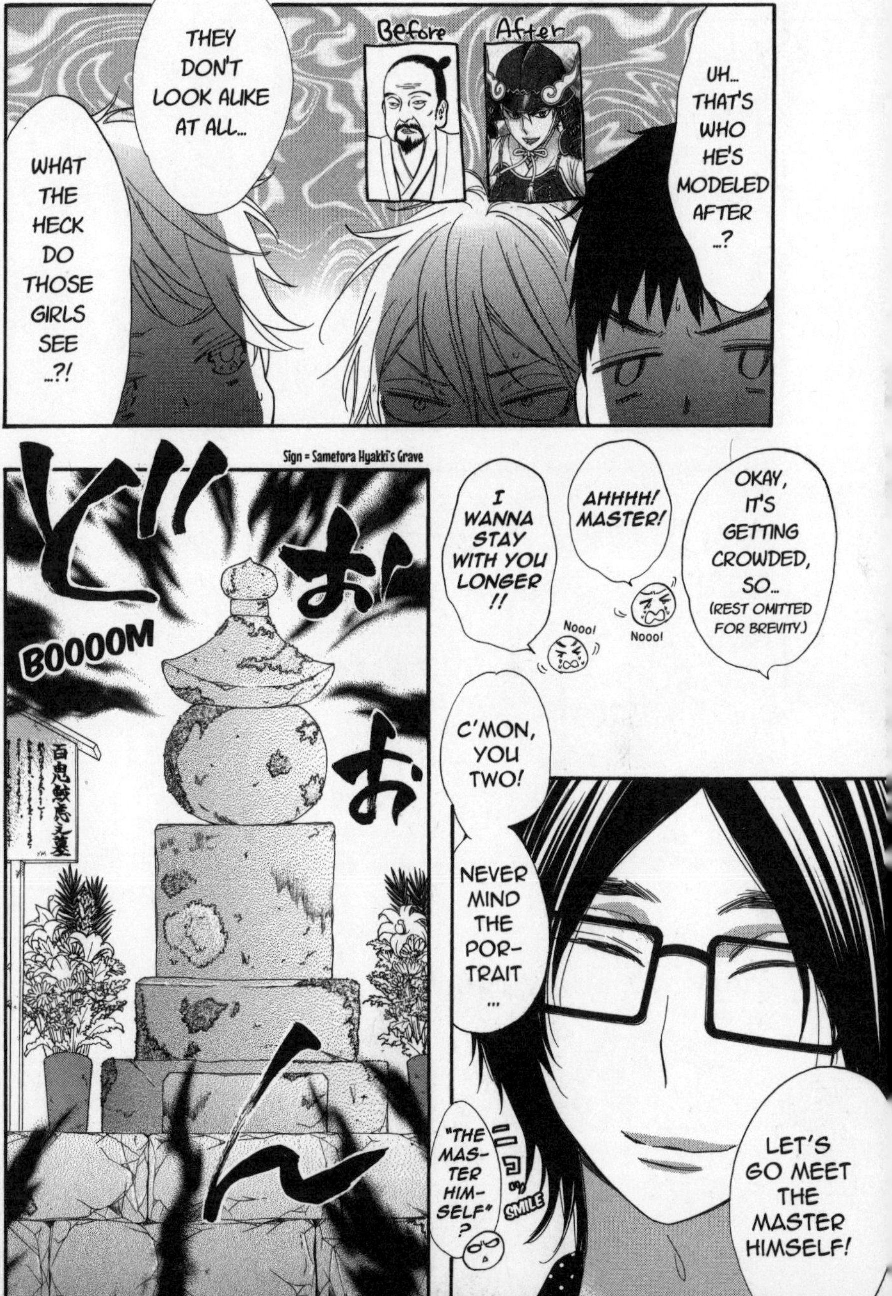
UH... THAT'S WHO HE'S MODELED AFTER ...?
Before
After
THEY DON'T LOOK ALIKE AT ALL...
WHAT THE HECK DO THOSE GIRLS SEE ...?!
OKAY, IT'S GETTING CROWDED, SO... (REST OMITTED FOR BREVITY.)
AHHHH! MASTER!
Nooo!
I WANNA STAY WITH YOU LONGER !!
Nooo!
C'MON, YOU TWO!
NEVER MIND THE POR-TRAIT ...
LET'S GO MEET THE MASTER HIMSELF!
SMILE
"THE MAS-TER HIM-SELF" ?
Sign = Sametora Hyakki's Grave
BOOOOM
百鬼鮫虎之墓

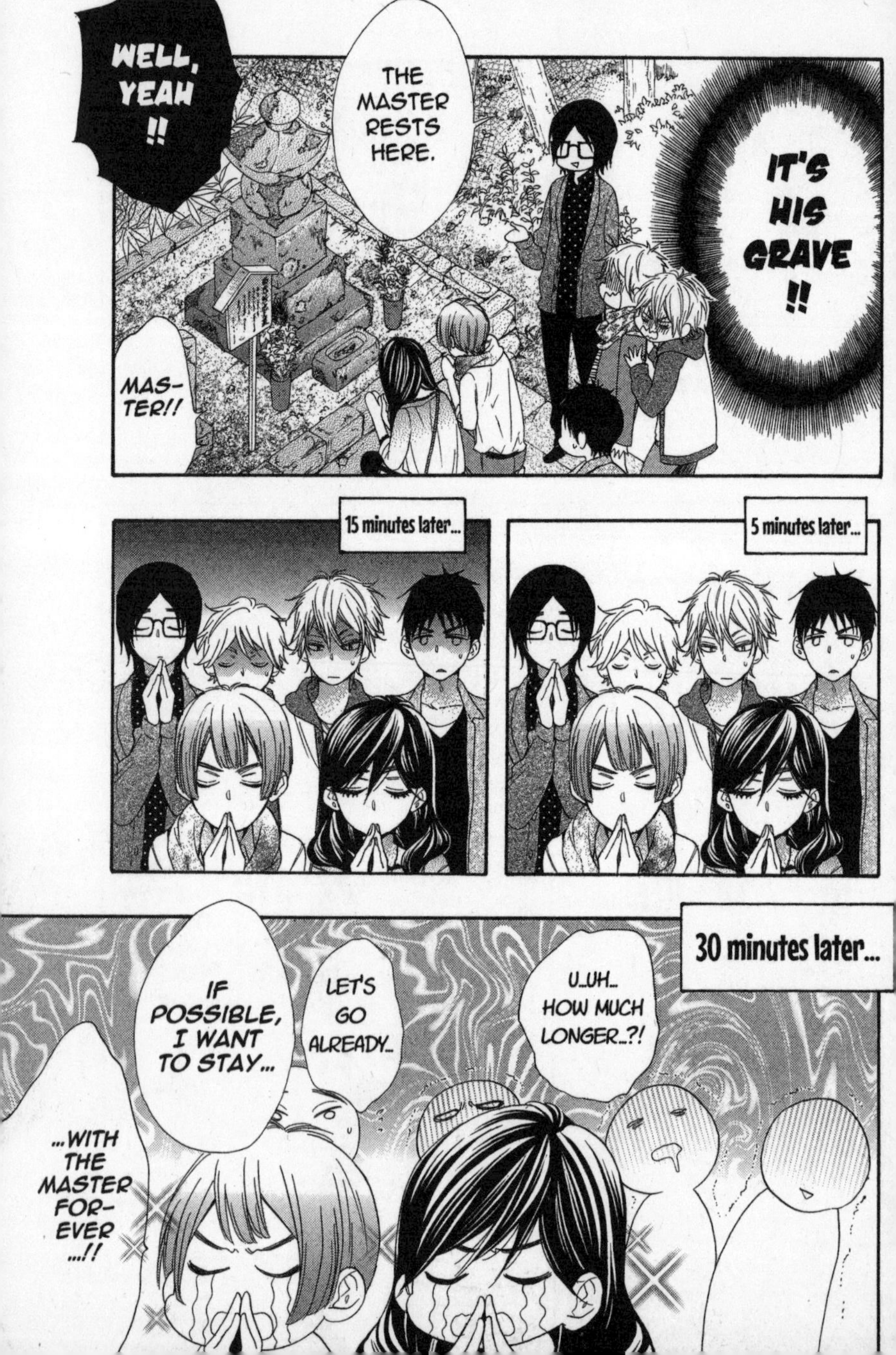
THE MASTER RESTS HERE.
IT'S HIS GRAVE!!
WELL, YEAH!!
MASTER!!
5 minutes later...
15 minutes later...
30 minutes later...
U..UH.. HOW MUCH LONGER..?!
LET'S GO ALREADY..
IF POSSIBLE, I WANT TO STAY...
...WITH THE MASTER FOREVER...!!

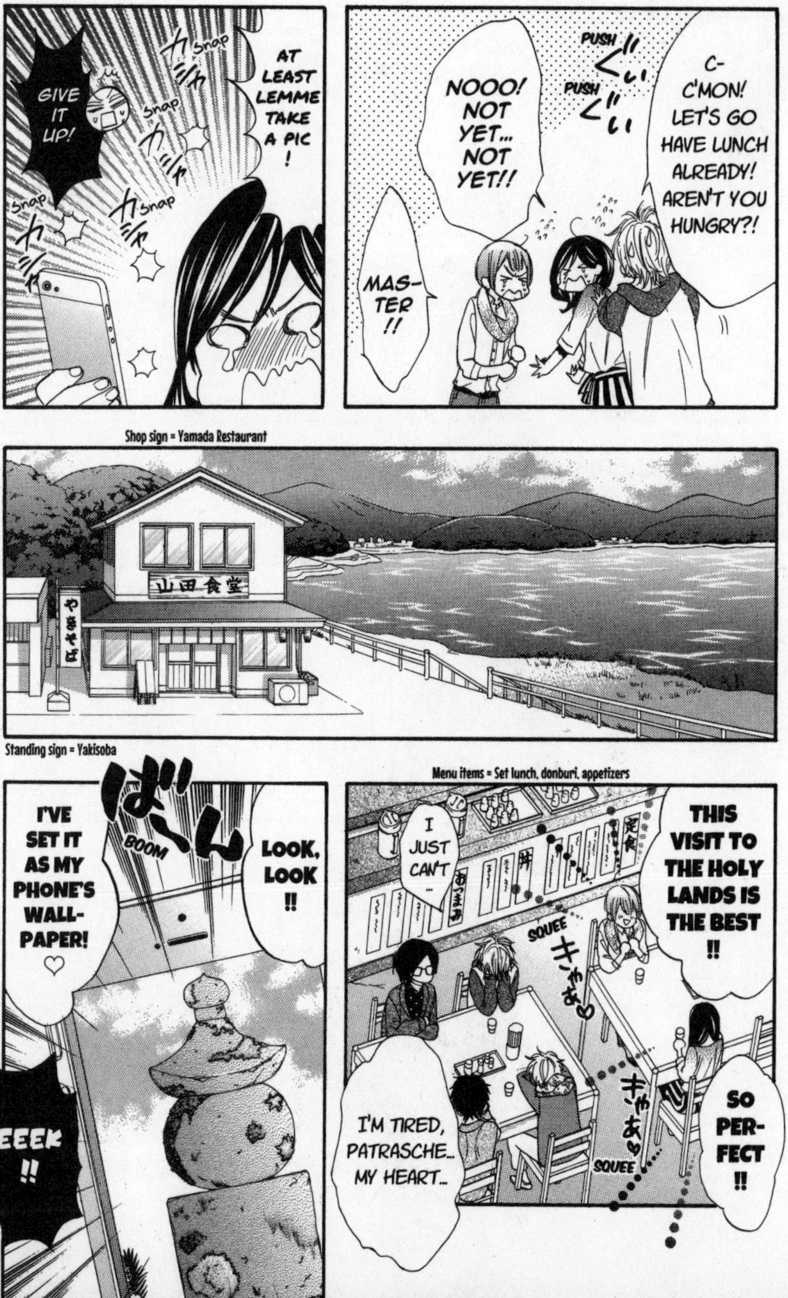
C- C'MON! LET'S GO HAVE LUNCH ALREADY! AREN'T YOU HUNGRY?!
PUSH
PUSH
NOOO! NOT YET... NOT YET!!
MAS-TER!!
AT LEAST LEMME TAKE A PIC!
Snap
Snap
Snap
Snap
GIVE IT UP!
Shop sign = Yamada Restaurant
山田食堂
やきそば
Standing sign = Yakisoba
Menu items = Set lunch, donburi, appetizers
THIS VISIT TO THE HOLY LANDS IS THE BEST!!
SQUEE
I JUST CAN'T...
SO PERFECT!!
SQUEE
I'M TIRED, PATRASCHE... MY HEART...
LOOK, LOOK!!
BOOM
I'VE SET IT AS MY PHONE'S WALL-PAPER! ♡
EEEK!!

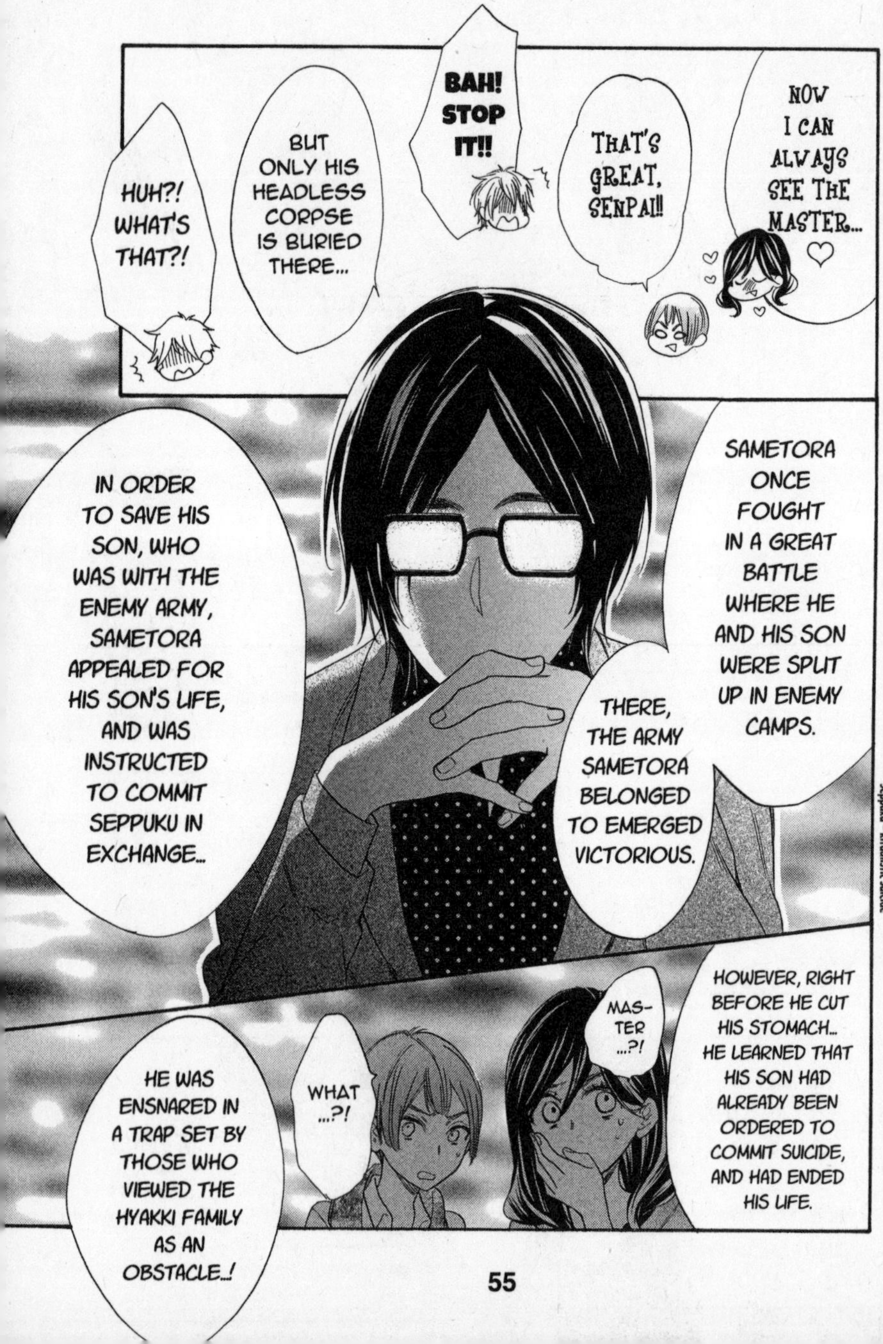
NOW I CAN ALWAYS SEE THE MASTER... ♡
THAT'S GREAT, SENPAI!!
BAH! STOP IT!!
BUT ONLY HIS HEADLESS CORPSE IS BURIED THERE...
HUH?! WHAT'S THAT?!
SAMETORA ONCE FOUGHT IN A GREAT BATTLE WHERE HE AND HIS SON WERE SPLIT UP IN ENEMY CAMPS.
THERE, THE ARMY SAMETORA BELONGED TO EMERGED VICTORIOUS.
IN ORDER TO SAVE HIS SON, WHO WAS WITH THE ENEMY ARMY, SAMETORA APPEALED FOR HIS SON'S LIFE, AND WAS INSTRUCTED TO COMMIT SEPPUKU IN EXCHANGE...
HOWEVER, RIGHT BEFORE HE CUT HIS STOMACH... HE LEARNED THAT HIS SON HAD ALREADY BEEN ORDERED TO COMMIT SUICIDE, AND HAD ENDED HIS LIFE.
MASTER ...?!
WHAT ...?!
HE WAS ENSNARED IN A TRAP SET BY THOSE WHO VIEWED THE HYAKKI FAMILY AS AN OBSTACLE...!

Seppuku = Ritualistic suicide

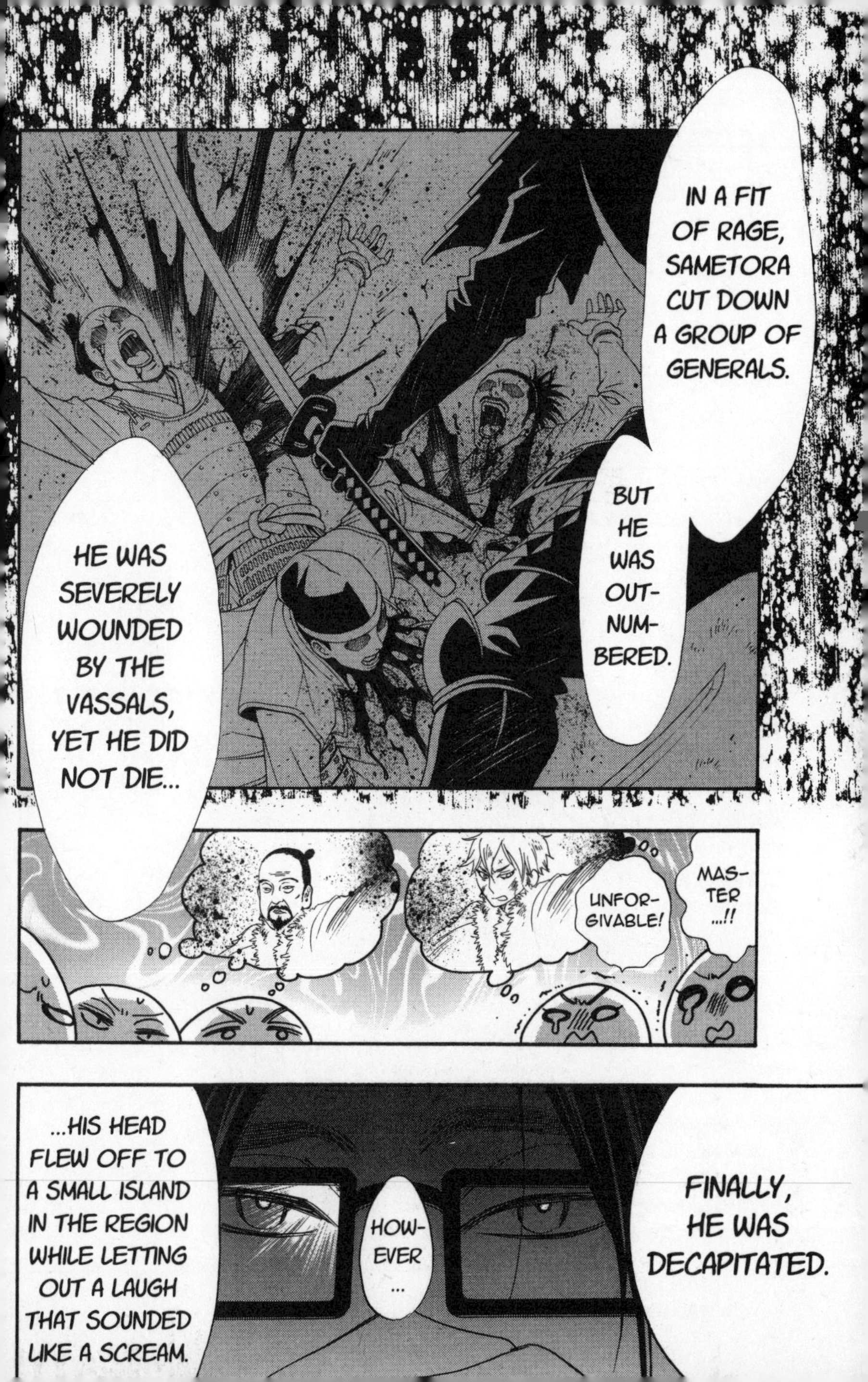
IN A FIT OF RAGE, SAMETORA CUT DOWN A GROUP OF GENERALS.
BUT HE WAS OUT-NUMBERED.
HE WAS SEVERELY WOUNDED BY THE VASSALS, YET HE DID NOT DIE...
MAS-TER ...!!
UNFOR-GIVABLE!
FINALLY, HE WAS DECAPITATED.
HOW-EVER ...
...HIS HEAD FLEW OFF TO A SMALL ISLAND IN THE REGION WHILE LETTING OUT A LAUGH THAT SOUNDED LIKE A SCREAM.

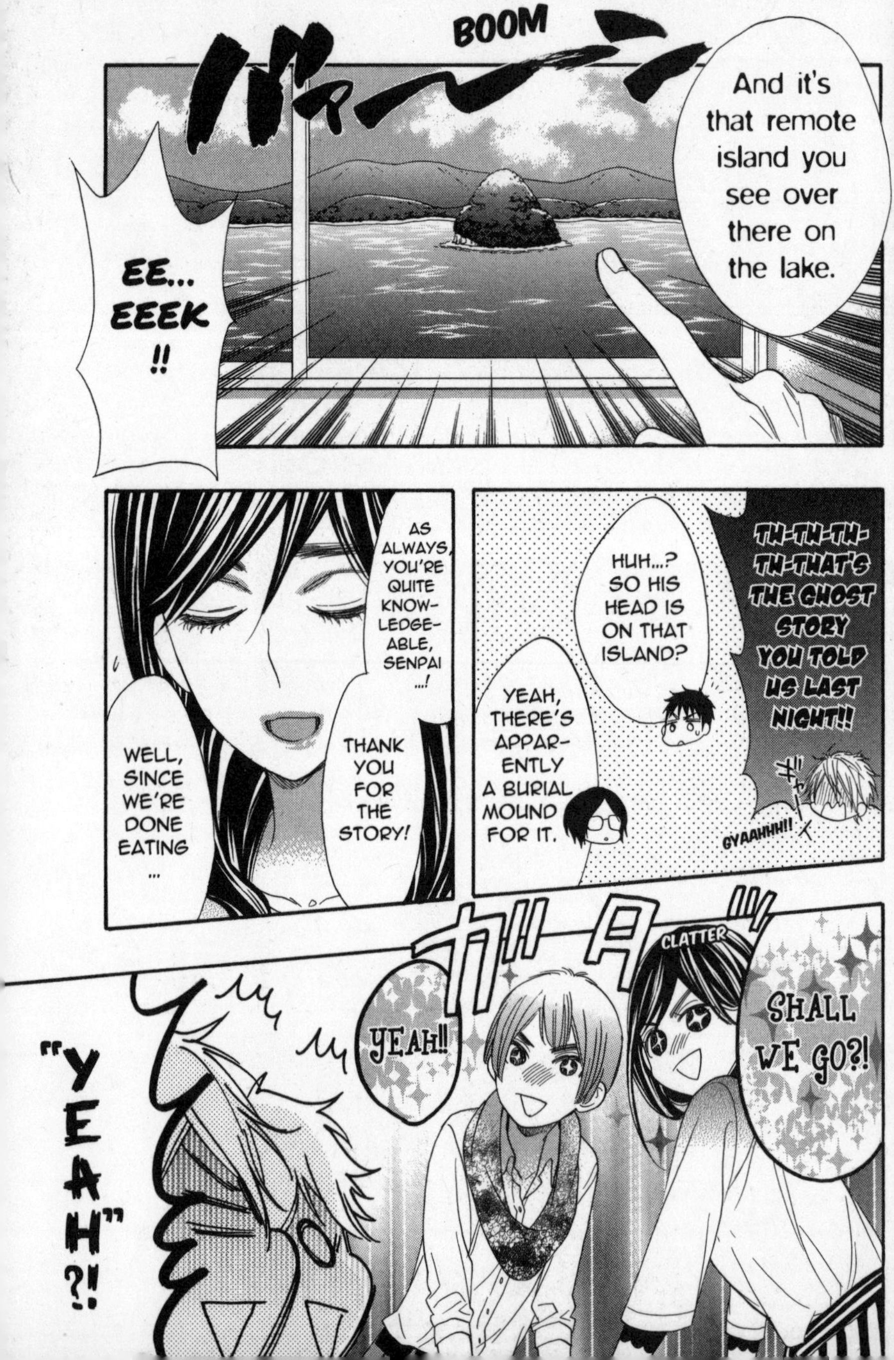

BOOM
And it's that remote island you see over there on the lake.
EE... EEEK!!
TH-TH-TH-TH-THAT'S THE GHOST STORY YOU TOLD US LAST NIGHT!!
HUH...? SO HIS HEAD IS ON THAT ISLAND?
YEAH, THERE'S APPARENTLY A BURIAL MOUND FOR IT.
GYAAHHH!!
AS ALWAYS, YOU'RE QUITE KNOWLEDGEABLE, SENPAI...!
THANK YOU FOR THE STORY!
WELL, SINCE WE'RE DONE EATING...
CLATTER
SHALL WE GO?!
YEAH!!
"YEAH"?!

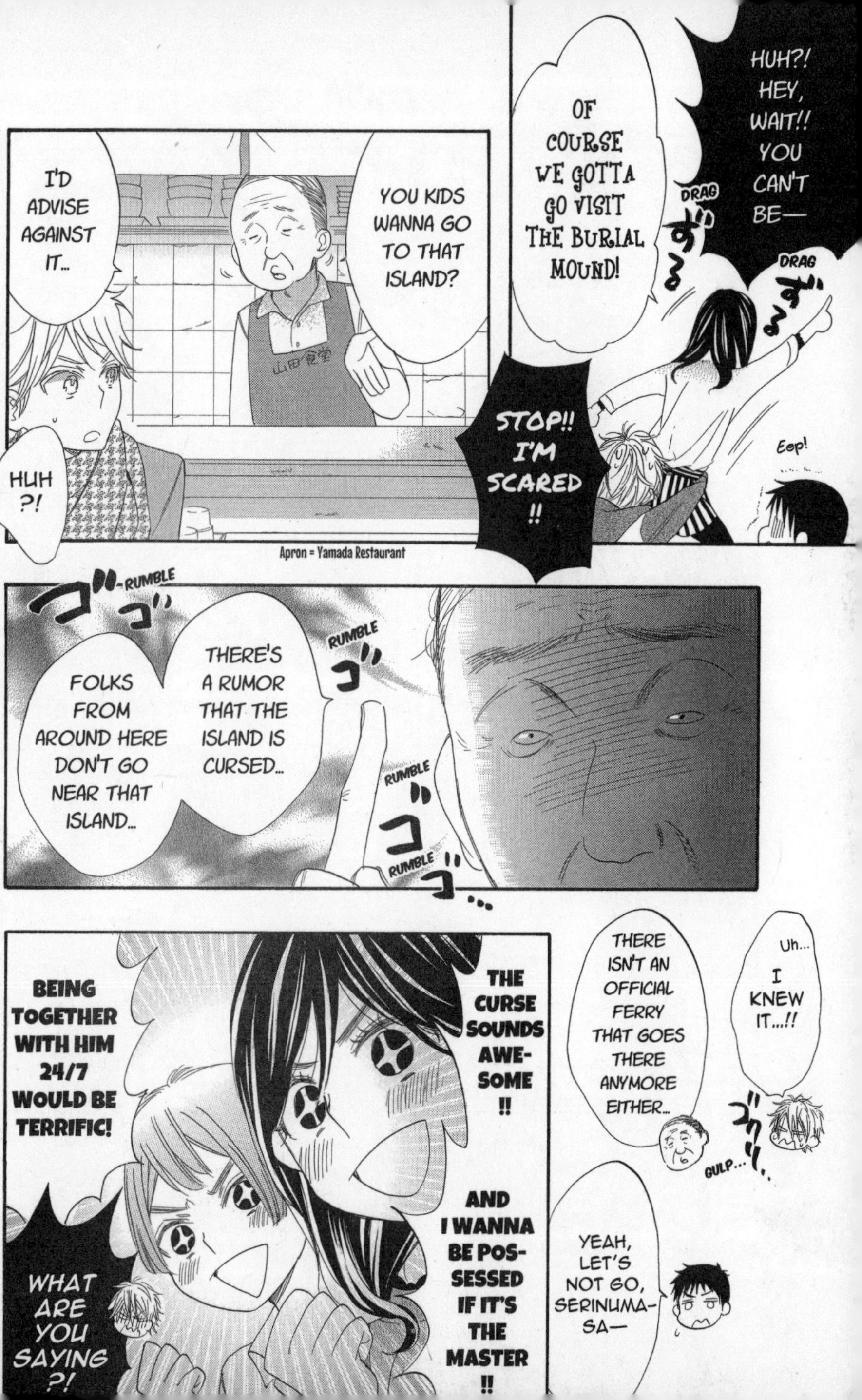
HUH?! HEY, WAIT!! YOU CAN'T BE—
OF COURSE WE GOTTA GO VISIT THE BURIAL MOUND!
DRAG
DRAG
STOP!! I'M SCARED!!
Eep!
YOU KIDS WANNA GO TO THAT ISLAND?
I'D ADVISE AGAINST IT...
HUH?!
Apron = Yamada Restaurant
RUMBLE
RUMBLE
THERE'S A RUMOR THAT THE ISLAND IS CURSED...
FOLKS FROM AROUND HERE DON'T GO NEAR THAT ISLAND...
RUMBLE
RUMBLE
Uh... I KNEW IT...!!
THERE ISN'T AN OFFICIAL FERRY THAT GOES THERE ANYMORE EITHER...
GULP...
YEAH, LET'S NOT GO, SERINUMA-SA—
THE CURSE SOUNDS AWESOME!!
BEING TOGETHER WITH HIM 24/7 WOULD BE TERRIFIC!
AND I WANNA BE POSSESSED IF IT'S THE MASTER!!
WHAT ARE YOU SAYING?!

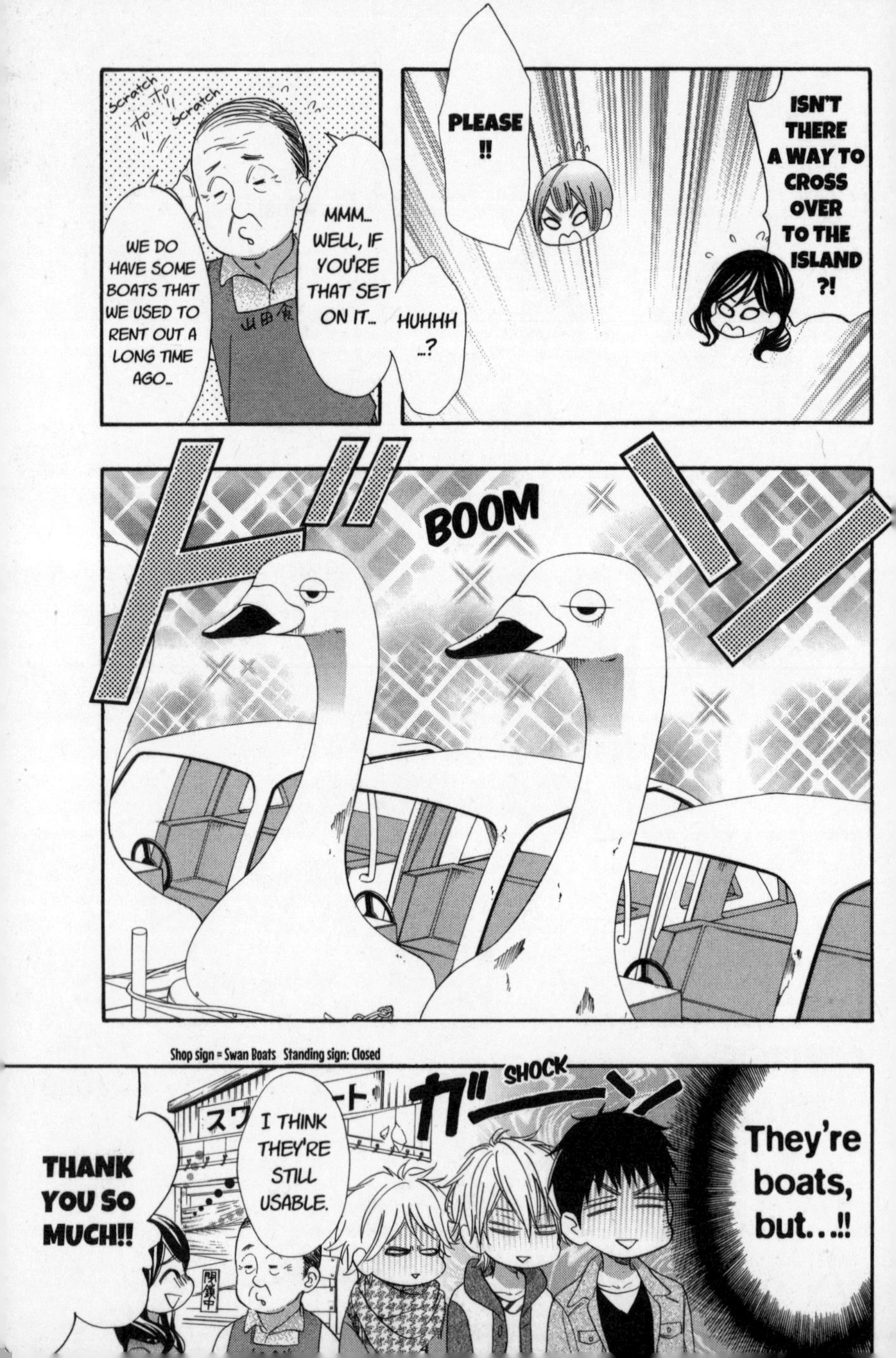
ISN'T THERE A WAY TO CROSS OVER TO THE ISLAND ?!
PLEASE !!
HUHHH ...?
Scratch Scratch
MMM... WELL, IF YOU'RE THAT SET ON IT...
WE DO HAVE SOME BOATS THAT WE USED TO RENT OUT A LONG TIME AGO...
BOOM
Shop sign = Swan Boats Standing sign: Closed
They're boats, but. . .!!
SHOCK
I THINK THEY'RE STILL USABLE.
THANK YOU SO MUCH!!

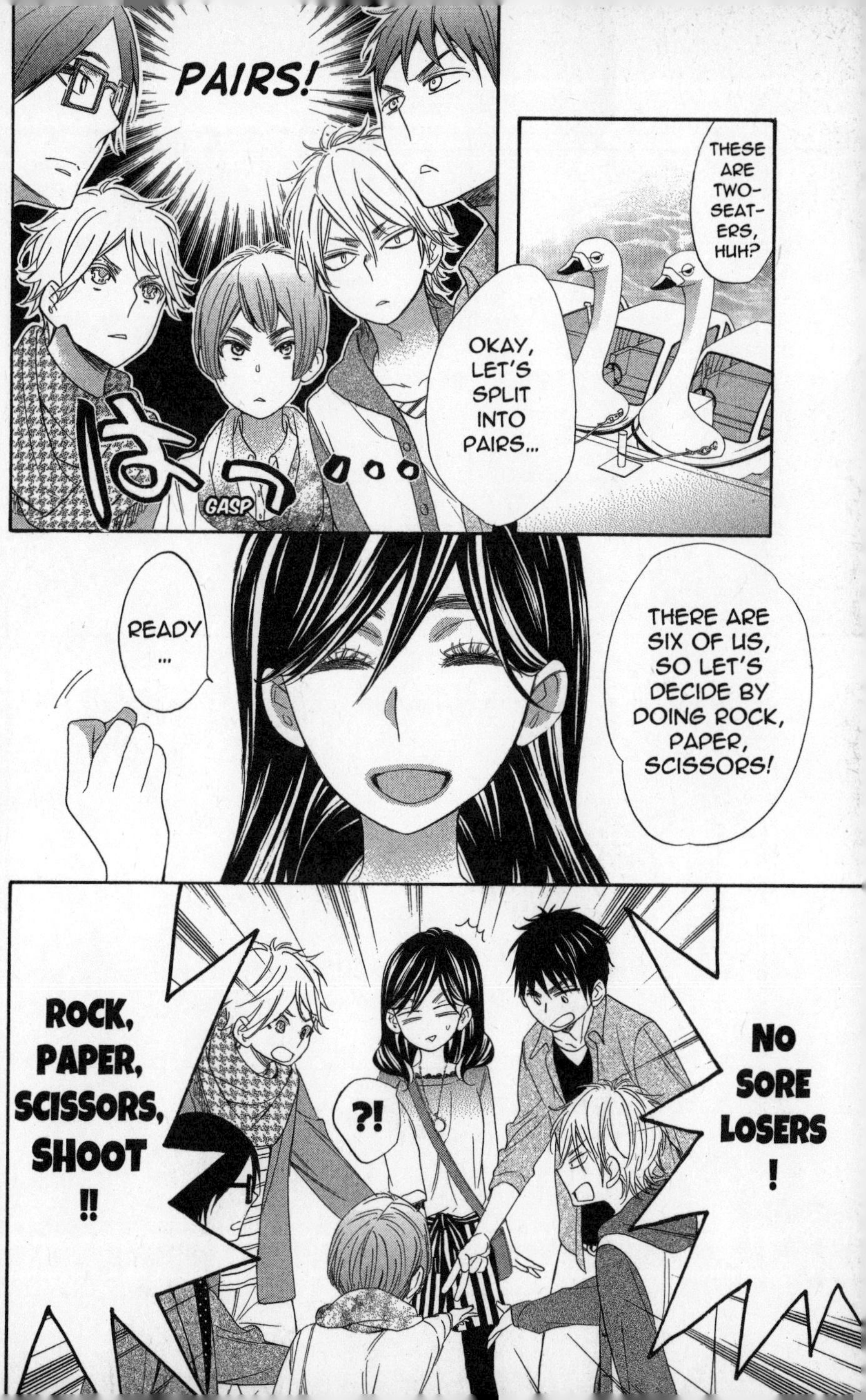
THESE ARE TWO-SEATERS, HUH?
OKAY, LET'S SPLIT INTO PAIRS...
PAIRS!
はっ
GASP
...
THERE ARE SIX OF US, SO LET'S DECIDE BY DOING ROCK, PAPER, SCISSORS!
READY ...
NO SORE LOSERS!
?!
ROCK, PAPER, SCISSORS, SHOOT!!

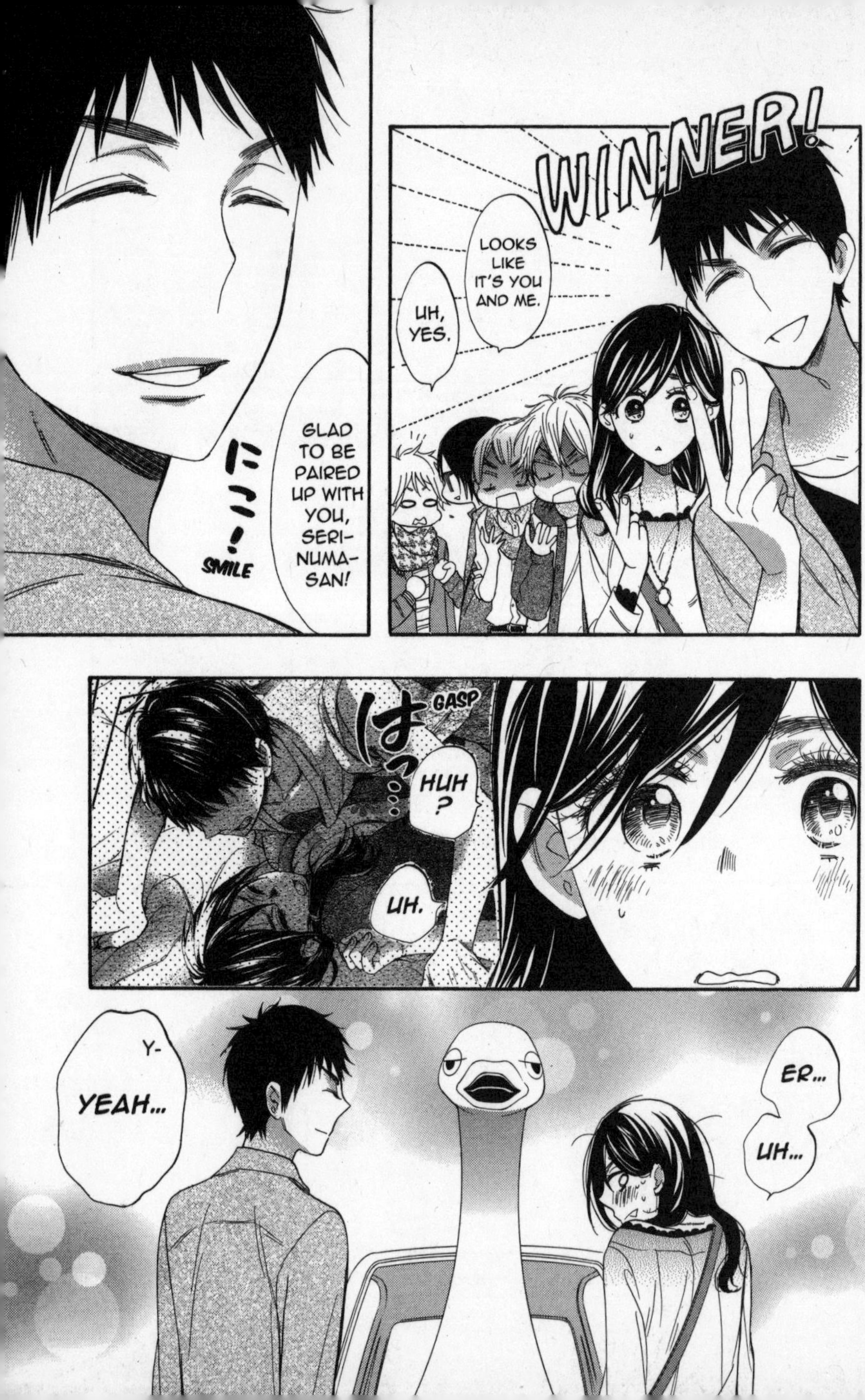
WINNER!
LOOKS LIKE IT'S YOU AND ME.
UH, YES.
GLAD TO BE PAIRED UP WITH YOU, SERI-NUMA-SAN!
にこ!
SMILE
はっ
GASP
HUH?
UH.
ER...
UH...
Y-
YEAH...

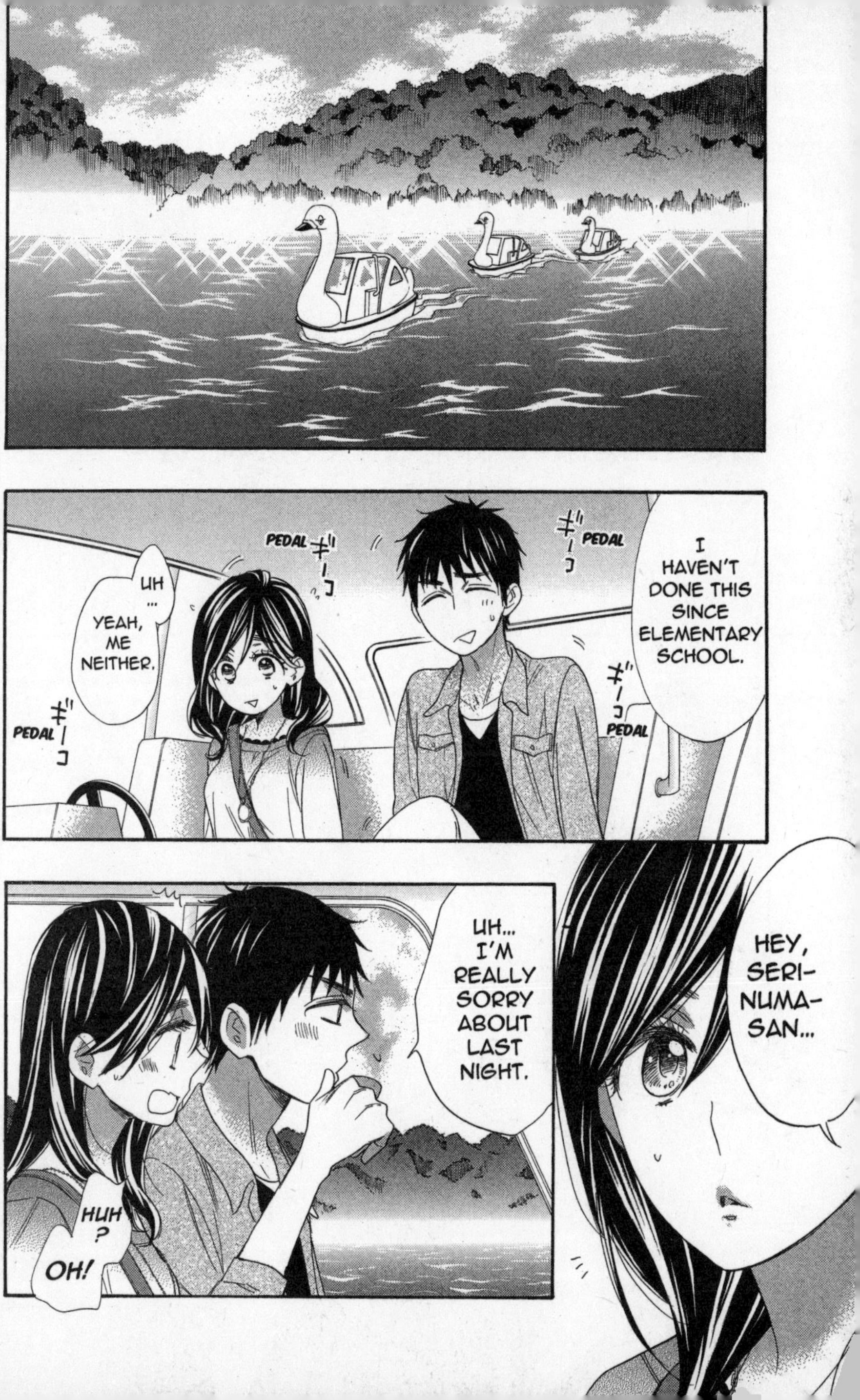

I HAVEN'T DONE THIS SINCE ELEMENTARY SCHOOL.
PEDAL
PEDAL
UH... YEAH, ME NEITHER.
PEDAL
PEDAL
HEY, SERI-NUMA-SAN...
UH... I'M REALLY SORRY ABOUT LAST NIGHT.
HUH? OH!

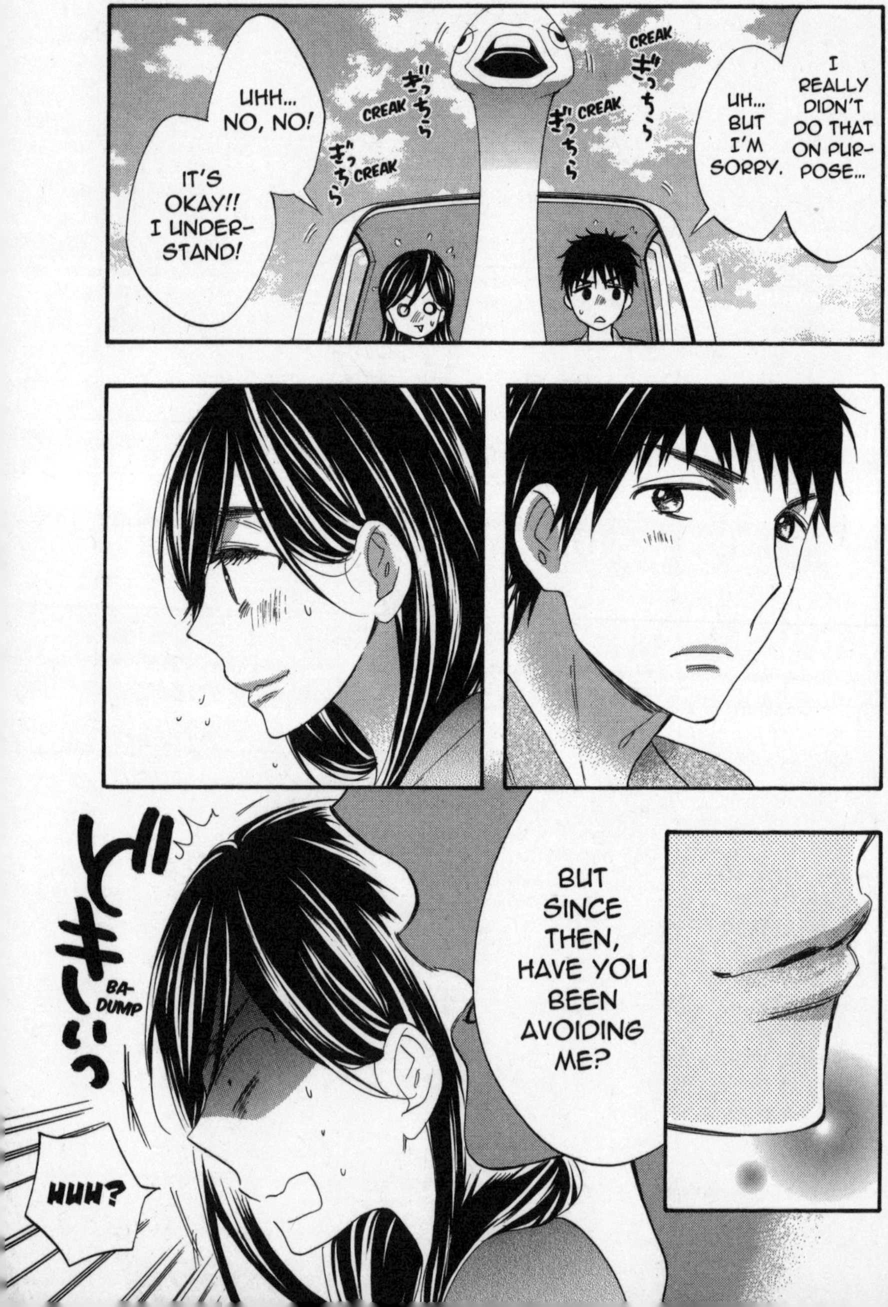
I REALLY DIDN'T DO THAT ON PURPOSE...
UH... BUT I'M SORRY.
CREAK
ぎっちら
CREAK
ぎっちら
CREAK
ぎっちら
CREAK
ぎっちら
UHH... NO, NO!
IT'S OKAY!! I UNDERSTAND!
BUT SINCE THEN, HAVE YOU BEEN AVOIDING ME?
BA-DUMP
HUH?

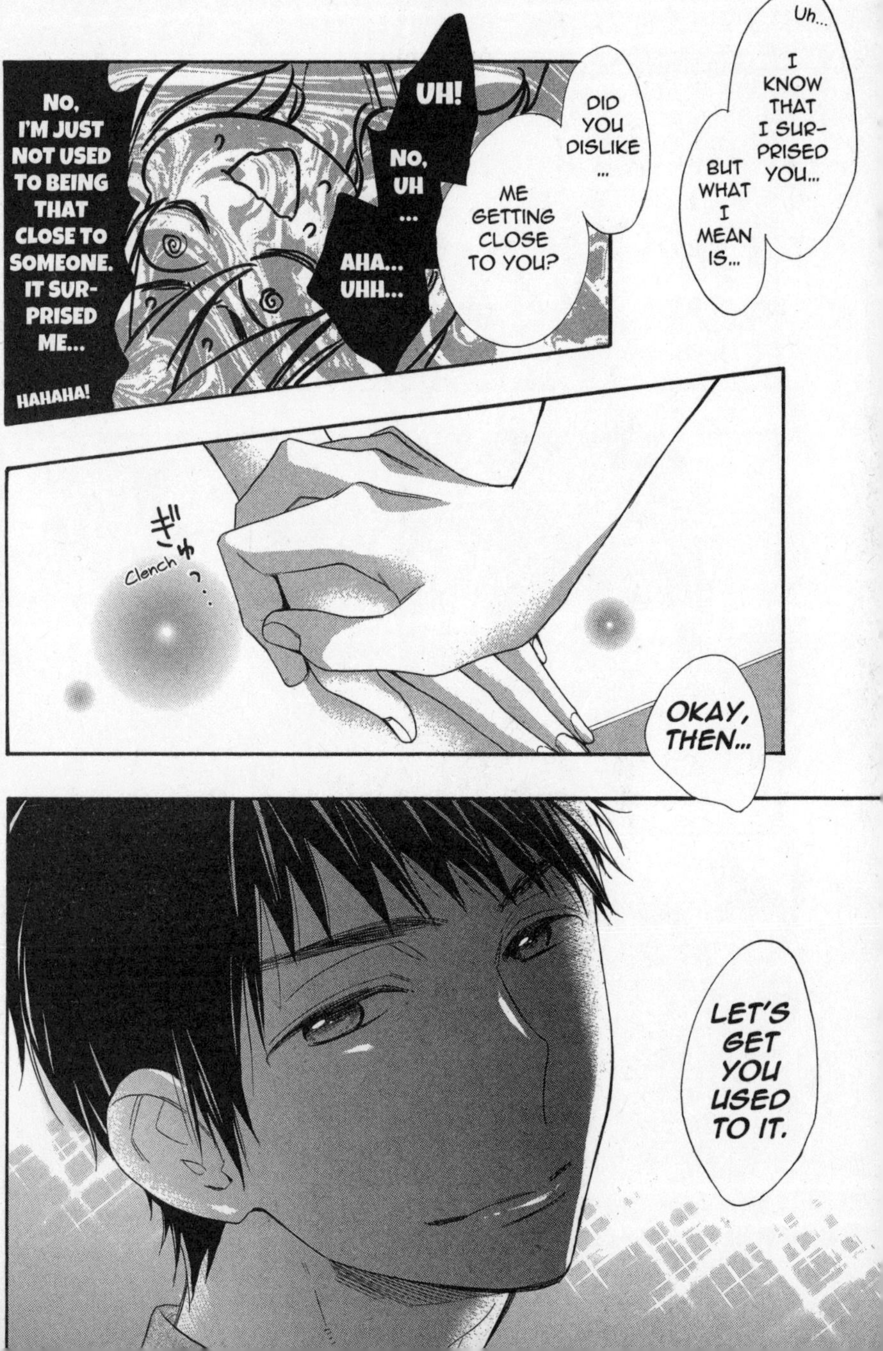
Uh...
I KNOW THAT I SURPRISED YOU...
BUT WHAT I MEAN IS...
DID YOU DISLIKE...
ME GETTING CLOSE TO YOU?
UH!
NO, UH...
AHA... UHH...
NO, I'M JUST NOT USED TO BEING THAT CLOSE TO SOMEONE. IT SURPRISED ME...
HAHAHA!
ぎゅっ...
Clench
OKAY, THEN...
LET'S GET YOU USED TO IT.

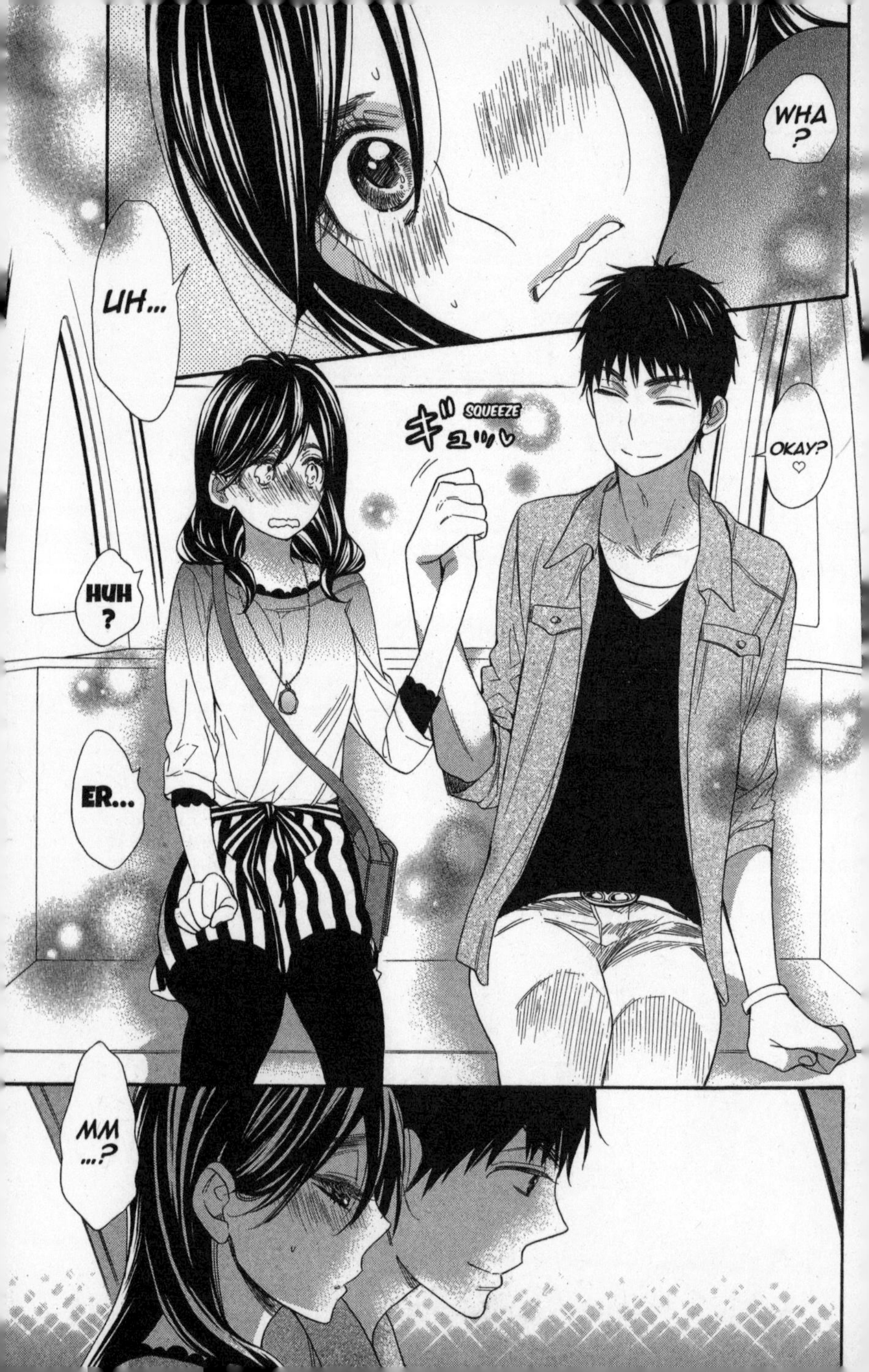
WHA?
UH...
OKAY? ♡
ギュッ♡ SQUEEZE
HUH?
ER...
MM ...?

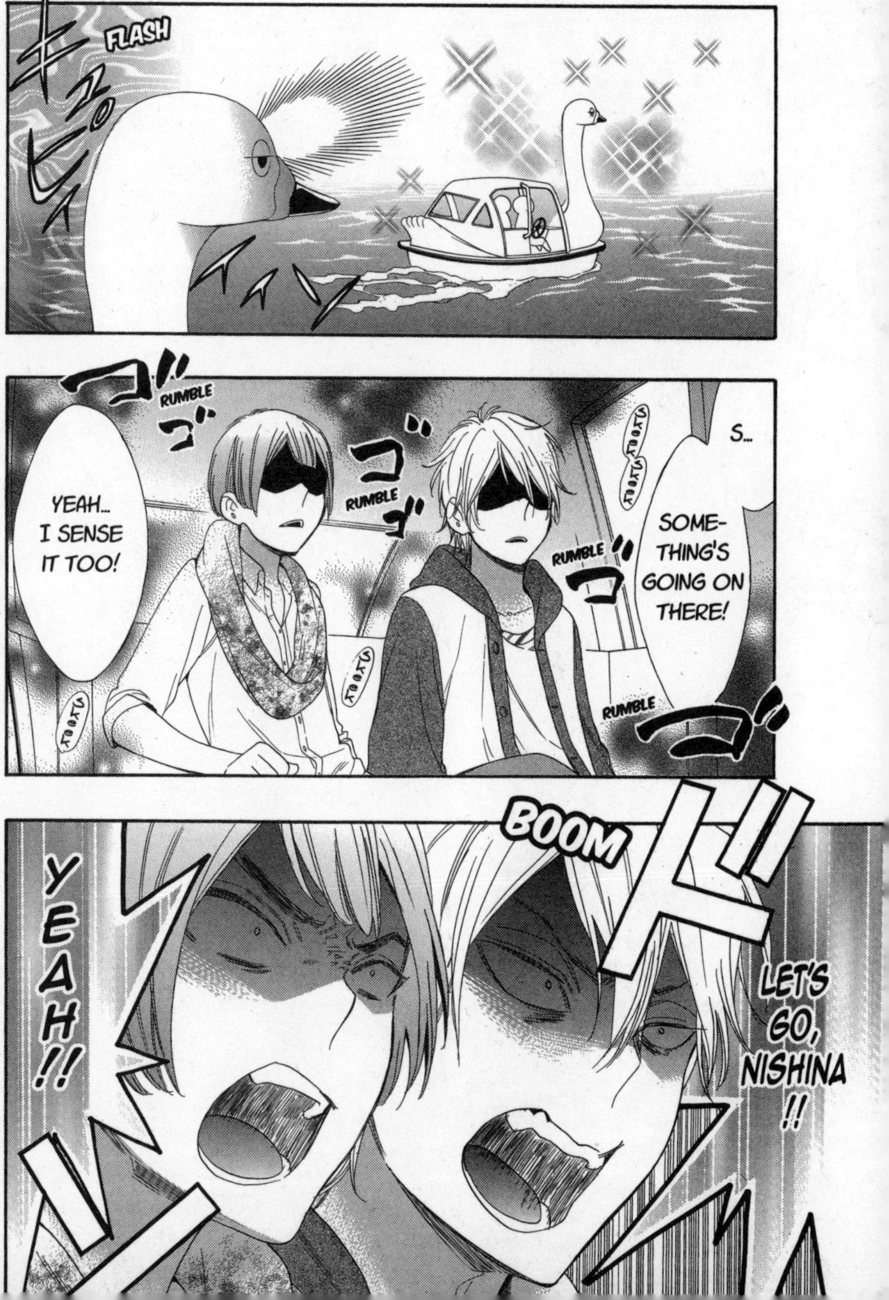
FLASH
RUMBLE
RUMBLE
RUMBLE
RUMBLE
S...
SOMETHING'S GOING ON THERE!
YEAH... I SENSE IT TOO!
BOOM
LET'S GO, NISHINA!!
YEAH!!

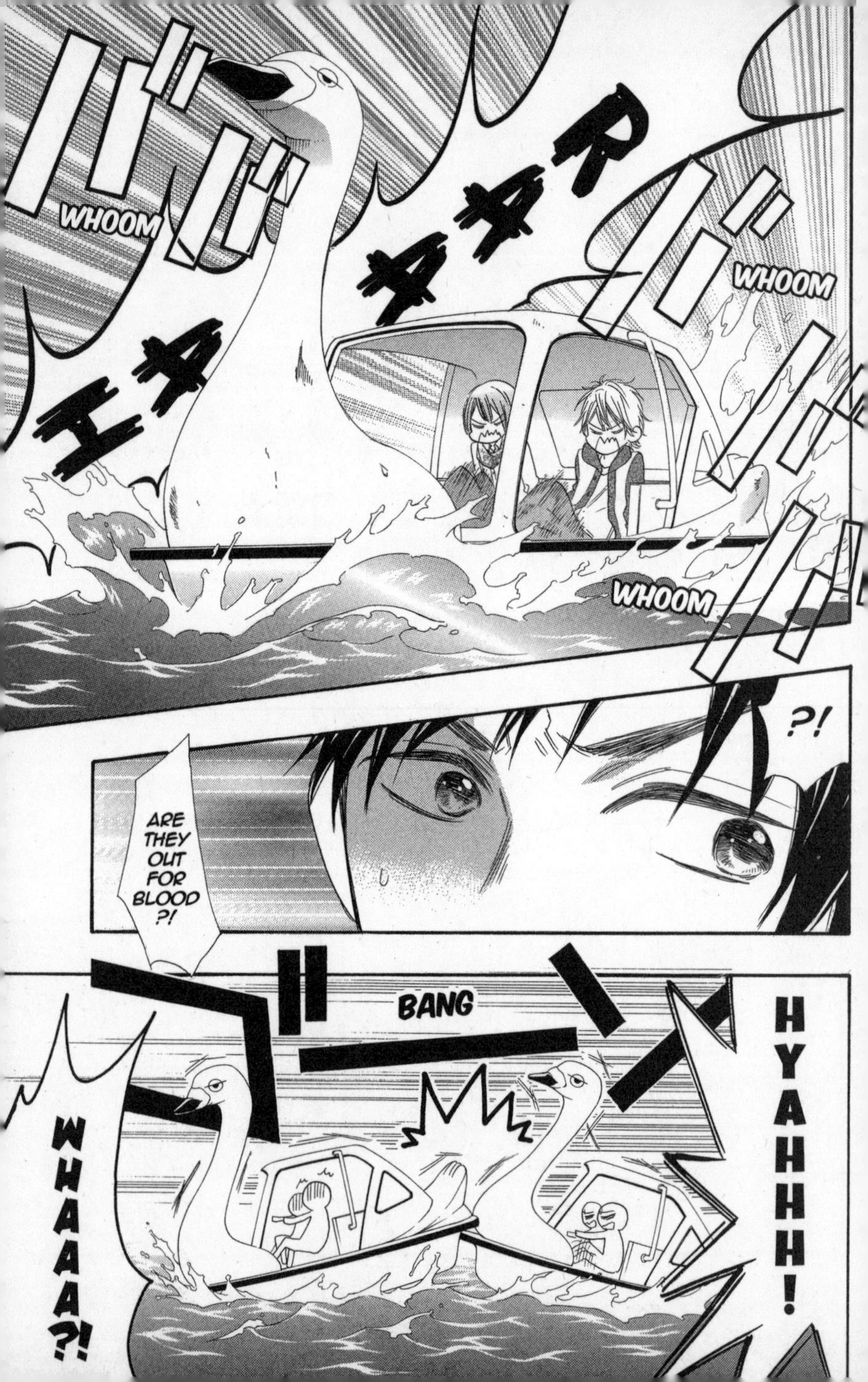
WHOOM
WHOOM
WHOOM
?!
ARE THEY OUT FOR BLOOD ?!
HYAHHH!
BANG
WHAAAA?!

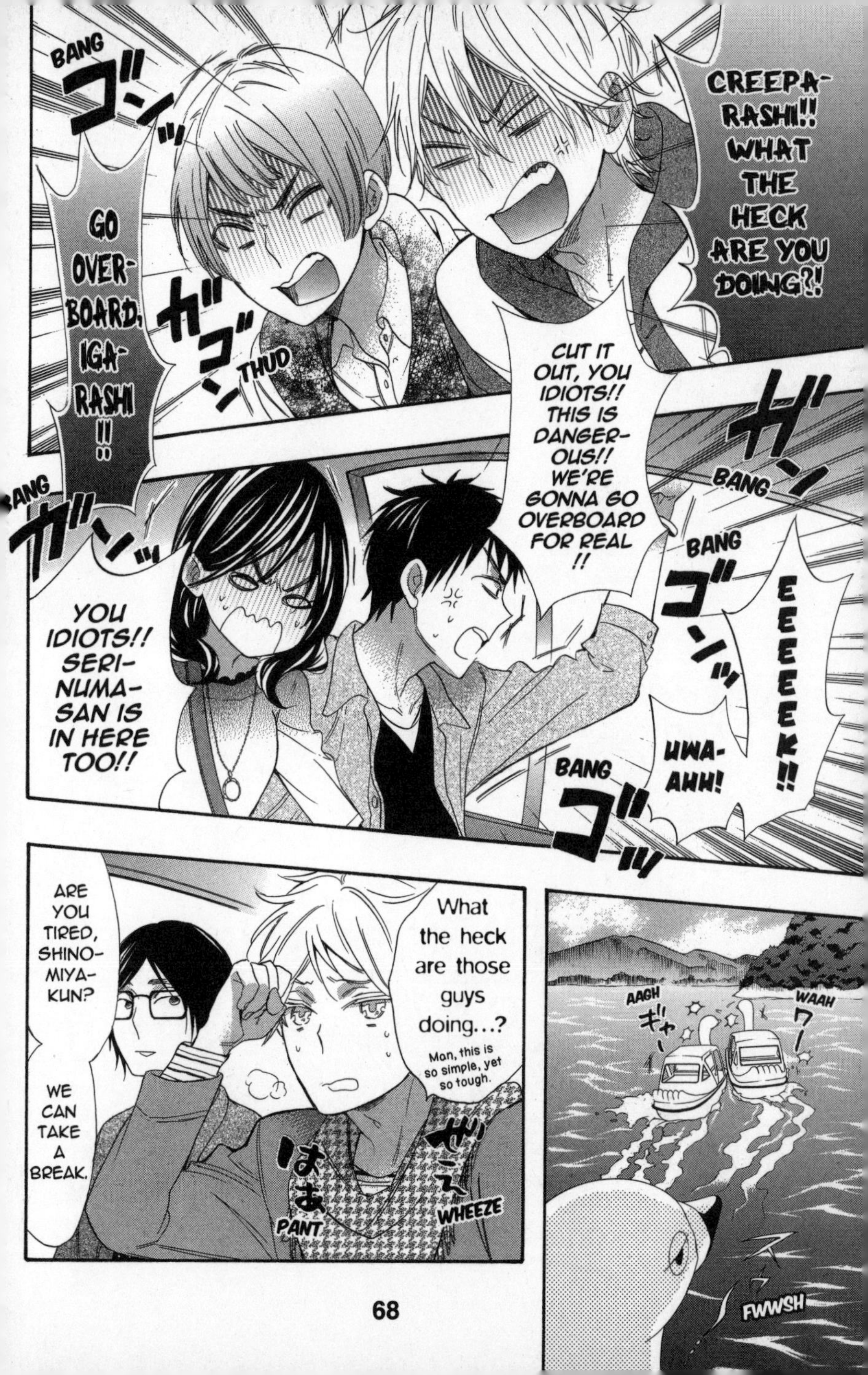
CREEPA-RASHI!! WHAT THE HECK ARE YOU DOING?!
BANG
GO OVER-BOARD, IGA-RASHI!!
THUD
BANG
CUT IT OUT, YOU IDIOTS!! THIS IS DANGER-OUS!! WE'RE GONNA GO OVERBOARD FOR REAL!!
EEEEEEK!!
BANG
UWA-AHH!
BANG
YOU IDIOTS!! SERI-NUMA-SAN IS IN HERE TOO!!
BANG
WAAH
AAGH
FWWSH
What the heck are those guys doing...?
Man, this is so simple, yet so tough.
ARE YOU TIRED, SHINO-MIYA-KUN?
WE CAN TAKE A BREAK.
WHEEZE
PANT

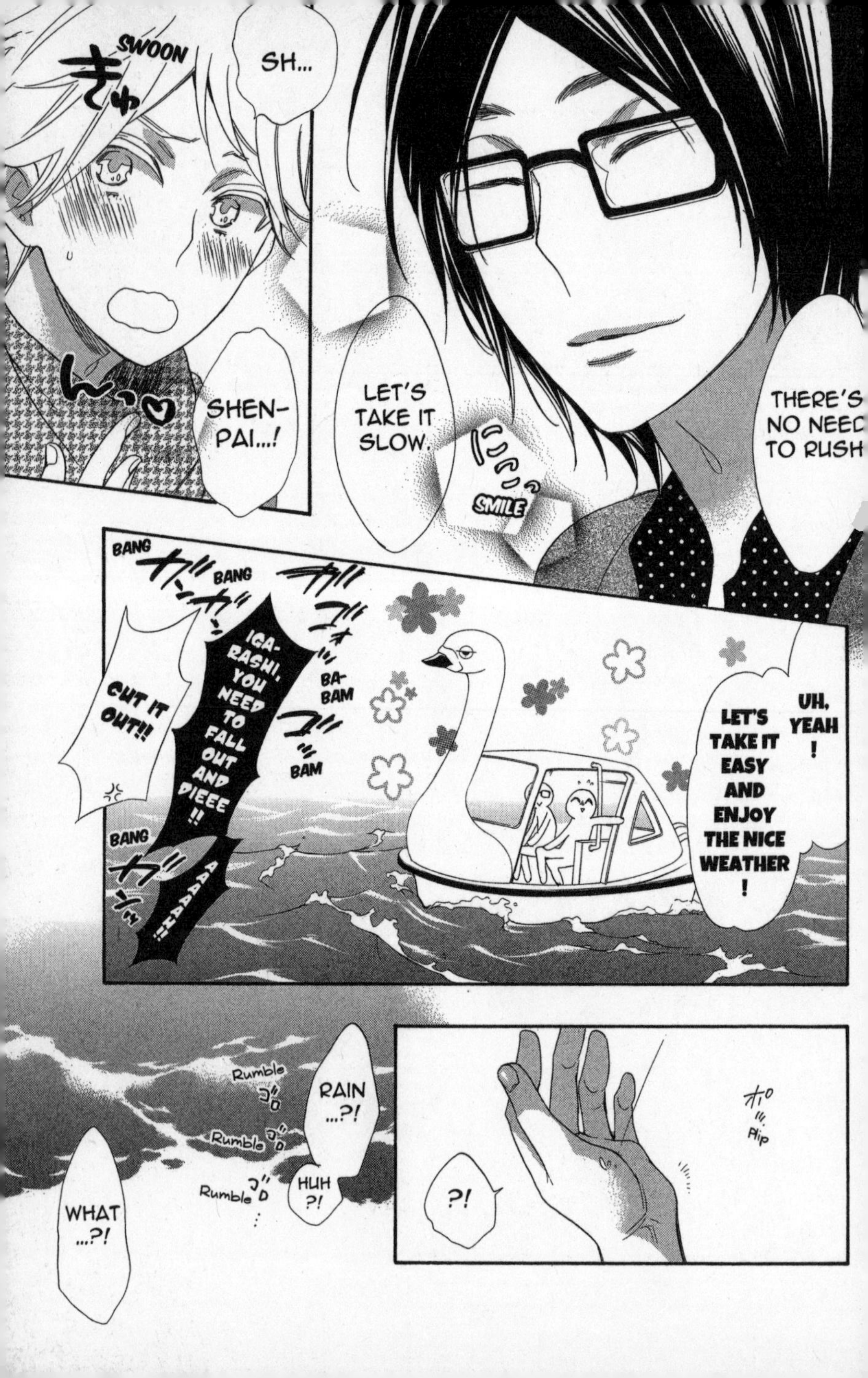
THERE'S NO NEED TO RUSH
LET'S TAKE IT SLOW.
SMILE
SH...
SWOON
SHEN-PAI...!
UH, YEAH!
LET'S TAKE IT EASY AND ENJOY THE NICE WEATHER!
BANG
BANG
BA-BAM
BAM
IGA-RASHI, YOU NEED TO FALL OUT AND DIEEE!!
CUT IT OUT!!
BANG
AAAAAH!!
Flip
?!
RAIN...?!
HUH?!
Rumble
Rumble
Rumble
WHAT...?!

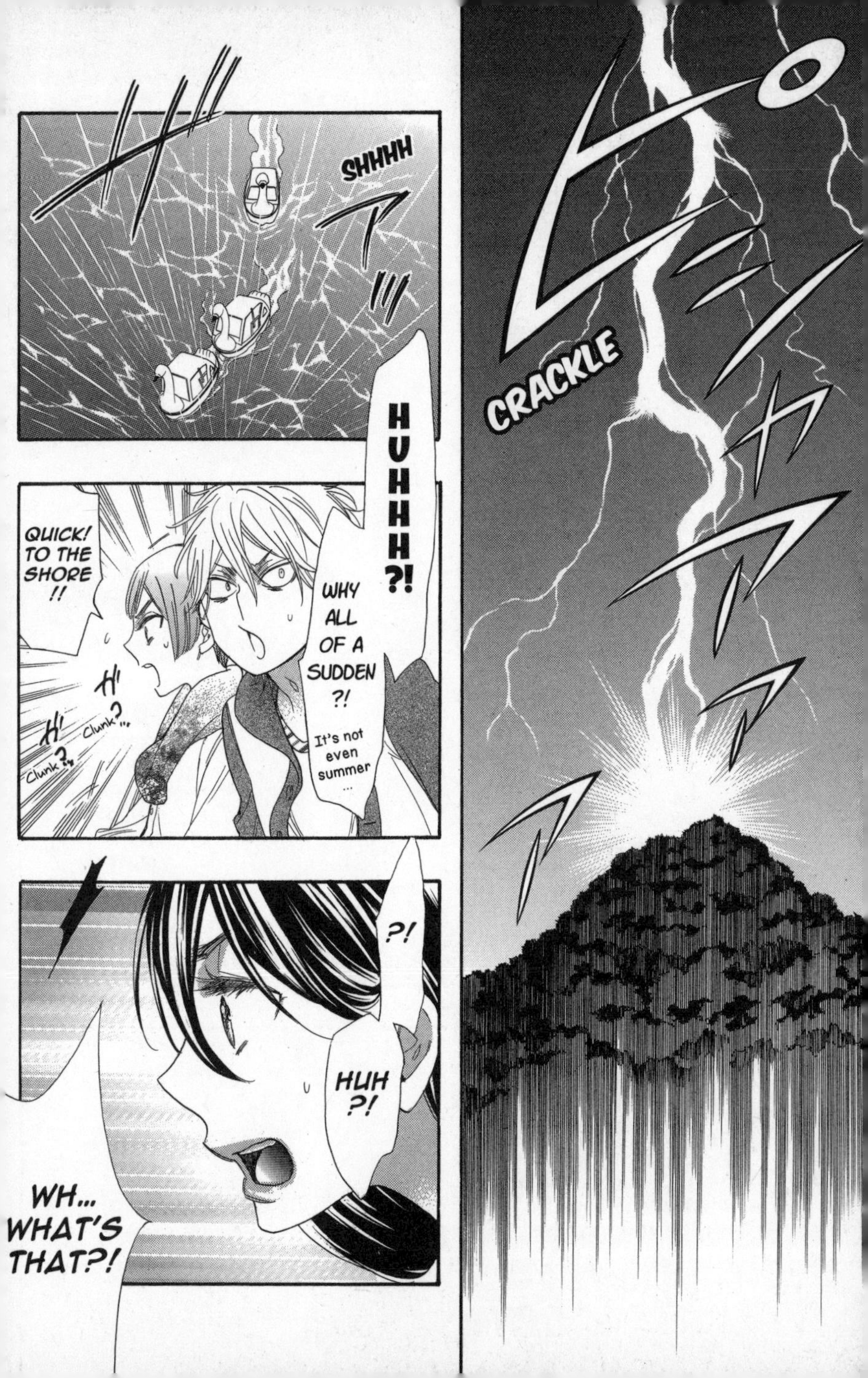
CRACKLE
SHHHH
HUHHHH?!
WHY ALL OF A SUDDEN?!
It's not even summer...
QUICK! TO THE SHORE!!
Clunk
Clunk
?!
HUH?!
WH... WHAT'S THAT?!

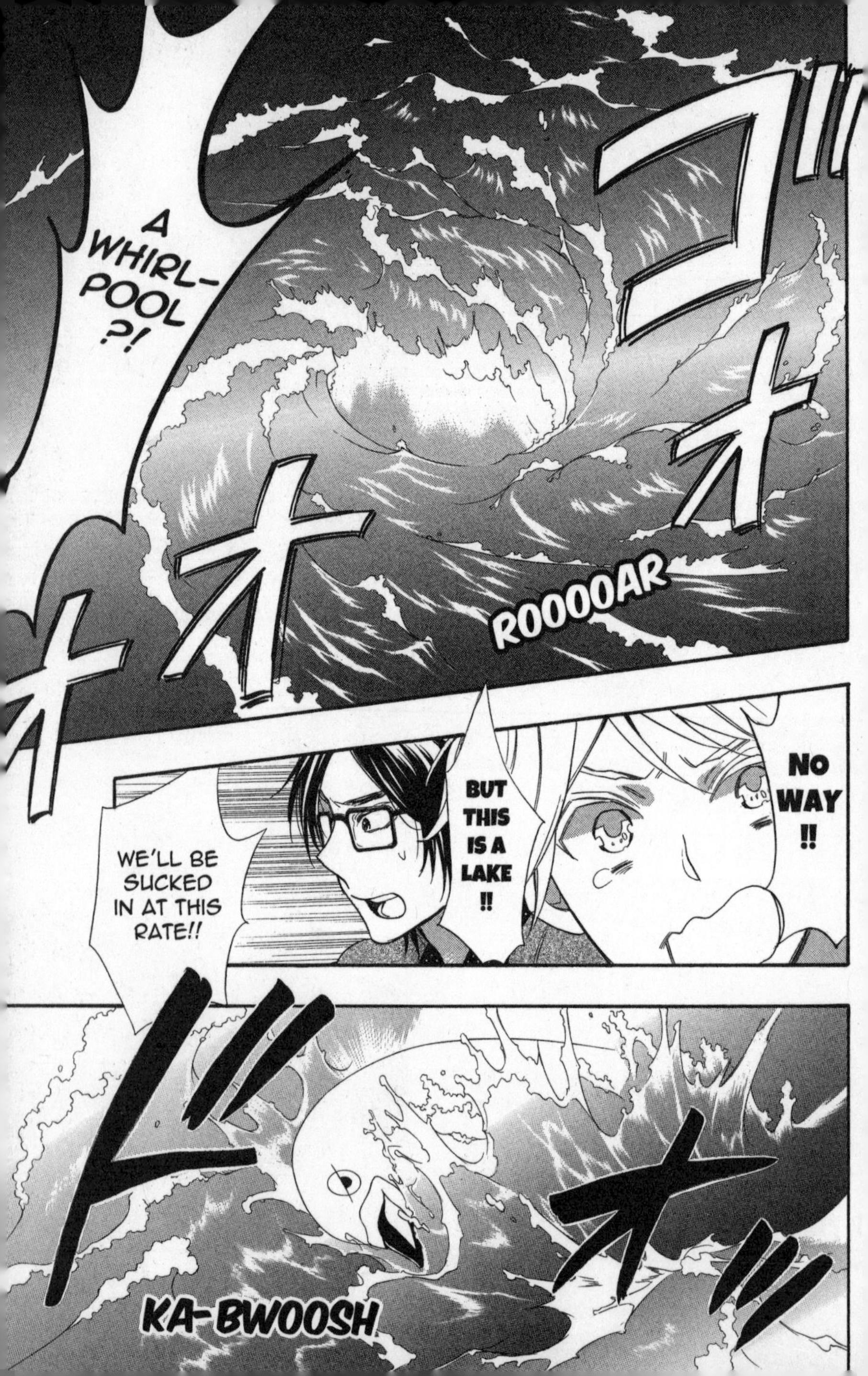
A WHIRLPOOL?!
ROOOOAR
NO WAY!!
BUT THIS IS A LAKE!!
WE'LL BE SUCKED IN AT THIS RATE!!
KA-BWOOSH

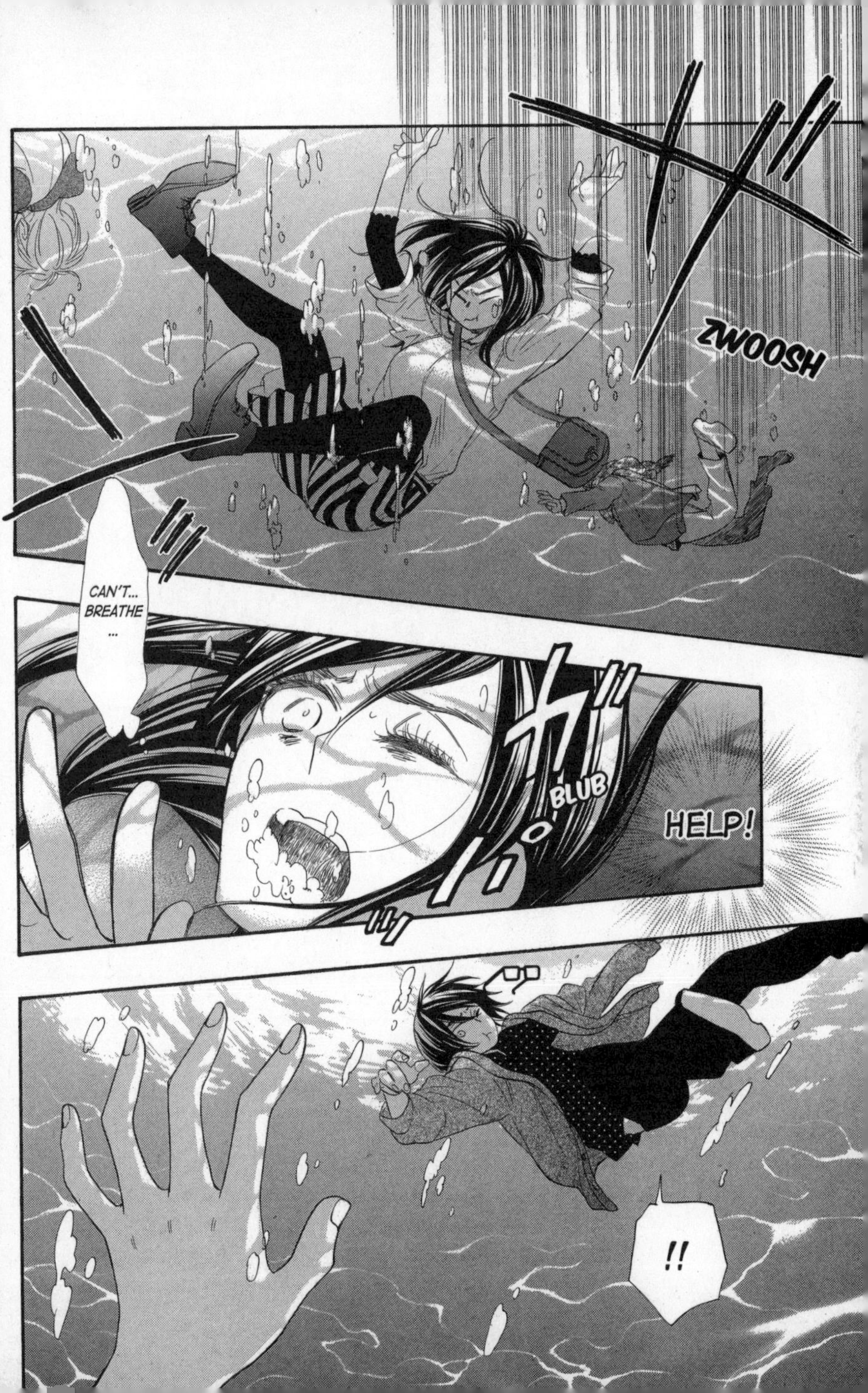
ZWOOSH
HELP!
BLUB
CAN'T... BREATHE ...
!!

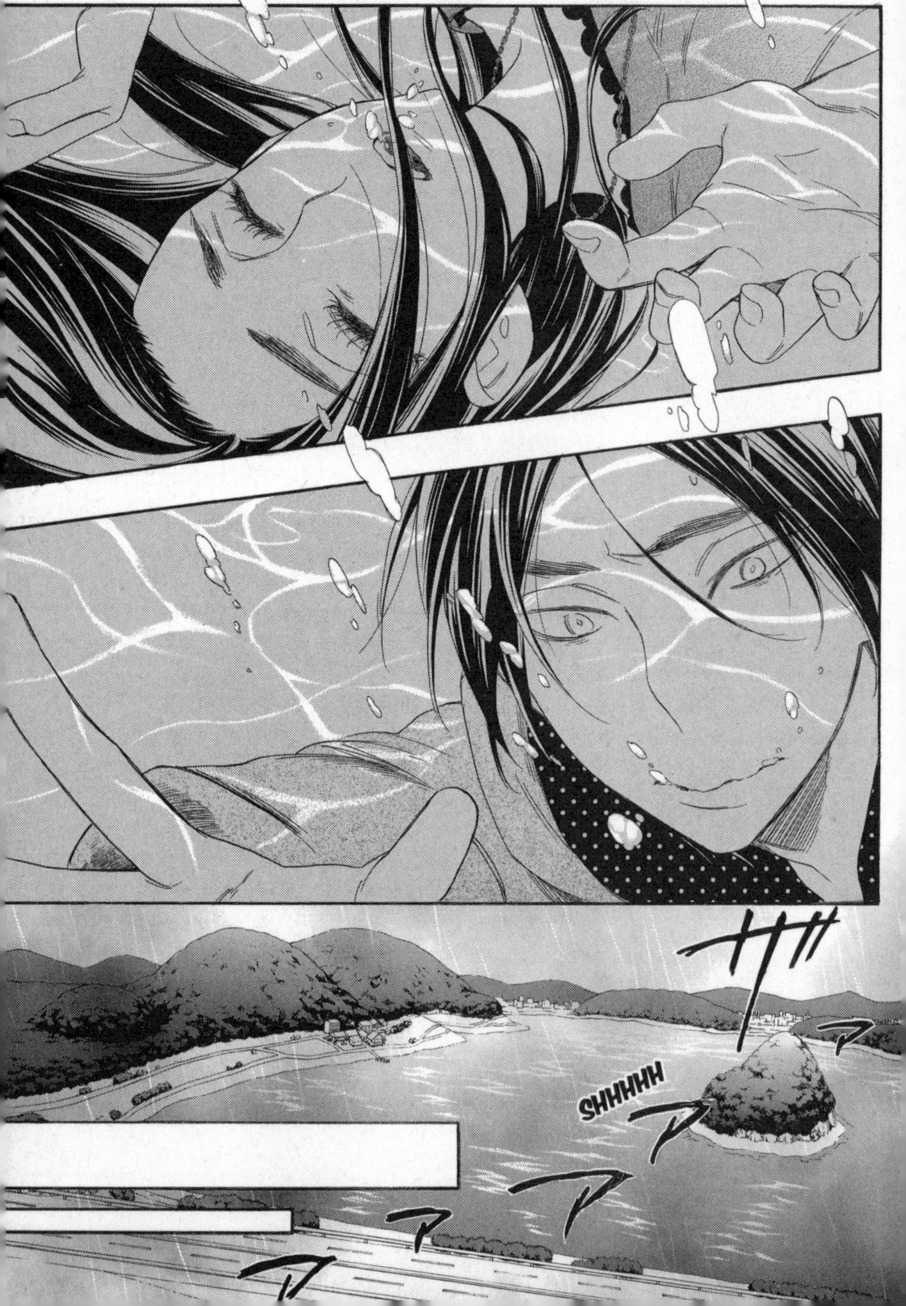
SHHHHH

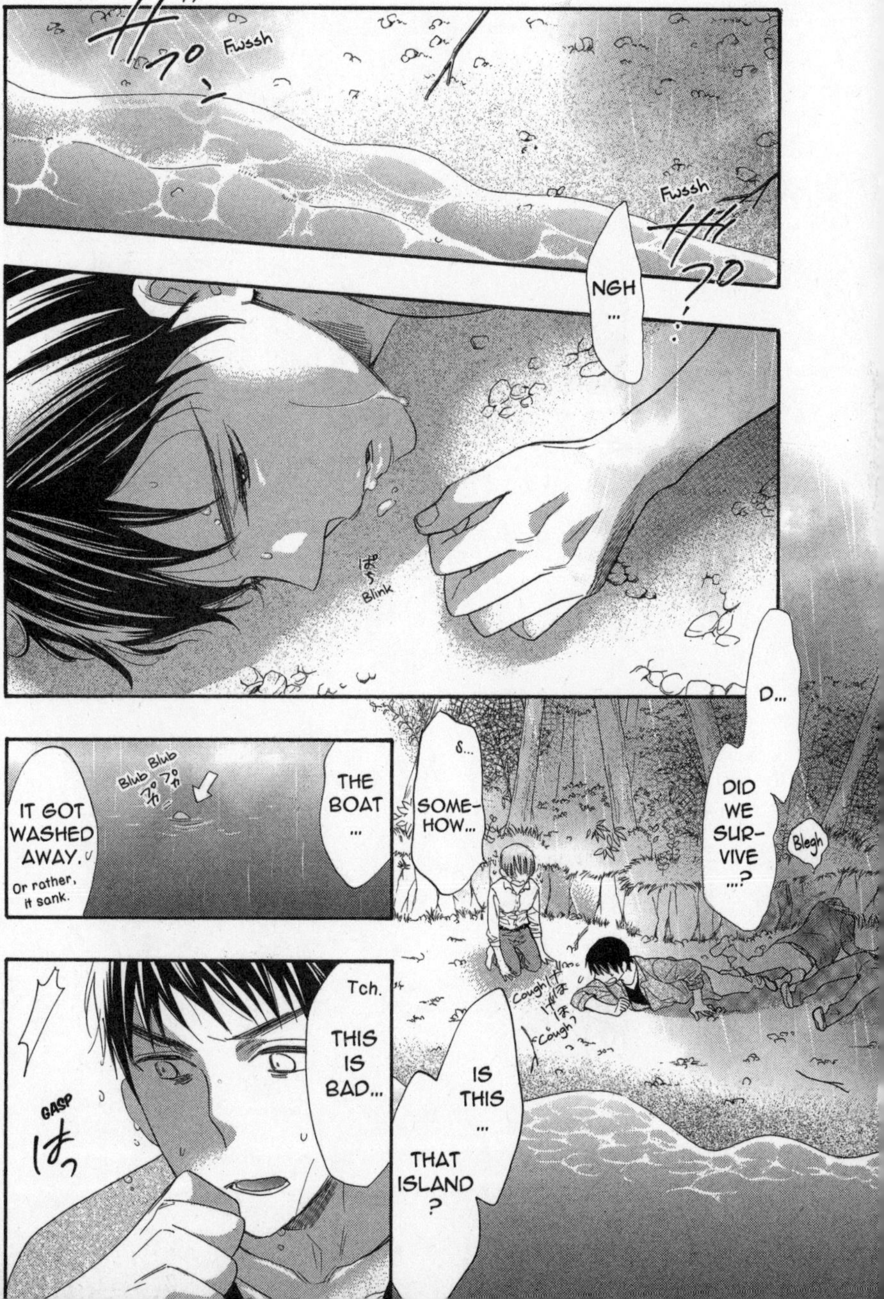
Fwssh
Fwssh
NGH...
Blink
D...
DID WE SURVIVE...?
Blegh
S...
SOMEHOW...
Cough
Cough
THE BOAT...
IS THIS... THAT ISLAND?
Blub Blub
IT GOT WASHED AWAY.
Or rather, it sank.
Tch.
THIS IS BAD...
GASP

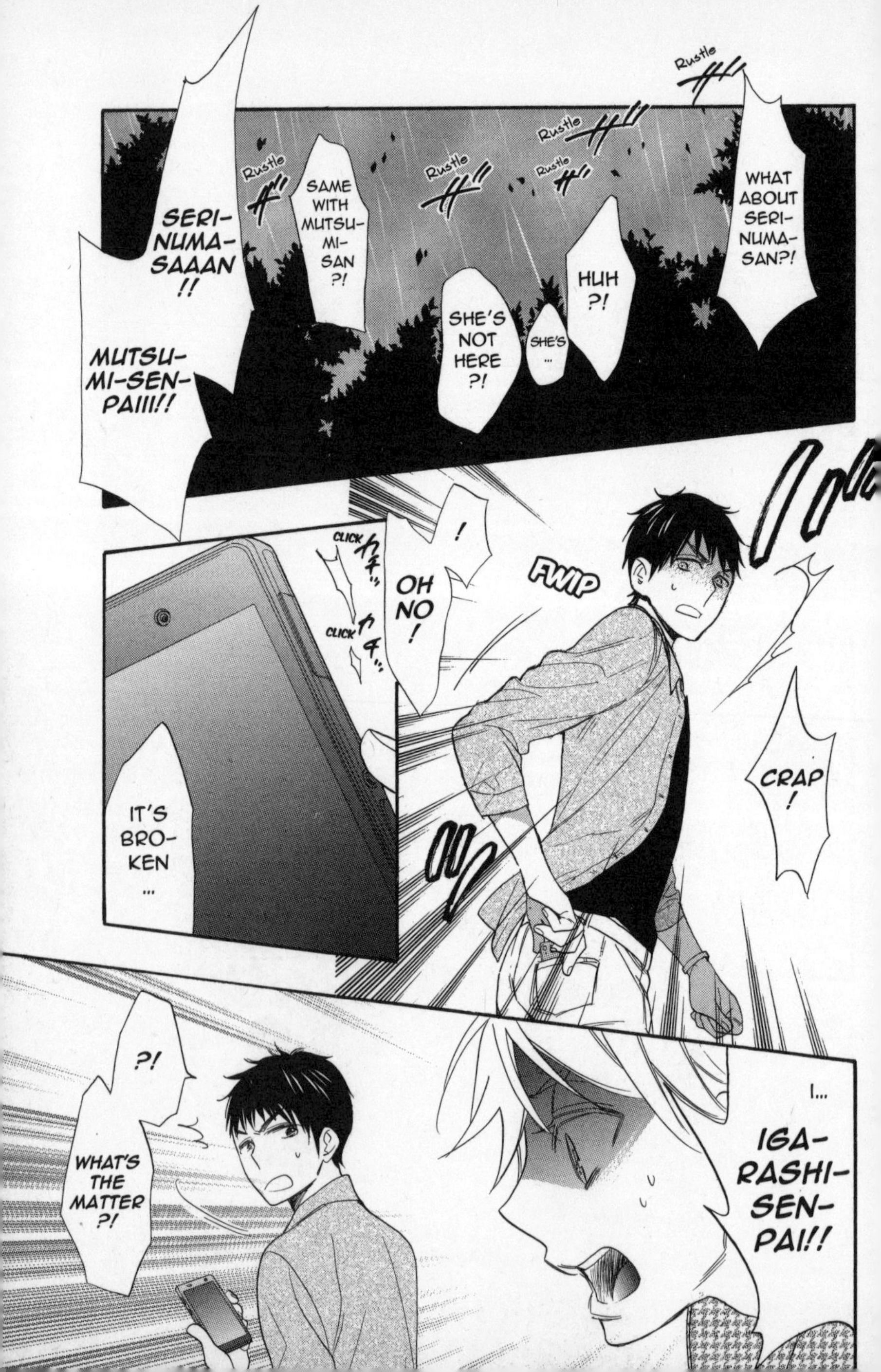
Rustle
WHAT ABOUT SERI-NUMA-SAN?!
Rustle
Rustle
HUH?!
SHE'S...
SHE'S NOT HERE?!
Rustle
SAME WITH MUTSU-MI-SAN?!
Rustle
SERI-NUMA-SAAAN!!
MUTSU-MI-SEN-PAIII!!
CRAP!
FWIP
OH NO!
!
CLICK
CLICK
IT'S BRO-KEN...
I...
IGA-RASHI-SEN-PAI!!
?!
WHAT'S THE MATTER?!

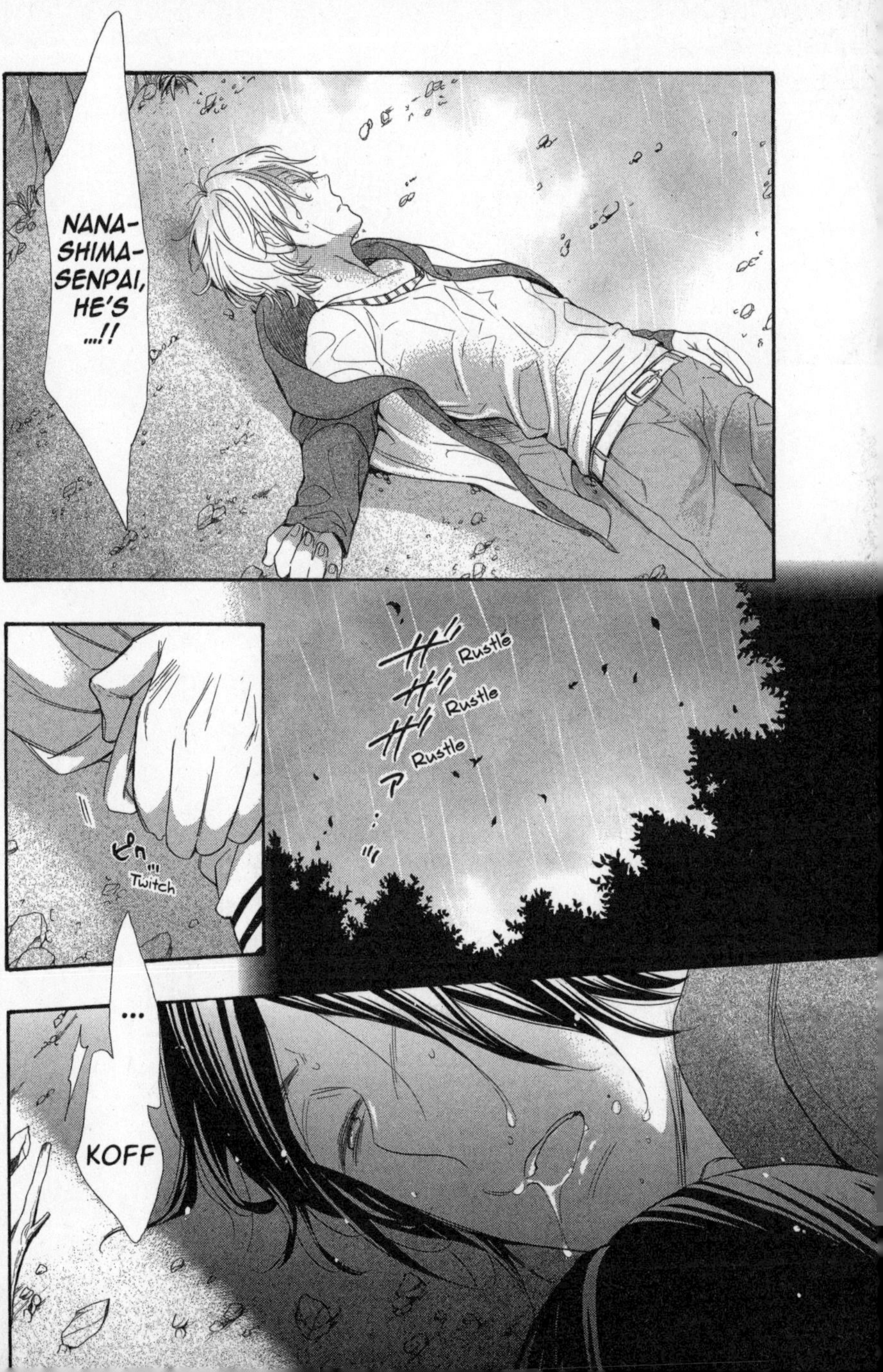

NANA-SHIMA-SENPAI, HE'S ...!!
Rustle
Rustle
Rustle
Twitch
...
KOFF

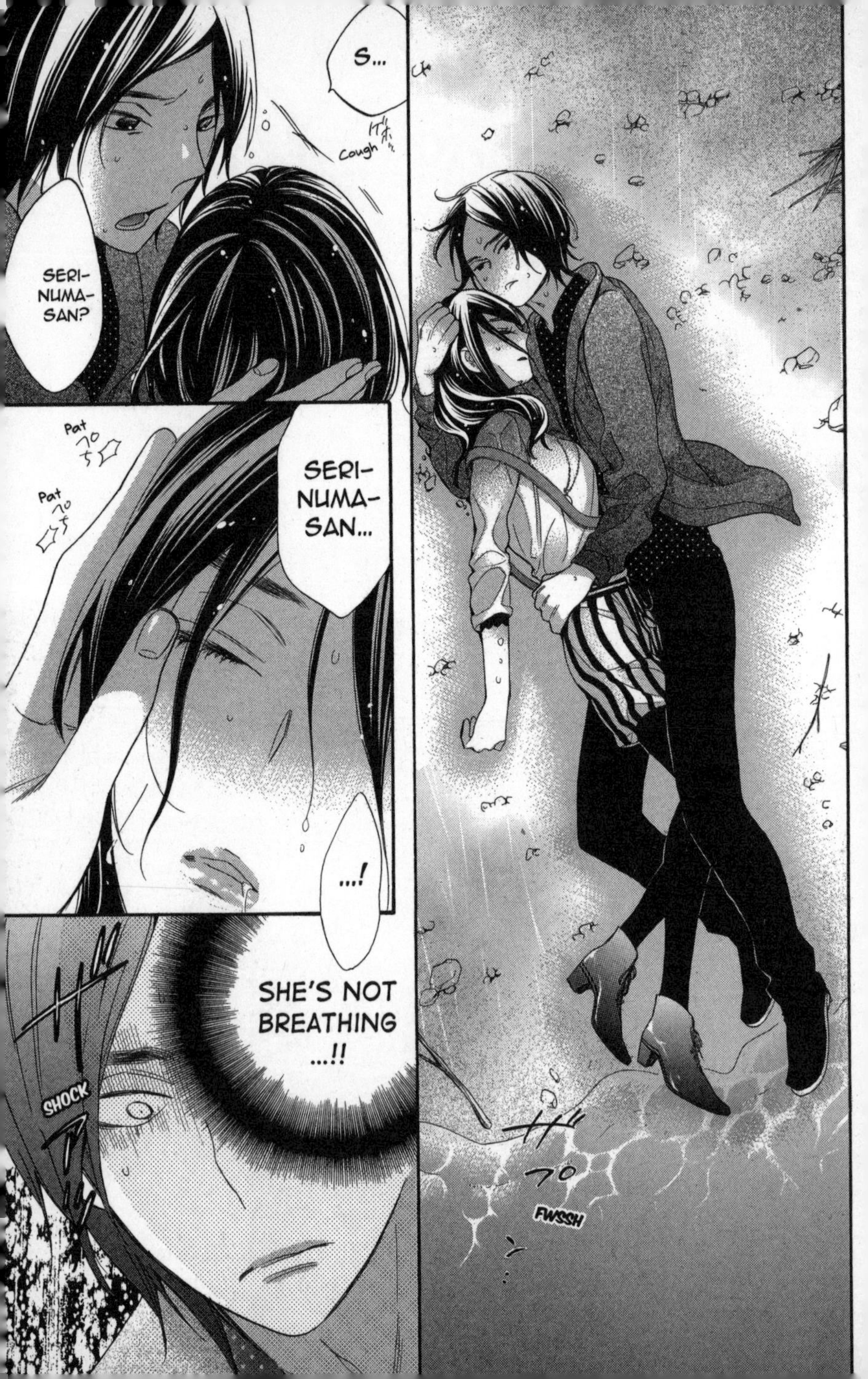
FWSSH
S...
Cough
SERI-NUMA-SAN?
Pat
Pat
SERI-NUMA-SAN...
...!
SHE'S NOT BREATHING ...!!
SHOCK

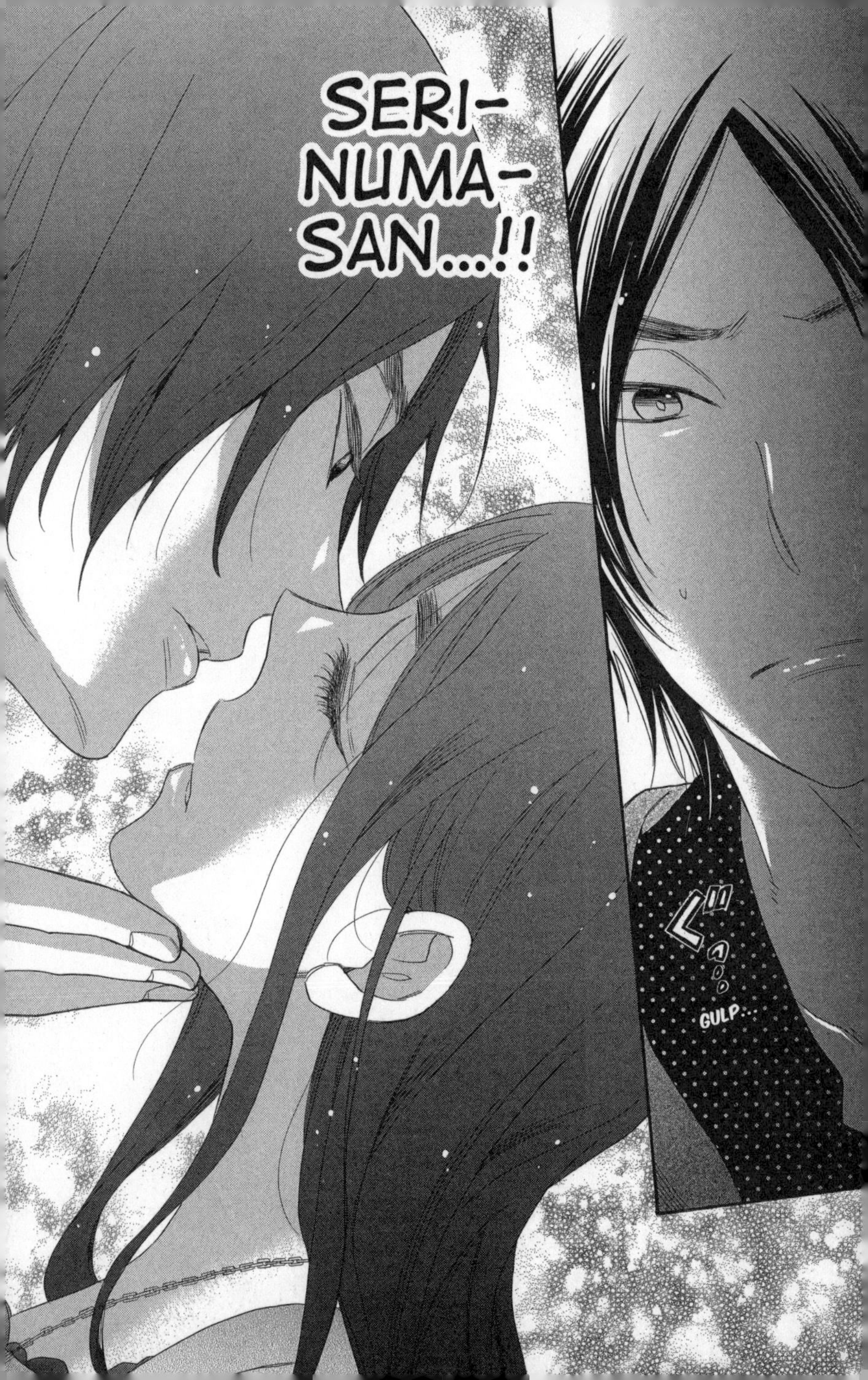
SERI-NUMA-SAN...!!
GULP...

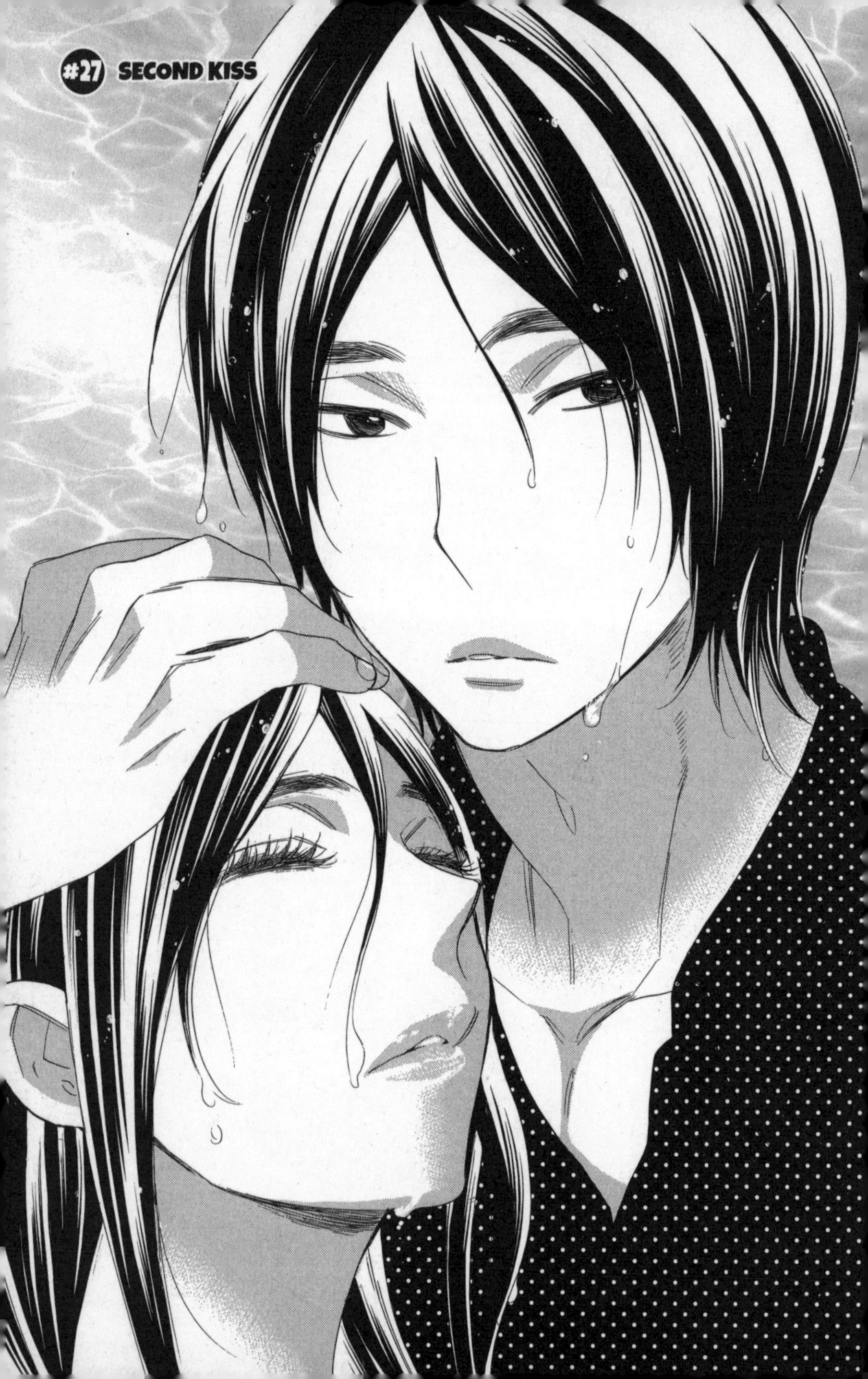
#27 SECOND KISS

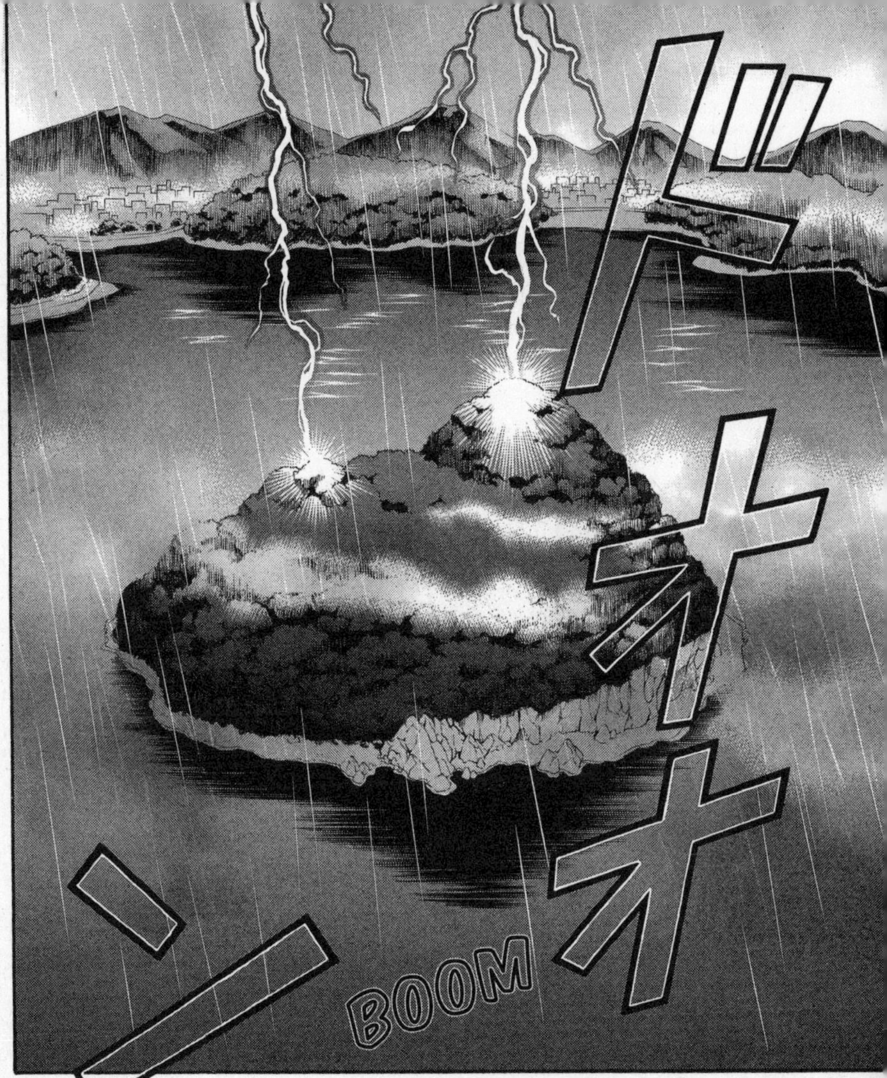
ドオオン
BOOM

KiSS HiM, NOT ME!

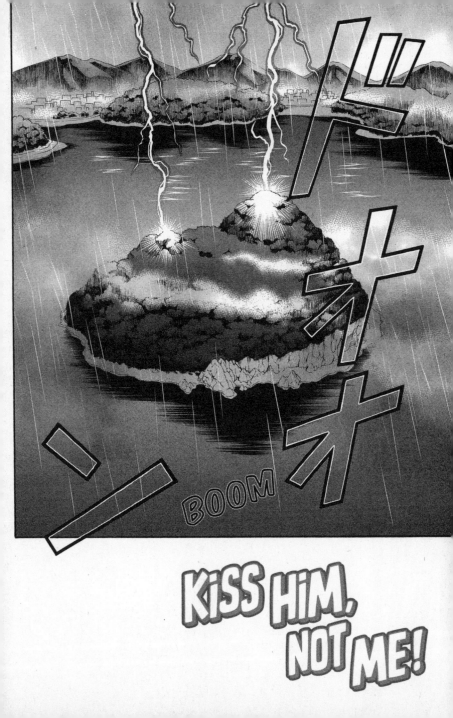

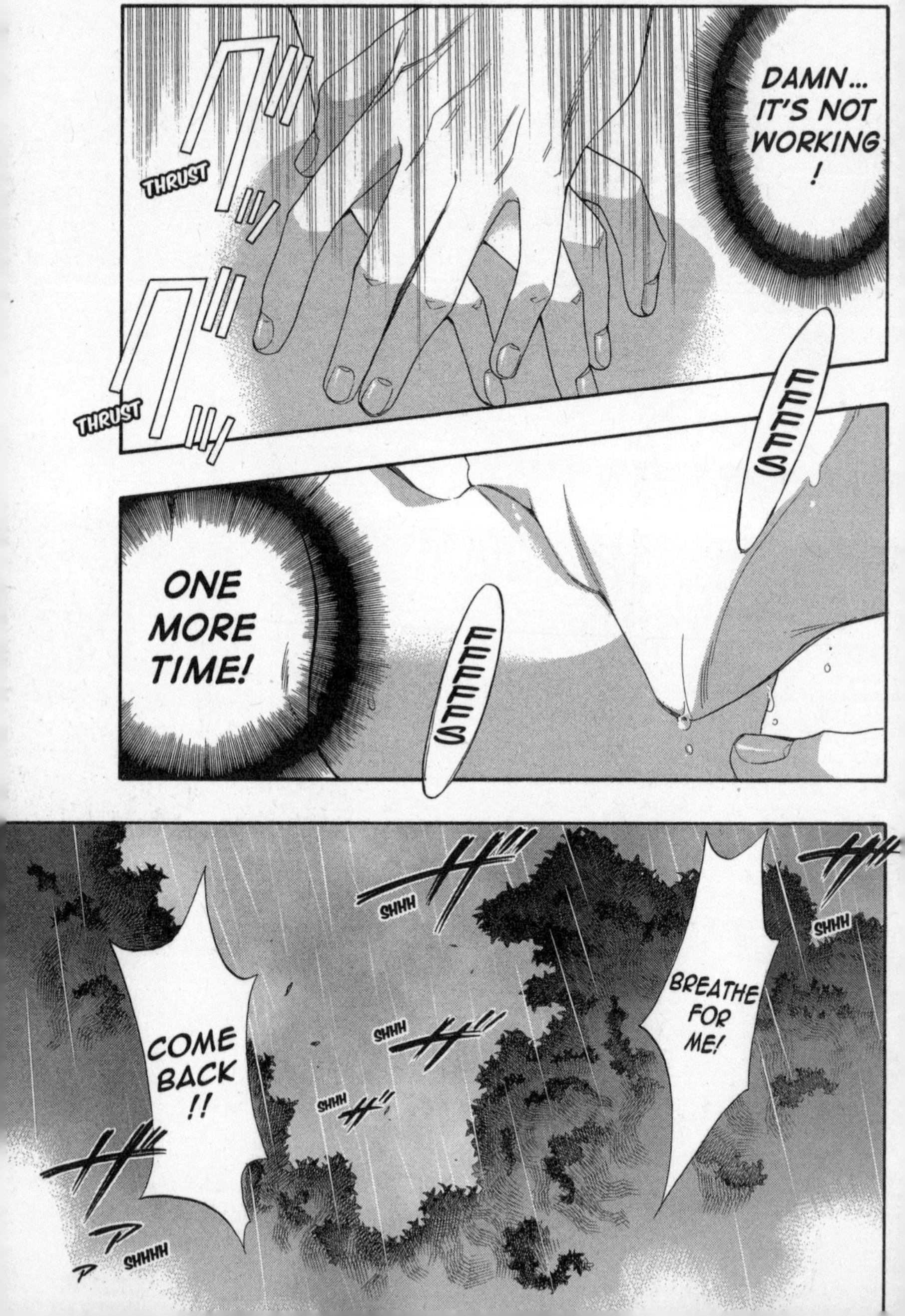
DAMN... IT'S NOT WORKING!
THRUST
THRUST
FFFFS
FFFFS
ONE MORE TIME!
BREATHE FOR ME!
SHHH
SHHH
SHHH
SHHH
COME BACK!!
SHHHH

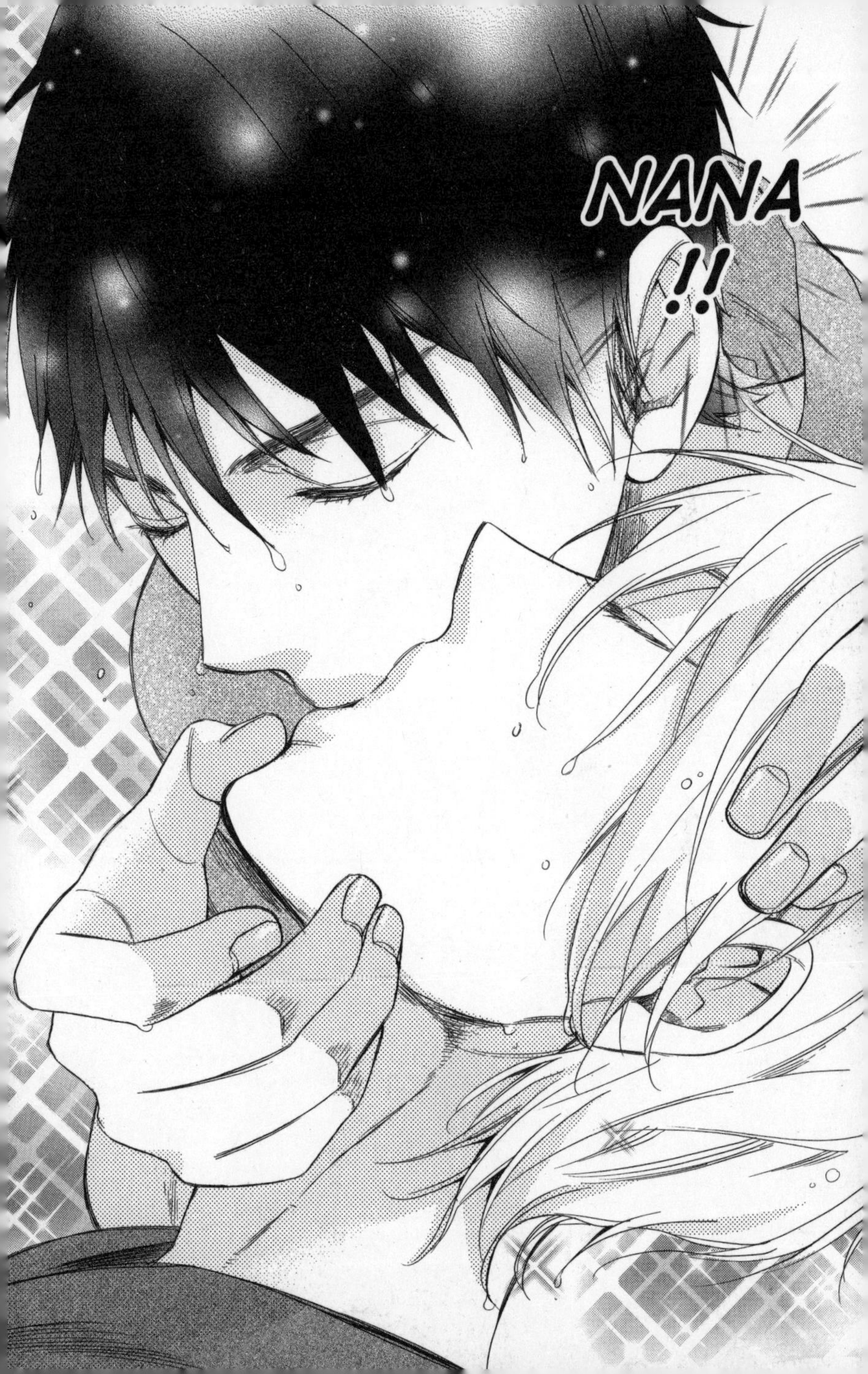
NANA!!

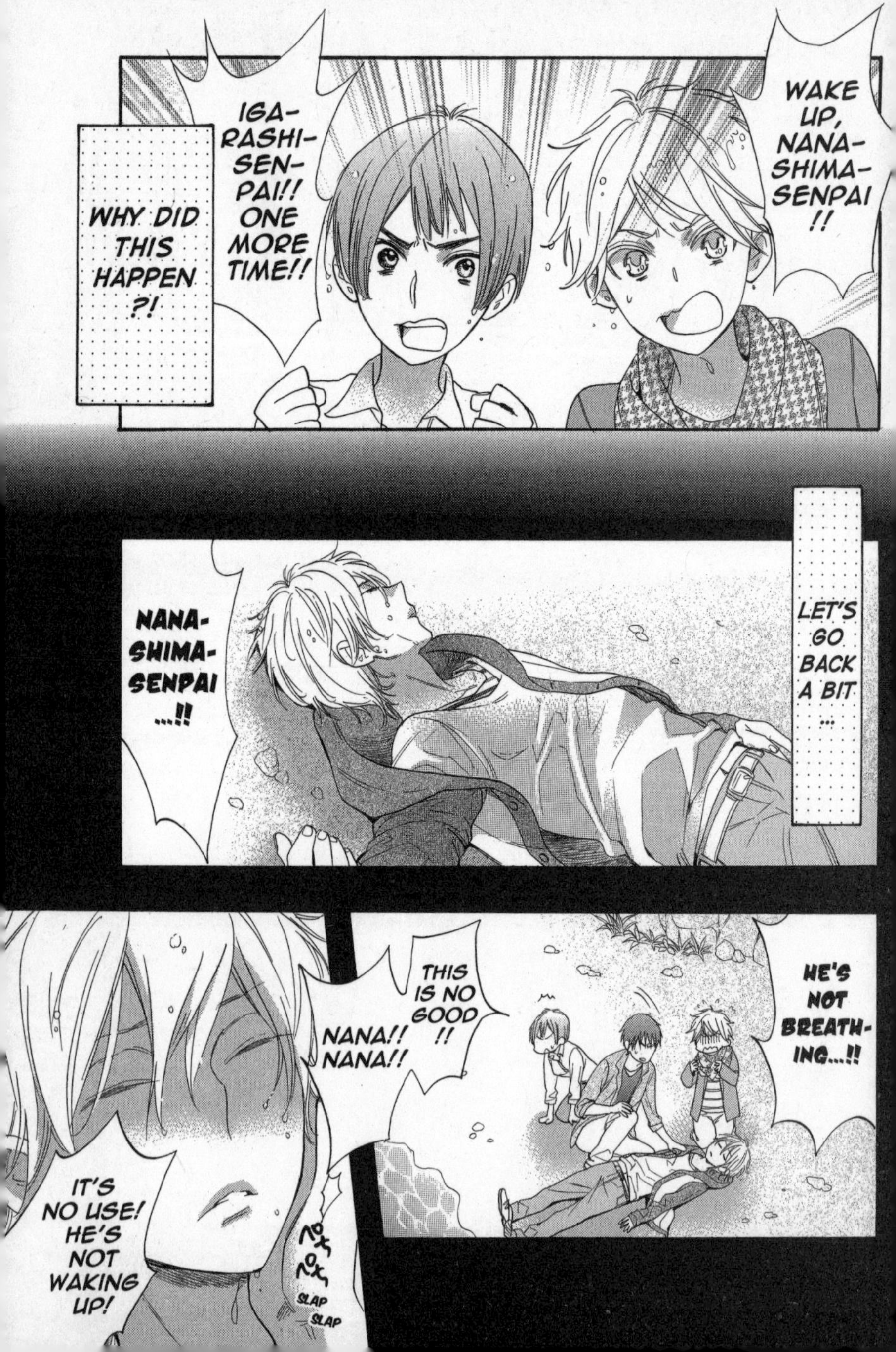
WAKE UP, NANA-SHIMA-SENPAI!!
IGA-RASHI-SENPAI!! ONE MORE TIME!!
WHY DID THIS HAPPEN?!
LET'S GO BACK A BIT...
NANA-SHIMA-SENPAI...!!
HE'S NOT BREATH-ING...!!
THIS IS NO GOOD!!
NANA!! NANA!!
IT'S NO USE! HE'S NOT WAKING UP!
SLAP SLAP

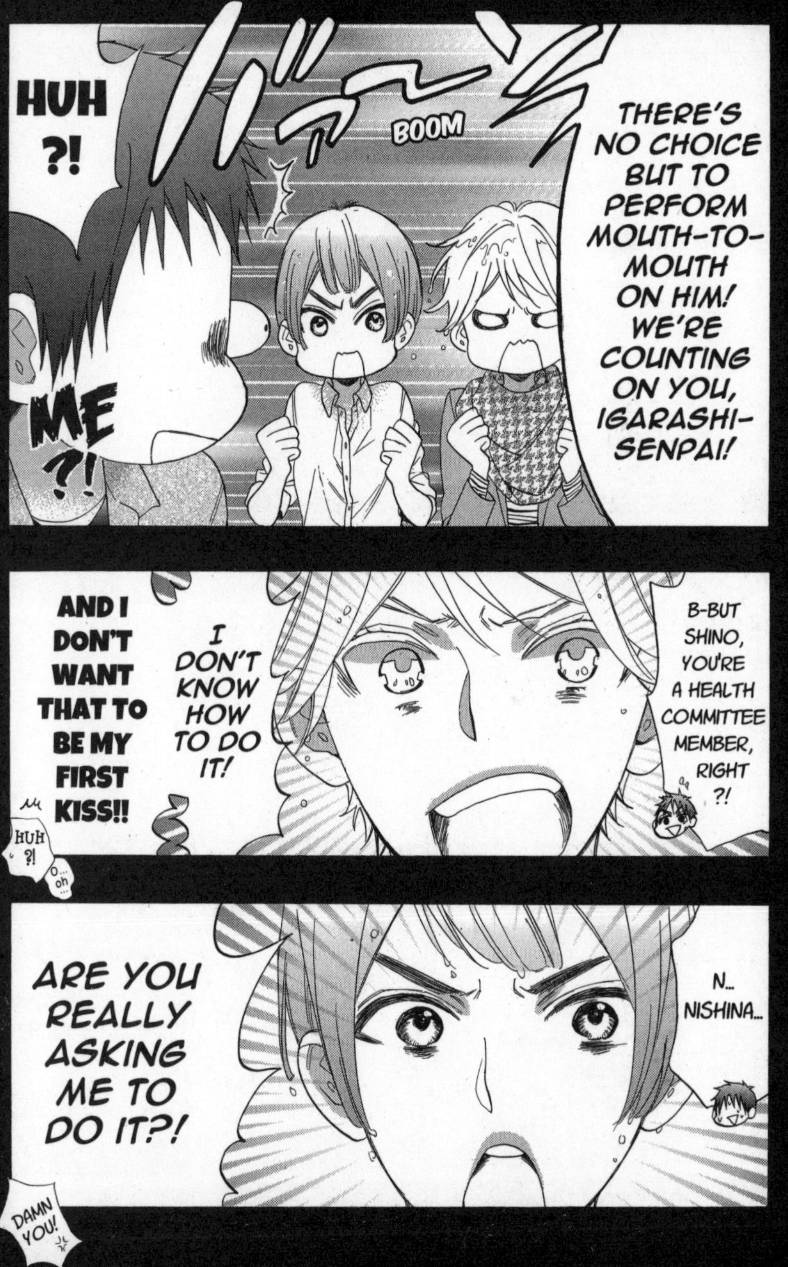
THERE'S NO CHOICE BUT TO PERFORM MOUTH-TO-MOUTH ON HIM! WE'RE COUNTING ON YOU, IGARASHI-SENPAI!
BOOM
HUH ?!
ME ?!
B-BUT SHINO, YOU'RE A HEALTH COMMITTEE MEMBER, RIGHT ?!
I DON'T KNOW HOW TO DO IT!
AND I DON'T WANT THAT TO BE MY FIRST KISS!!
HUH ?!
O... oh...
N... NISHINA...
ARE YOU REALLY ASKING ME TO DO IT?!
DAMN YOU!

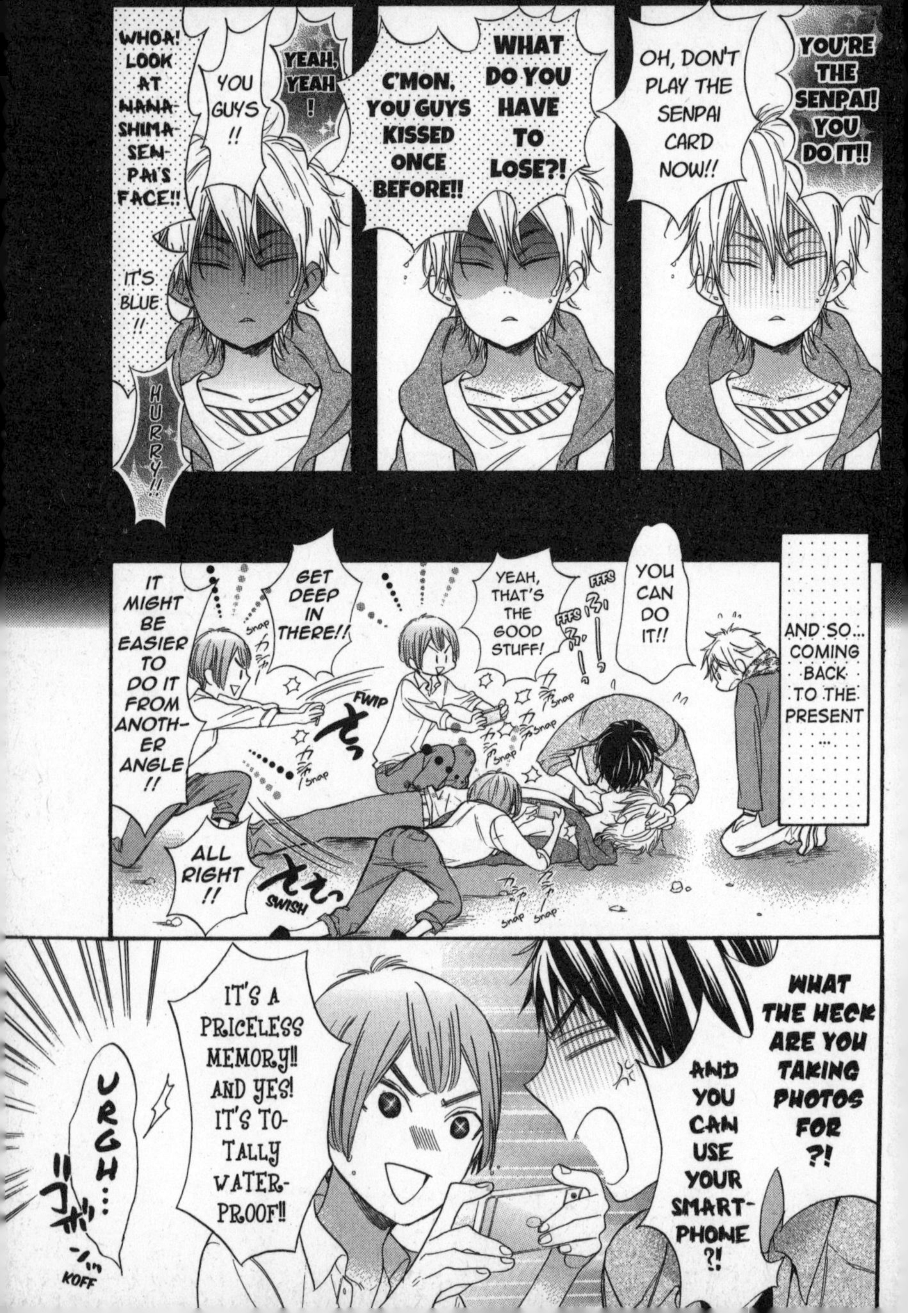

YOU'RE THE SENPAI! YOU DO IT!!
OH, DON'T PLAY THE SENPAI CARD NOW!!
WHAT DO YOU HAVE TO LOSE?!
C'MON, YOU GUYS KISSED ONCE BEFORE!!
YEAH, YEAH!
YOU GUYS!!
WHOA! LOOK AT NANASHIMA-SENPAI'S FACE!!
IT'S BLUE!!
HURRY!!
AND SO... COMING BACK TO THE PRESENT...
YOU CAN DO IT!!
FFFS
FFFS
YEAH, THAT'S THE GOOD STUFF!
SNAP
SNAP
SNAP
GET DEEP IN THERE!!
IT MIGHT BE EASIER TO DO IT FROM ANOTHER ANGLE!!
SNAP
FWIP
SNAP
ALL RIGHT!!
SWISH
SNAP
SNAP
WHAT THE HECK ARE YOU TAKING PHOTOS FOR?!
AND YOU CAN USE YOUR SMARTPHONE?!
IT'S A PRICELESS MEMORY!! AND YES! IT'S TOTALLY WATERPROOF!!
URGH...
KOFF

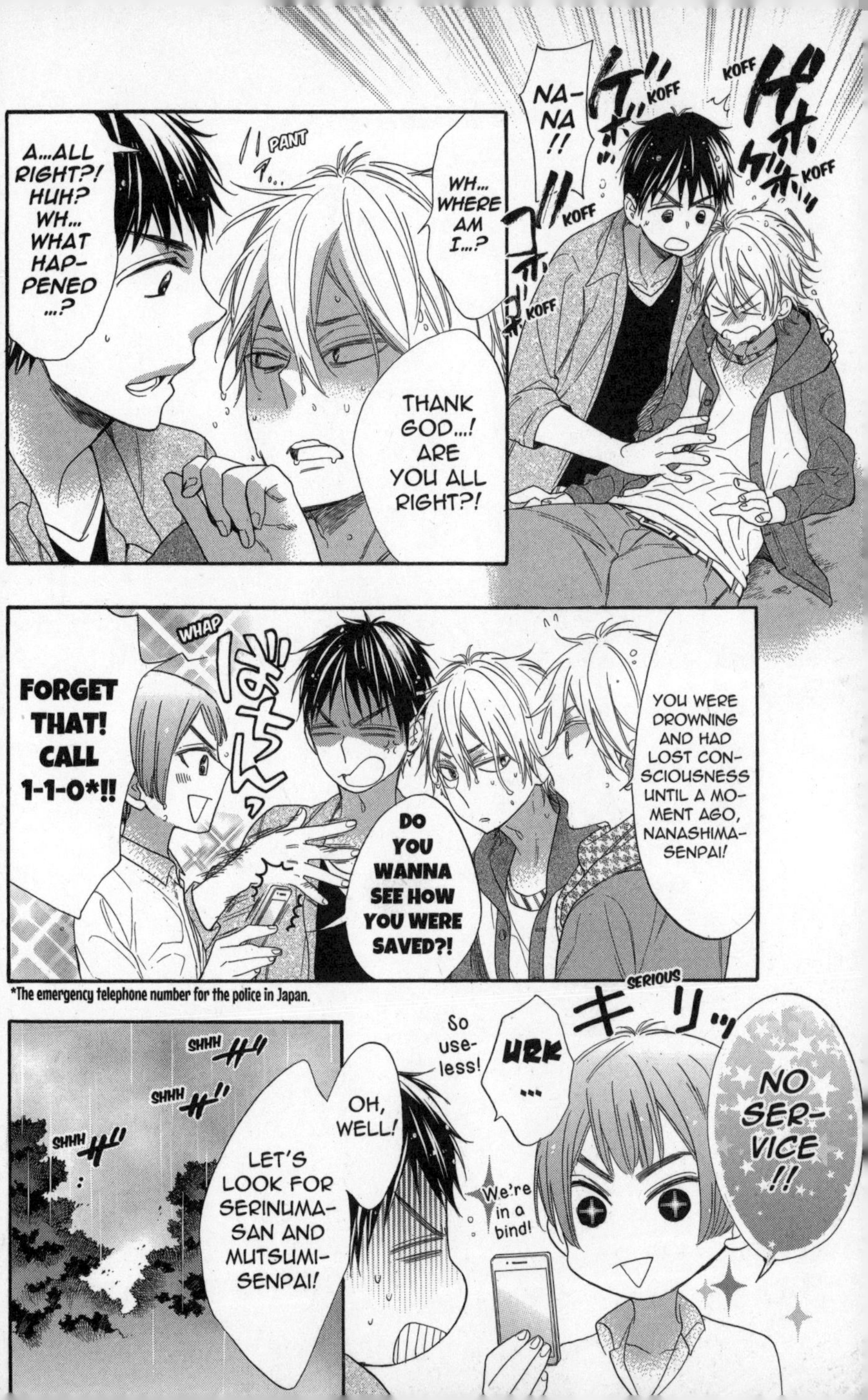
NA-NA!!
KOFF
KOFF
KOFF
KOFF
KOFF
WH... WHERE AM I...?
PANT
A...ALL RIGHT?! HUH? WH... WHAT HAP-PENED ...?
THANK GOD...! ARE YOU ALL RIGHT?!
YOU WERE DROWNING AND HAD LOST CON-SCIOUSNESS UNTIL A MO-MENT AGO, NANASHIMA-SENPAI!
DO YOU WANNA SEE HOW YOU WERE SAVED?!
WHAP
FORGET THAT! CALL 1-1-0*!!
SERIOUS
NO SER-VICE!!
We're in a bind!
URK ...
So use-less!
OH, WELL!
LET'S LOOK FOR SERINUMA-SAN AND MUTSUMI-SENPAI!
SHHH
SHHH
SHHH

*The emergency telephone number for the police in Japan.

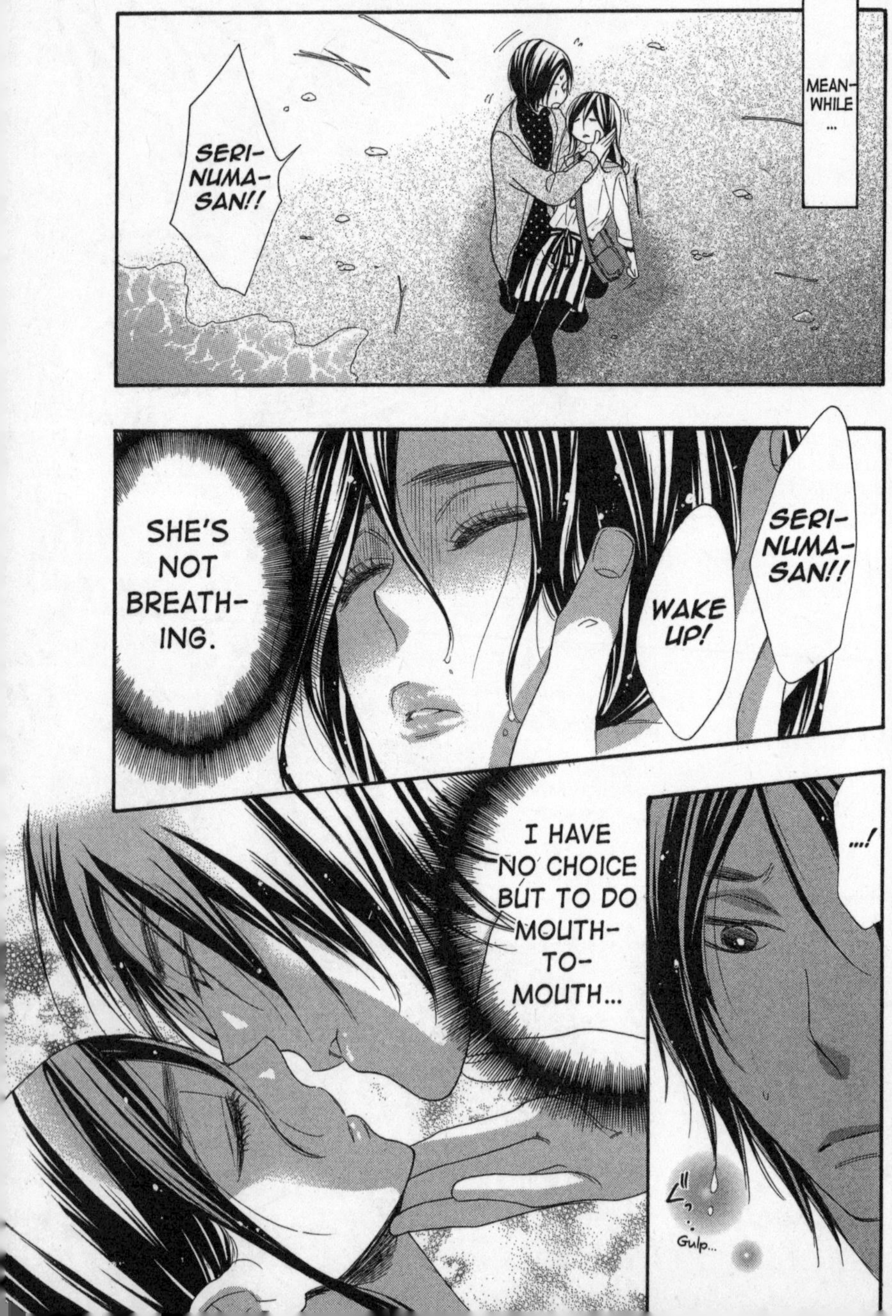
MEAN-WHILE ...
SERI-NUMA-SAN!!
SERI-NUMA-SAN!!
WAKE UP!
SHE'S NOT BREATH-ING.
...!
Gulp...
I HAVE NO CHOICE BUT TO DO MOUTH-TO-MOUTH...

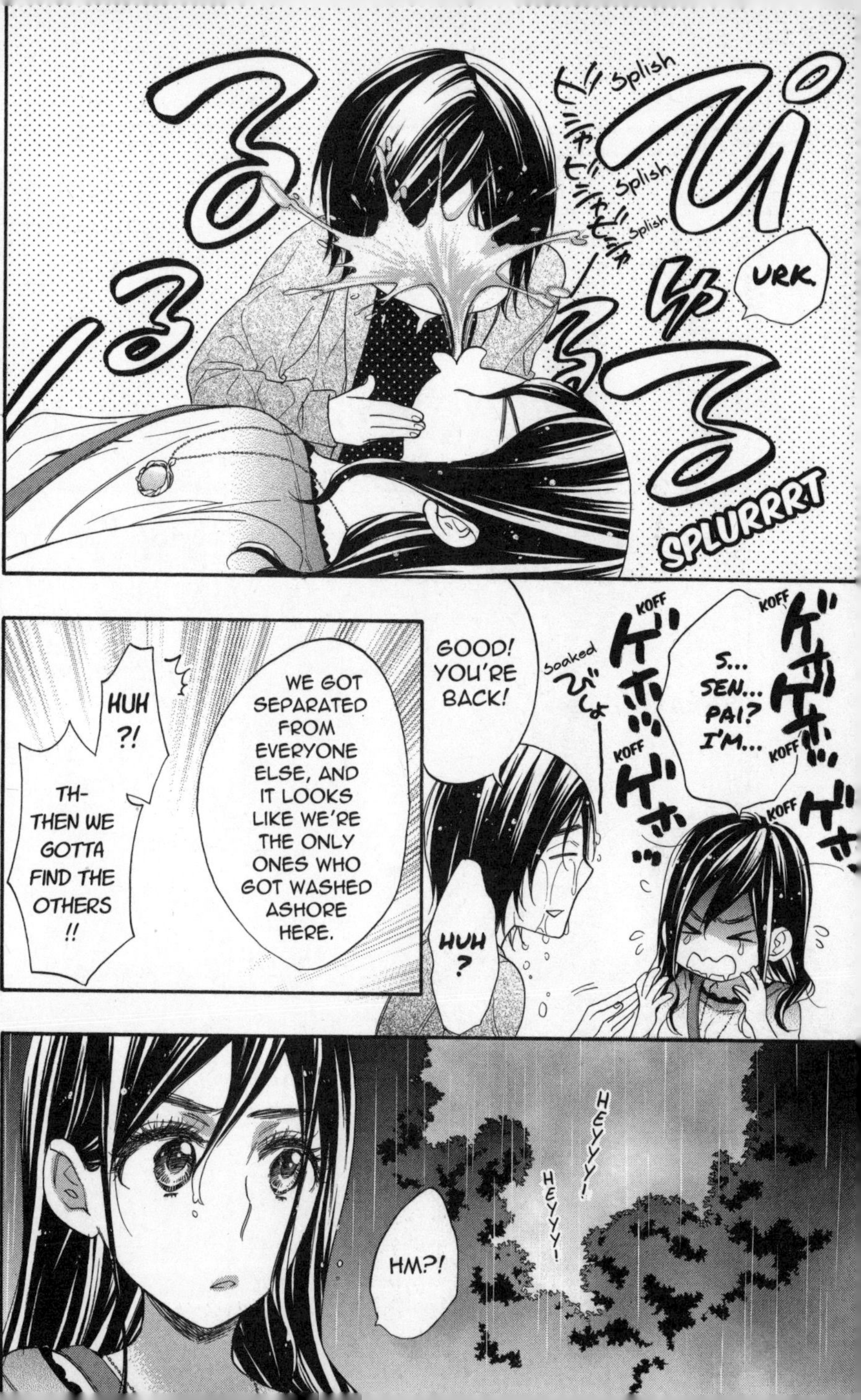
Splish
Splish
Splish
URK.
SPLURRRT
KOFF
KOFF
KOFF
KOFF
S... SEN... PAI? I'M...
Soaked
GOOD! YOU'RE BACK!
HUH?
WE GOT SEPARATED FROM EVERYONE ELSE, AND IT LOOKS LIKE WE'RE THE ONLY ONES WHO GOT WASHED ASHORE HERE.
HUH?!
TH- THEN WE GOTTA FIND THE OTHERS!!
HEYYY!
HEYYY!
HM?!

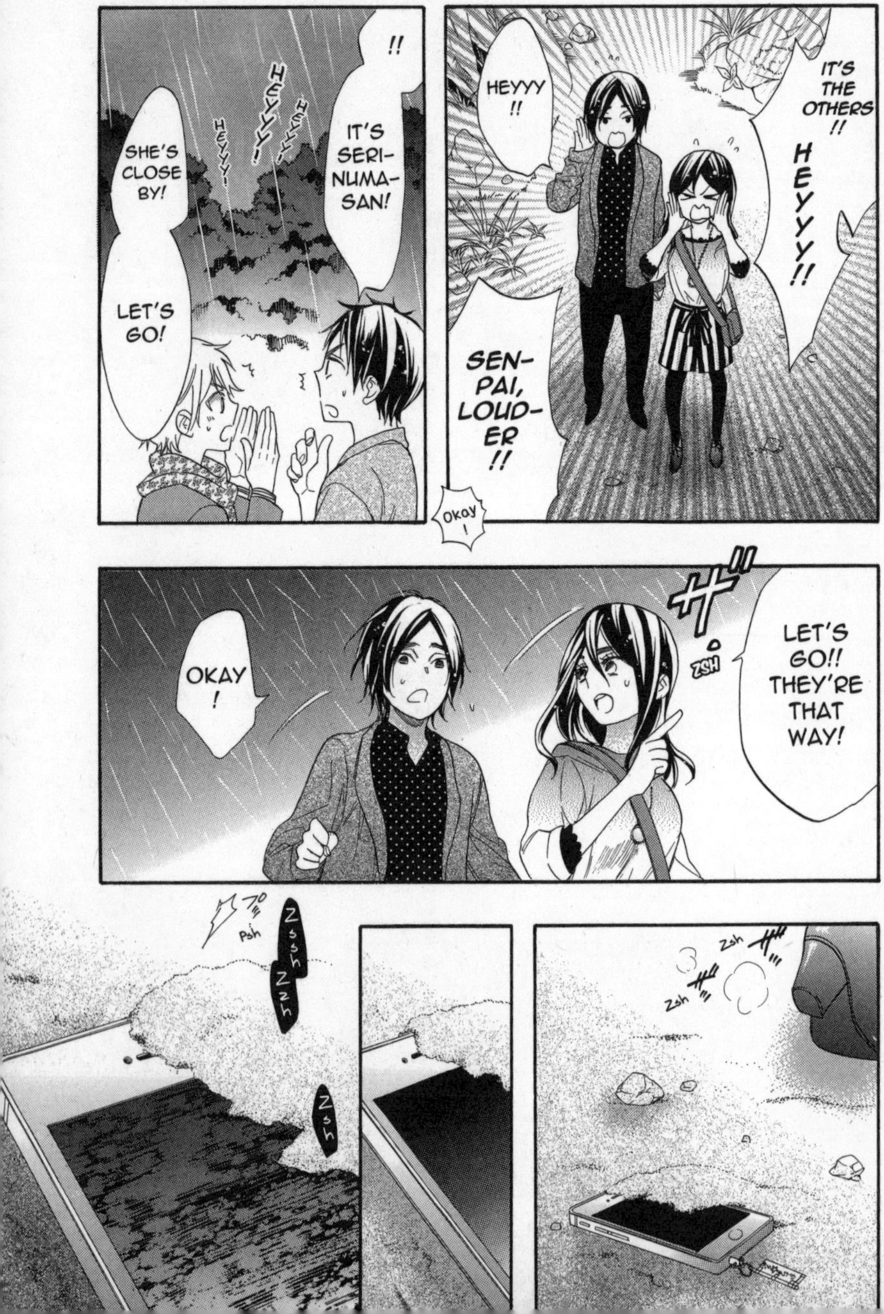
IT'S THE OTHERS!!
HEYYY!!
HEYYY!!
SENPAI, LOUDER!!
Okay!
!!
IT'S SERINUMA-SAN!
HEYYY!
HEYYY!
HEYYY!
SHE'S CLOSE BY!
LET'S GO!
LET'S GO!! THEY'RE THAT WAY!
ZSH
OKAY!
Zsh
Zsh
Psh
Zssh
Zsh
Zsh

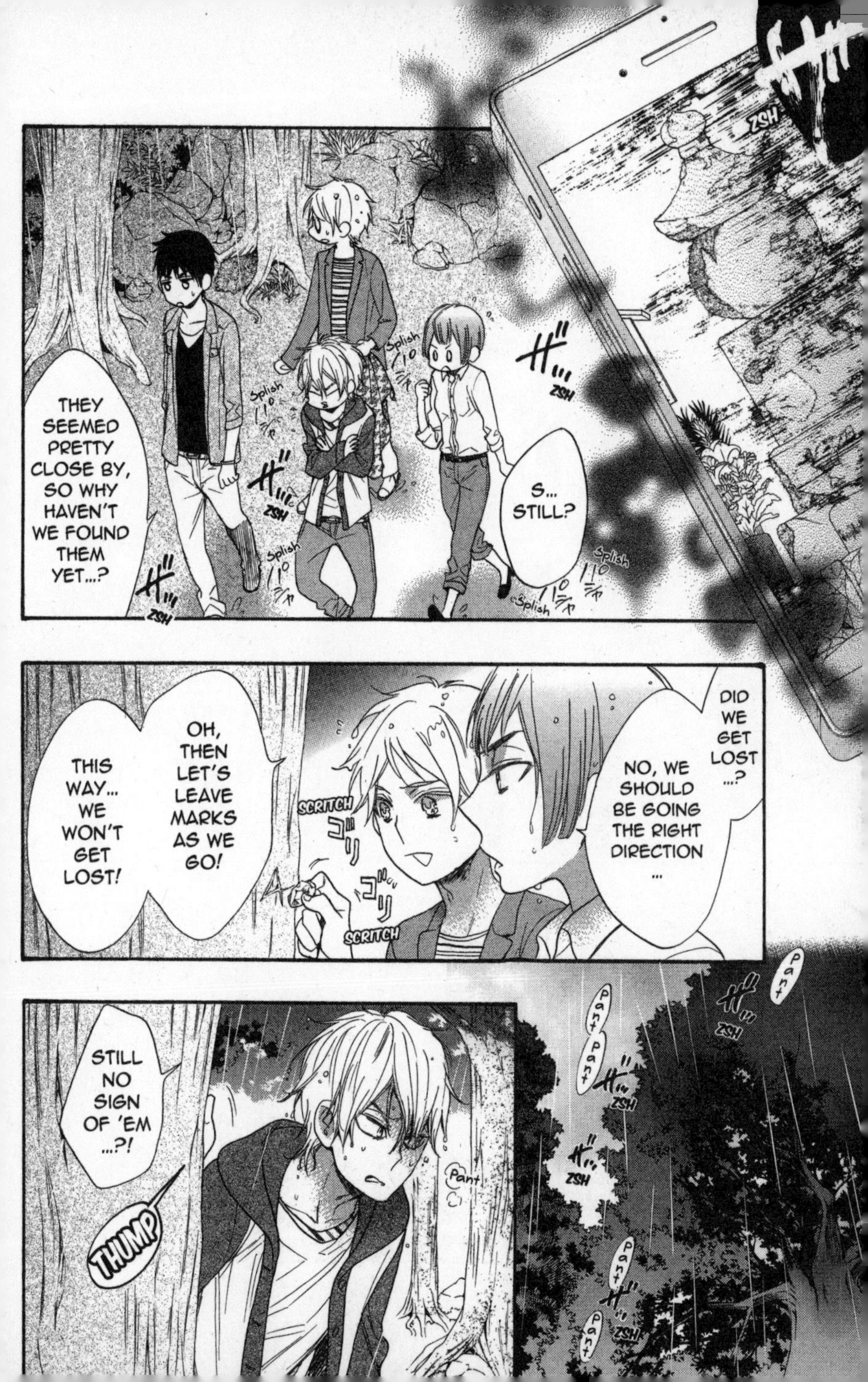
ZSH
S... STILL?
Splish
Splish
ZSH
Splish
THEY SEEMED PRETTY CLOSE BY, SO WHY HAVEN'T WE FOUND THEM YET...?
ZSH
DID WE GET LOST ...?
NO, WE SHOULD BE GOING THE RIGHT DIRECTION ...
SCRITCH
SCRITCH
OH, THEN LET'S LEAVE MARKS AS WE GO!
THIS WAY... WE WON'T GET LOST!
Pant
ZSH
Pant pant
ZSH
ZSH
Pant
ZSH
Pant
STILL NO SIGN OF 'EM ...?!
Pant
THUMP

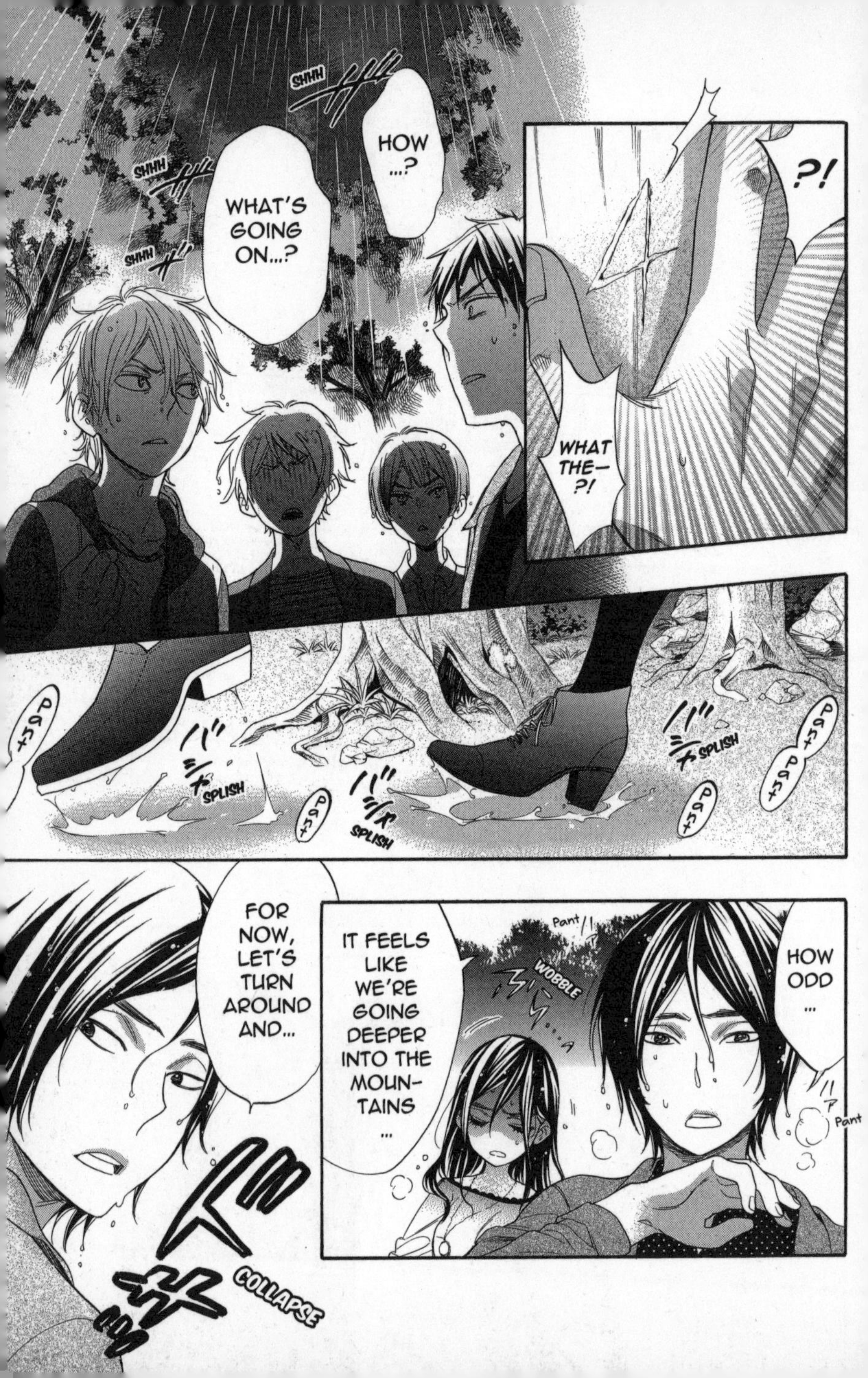
?!
WHAT THE—?!
HOW ...?
WHAT'S GOING ON...?
SHHH
SHHH
SHHH
Pant Pant
SPLISH
Pant
SPLISH
Pant
SPLISH
Pant
HOW ODD ...
Pant
Pant
WOBBLE
IT FEELS LIKE WE'RE GOING DEEPER INTO THE MOUN-TAINS ...
FOR NOW, LET'S TURN AROUND AND...
COLLAPSE

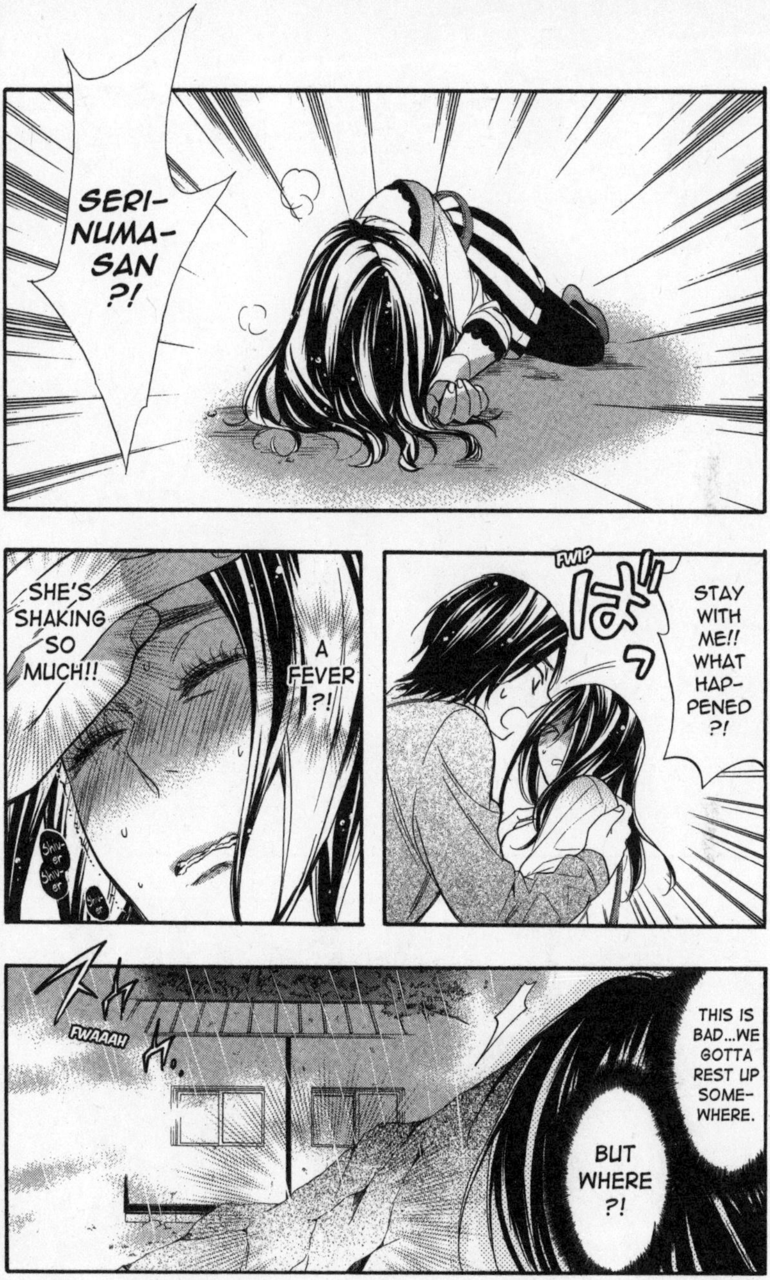
SERI-NUMA-SAN?!
FWIP
ばっ
STAY WITH ME!! WHAT HAP-PENED?!
SHE'S SHAKING SO MUCH!!
A FEVER?!
Shiv-er Shiv-er
FWAAAH
THIS IS BAD...WE GOTTA REST UP SOME-WHERE.
BUT WHERE?!

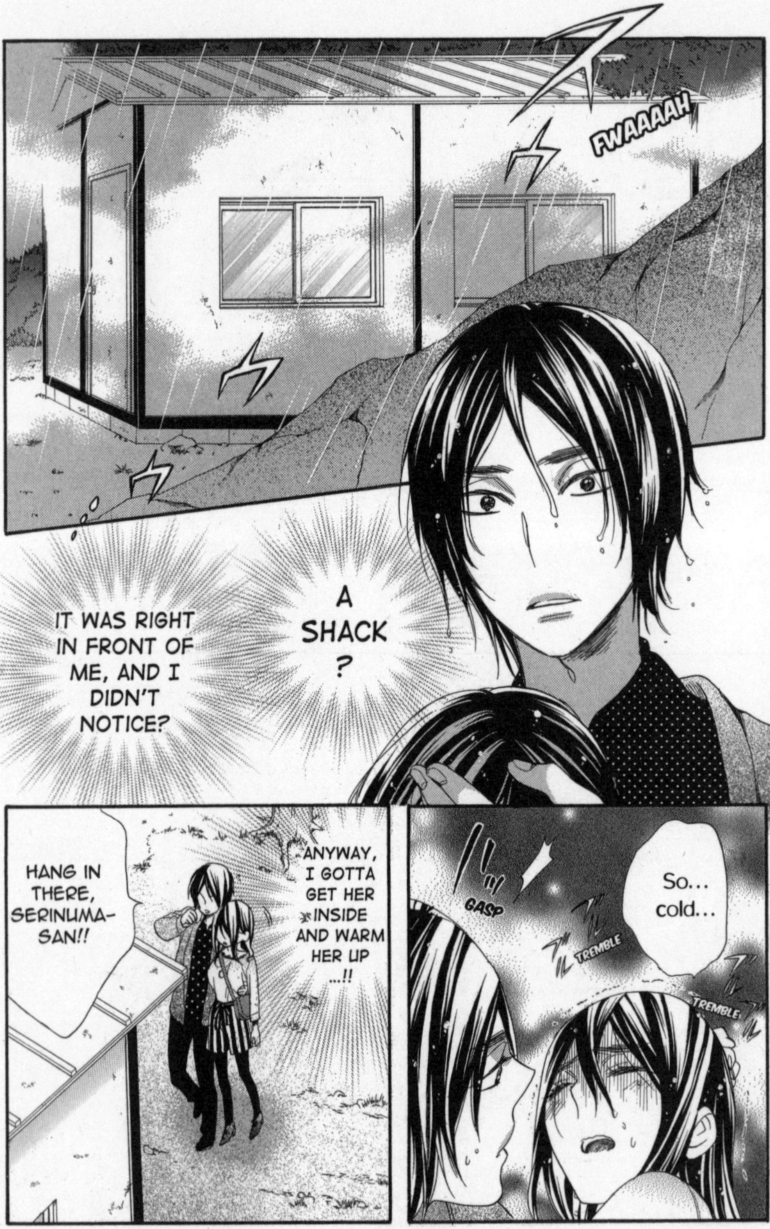
FWAAAAH
A SHACK?
IT WAS RIGHT IN FRONT OF ME, AND I DIDN'T NOTICE?
GASP
So... cold...
TREMBLE
TREMBLE
ANYWAY, I GOTTA GET HER INSIDE AND WARM HER UP ...!!
HANG IN THERE, SERINUMA-SAN!!

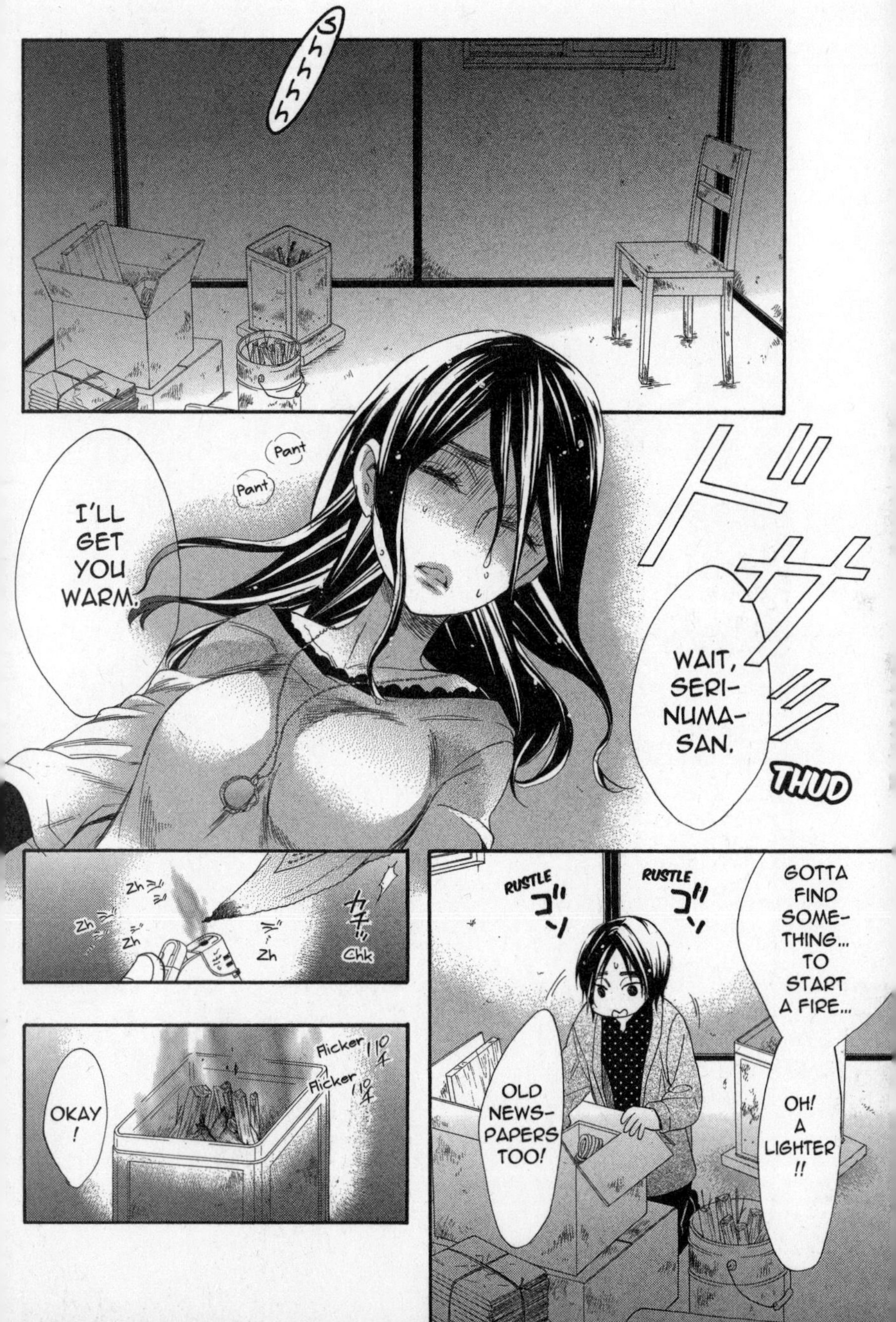
ううううう
WAIT, SERI-NUMA-SAN.
ドサッ
THUD
Pant
Pant
I'LL GET YOU WARM.
GOTTA FIND SOME-THING... TO START A FIRE...
RUSTLE
ゴソ
RUSTLE
ゴソ
OH! A LIGHTER !!
OLD NEWS-PAPERS TOO!
カチッ
Chk
Zh
Zh
Zh
Zh
Flicker
Flicker
OKAY!

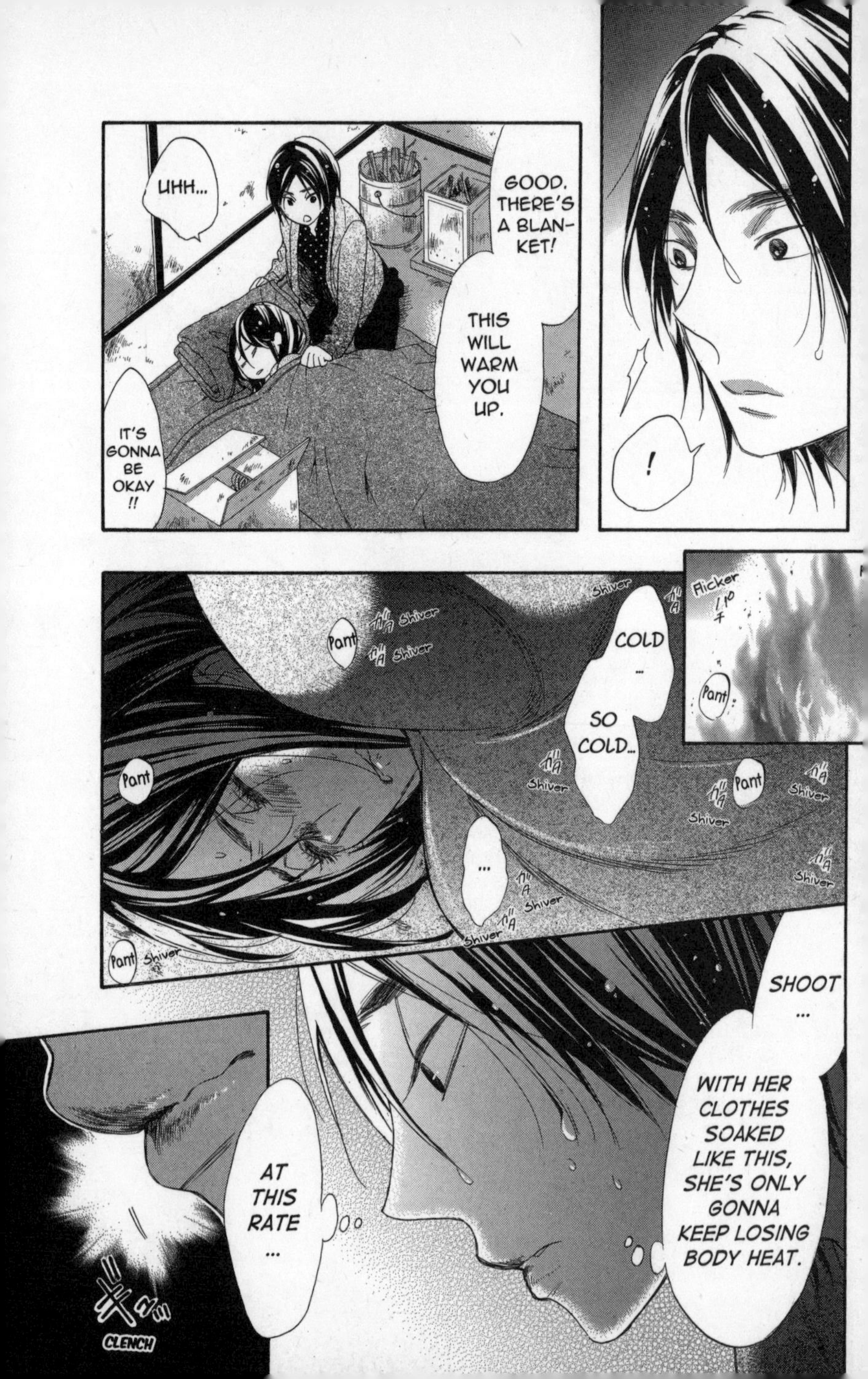
!
GOOD. THERE'S A BLAN-KET!
UHH...
THIS WILL WARM YOU UP.
IT'S GONNA BE OKAY!!
Flicker
Pant
Shiver
COLD... SO COLD...
Shiver
Pant
Shiver
Shiver
Shiver
Pant
Shiver
...
Shiver
Shiver
Pant
Shiver
SHOOT...
WITH HER CLOTHES SOAKED LIKE THIS, SHE'S ONLY GONNA KEEP LOSING BODY HEAT.
AT THIS RATE...
CLENCH

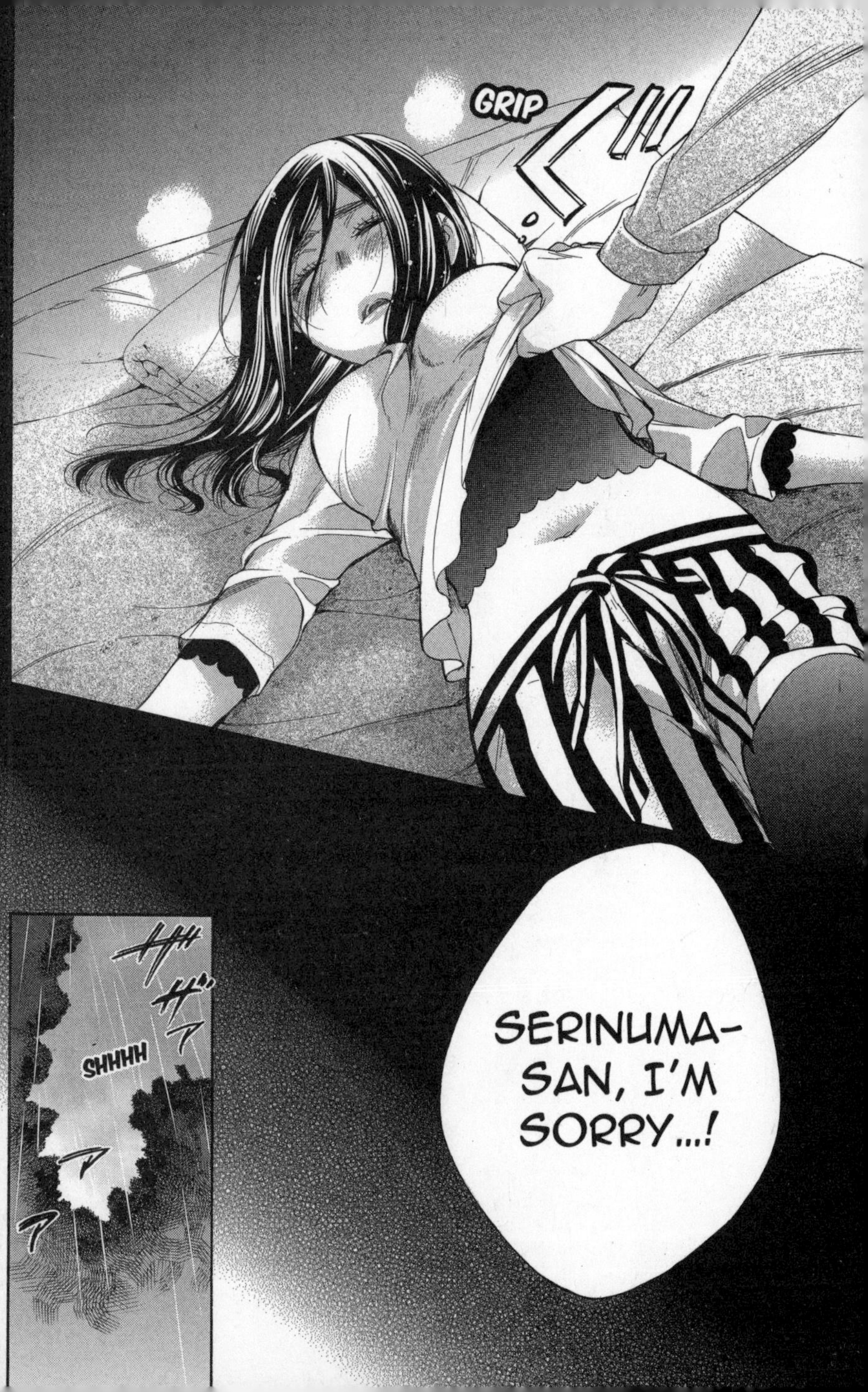
GRIP
SERINUMA-SAN, I'M SORRY...!
SHHHH

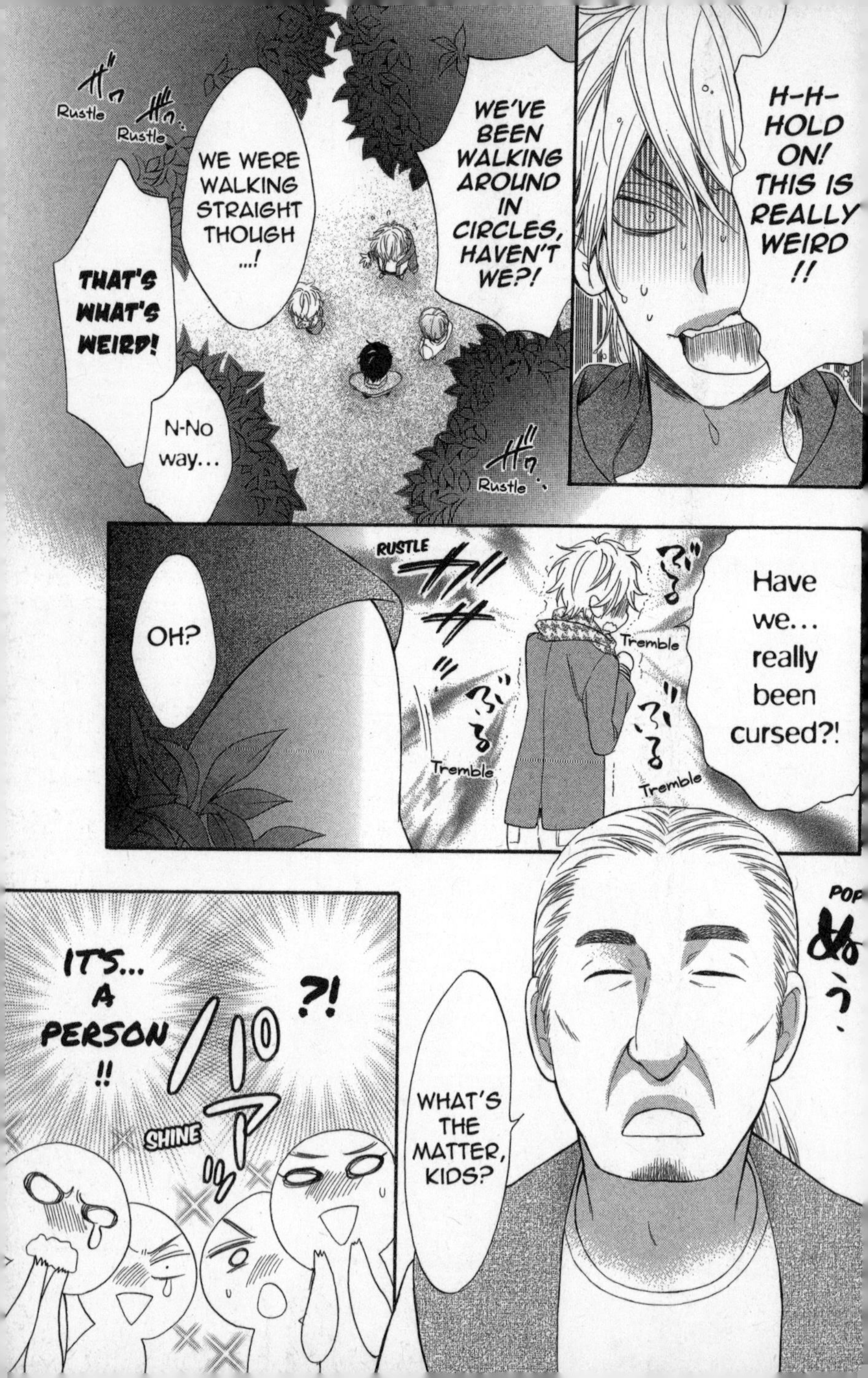
H-H-HOLD ON! THIS IS REALLY WEIRD!!
WE'VE BEEN WALKING AROUND IN CIRCLES, HAVEN'T WE?!
WE WERE WALKING STRAIGHT THOUGH ...!
Rustle
Rustle
THAT'S WHAT'S WEIRD!
N-No way...
Rustle
Have we... really been cursed?!
Tremble
Tremble
Tremble
RUSTLE
OH?
POP
WHAT'S THE MATTER, KIDS?
?!
IT'S... A PERSON!!
SHINE

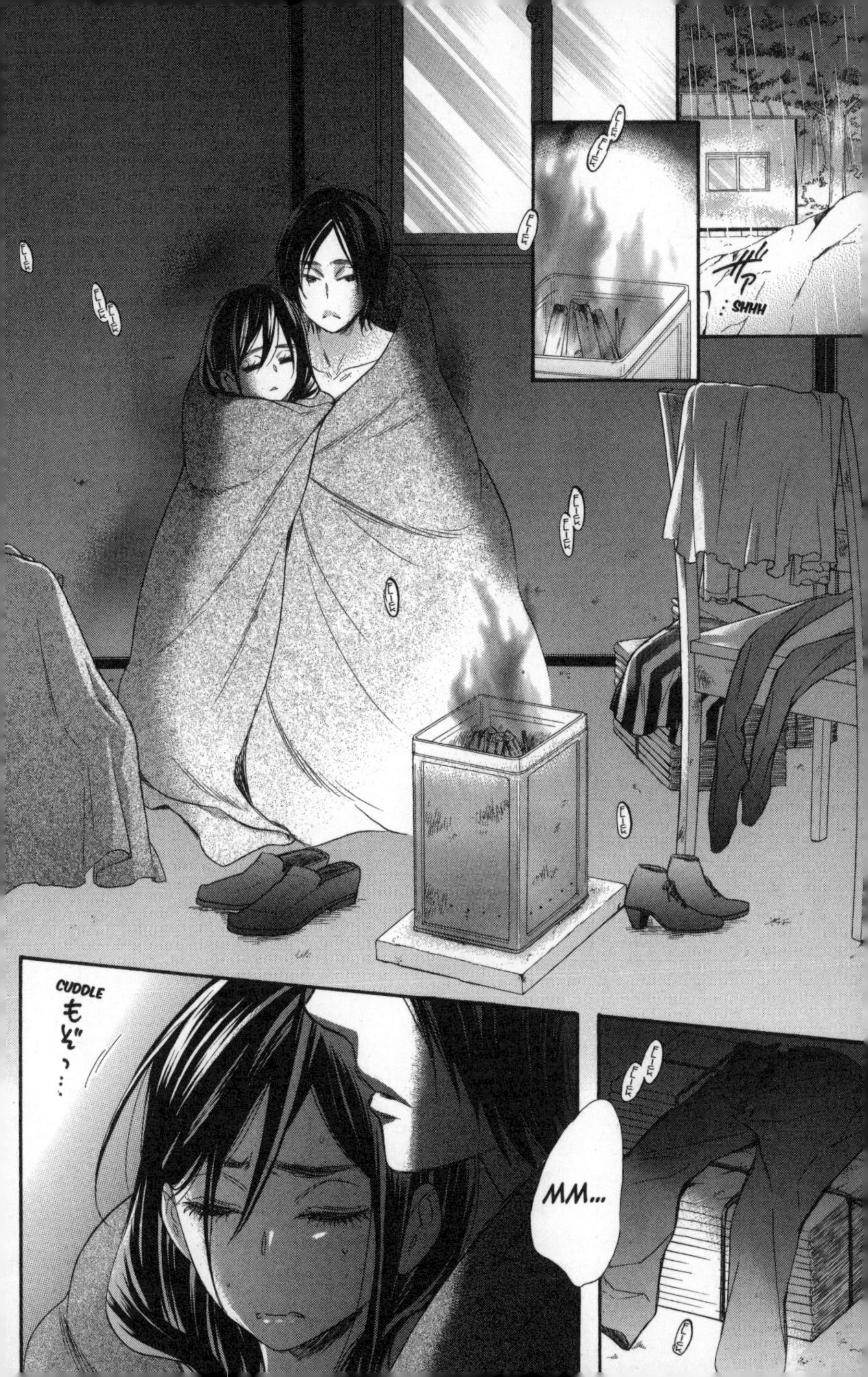
SHHH
FLICK FLICK
FLICK
FLICK
FLICK FLICK
FLICK FLICK
FLICK
FLICK
FLICK FLICK
MM...
FLICK
CUDDLE
もぞっ…

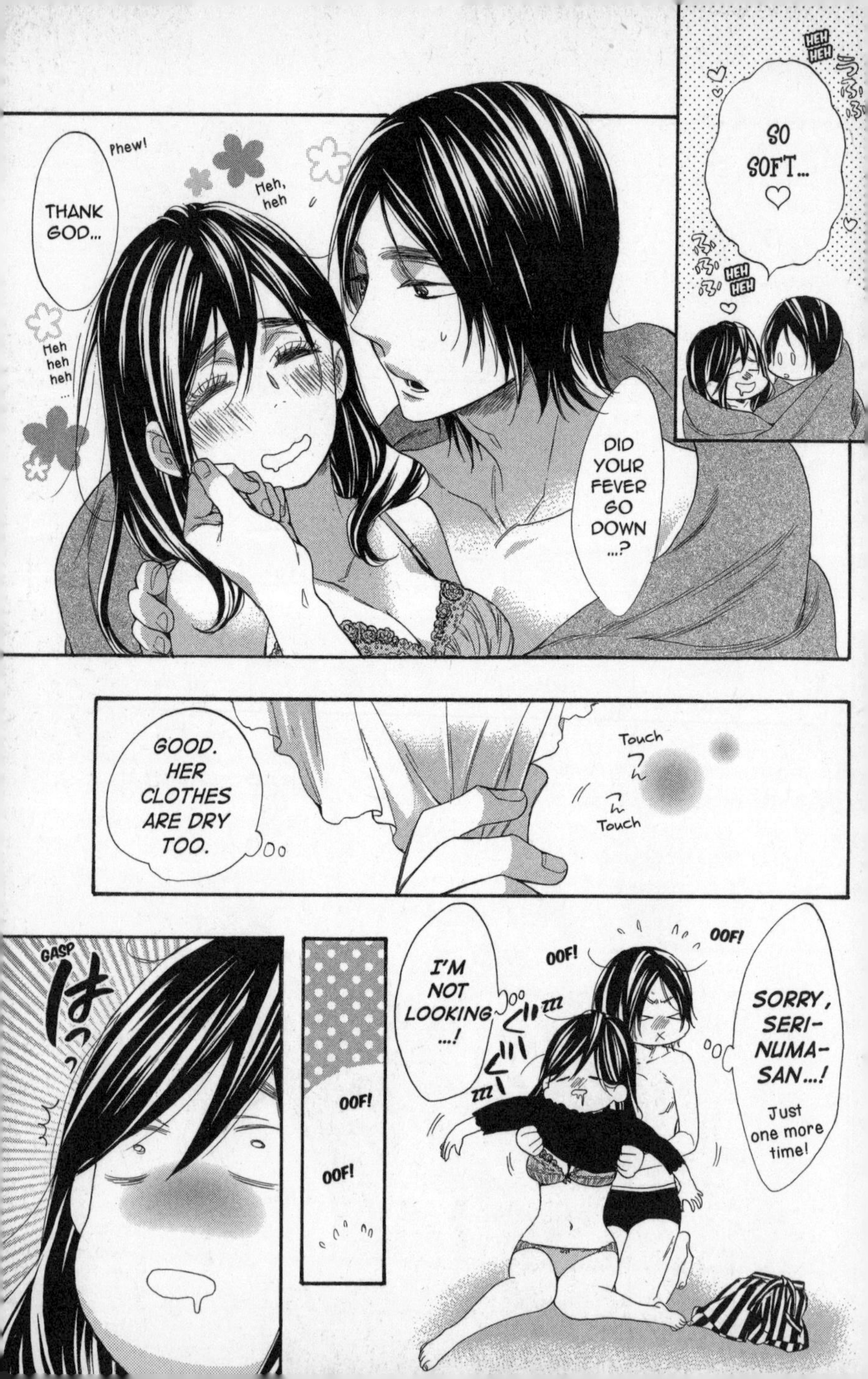
HEH HEH
うふふ
SO SOFT... ♡
ふふふ
HEH HEH
DID YOUR FEVER GO DOWN ...?
Heh, heh
Phew!
THANK GOD...
Heh heh heh ...
Touch
Touch
GOOD. HER CLOTHES ARE DRY TOO.
SORRY, SERI-NUMA-SAN...!
Just one more time!
OOF!
OOF!
I'M NOT LOOKING ...!
ぐい ぐい
zzz
zzz
OOF!
OOF!
GASP
はっ

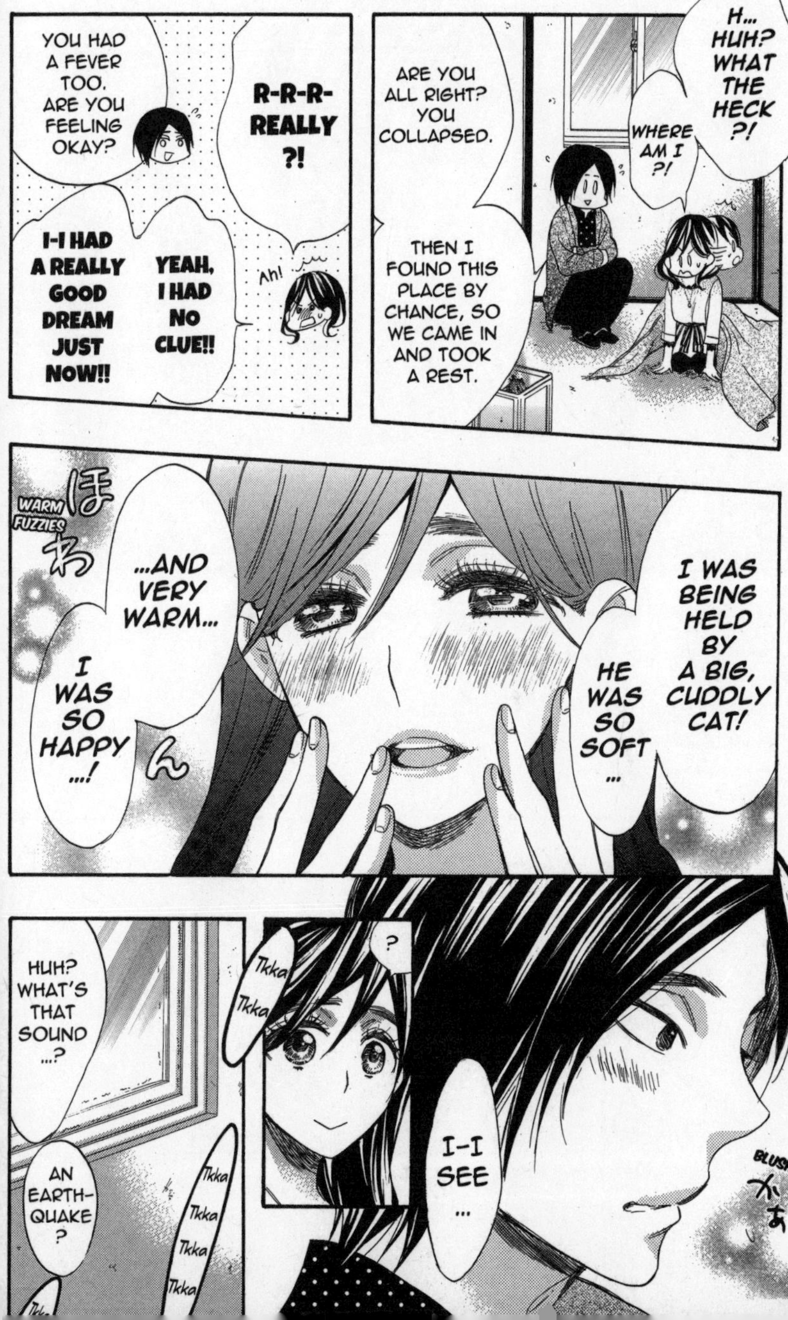
H... HUH? WHAT THE HECK ?!
WHERE AM I ?!
ARE YOU ALL RIGHT? YOU COLLAPSED.
THEN I FOUND THIS PLACE BY CHANCE, SO WE CAME IN AND TOOK A REST.
R-R-R-REALLY ?!
YOU HAD A FEVER TOO. ARE YOU FEELING OKAY?
Ah!
YEAH, I HAD NO CLUE!!
I-I HAD A REALLY GOOD DREAM JUST NOW!!
I WAS BEING HELD BY A BIG, CUDDLY CAT!
HE WAS SO SOFT ...
...AND VERY WARM...
I WAS SO HAPPY ...!
WARM FUZZIES
ほわん
...
BLUSH
かぁ
I-I SEE ...
?
Tkka
Tkka
HUH? WHAT'S THAT SOUND ...?
AN EARTH-QUAKE ?
Tkka
Tkka
Tkka
Tkka

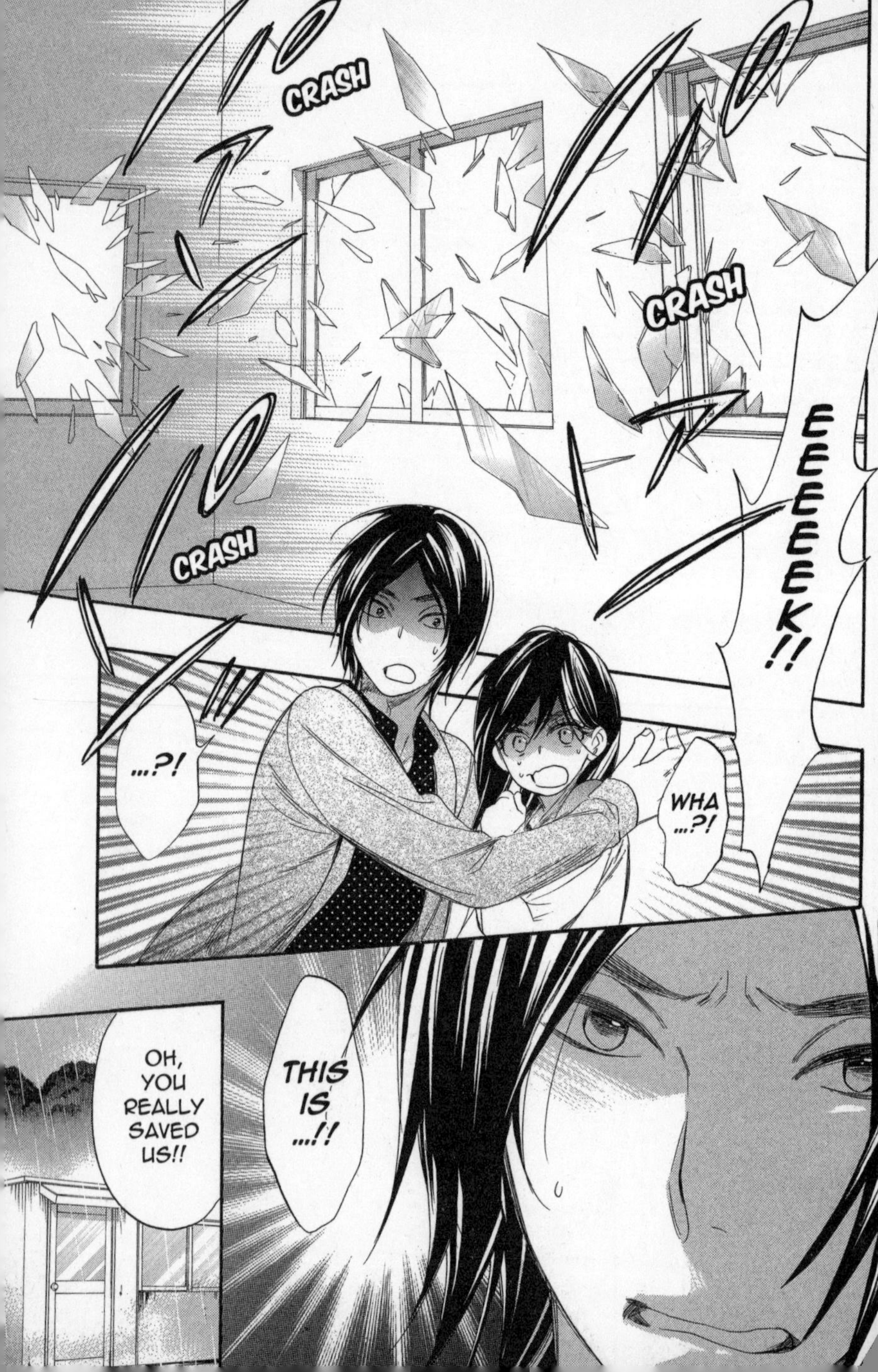
EEEEEEK!!
CRASH
CRASH
CRASH
WHA ...?!
...?!
THIS IS ...!!
OH, YOU REALLY SAVED US!!

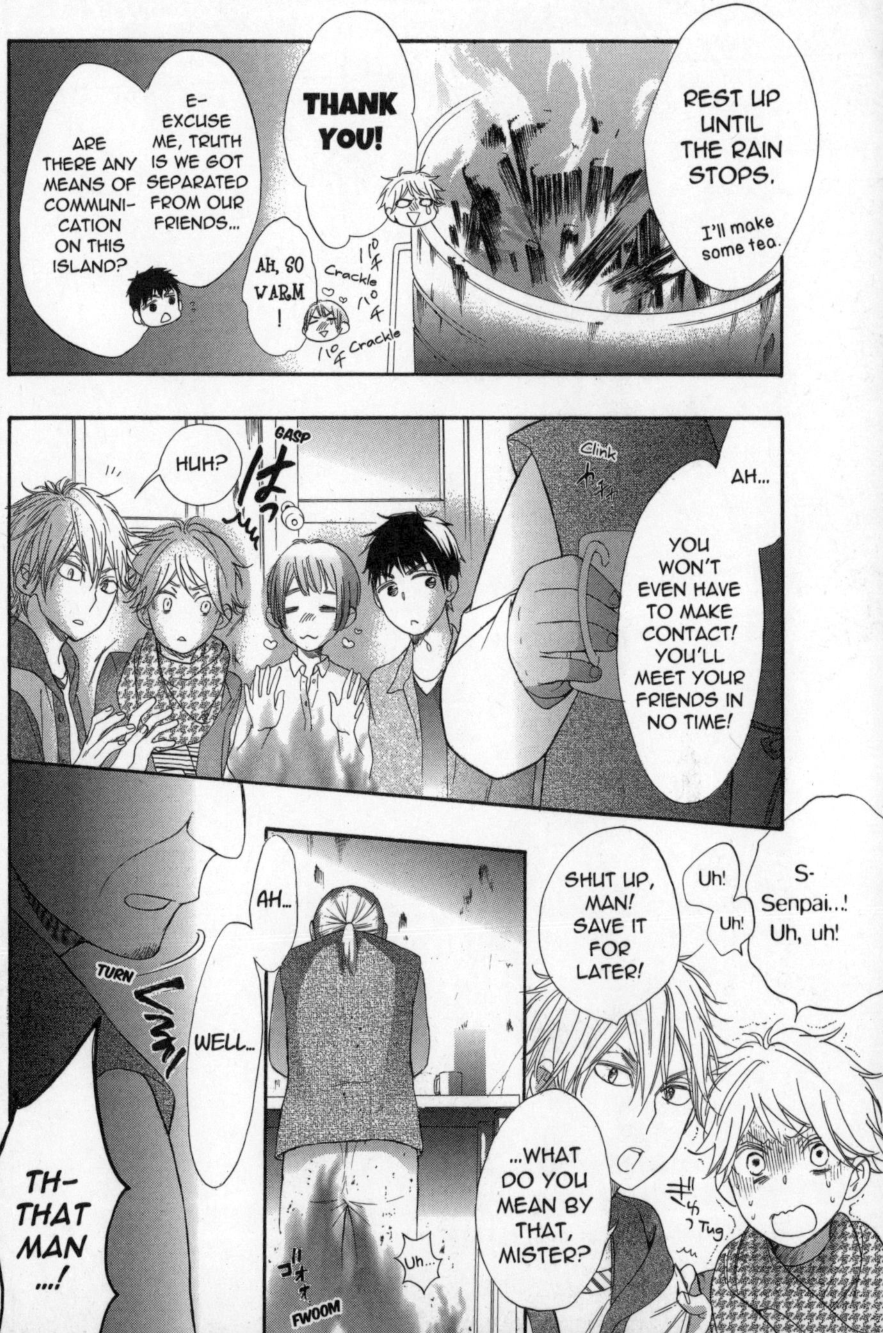
REST UP UNTIL THE RAIN STOPS.
I'll make some tea.
THANK YOU!
Crackle
AH, SO WARM!
Crackle
E-EXCUSE ME, TRUTH IS WE GOT SEPARATED FROM OUR FRIENDS...
ARE THERE ANY MEANS OF COMMUNICATION ON THIS ISLAND?
Clink
AH...
YOU WON'T EVEN HAVE TO MAKE CONTACT! YOU'LL MEET YOUR FRIENDS IN NO TIME!
GASP
HUH?
S-Senpai...! Uh, uh!
Uh!
Uh!
SHUT UP, MAN! SAVE IT FOR LATER!
Tug
...WHAT DO YOU MEAN BY THAT, MISTER?
AH...
WELL...
Uh...
FWOOM
TURN
TH-THAT MAN...!

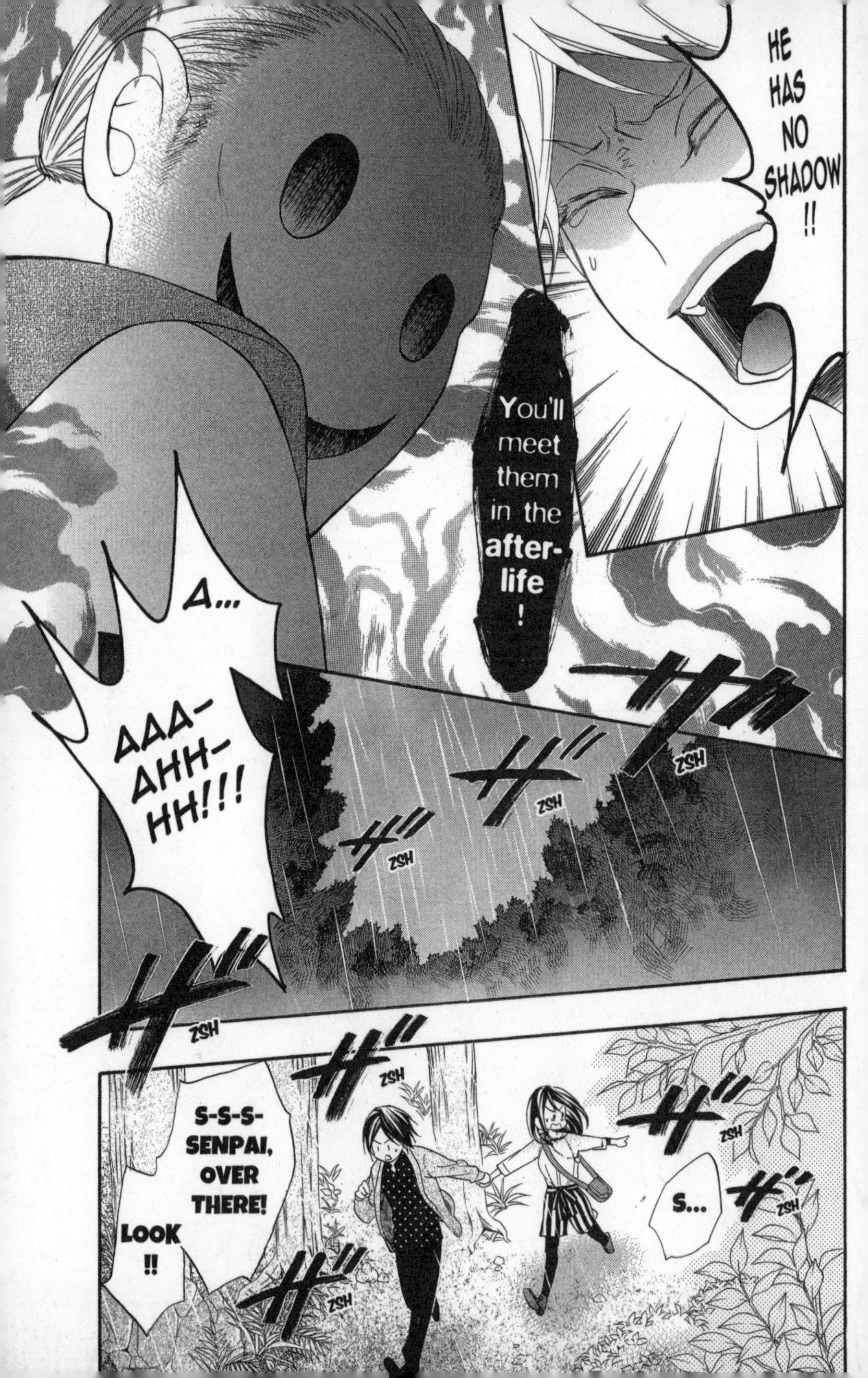
HE HAS NO SHADOW!!
You'll meet them in the after-life!
A...
AAA-AHH-HH!!!
ZSH
ZSH
ZSH
ZSH
ZSH
S...
ZSH
ZSH
S-S-S-SENPAI, OVER THERE!
LOOK!!
ZSH

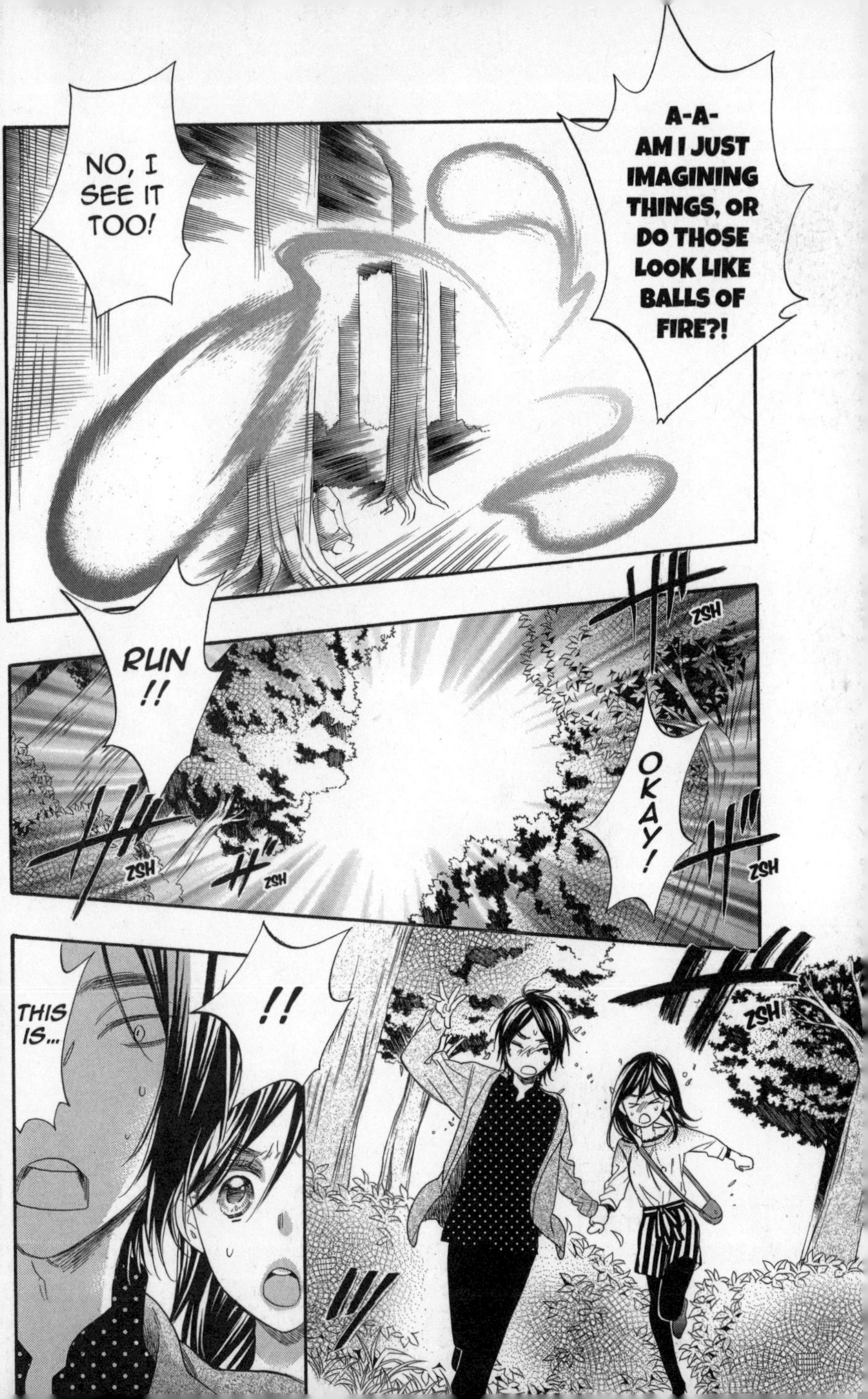
A-A-
AM I JUST IMAGINING THINGS, OR DO THOSE LOOK LIKE BALLS OF FIRE?!
NO, I SEE IT TOO!
ZSH
RUN!!
OKAY!
ZSH
ZSH
ZSH
ZSH
!!
THIS IS...

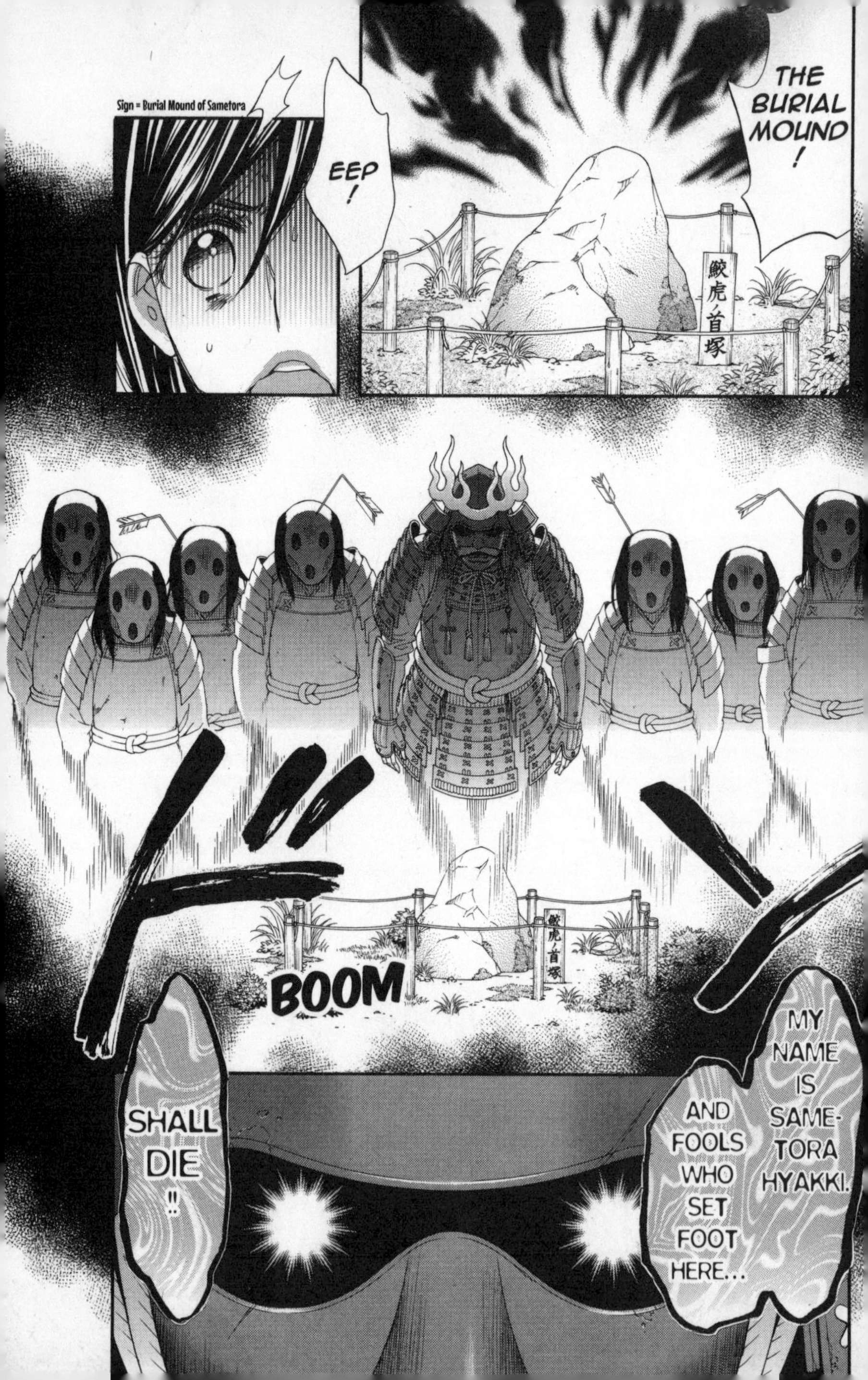
THE BURIAL MOUND!
鮫虎ノ首塚
Sign = Burial Mound of Sametora
EEP!
BOOM
MY NAME IS SAME-TORA HYAKKI.
AND FOOLS WHO SET FOOT HERE...
SHALL DIE!!

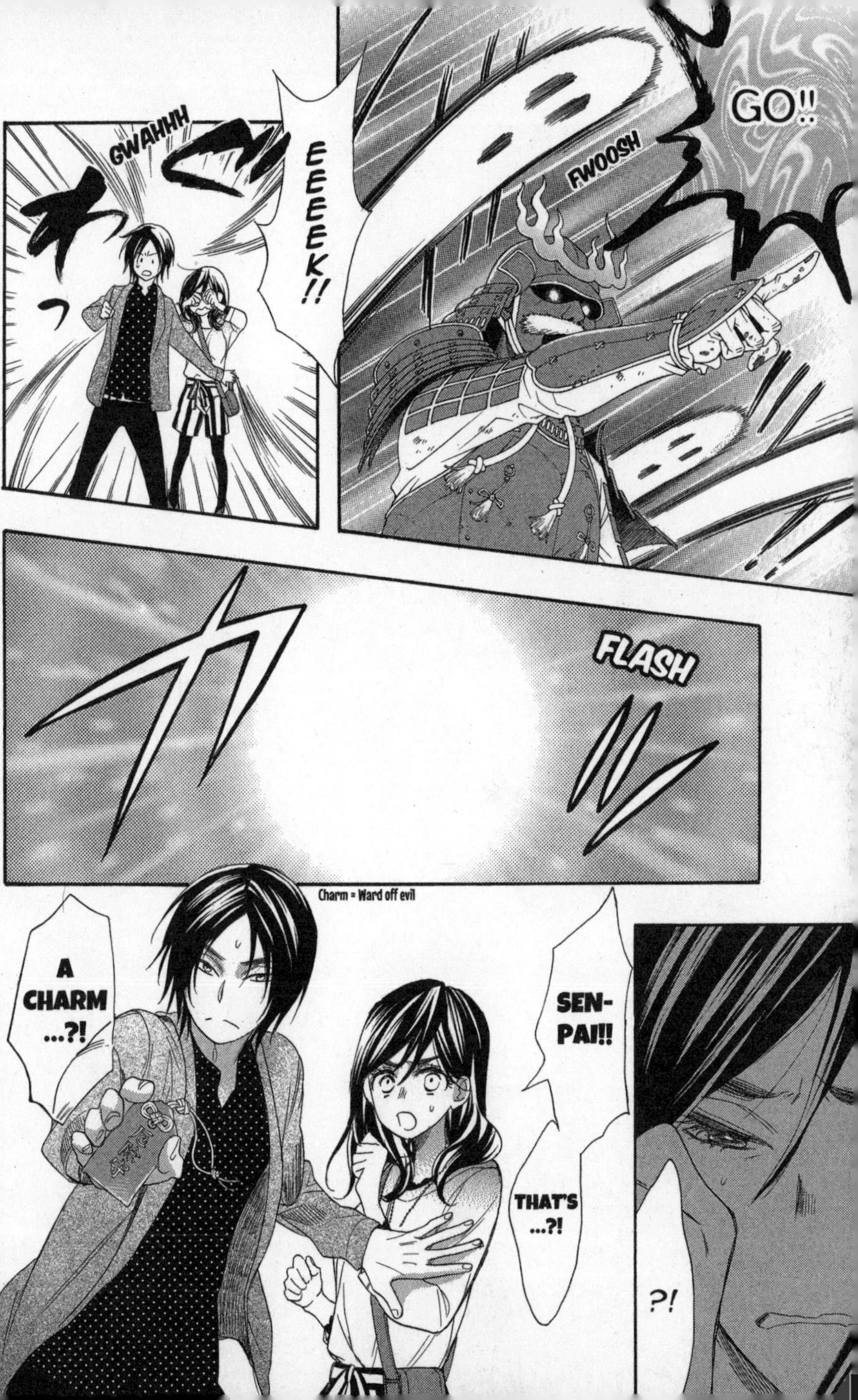
GO!!
FWOOSH
EEEEEK!!
GWAHHH
FLASH
?!
Charm = Ward off evil
SEN-PAI!!
THAT'S ...?!
A CHARM ...?!

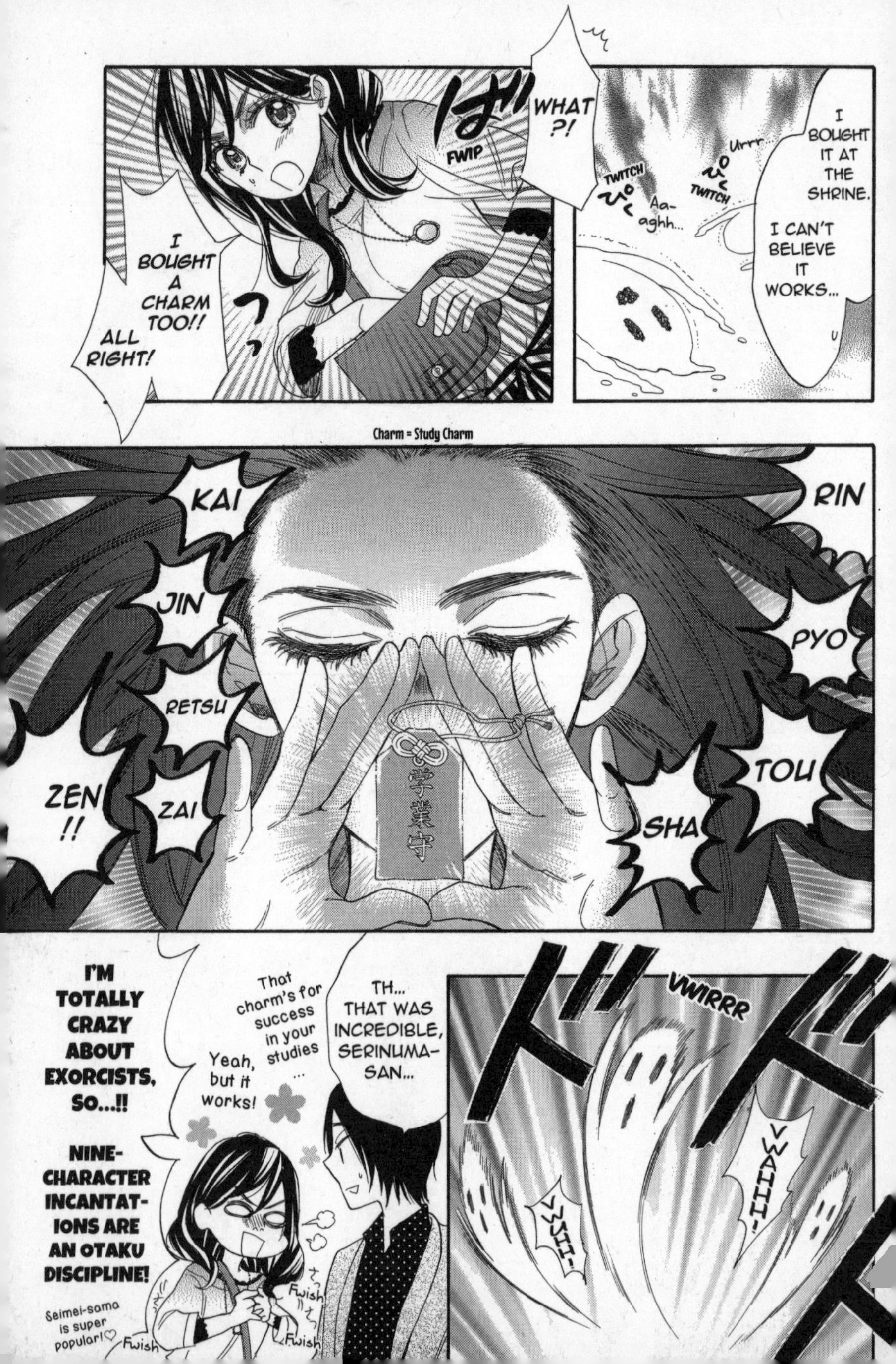
I BOUGHT IT AT THE SHRINE.
I CAN'T BELIEVE IT WORKS...
Urrr...
TWITCH
Aa-aghh...
TWITCH
WHAT?!
FWIP
I BOUGHT A CHARM TOO!! ALL RIGHT!
Charm = Study Charm
RIN
PYO
TOU
SHA
KAI
JIN
RETSU
ZAI
ZEN!!
学業守
VWIRRR
VWAHHH!
VWAHH!
TH... THAT WAS INCREDIBLE, SERINUMA-SAN...
That charm's for success in your studies...
Yeah, but it works!
I'M TOTALLY CRAZY ABOUT EXORCISTS, SO...!!
NINE-CHARACTER INCANTATIONS ARE AN OTAKU DISCIPLINE!
Fwish
Fwish
Seimei-sama is super popular!♡

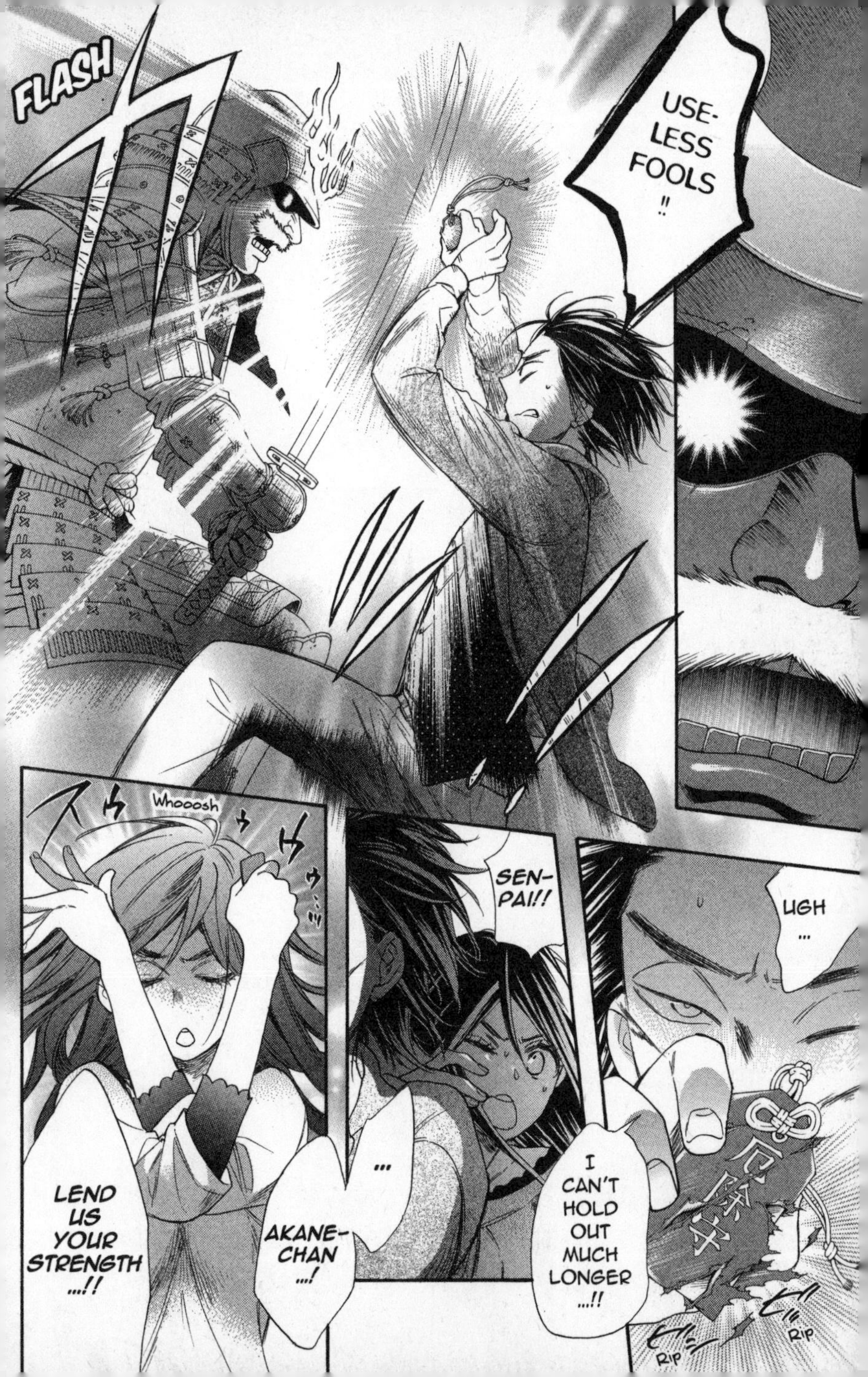
USE-LESS FOOLS!!
FLASH
UGH...
I CAN'T HOLD OUT MUCH LONGER...!!
Rip
Rip
SEN-PAI!!
...
AKANE-CHAN...!
Whoooosh
LEND US YOUR STRENGTH...!!

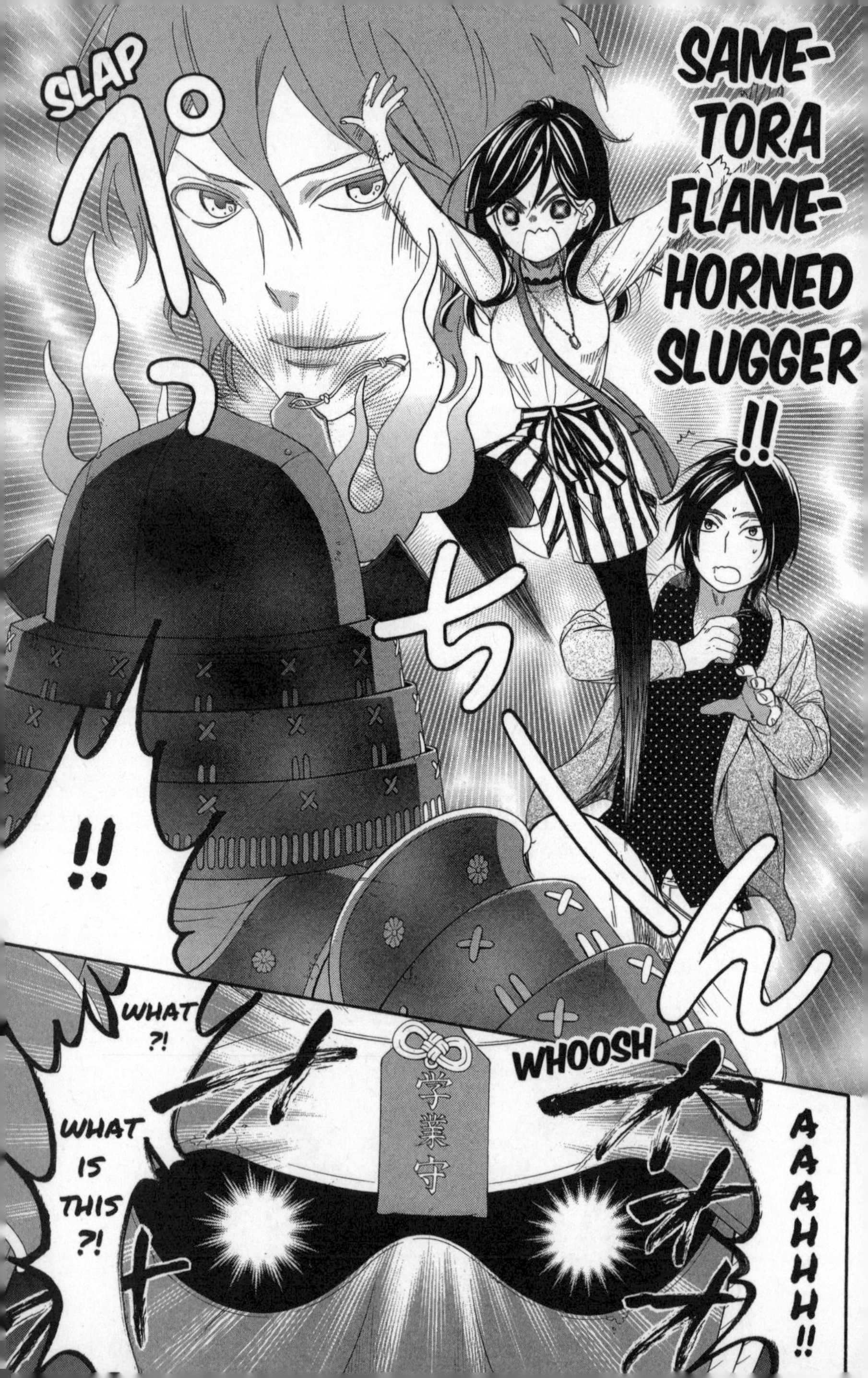
SAME-TORA FLAME-HORNED SLUGGER!!
SLAP
ぺちーん
!!
AAAHHH!!
WHOOSH
学業守
WHAT?!
WHAT IS THIS?!

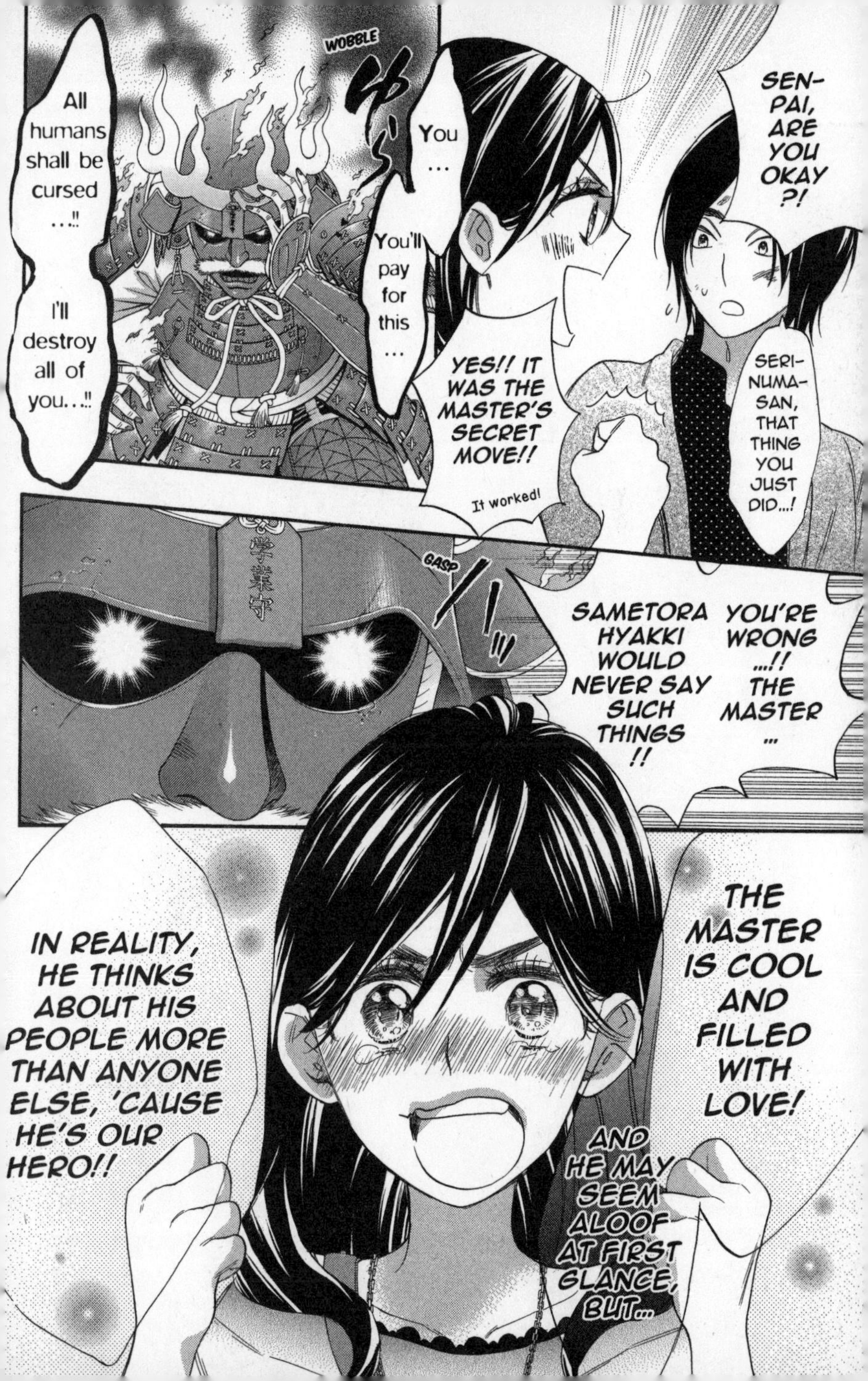
SEN-PAI, ARE YOU OKAY?!
SERI-NUMA-SAN, THAT THING YOU JUST DID...!
YES!! IT WAS THE MASTER'S SECRET MOVE!!
It worked!
WOBBLE
You ...
You'll pay for this ...
All humans shall be cursed ...!!
I'll destroy all of you...!!
GASP
YOU'RE WRONG ...!! THE MASTER ...
SAMETORA HYAKKI WOULD NEVER SAY SUCH THINGS !!
THE MASTER IS COOL AND FILLED WITH LOVE!
AND HE MAY SEEM ALOOF AT FIRST GLANCE, BUT...
IN REALITY, HE THINKS ABOUT HIS PEOPLE MORE THAN ANYONE ELSE, 'CAUSE HE'S OUR HERO!!

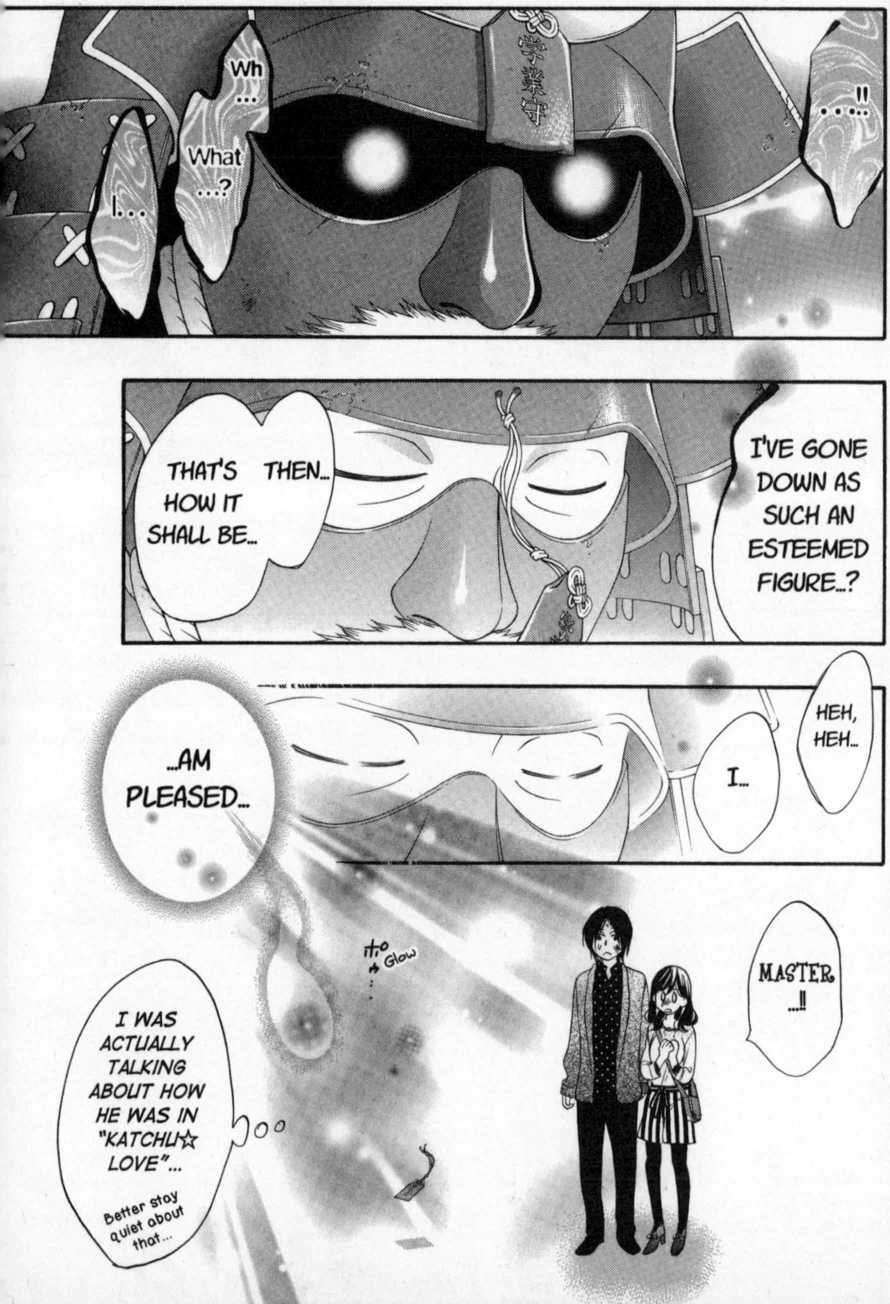
...!!
Wh... What...?
I...
学業守
I'VE GONE DOWN AS SUCH AN ESTEEMED FIGURE...?
THEN... THAT'S HOW IT SHALL BE...
HEH, HEH...
I...
...AM PLEASED...
MASTER...!!
Glow
I WAS ACTUALLY TALKING ABOUT HOW HE WAS IN "KATCHU☆ LOVE"...
Better stay quiet about that...

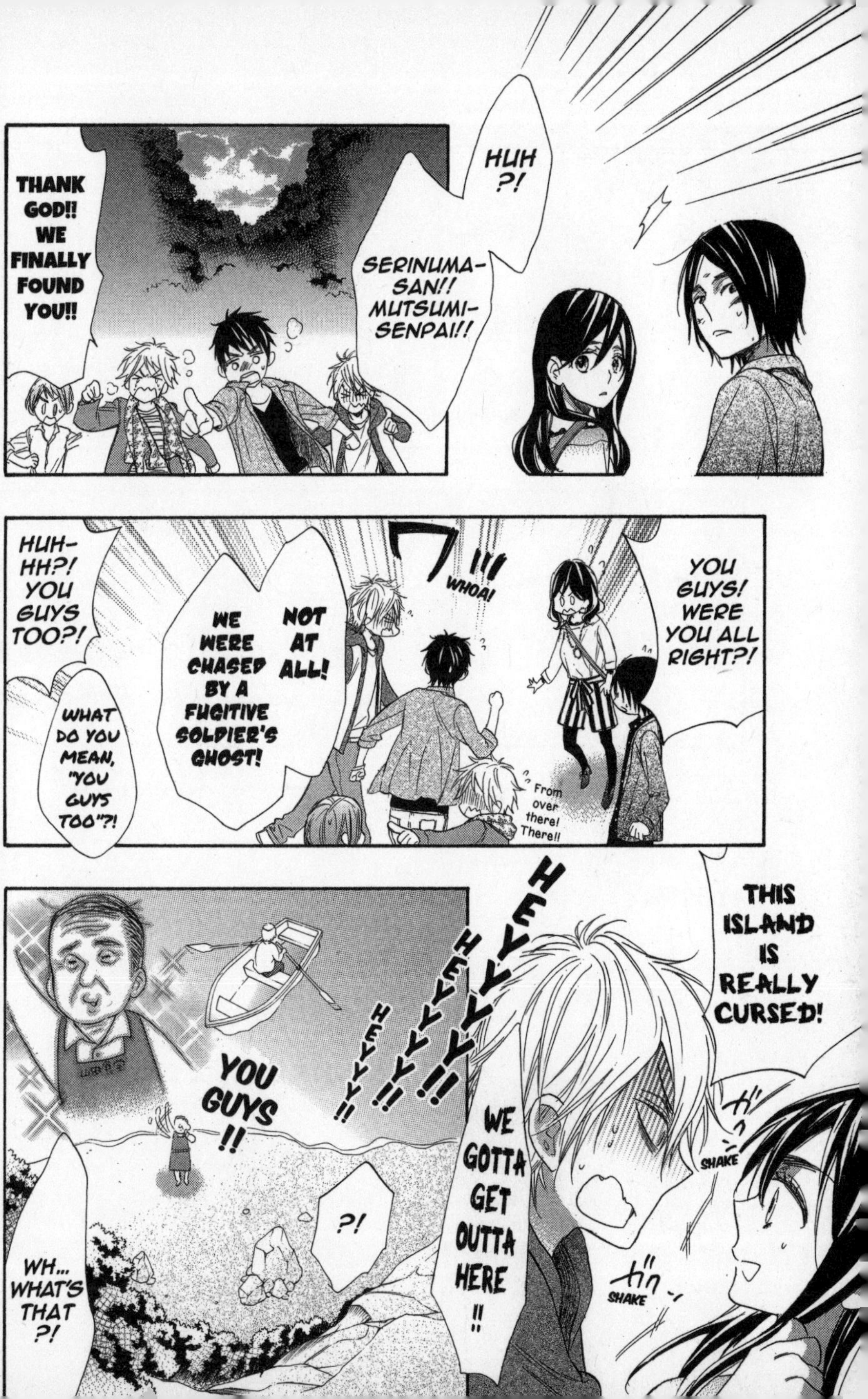
HUH ?!
SERINUMA-SAN!! MUTSUMI-SENPAI!!
THANK GOD!! WE FINALLY FOUND YOU!!
YOU GUYS! WERE YOU ALL RIGHT?!
WHOA!
NOT AT ALL!
WE WERE CHASED BY A FUGITIVE SOLDIER'S GHOST!
HUHH-HH?! YOU GUYS TOO?!
WHAT DO YOU MEAN, "YOU GUYS TOO"?!
From over there! There!!
THIS ISLAND IS REALLY CURSED!
SHAKE
SHAKE
WE GOTTA GET OUTTA HERE !!
HEYYY!!
HEYYY!!
HEYYY!!
YOU GUYS !!
?!
WH... WHAT'S THAT ?!

Shop sign = Yamada Restaurant

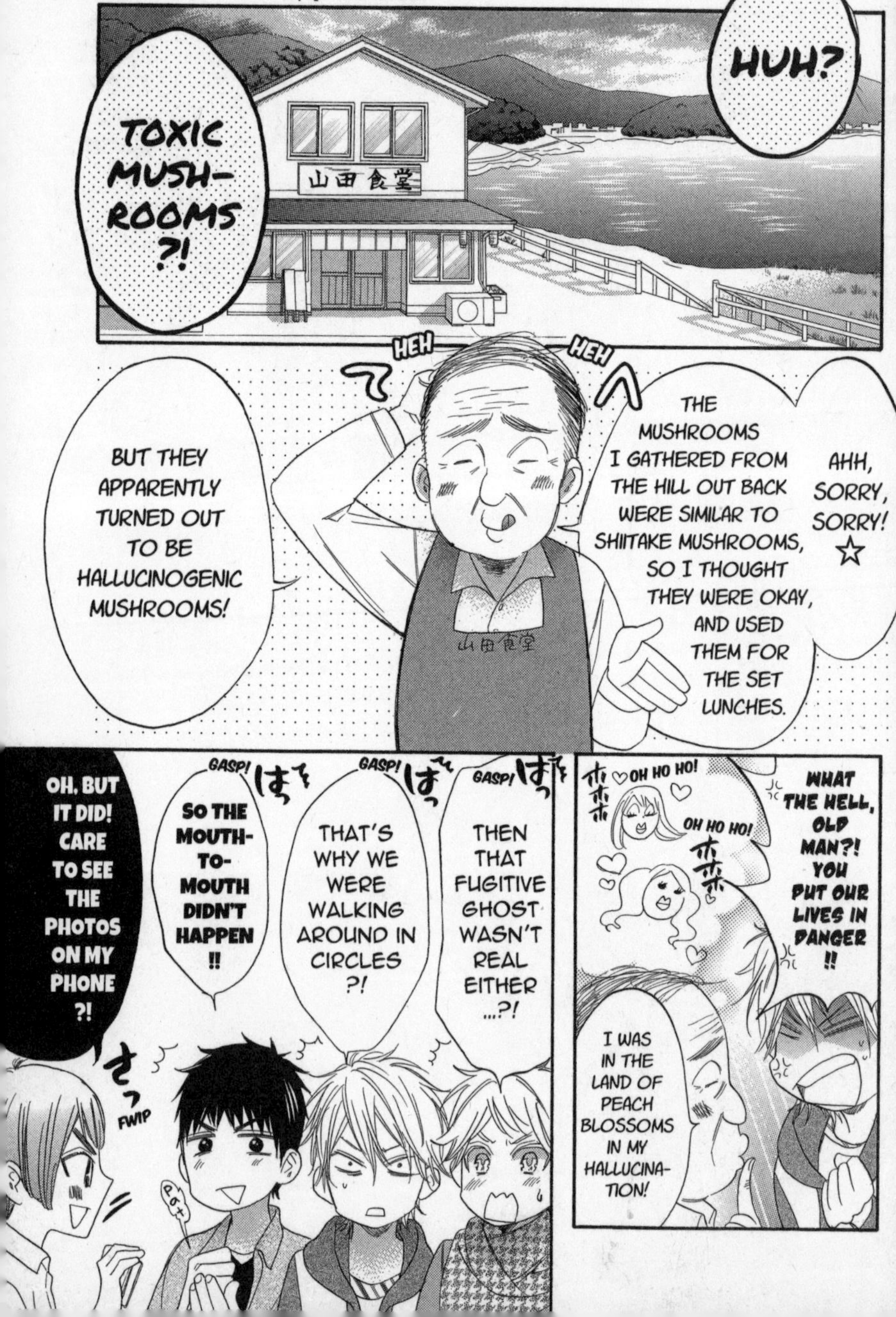
HUH?
TOXIC MUSH-ROOMS?!
山田食堂
HEH HEH
AHH, SORRY, SORRY! ☆
THE MUSHROOMS I GATHERED FROM THE HILL OUT BACK WERE SIMILAR TO SHIITAKE MUSHROOMS, SO I THOUGHT THEY WERE OKAY, AND USED THEM FOR THE SET LUNCHES.
BUT THEY APPARENTLY TURNED OUT TO BE HALLUCINOGENIC MUSHROOMS!
WHAT THE HELL, OLD MAN?! YOU PUT OUR LIVES IN DANGER!!
OH HO HO!
OH HO HO!
I WAS IN THE LAND OF PEACH BLOSSOMS IN MY HALLUCINATION!
GASP!
THEN THAT FUGITIVE GHOST WASN'T REAL EITHER ...?!
GASP!
THAT'S WHY WE WERE WALKING AROUND IN CIRCLES?!
GASP!
SO THE MOUTH-TO-MOUTH DIDN'T HAPPEN!!
OH, BUT IT DID! CARE TO SEE THE PHOTOS ON MY PHONE?!
FWIP

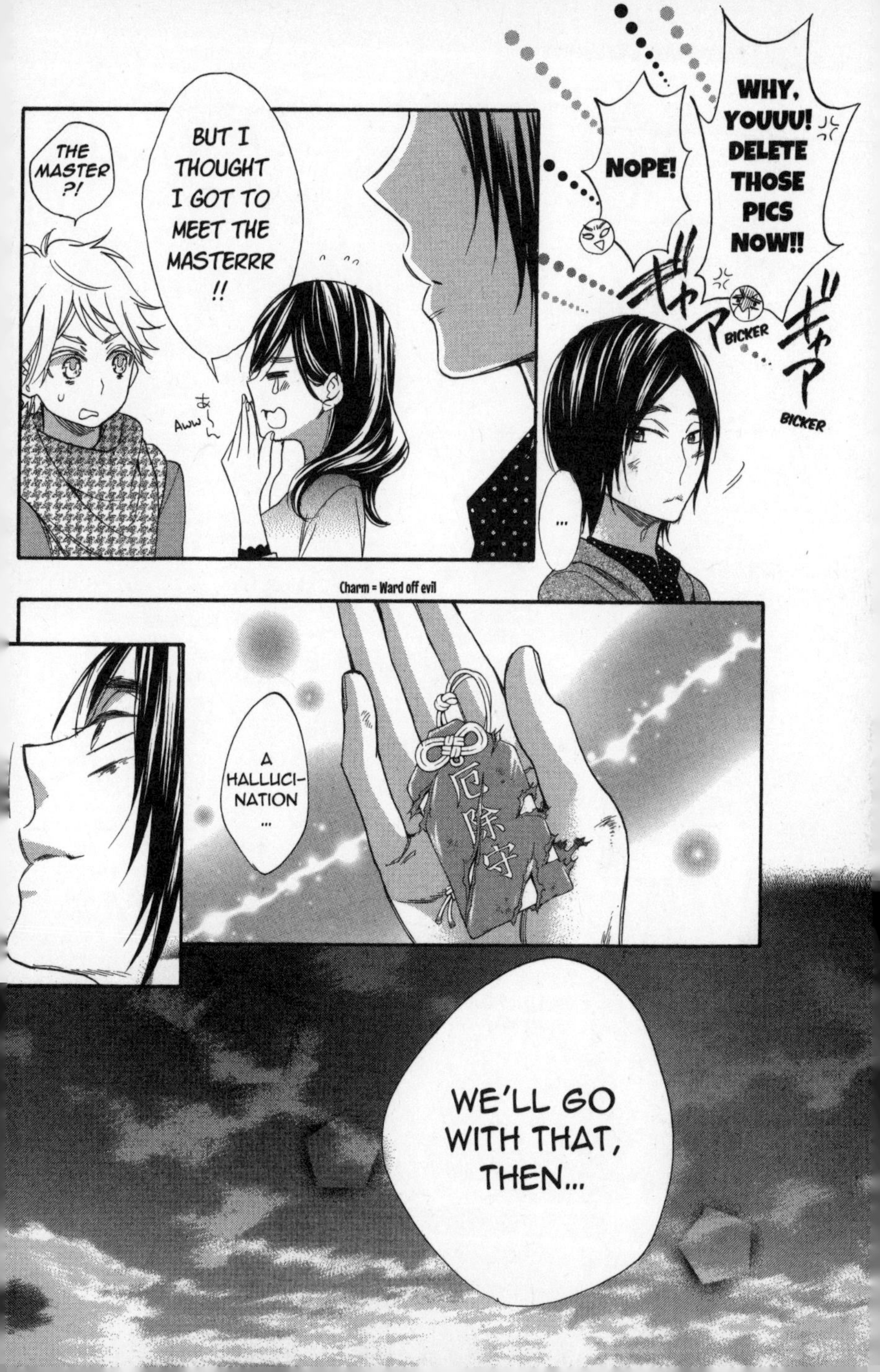
WHY, YOUUU! DELETE THOSE PICS NOW!!
NOPE!
ギャア BICKER
ギャア BICKER
...
BUT I THOUGHT I GOT TO MEET THE MASTERRR!!
あ〜ん AWW
THE MASTER?!
Charm = Ward off evil
厄除守
A HALLUCINATION...
WE'LL GO WITH THAT, THEN...

#28 I'M FALLING BEHIND

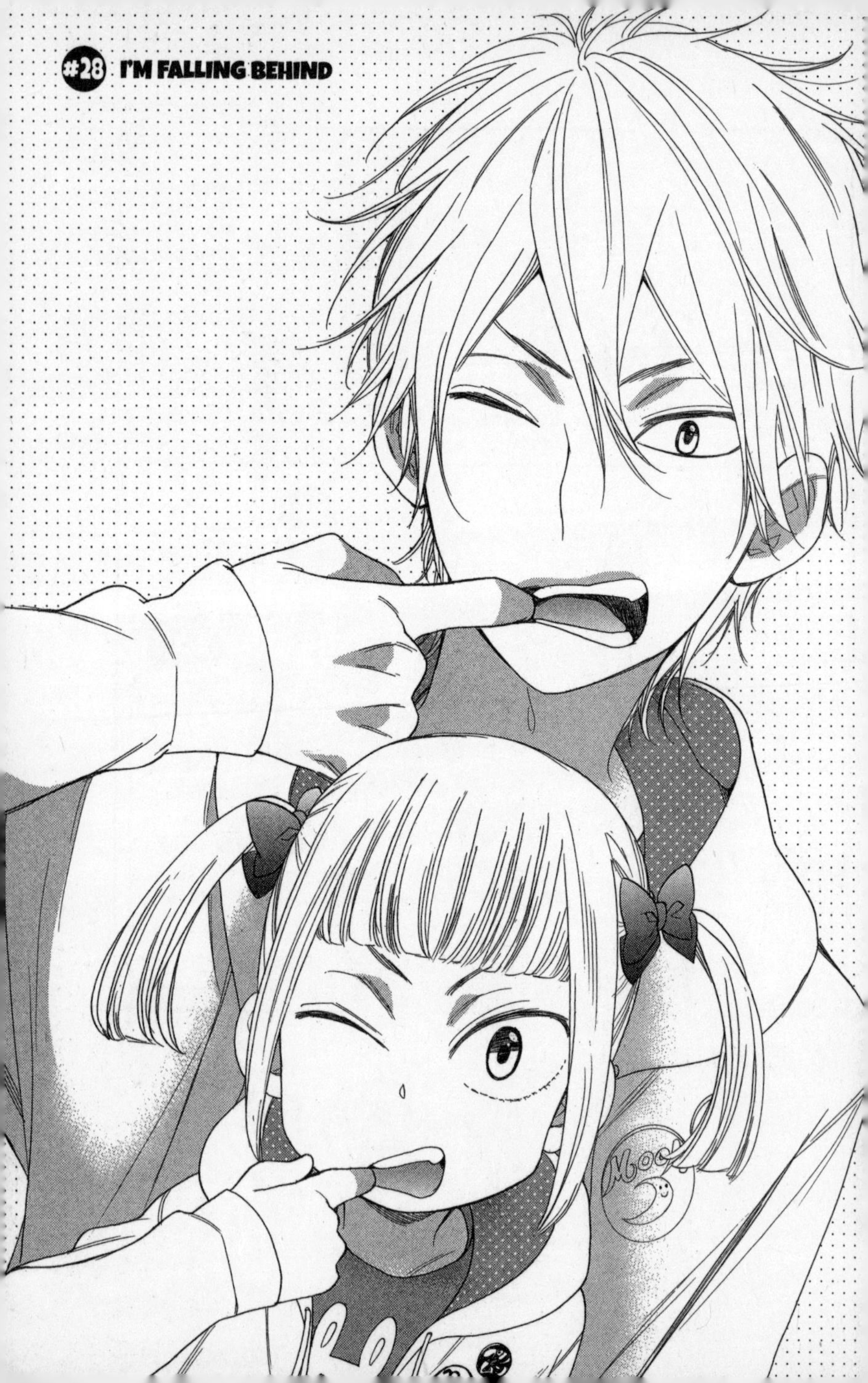

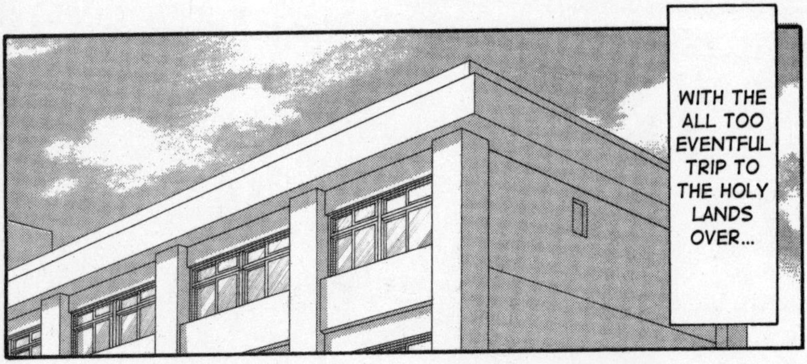
WITH THE ALL TOO EVENTFUL TRIP TO THE HOLY LANDS OVER...
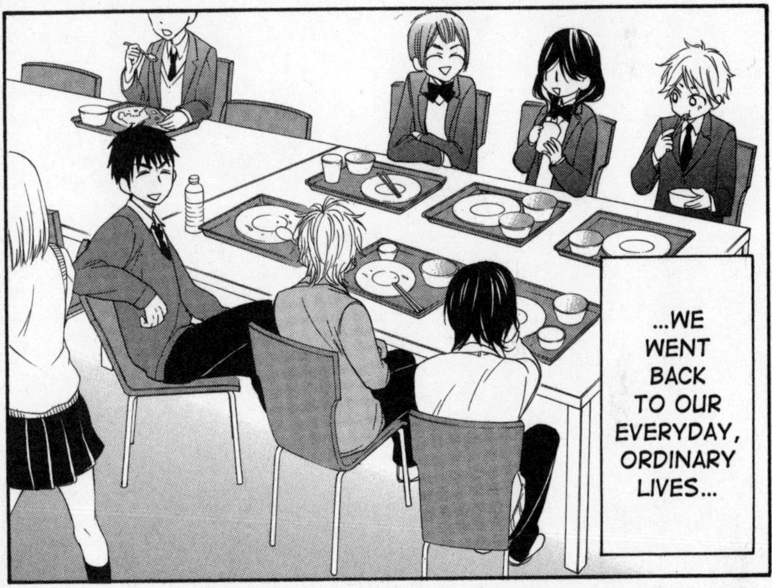
...WE WENT BACK TO OUR EVERYDAY, ORDINARY LIVES...

KiSS HiM, NOT ME!

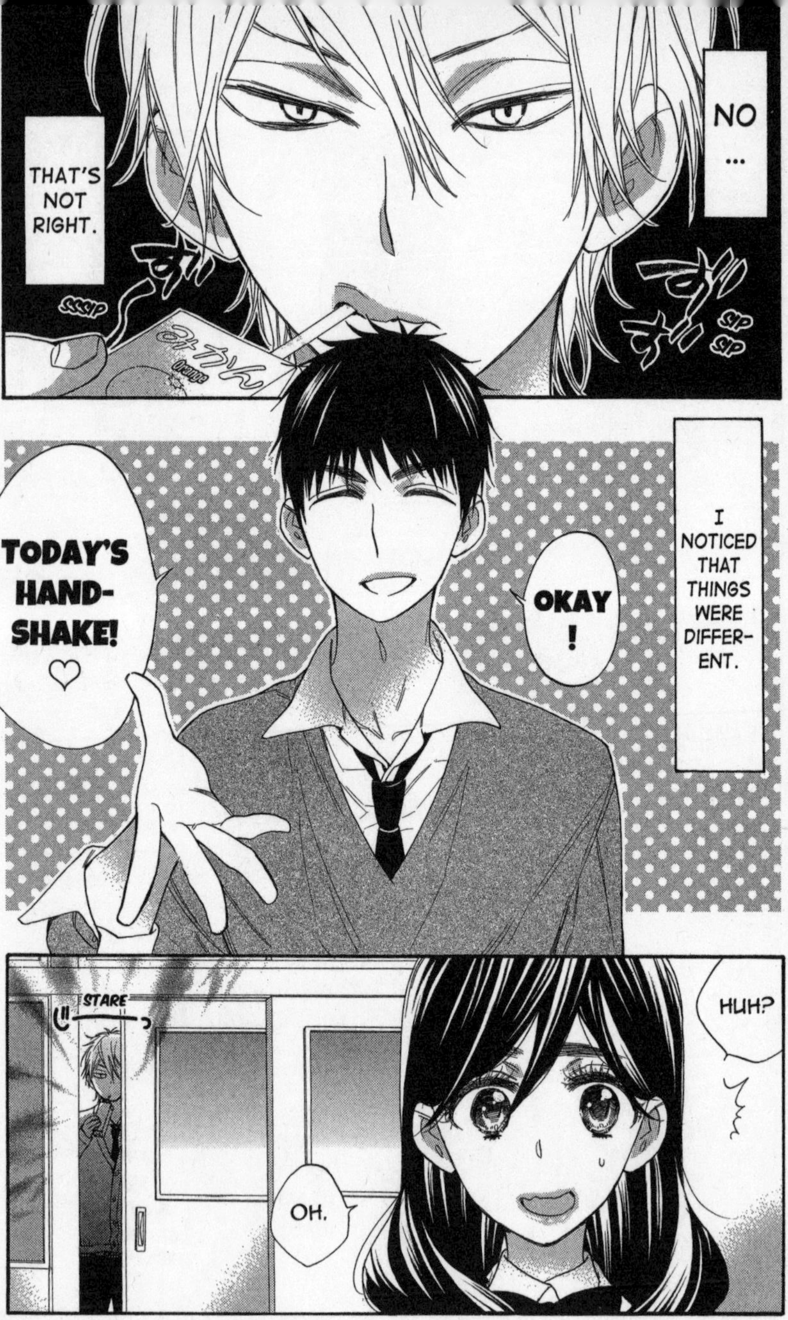
NO ...
SIP SIP
THAT'S NOT RIGHT.
SSSIP
I NOTICED THAT THINGS WERE DIFFER-ENT.
OKAY!
TODAY'S HAND-SHAKE! ♡
HUH?
OH.
STARE

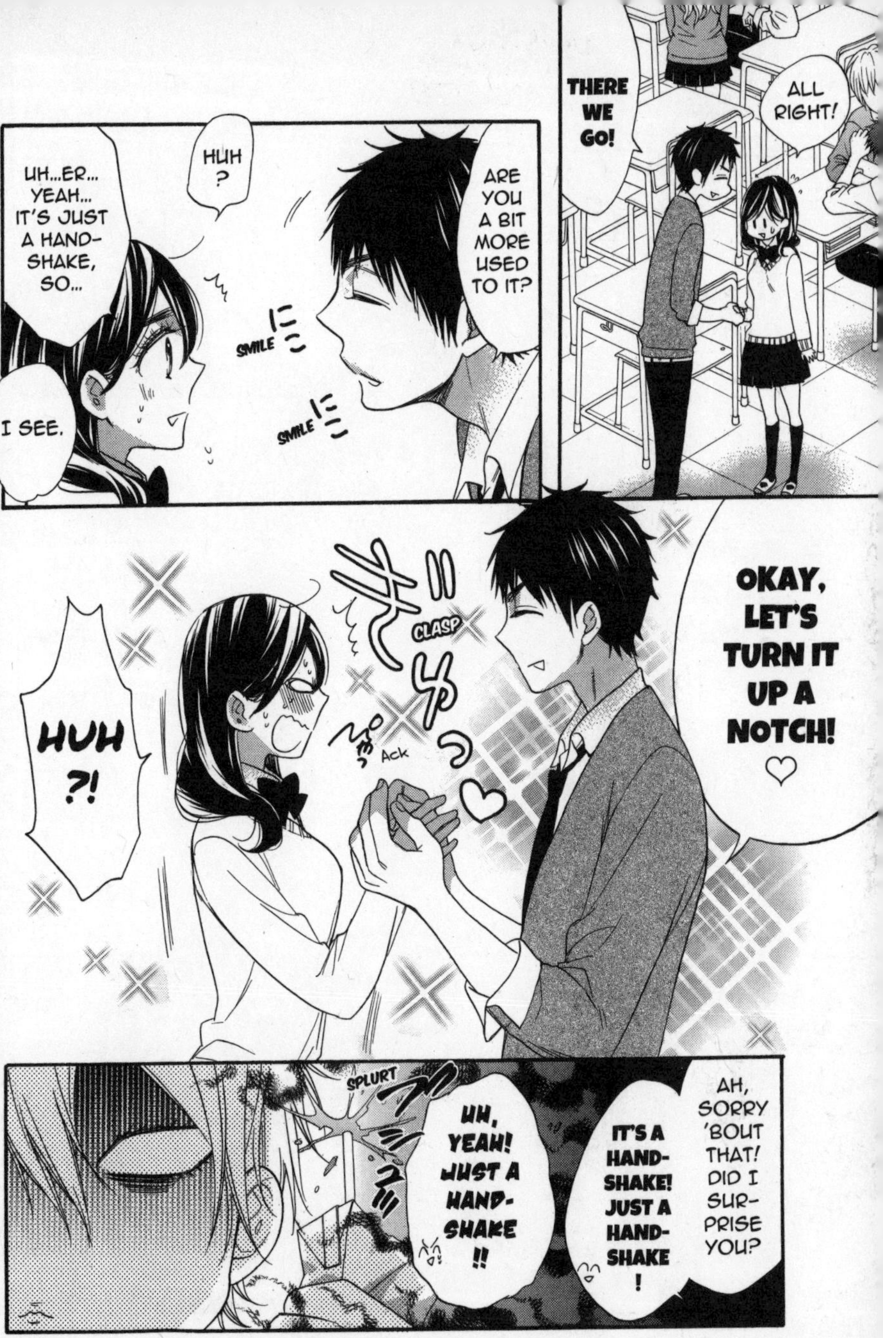
ALL RIGHT!
THERE WE GO!
ARE YOU A BIT MORE USED TO IT?
SMILE
SMILE
HUH?
UH...ER... YEAH... IT'S JUST A HANDSHAKE, SO...
I SEE.
OKAY, LET'S TURN IT UP A NOTCH! ♡
CLASP
Ack
HUH?!
AH, SORRY 'BOUT THAT! DID I SURPRISE YOU?
IT'S A HANDSHAKE! JUST A HANDSHAKE!
UH, YEAH! JUST A HANDSHAKE!!
SPLURT

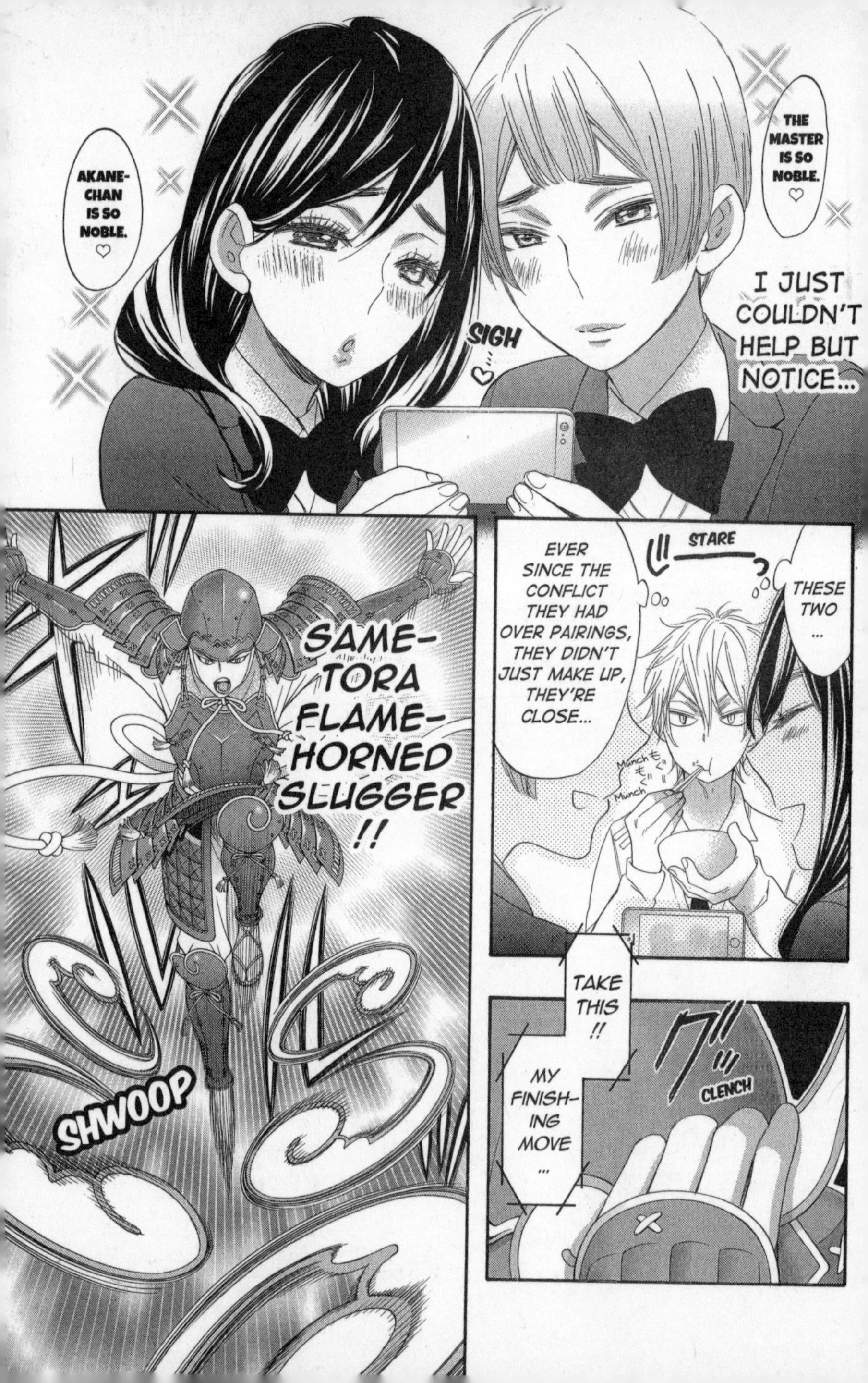
THE MASTER IS SO NOBLE. ♡
I JUST COULDN'T HELP BUT NOTICE...
SIGH ...♡
AKANE-CHAN IS SO NOBLE. ♡
THESE TWO ...
STARE
EVER SINCE THE CONFLICT THEY HAD OVER PAIRINGS, THEY DIDN'T JUST MAKE UP, THEY'RE CLOSE...
Munch
Munch
TAKE THIS !!
MY FINISH-ING MOVE ...
CLENCH
SAME-TORA FLAME-HORNED SLUGGER !!
SHWOOP

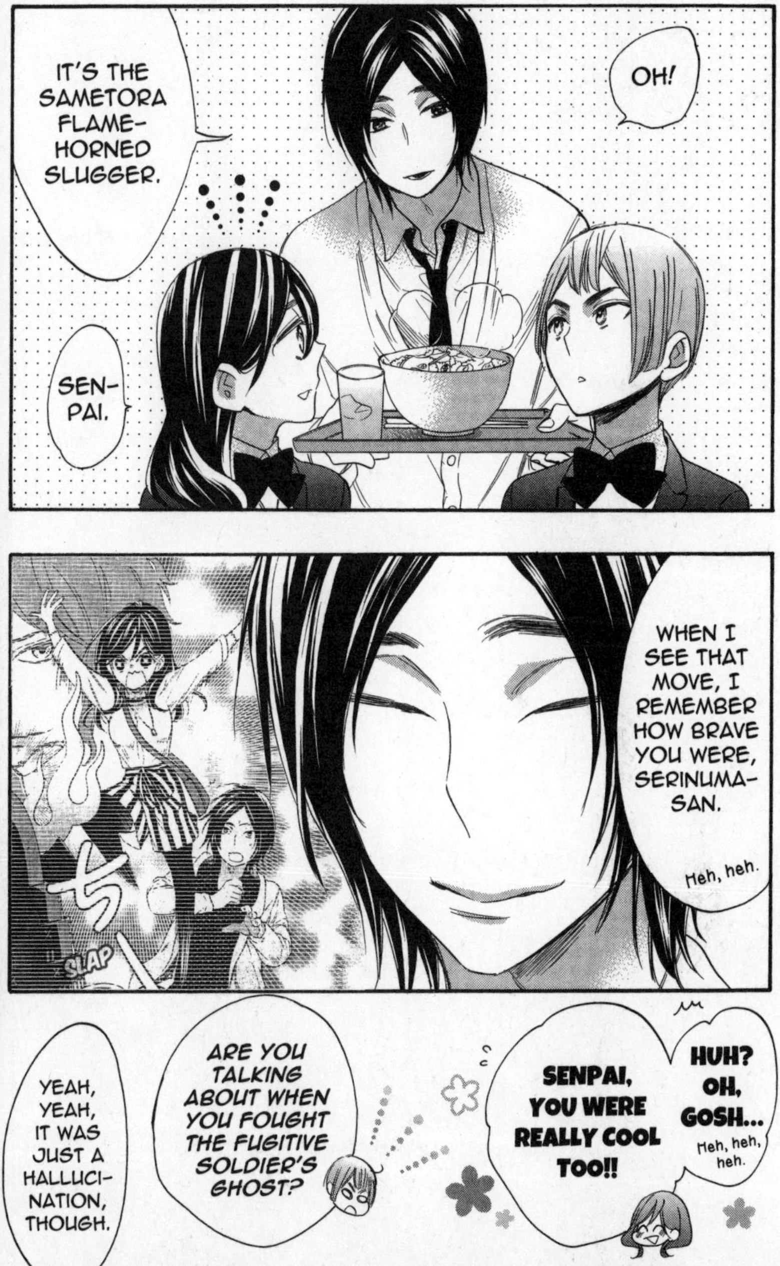
OH!
IT'S THE SAMETORA FLAME-HORNED SLUGGER.
SEN-PAI.
WHEN I SEE THAT MOVE, I REMEMBER HOW BRAVE YOU WERE, SERINUMA-SAN.
Heh, heh.
SLAP
HUH? OH, GOSH...
Heh, heh, heh.
SENPAI, YOU WERE REALLY COOL TOO!!
ARE YOU TALKING ABOUT WHEN YOU FOUGHT THE FUGITIVE SOLDIER'S GHOST?
YEAH, YEAH, IT WAS JUST A HALLUCI-NATION, THOUGH.

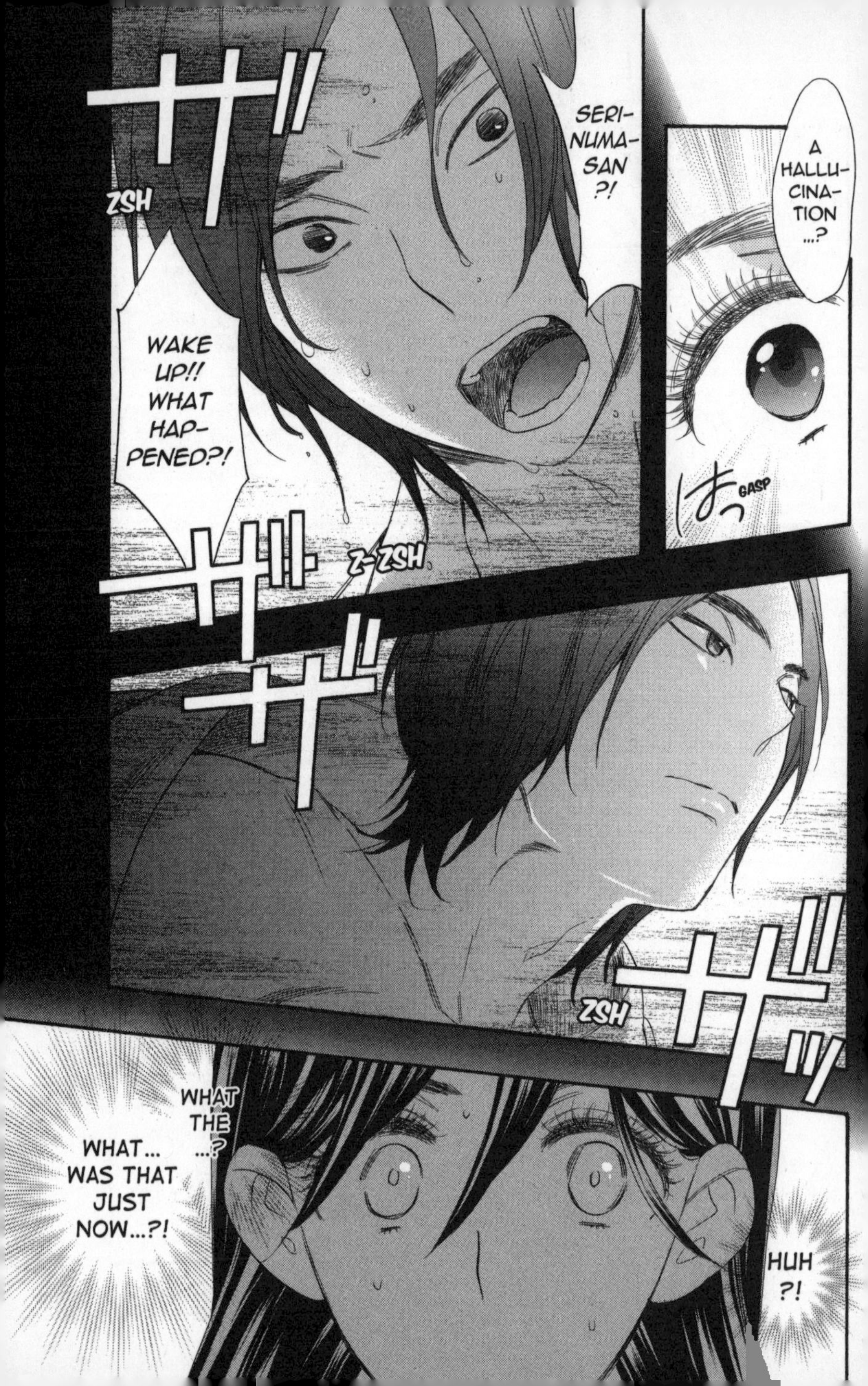
A HALLUCINATION...?
GASP
SERINUMA-SAN?!
ZSH
WAKE UP!! WHAT HAPPENED?!
Z-ZSH
ZSH
HUH?!
WHAT THE...?
WHAT... WAS THAT JUST NOW...?!

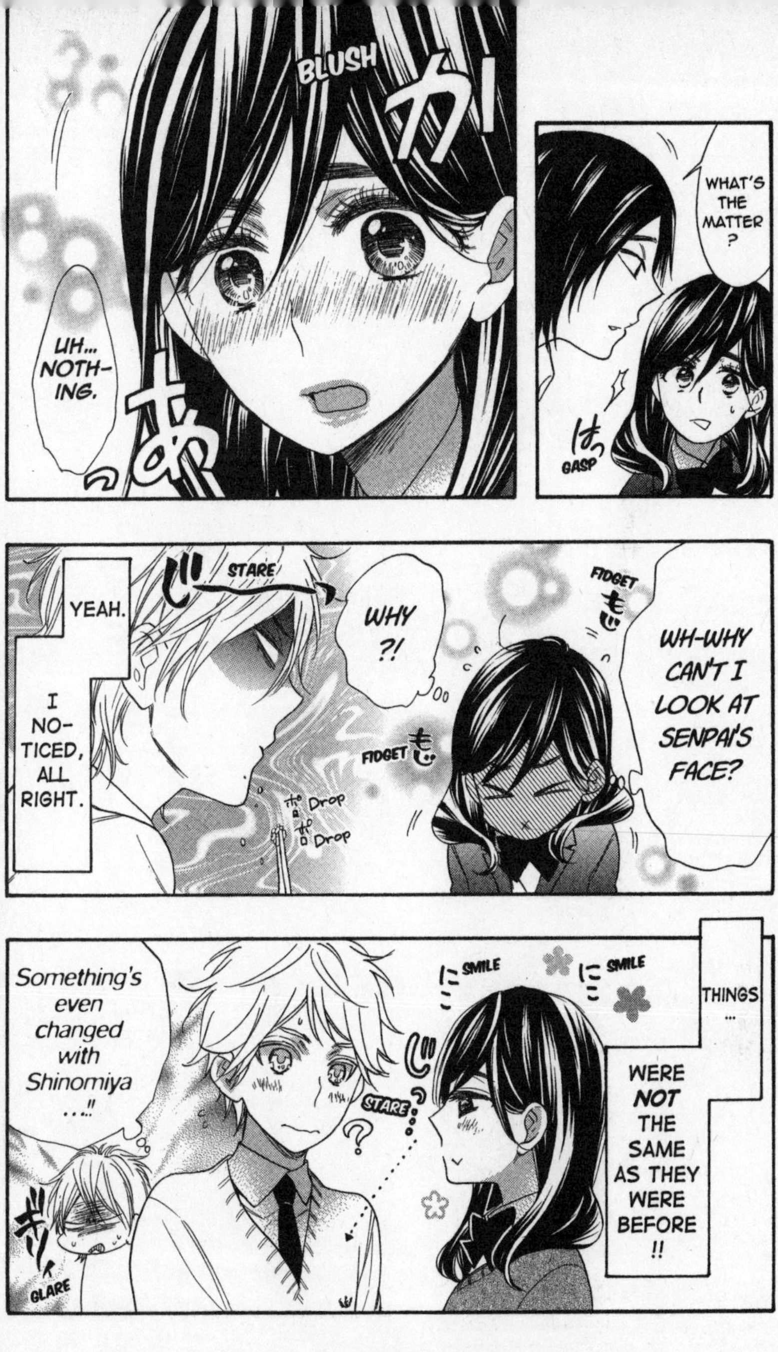
WHAT'S THE MATTER?
GASP
BLUSH
UH... NOTHING.
FIDGET
WH-WHY CAN'T I LOOK AT SENPAI'S FACE?
FIDGET
WHY?!
STARE
YEAH.
I NOTICED, ALL RIGHT.
Drop
Drop
THINGS...
WERE **NOT** THE SAME AS THEY WERE BEFORE!!
SMILE
SMILE
STARE
Something's even changed with Shinomiya...!!
GLARE

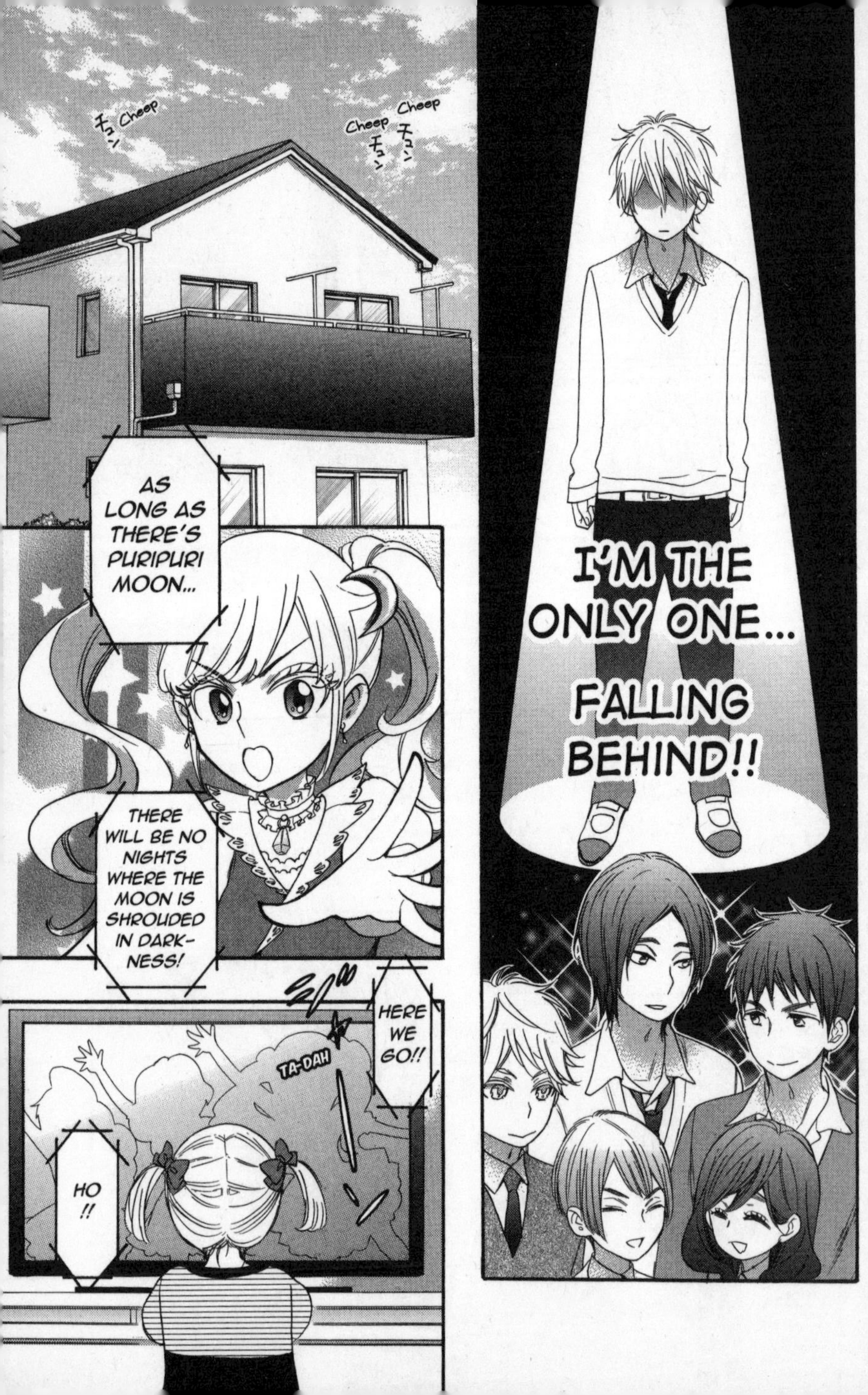
I'M THE ONLY ONE...
FALLING BEHIND!!
Cheep
Cheep
Cheep
AS LONG AS THERE'S PURIPURI MOON...
THERE WILL BE NO NIGHTS WHERE THE MOON IS SHROUDED IN DARK-NESS!
HERE WE GO!!
TA-DAH
HO!!

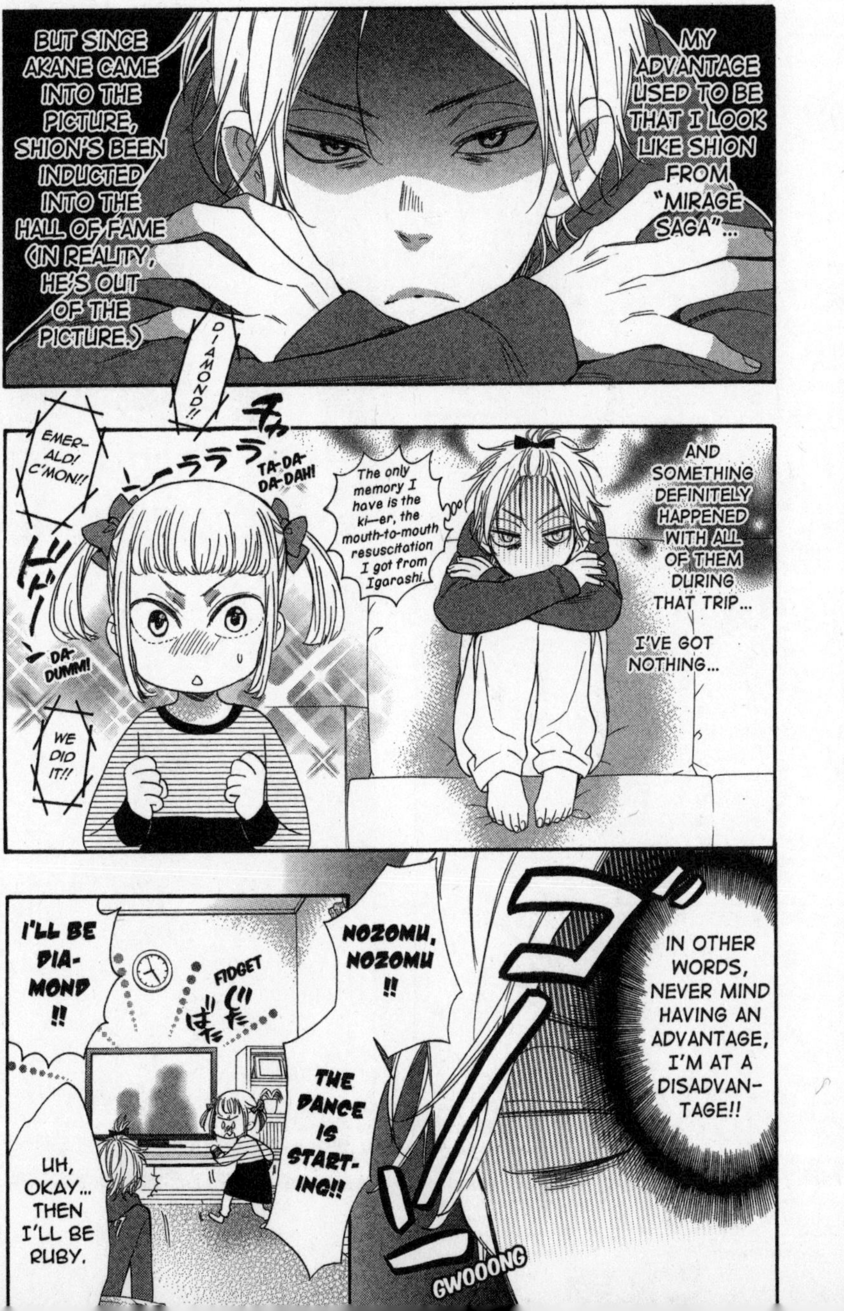
MY ADVANTAGE USED TO BE THAT I LOOK LIKE SHION FROM "MIRAGE SAGA"...
BUT SINCE AKANE CAME INTO THE PICTURE, SHION'S BEEN INDUCTED INTO THE HALL OF FAME (IN REALITY, HE'S OUT OF THE PICTURE.)
AND SOMETHING DEFINITELY HAPPENED WITH ALL OF THEM DURING THAT TRIP...
I'VE GOT NOTHING...
The only memory I have is the ki—er, the mouth-to-mouth resuscitation I got from Igarashi.
DIAMOND!!
TA-DA-DA-DAH!
EMERALD! C'MON!!
DA-DUMM!
WE DID IT!!
IN OTHER WORDS, NEVER MIND HAVING AN ADVANTAGE, I'M AT A DISADVANTAGE!!
GWOOONG
NOZOMU, NOZOMU!!
THE DANCE IS STARTING!!
I'LL BE DIAMOND!!
FIDGET
UH, OKAY... THEN I'LL BE RUBY.

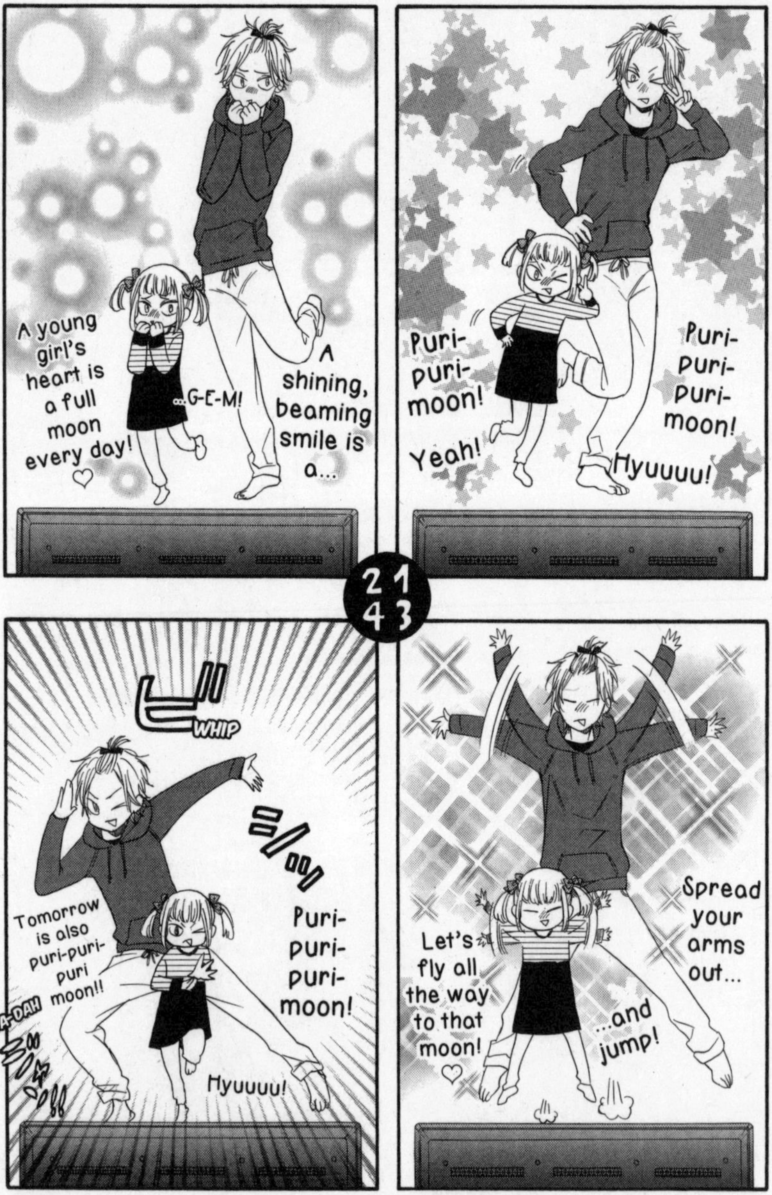
Puri-puri-puri-moon!
Hyuuuu!
Puri-puri-moon!
Yeah!
A shining, beaming smile is a...
...G-E-M!
A young girl's heart is a full moon every day! ♡
Spread your arms out...
...and jump!
Let's fly all the way to that moon! ♡
WHIP
Puri-puri-puri-moon!
Hyuuuu!
Tomorrow is also puri-puri-puri moon!!
TA-DAH

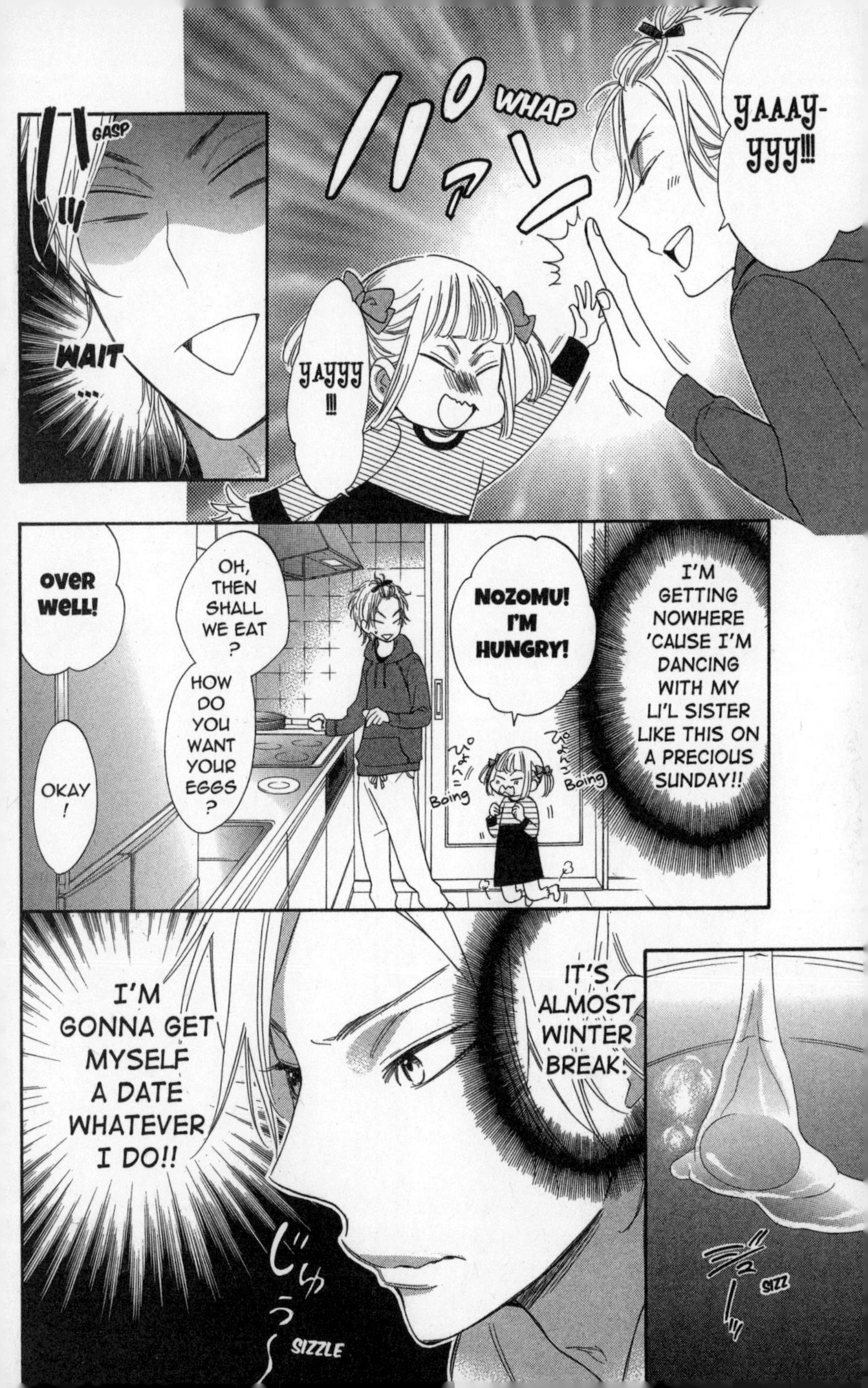
YAAAY-YYY!!!
WHAP
YAYYY !!!
GASP
WAIT ...
I'M GETTING NOWHERE 'CAUSE I'M DANCING WITH MY LI'L SISTER LIKE THIS ON A PRECIOUS SUNDAY!!
NOZOMU! I'M HUNGRY!
Boing
Boing
OH, THEN SHALL WE EAT?
HOW DO YOU WANT YOUR EGGS?
OVER WELL!
OKAY!
SIZZ
IT'S ALMOST WINTER BREAK.
I'M GONNA GET MYSELF A DATE WHATEVER I DO!!
SIZZLE

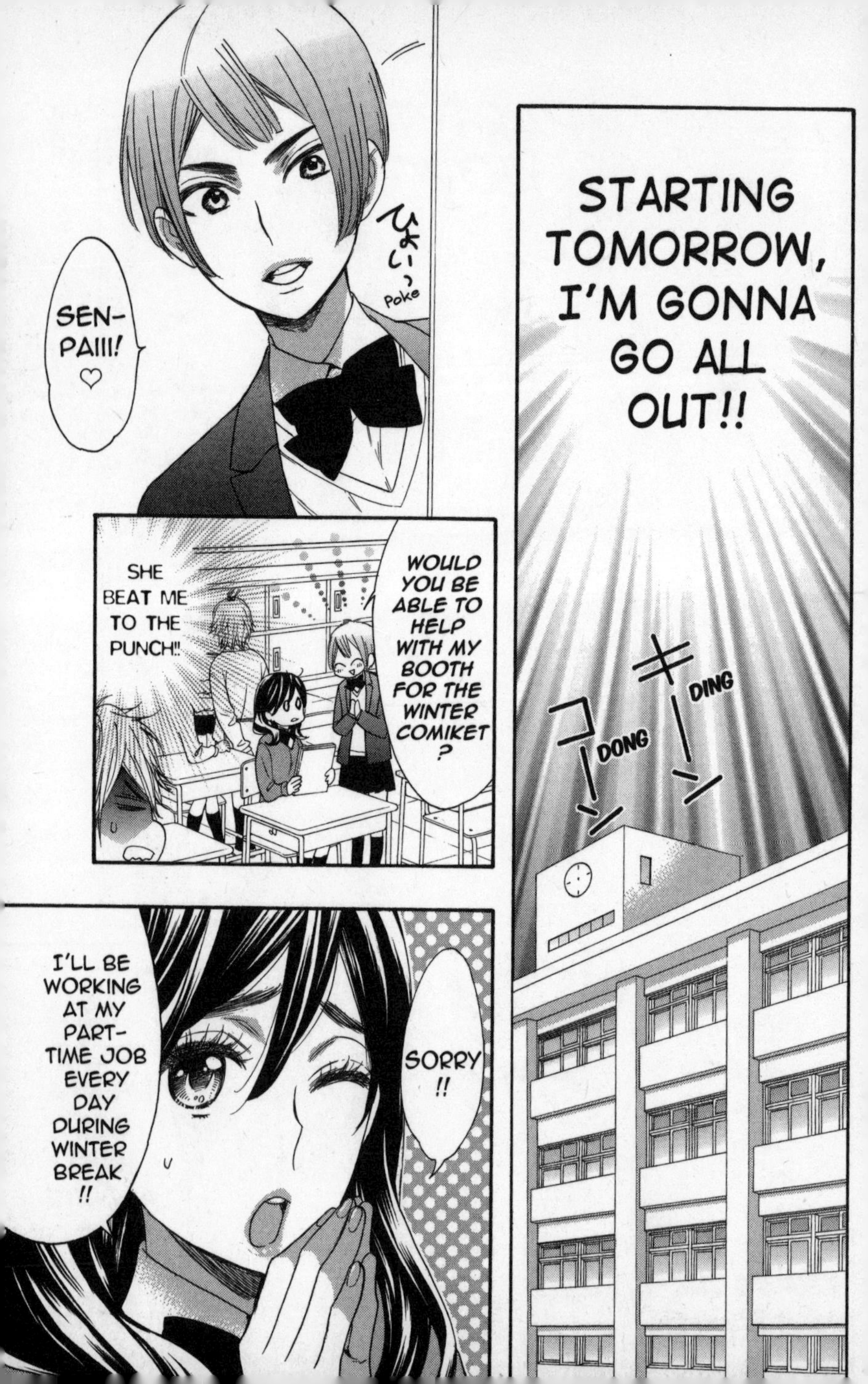
STARTING TOMORROW, I'M GONNA GO ALL OUT!!
キーン
DING
コーン
DONG
ひょいっ
Poke
SEN-PAIII! ♡
WOULD YOU BE ABLE TO HELP WITH MY BOOTH FOR THE WINTER COMIKET ?
SHE BEAT ME TO THE PUNCH!!
SORRY !!
I'LL BE WORKING AT MY PART-TIME JOB EVERY DAY DURING WINTER BREAK !!

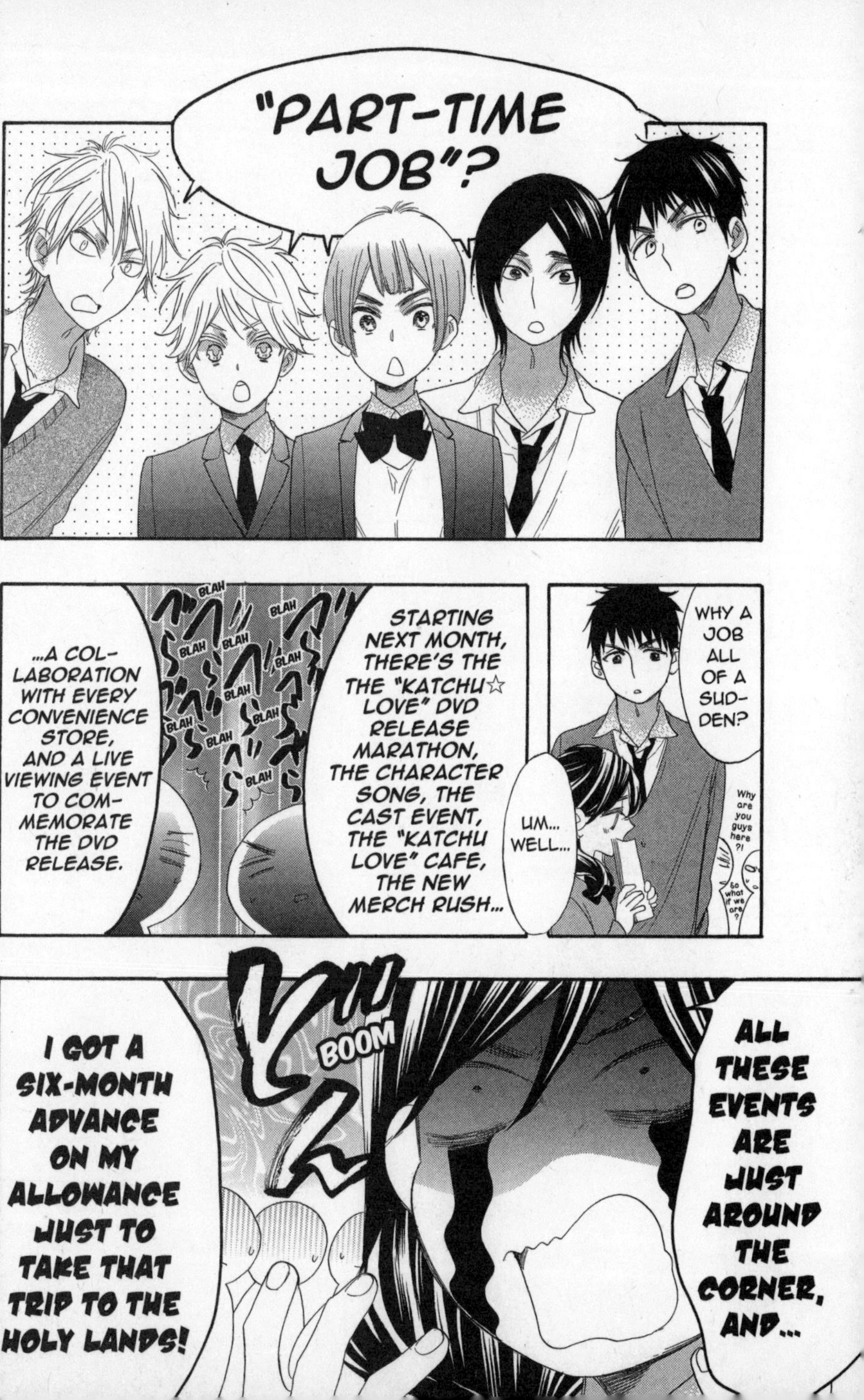
"PART-TIME JOB"?
WHY A JOB ALL OF A SUD-DEN?
Why are you guys here?!
So what if we are?
UM... WELL...
STARTING NEXT MONTH, THERE'S THE THE "KATCHU☆LOVE" DVD RELEASE MARATHON, THE CHARACTER SONG, THE CAST EVENT, THE "KATCHU LOVE" CAFE, THE NEW MERCH RUSH...
BLAH BLAH BLAH BLAH BLAH BLAH BLAH BLAH BLAH BLAH
...A COL-LABORATION WITH EVERY CONVENIENCE STORE, AND A LIVE VIEWING EVENT TO COM-MEMORATE THE DVD RELEASE.
ALL THESE EVENTS ARE JUST AROUND THE CORNER, AND...
BOOM
I GOT A SIX-MONTH ADVANCE ON MY ALLOWANCE JUST TO TAKE THAT TRIP TO THE HOLY LANDS!

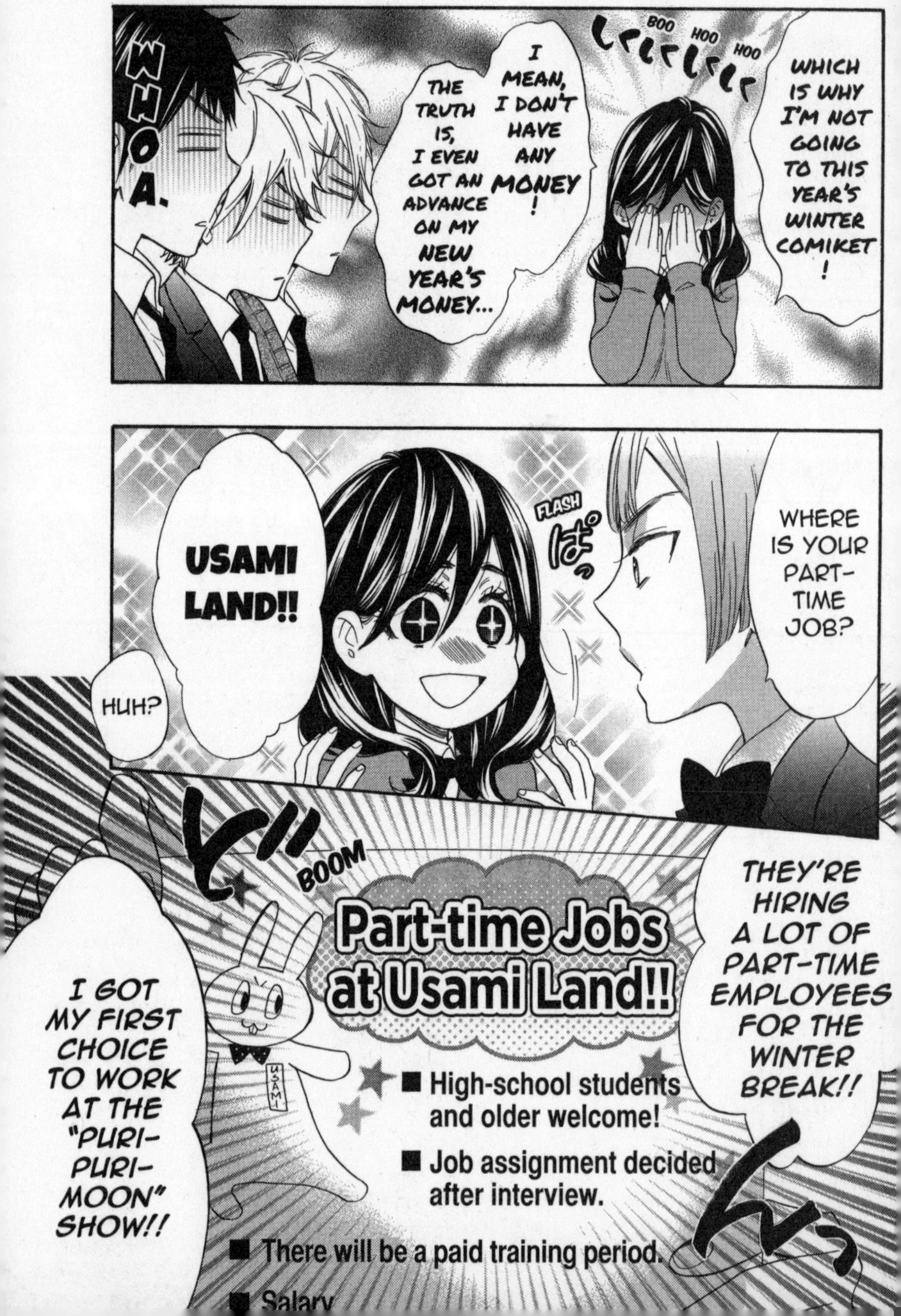
WHICH IS WHY I'M NOT GOING TO THIS YEAR'S WINTER COMIKET!
BOO HOO HOO
I MEAN, I DON'T HAVE ANY MONEY!
THE TRUTH IS, I EVEN GOT AN ADVANCE ON MY NEW YEAR'S MONEY...
WHOA.
WHERE IS YOUR PART-TIME JOB?
FLASH
USAMI LAND!!
HUH?
THEY'RE HIRING A LOT OF PART-TIME EMPLOYEES FOR THE WINTER BREAK!!
BOOM
Part-time Jobs at Usami Land!!
■ High-school students and older welcome!
■ Job assignment decided after interview.
■ There will be a paid training period.
■ Salary
USAMI
I GOT MY FIRST CHOICE TO WORK AT THE "PURI-PURI-MOON" SHOW!!

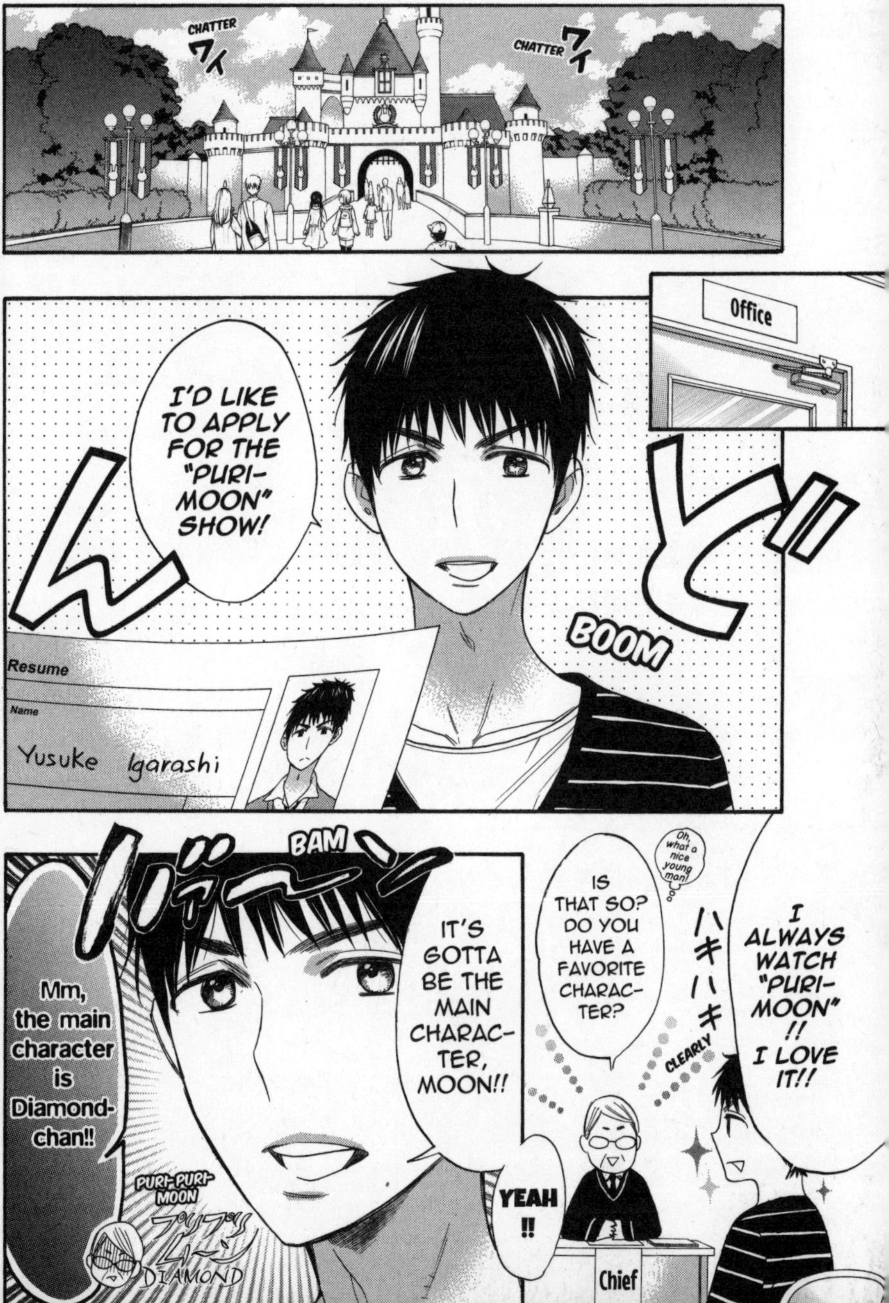

CHATTER
ワイ
CHATTER
ワイ
Office
I'D LIKE TO APPLY FOR THE "PURI-MOON" SHOW!
BOOM
Resume
Name
Yusuke Igarashi
I ALWAYS WATCH "PURI-MOON"!! I LOVE IT!!
ハキハキ
CLEARLY
Oh, what a nice young man!
IS THAT SO? DO YOU HAVE A FAVORITE CHARAC-TER?
YEAH !!
Chief
BAM
IT'S GOTTA BE THE MAIN CHARAC-TER, MOON!!
Mm, the main character is Diamond-chan!!
PURI-PURI MOON
DIAMOND

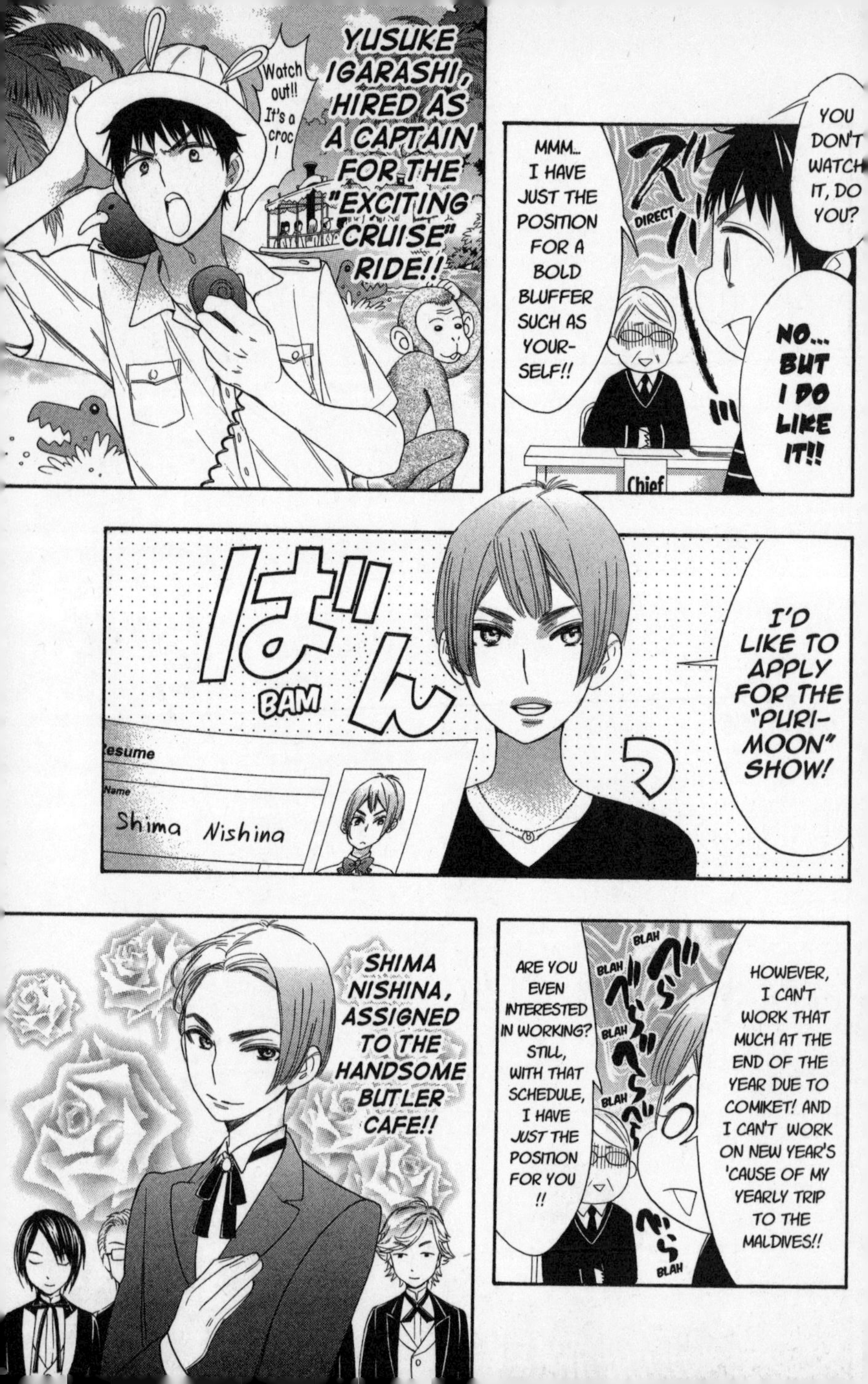
YOU DON'T WATCH IT, DO YOU?
MMM... I HAVE JUST THE POSITION FOR A BOLD BLUFFER SUCH AS YOURSELF!!
DIRECT
NO... BUT I DO LIKE IT!!
Chief
YUSUKE IGARASHI, HIRED AS A CAPTAIN FOR THE "EXCITING CRUISE" RIDE!!
Watch out!! It's a croc!
I'D LIKE TO APPLY FOR THE "PURI-MOON" SHOW!
BAM
Resume
Name
Shima Nishina
HOWEVER, I CAN'T WORK THAT MUCH AT THE END OF THE YEAR DUE TO COMIKET! AND I CAN'T WORK ON NEW YEAR'S 'CAUSE OF MY YEARLY TRIP TO THE MALDIVES!!
BLAH
BLAH
BLAH
BLAH
BLAH
ARE YOU EVEN INTERESTED IN WORKING? STILL, WITH THAT SCHEDULE, I HAVE JUST THE POSITION FOR YOU!!
SHIMA NISHINA, ASSIGNED TO THE HANDSOME BUTLER CAFE!!

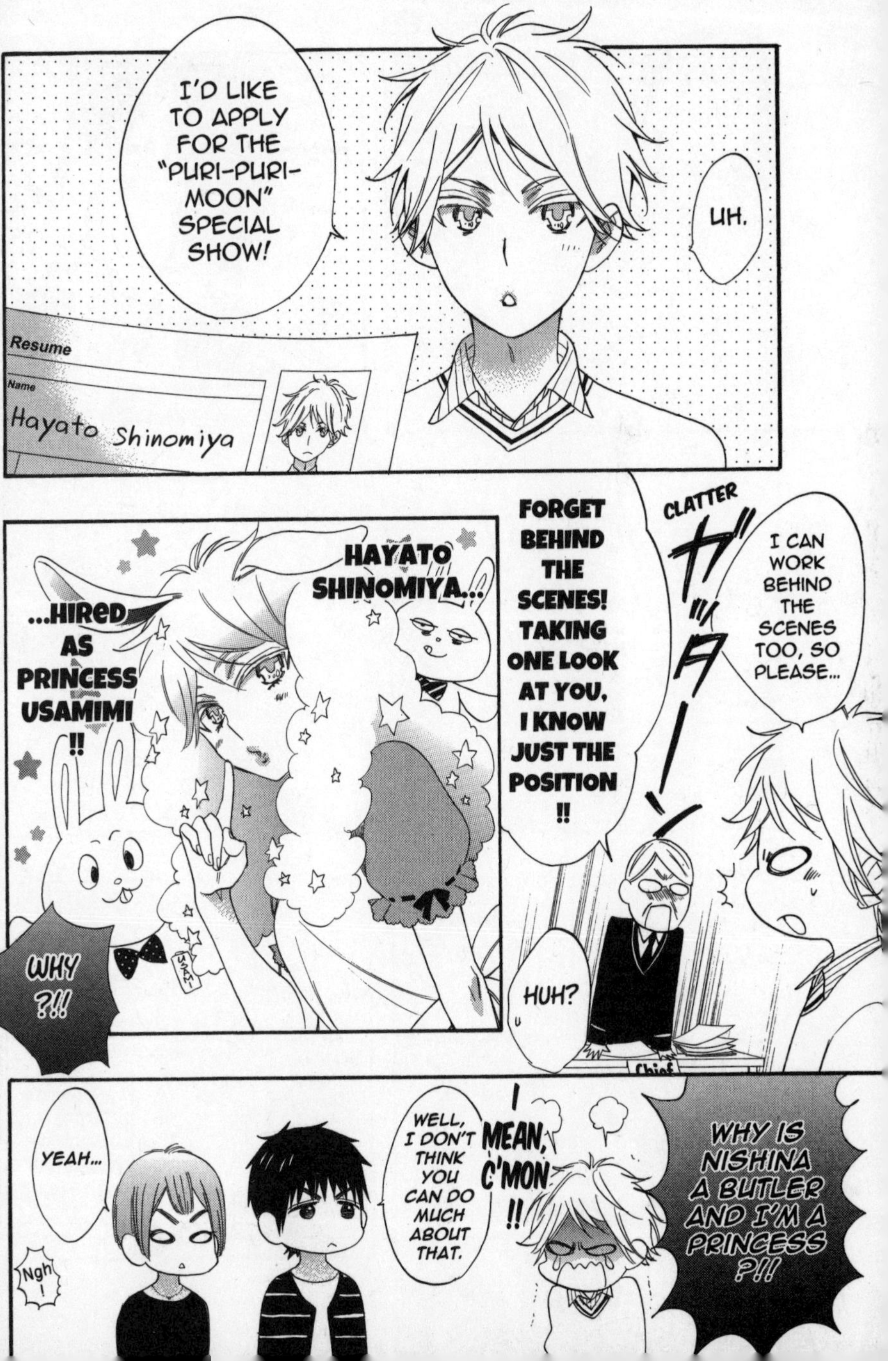
I'D LIKE TO APPLY FOR THE "PURI-PURI-MOON" SPECIAL SHOW!
UH.
Resume
Name
Hayato Shinomiya
CLATTER
I CAN WORK BEHIND THE SCENES TOO, SO PLEASE...
FORGET BEHIND THE SCENES! TAKING ONE LOOK AT YOU, I KNOW JUST THE POSITION!!
HUH?
Chief
HAYATO SHINOMIYA...
...HIRED AS PRINCESS USAMIMI!!
USAMI
WHY?!!
WHY IS NISHINA A BUTLER AND I'M A PRINCESS?!!
I MEAN, C'MON!!
WELL, I DON'T THINK YOU CAN DO MUCH ABOUT THAT.
YEAH...
Ngh!

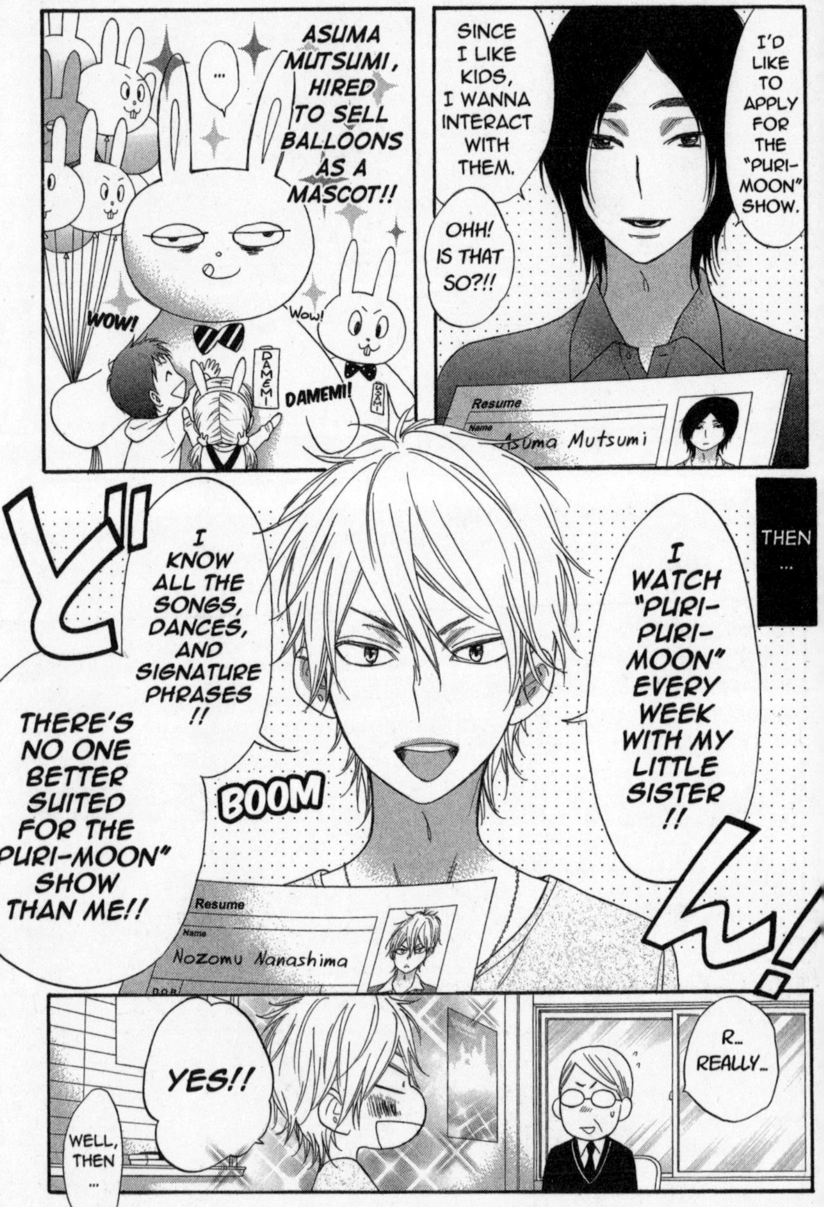
I'D LIKE TO APPLY FOR THE "PURI-MOON" SHOW.
SINCE I LIKE KIDS, I WANNA INTERACT WITH THEM.
OHH! IS THAT SO?!!
Resume
Name
Asuma Mutsumi
ASUMA MUTSUMI, HIRED TO SELL BALLOONS AS A MASCOT!!
...
Wow!
WOW!
DAMEMI
DAMEMI!
THEN ...
I WATCH "PURI-PURI-MOON" EVERY WEEK WITH MY LITTLE SISTER !!
I KNOW ALL THE SONGS, DANCES, AND SIGNATURE PHRASES !!
THERE'S NO ONE BETTER SUITED FOR THE "PURI-MOON" SHOW THAN ME!!
BOOM
どん!
Resume
Name
Nozomu Nanashima
R... REALLY...
YES!!
WELL, THEN ...

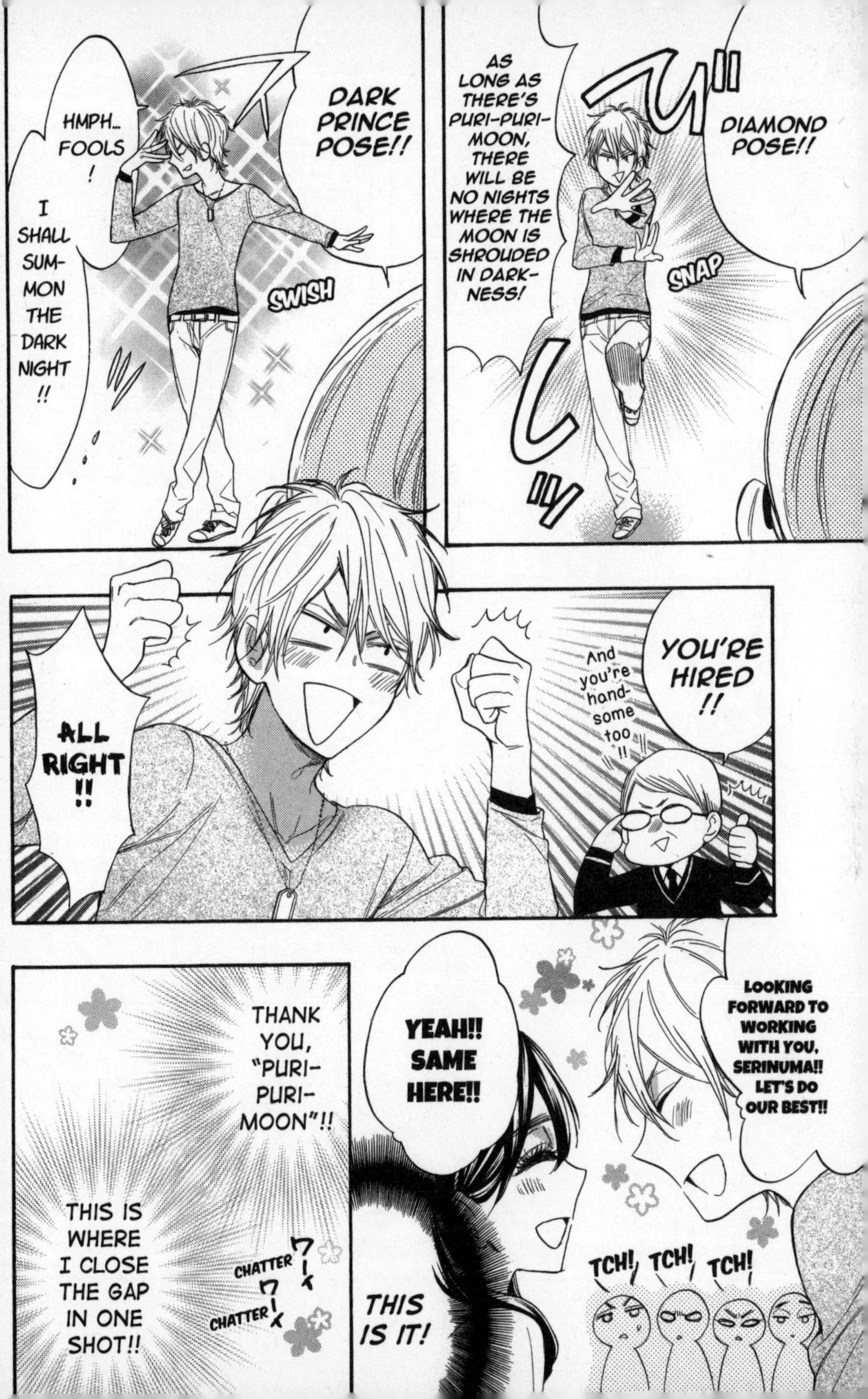
DIAMOND POSE!!
AS LONG AS THERE'S PURI-PURI-MOON, THERE WILL BE NO NIGHTS WHERE THE MOON IS SHROUDED IN DARKNESS!
SNAP
DARK PRINCE POSE!!
HMPH... FOOLS!
I SHALL SUMMON THE DARK NIGHT!!
SWISH
YOU'RE HIRED!!
And you're handsome too!!
ALL RIGHT!!
LOOKING FORWARD TO WORKING WITH YOU, SERINUMA!! LET'S DO OUR BEST!!
YEAH!! SAME HERE!!
TCH! TCH! TCH!
THIS IS IT!
THANK YOU, "PURI-PURI-MOON"!!
THIS IS WHERE I CLOSE THE GAP IN ONE SHOT!!
CHATTER
CHATTER

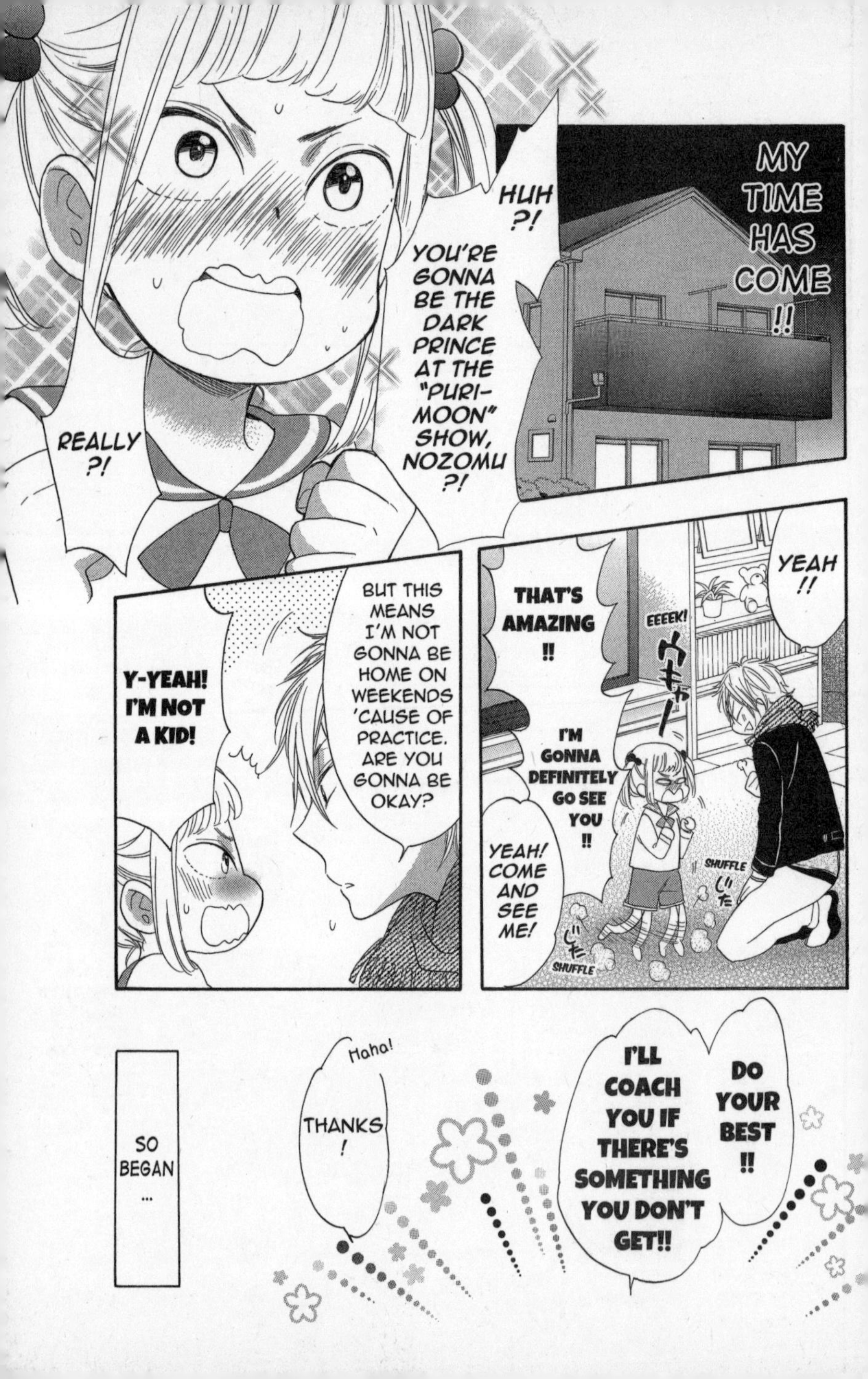
MY TIME HAS COME!!
HUH?!
YOU'RE GONNA BE THE DARK PRINCE AT THE "PURI-MOON" SHOW, NOZOMU?!
REALLY?!
YEAH!!
THAT'S AMAZING!!
EEEEK!
I'M GONNA DEFINITELY GO SEE YOU!!
YEAH! COME AND SEE ME!
SHUFFLE
SHUFFLE
BUT THIS MEANS I'M NOT GONNA BE HOME ON WEEKENDS 'CAUSE OF PRACTICE. ARE YOU GONNA BE OKAY?
Y-YEAH! I'M NOT A KID!
DO YOUR BEST!!
I'LL COACH YOU IF THERE'S SOMETHING YOU DON'T GET!!
Haha!
THANKS!
SO BEGAN ...

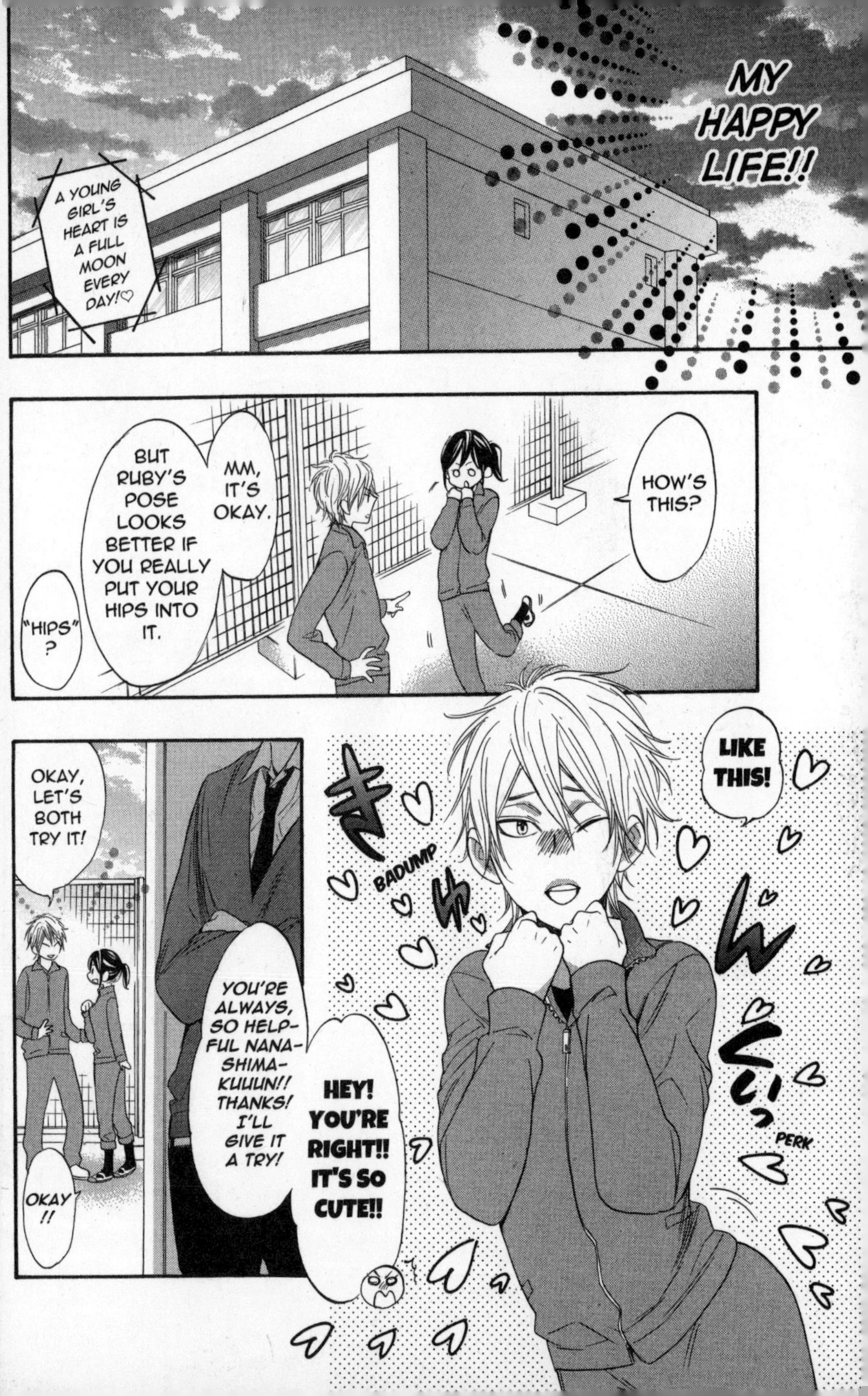
MY HAPPY LIFE!!
A YOUNG GIRL'S HEART IS A FULL MOON EVERY DAY!♡
HOW'S THIS?
MM, IT'S OKAY.
BUT RUBY'S POSE LOOKS BETTER IF YOU REALLY PUT YOUR HIPS INTO IT.
"HIPS"?
LIKE THIS!
BADUMP
PERK
HEY! YOU'RE RIGHT!! IT'S SO CUTE!!
YOU'RE ALWAYS, SO HELPFUL NANA-SHIMA-KUUUN!! THANKS! I'LL GIVE IT A TRY!
OKAY, LET'S BOTH TRY IT!
OKAY!!

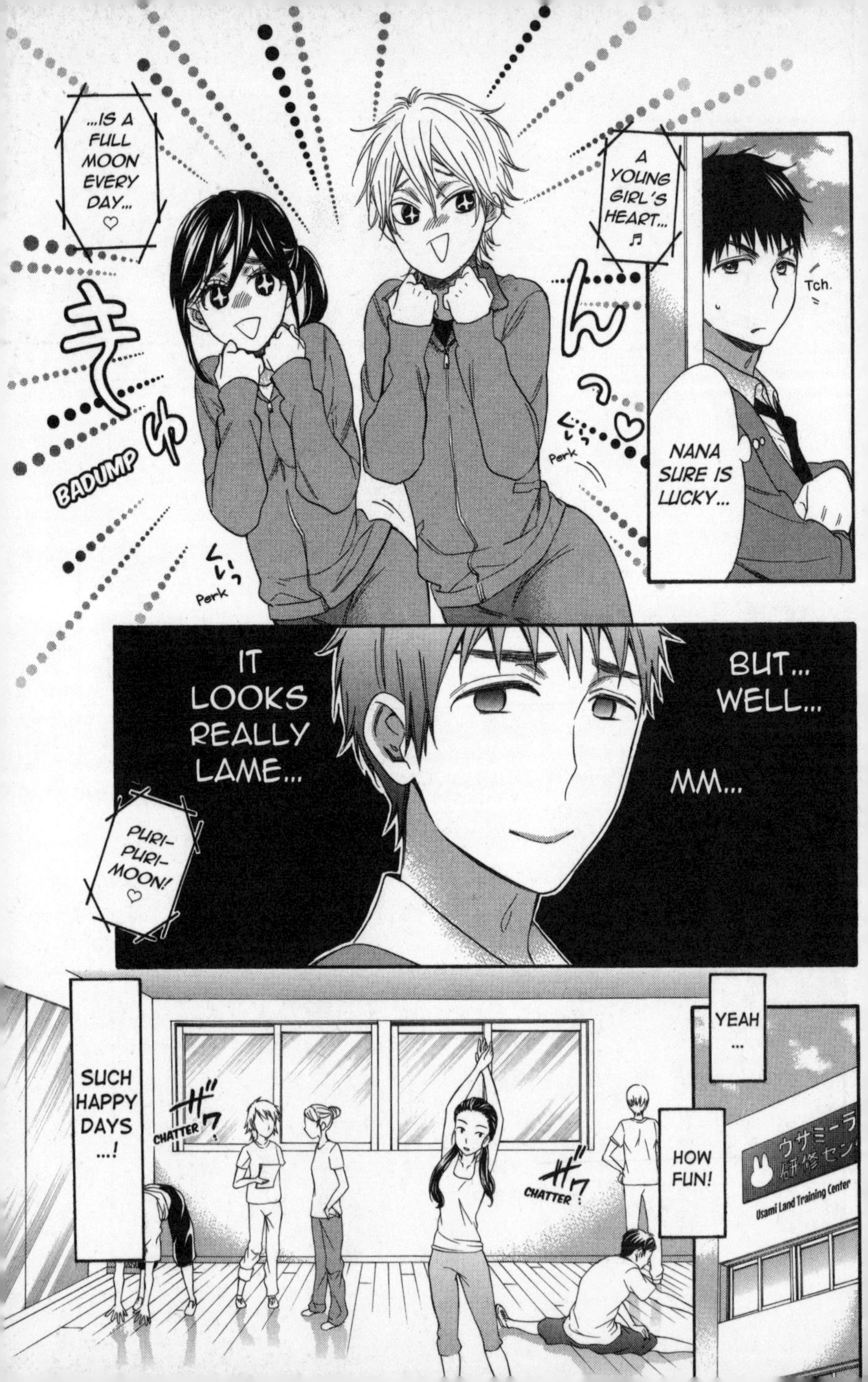

Tch.
NANA SURE IS LUCKY...
A YOUNG GIRL'S HEART... ♬
...IS A FULL MOON EVERY DAY... ♡
きゅんっ
BADUMP
ぐいっ
Perk
ぐいっ
Perk
BUT... WELL...
MM...
IT LOOKS REALLY LAME...
PURI-PURI-MOON! ♡
YEAH ...
HOW FUN!
Usami Land Training Center
ザワ
CHATTER
ザワ
CHATTER
SUCH HAPPY DAYS ...!

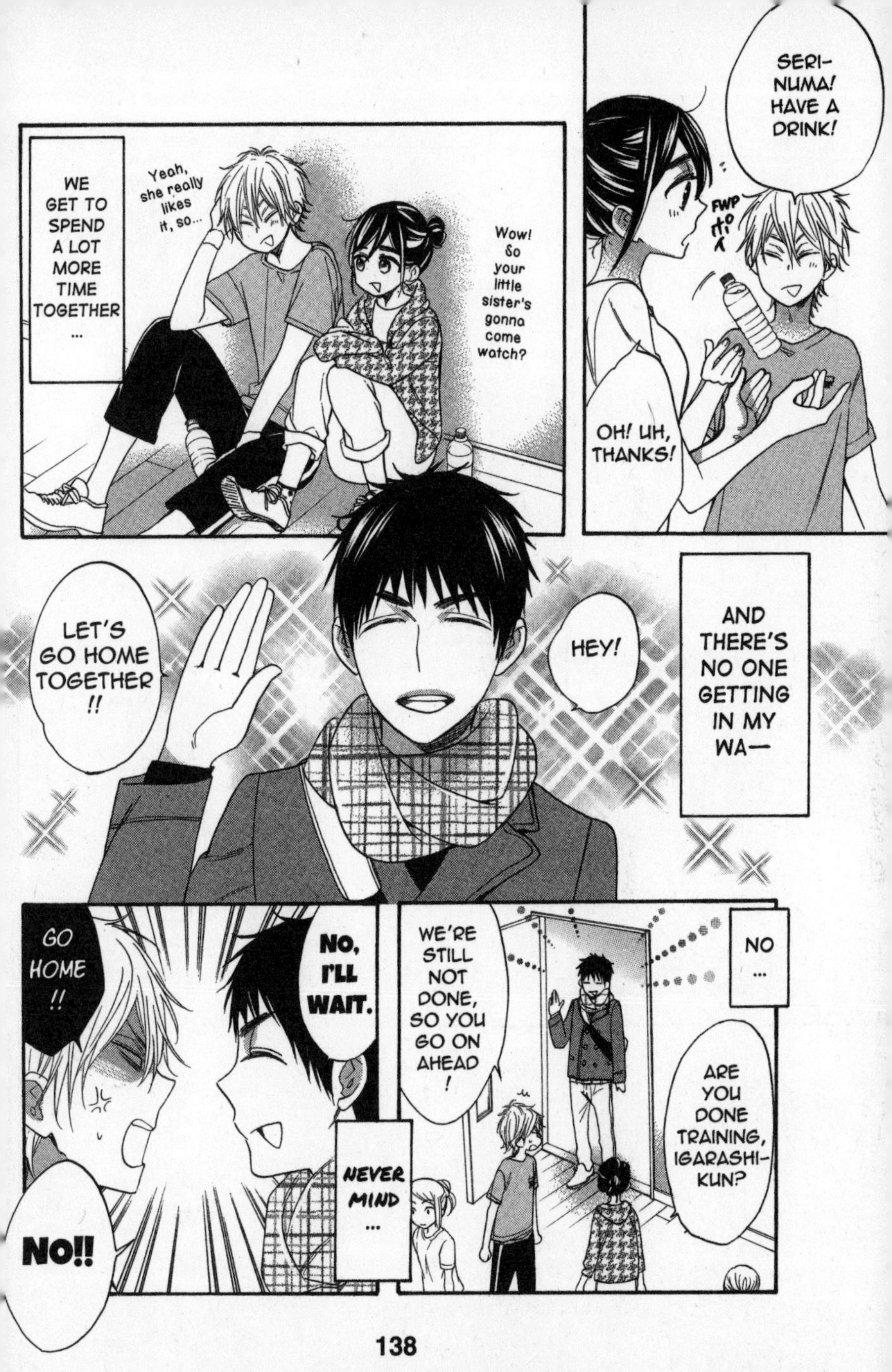
SERI-NUMA! HAVE A DRINK!
FWP
OH! UH, THANKS!
Wow! So your little sister's gonna come watch?
Yeah, she really likes it, so...
WE GET TO SPEND A LOT MORE TIME TOGETHER ...
AND THERE'S NO ONE GETTING IN MY WA—
HEY!
LET'S GO HOME TOGETHER !!
NO ...
ARE YOU DONE TRAINING, IGARASHI-KUN?
WE'RE STILL NOT DONE, SO YOU GO ON AHEAD !
NEVER MIND ...
NO, I'LL WAIT.
GO HOME !!
NO!!

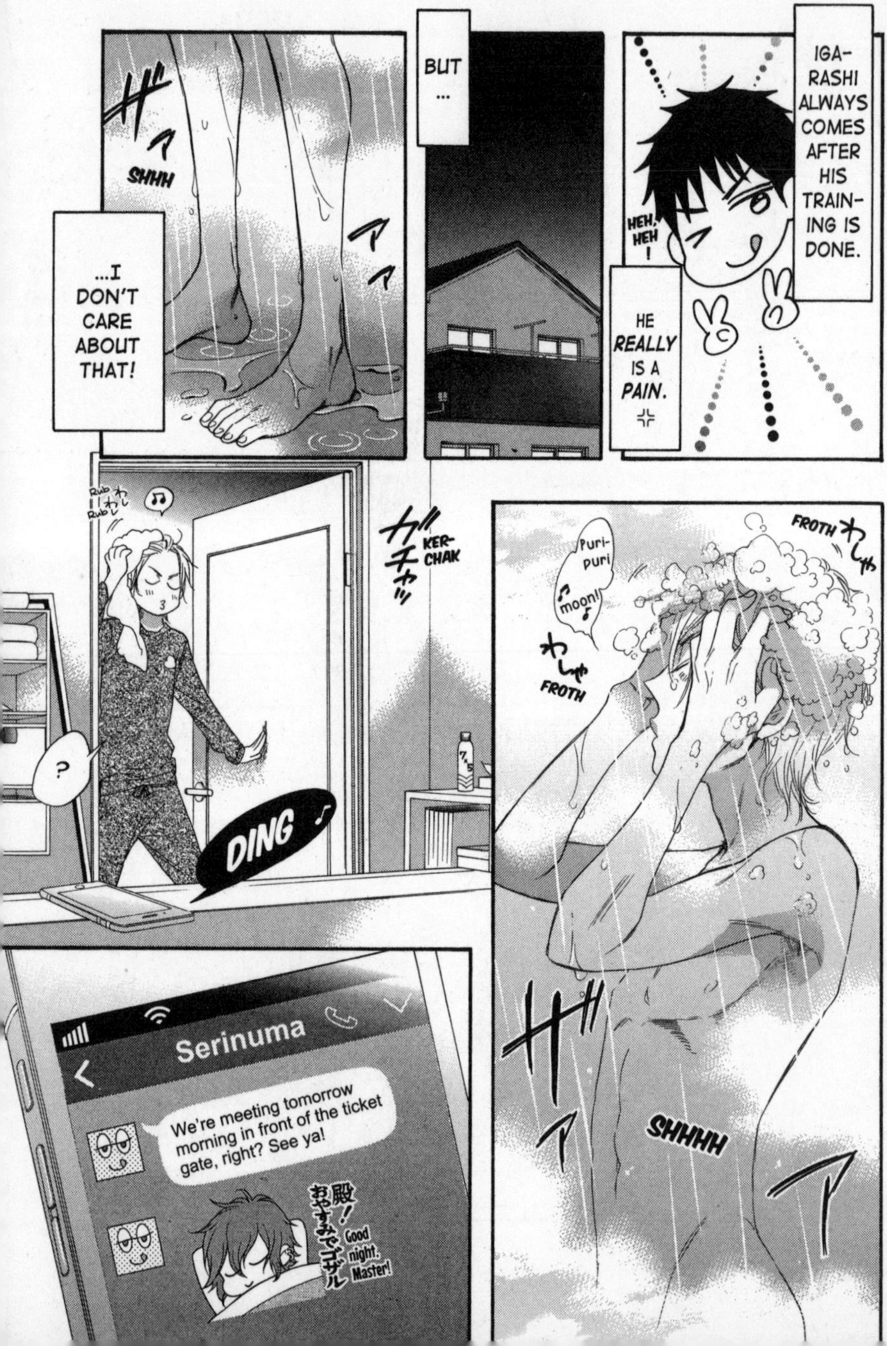
IGA-RASHI ALWAYS COMES AFTER HIS TRAIN-ING IS DONE.
HEH, HEH!
HE REALLY IS A PAIN.
BUT ...
SHHH
...I DON'T CARE ABOUT THAT!
FROTH
Puri-puri moon!
FROTH
SHHHH
Rub Rub
KER-CHAK
?
DING
Serinuma
We're meeting tomorrow morning in front of the ticket gate, right? See ya!
殿！おやすみでゴザル
Good night, Master!

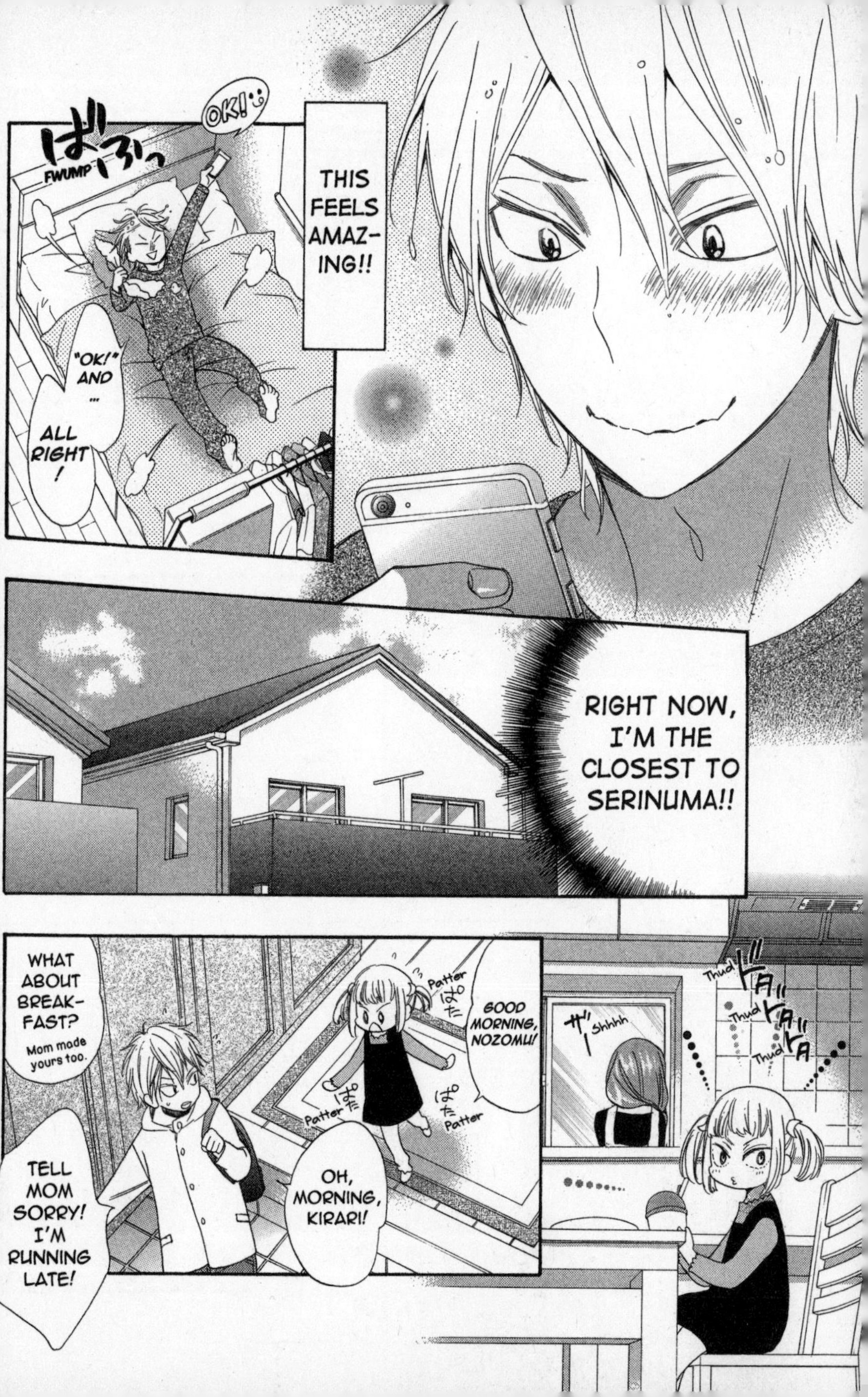
THIS FEELS AMAZ-ING!!
OK!
FWUMP
"OK!" AND ... ALL RIGHT!
RIGHT NOW, I'M THE CLOSEST TO SERINUMA!!
Thud Thud Thud
Shhhh
GOOD MORNING, NOZOMU!
Patter Patter Patter
OH, MORNING, KIRARI!
WHAT ABOUT BREAK-FAST?
Mom made yours too.
TELL MOM SORRY! I'M RUNNING LATE!

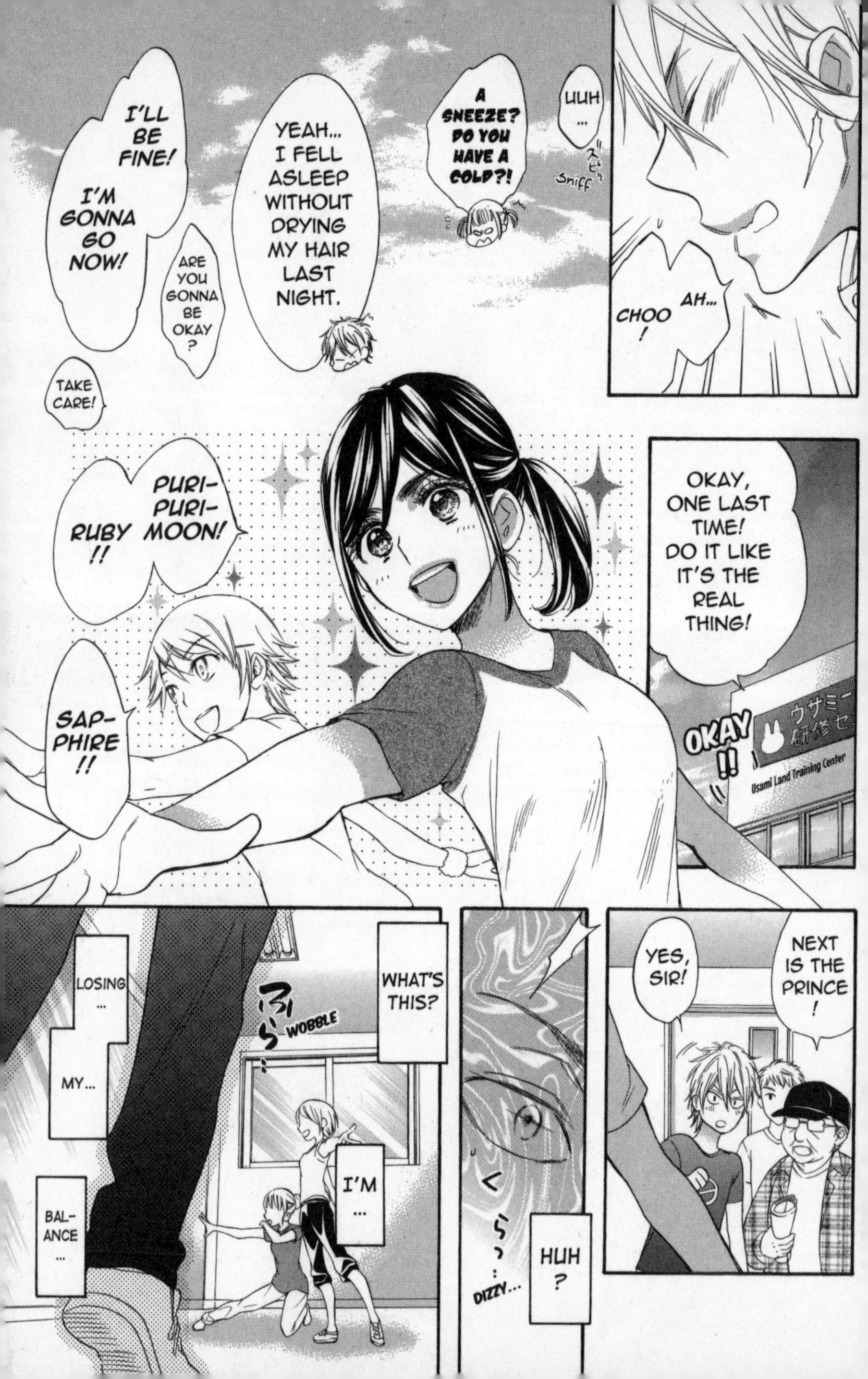
UUH ...
Sniff
AH... CHOO!
A SNEEZE? DO YOU HAVE A COLD?!
YEAH... I FELL ASLEEP WITHOUT DRYING MY HAIR LAST NIGHT.
ARE YOU GONNA BE OKAY?
I'LL BE FINE!
I'M GONNA GO NOW!
TAKE CARE!
OKAY, ONE LAST TIME! DO IT LIKE IT'S THE REAL THING!
OKAY!!
Usami Land Training Center
PURI-PURI-RUBY MOON!!
SAPPHIRE!!
NEXT IS THE PRINCE!
YES, SIR!
HUH?
DIZZY...
WHAT'S THIS?
I'M ...
WOBBLE
LOSING ...
MY...
BALANCE ...

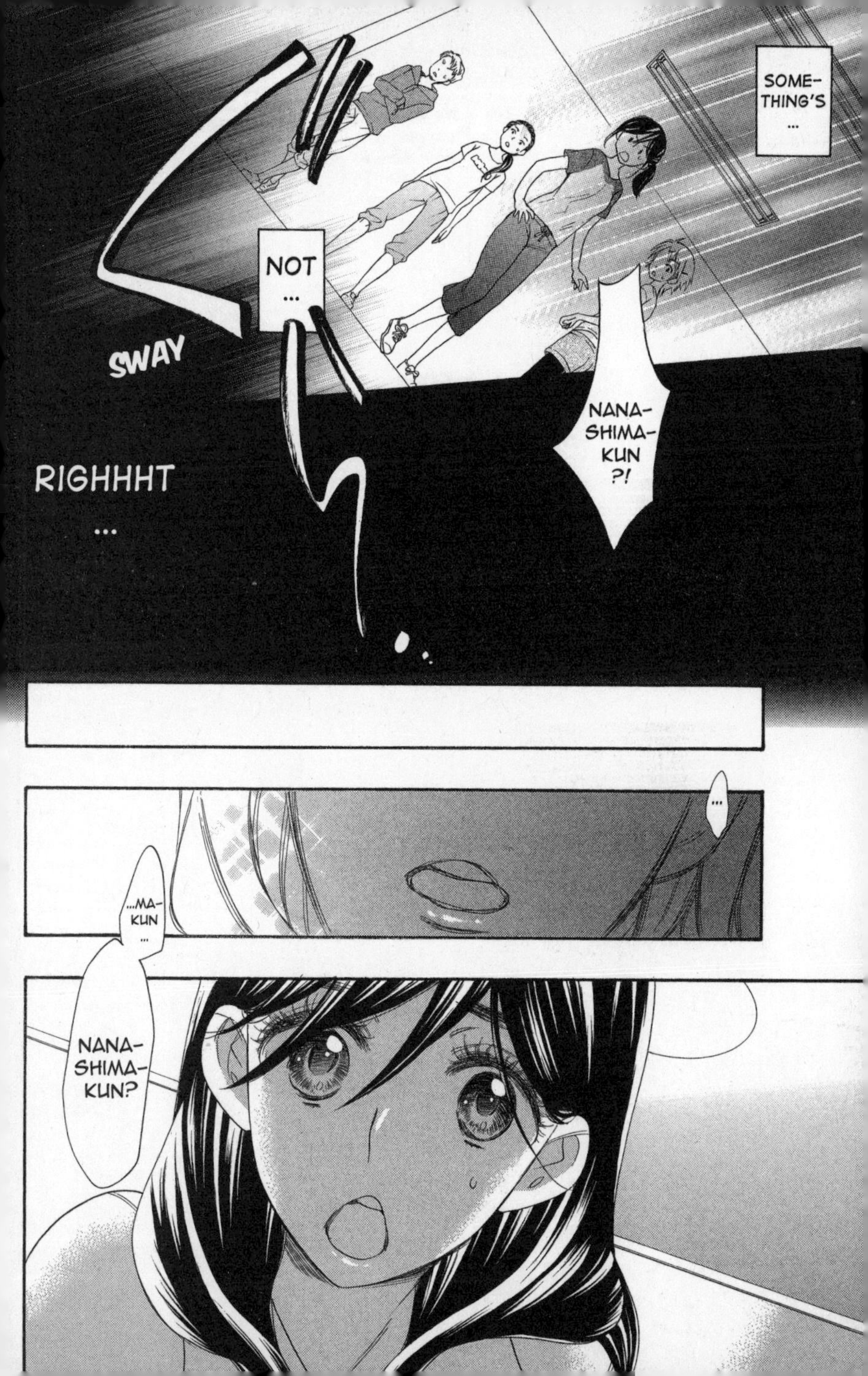
SOMETHING'S ...
NOT ...
SWAY
NANA-SHIMA-KUN ?!
RIGHHHT ...
...
...MA-KUN ...
NANA-SHIMA-KUN?

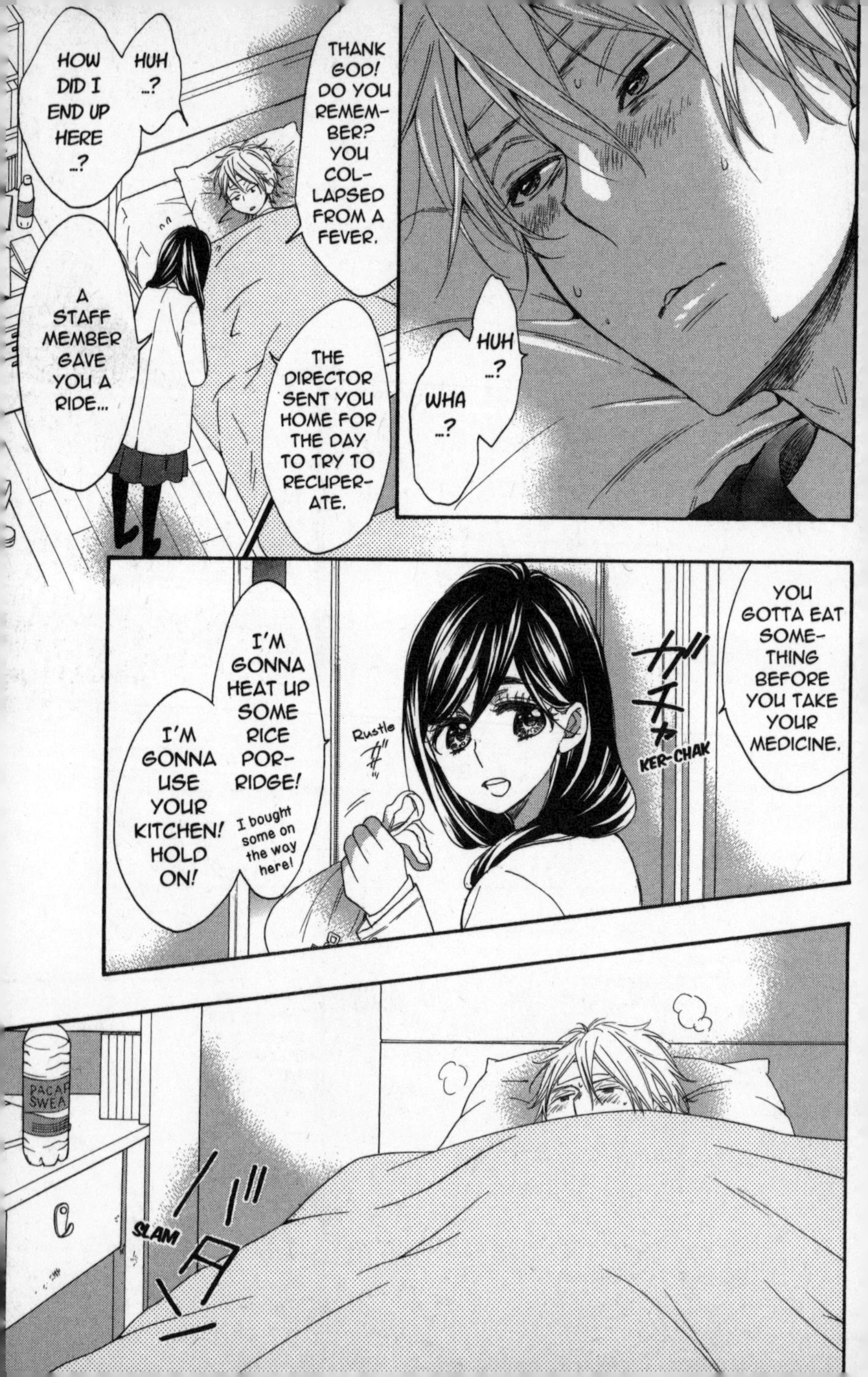
HUH ...?
WHA ...?
THANK GOD! DO YOU REMEMBER? YOU COLLAPSED FROM A FEVER.
HUH ...?
HOW DID I END UP HERE ...?
THE DIRECTOR SENT YOU HOME FOR THE DAY TO TRY TO RECUPERATE.
A STAFF MEMBER GAVE YOU A RIDE...
YOU GOTTA EAT SOMETHING BEFORE YOU TAKE YOUR MEDICINE.
KER-CHAK
Rustle
I'M GONNA HEAT UP SOME RICE PORRIDGE!
I bought some on the way here!
I'M GONNA USE YOUR KITCHEN! HOLD ON!
SLAM

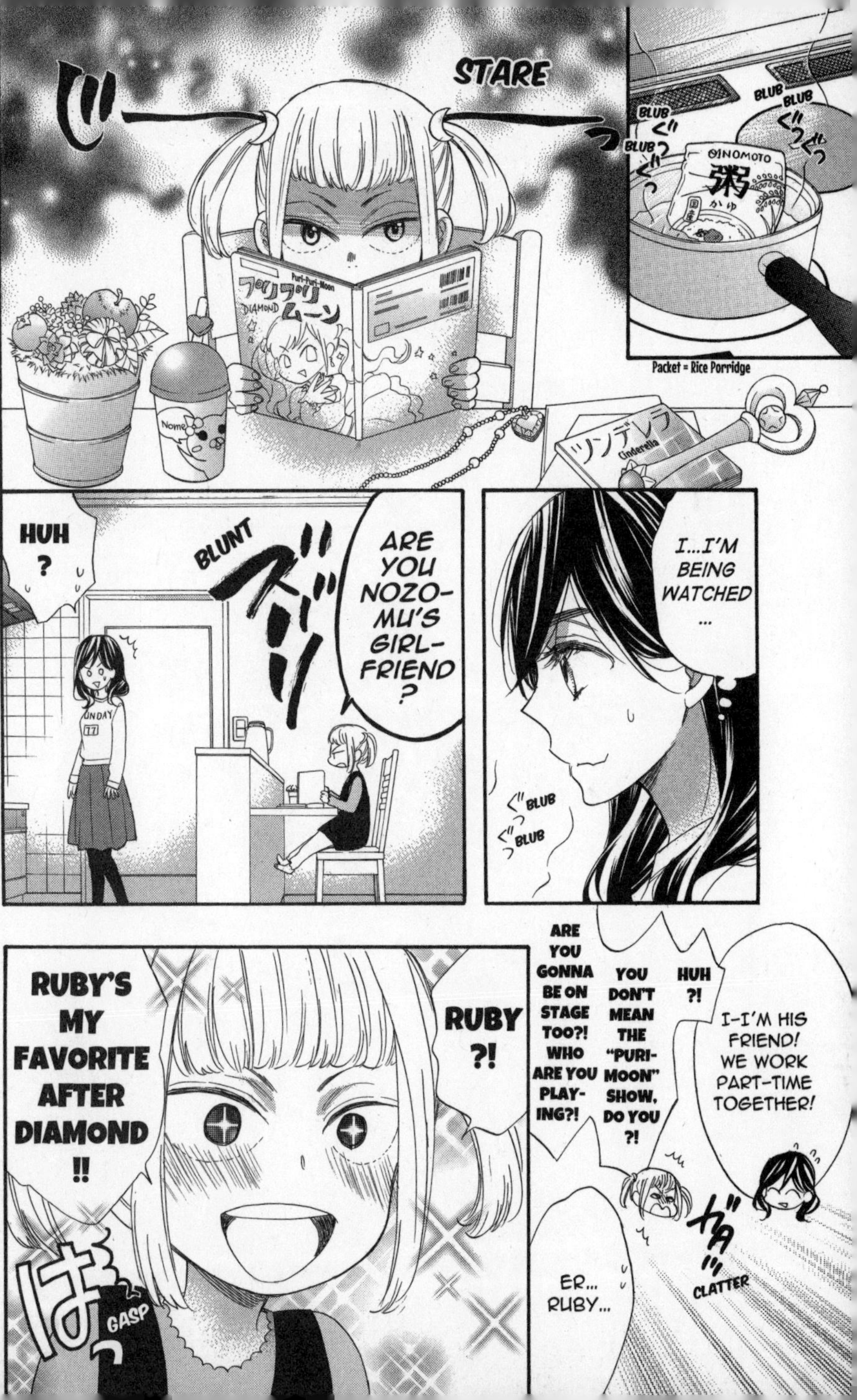
BLUB
BLUB
BLUB
BLUB
粥 かゆ
Packet = Rice Porridge
STARE
Puri-Puri-Moon
DIAMOND
Nome
ツンデレラ
Cinderella
I...I'M BEING WATCHED...
BLUB
BLUB
ARE YOU NOZOMU'S GIRLFRIEND?
BLUNT
HUH?
I-I'M HIS FRIEND! WE WORK PART-TIME TOGETHER!
HUH?!
YOU DON'T MEAN THE "PURI-MOON" SHOW, DO YOU?!
ARE YOU GONNA BE ON STAGE TOO?! WHO ARE YOU PLAYING?!
CLATTER
ER... RUBY...
RUBY?!
RUBY'S MY FAVORITE AFTER DIAMOND!!
GASP

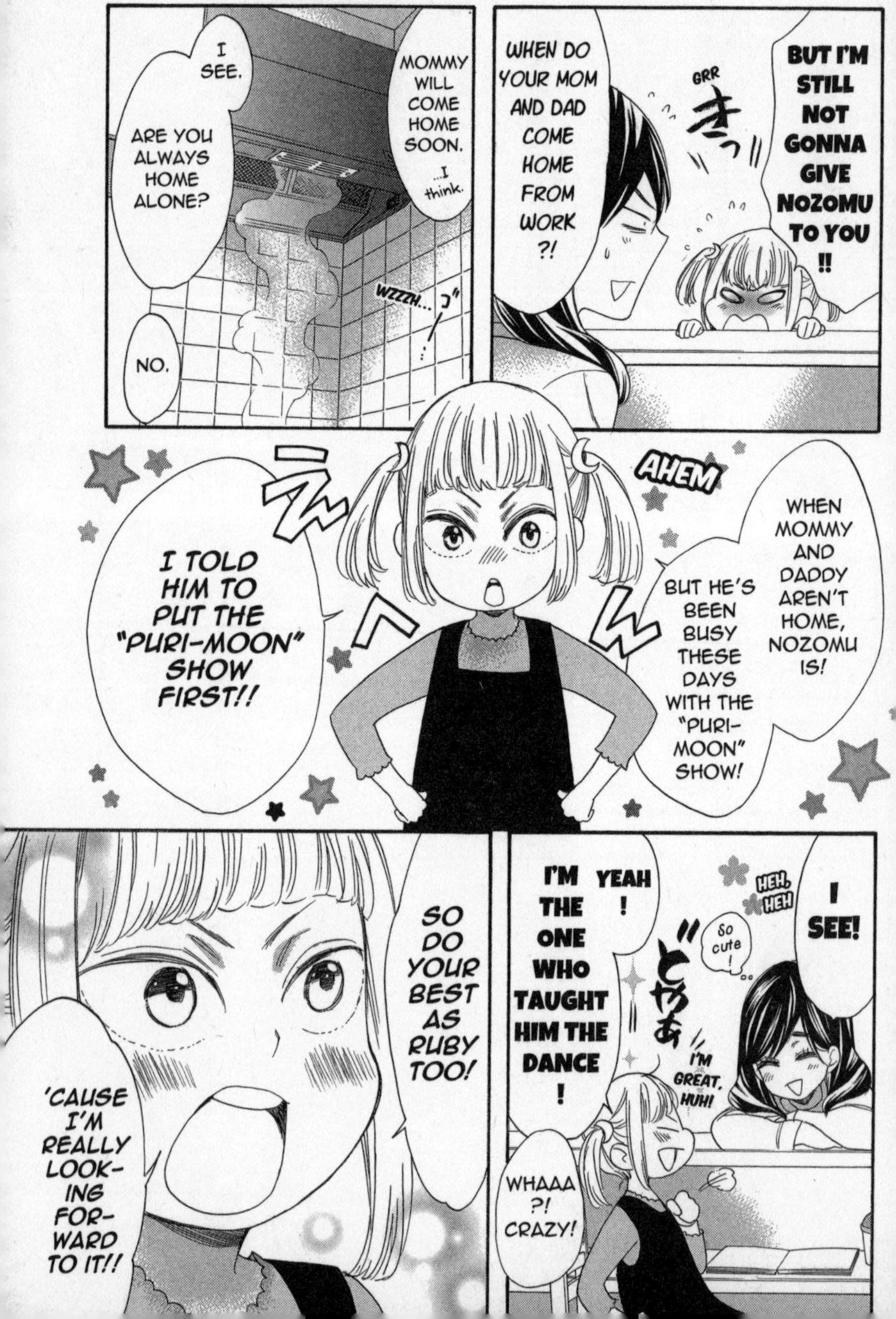
BUT I'M STILL NOT GONNA GIVE NOZOMU TO YOU!!
GRR
WHEN DO YOUR MOM AND DAD COME HOME FROM WORK?!
MOMMY WILL COME HOME SOON.
...I think.
I SEE.
ARE YOU ALWAYS HOME ALONE?
WZZZH...
NO.
AHEM
WHEN MOMMY AND DADDY AREN'T HOME, NOZOMU IS!
BUT HE'S BEEN BUSY THESE DAYS WITH THE "PURI-MOON" SHOW!
I TOLD HIM TO PUT THE "PURI-MOON" SHOW FIRST!!
I SEE!
HEH, HEH
So cute!
YEAH!
I'M THE ONE WHO TAUGHT HIM THE DANCE!
I'M GREAT, HUH!
WHAAA?! CRAZY!
SO DO YOUR BEST AS RUBY TOO!
'CAUSE I'M REALLY LOOKING FORWARD TO IT!!

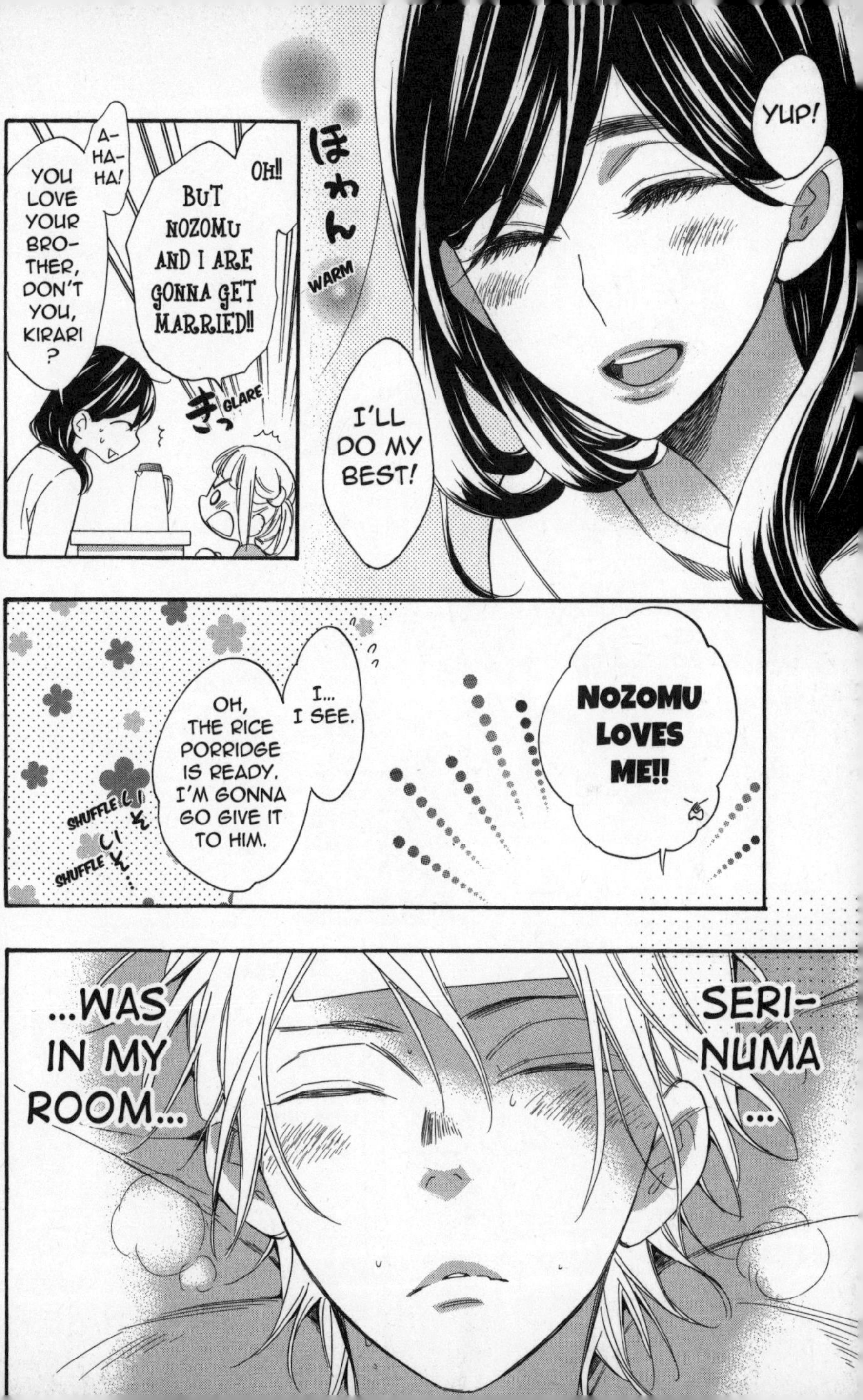
YUP!
I'LL DO MY BEST!
ほわん
WARM
OH!! BUT NOZOMU AND I ARE GONNA GET MARRIED!!
A-HA-HA!
YOU LOVE YOUR BROTHER, DON'T YOU, KIRARI?
きっ
GLARE
NOZOMU LOVES ME!!
I... I SEE.
OH, THE RICE PORRIDGE IS READY. I'M GONNA GO GIVE IT TO HIM.
じそ
SHUFFLE
じそ...
SHUFFLE
SERI-NUMA...
...WAS IN MY ROOM...

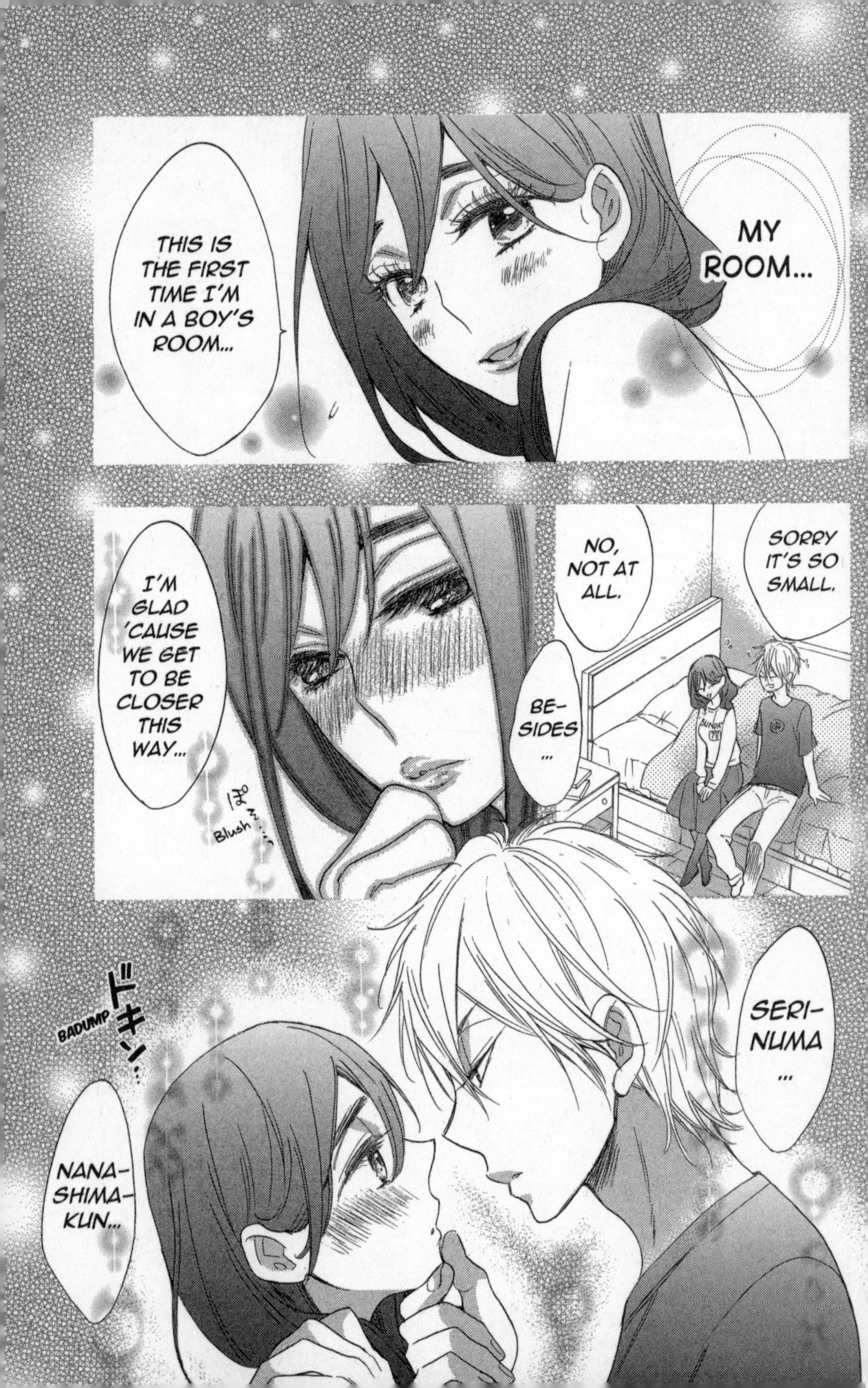
MY ROOM...
THIS IS THE FIRST TIME I'M IN A BOY'S ROOM...
SORRY IT'S SO SMALL.
NO, NOT AT ALL.
BE-SIDES...
I'M GLAD 'CAUSE WE GET TO BE CLOSER THIS WAY...
ぽ~
Blush
SERI-NUMA...
ドキン...
BADUMP
NANA-SHIMA-KUN...

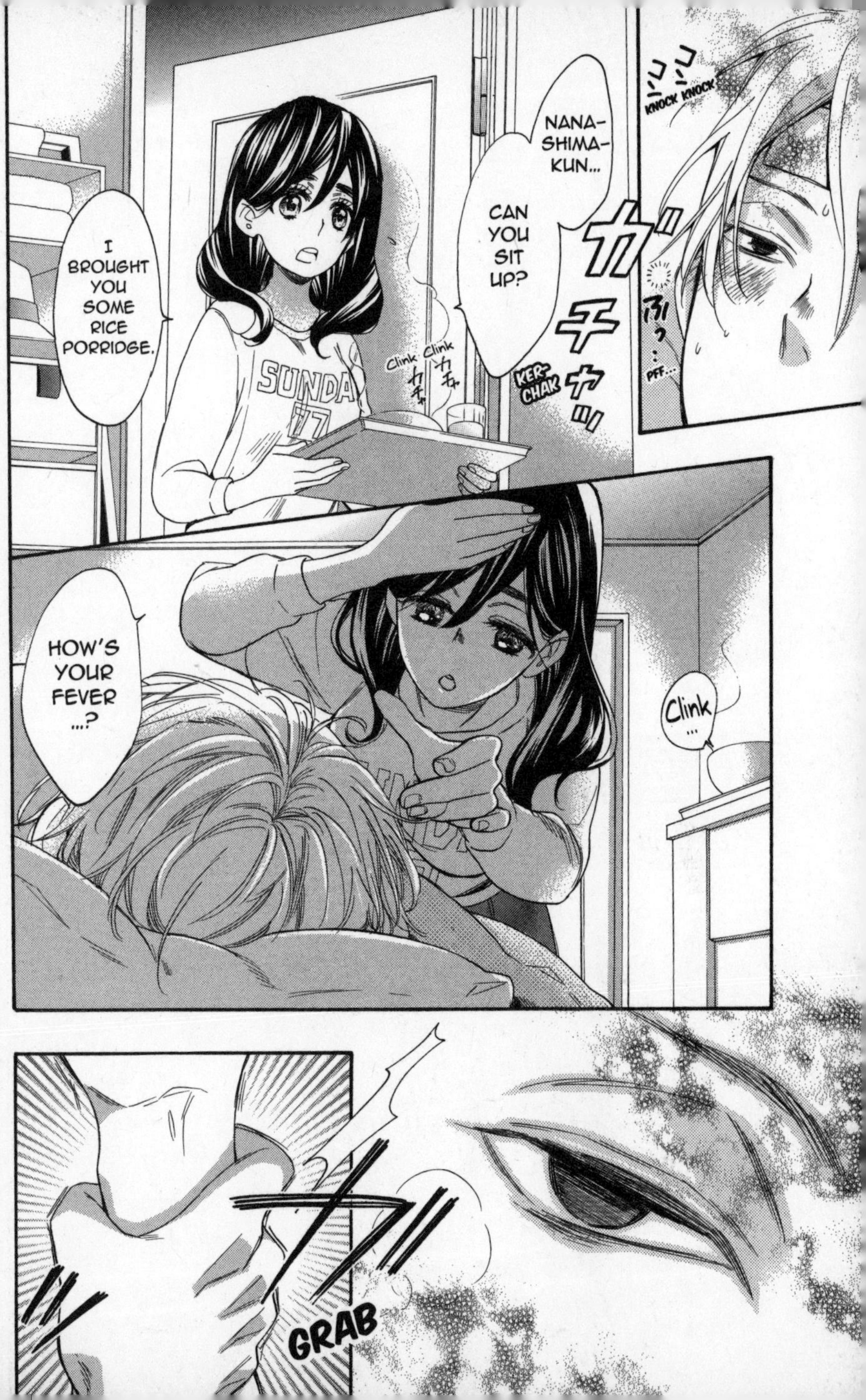
KNOCK KNOCK
PFF...
KER-CHAK
NANA-SHIMA-KUN...
CAN YOU SIT UP?
I BROUGHT YOU SOME RICE PORRIDGE.
Clink Clink
Clink ...
HOW'S YOUR FEVER ...?
GRAB

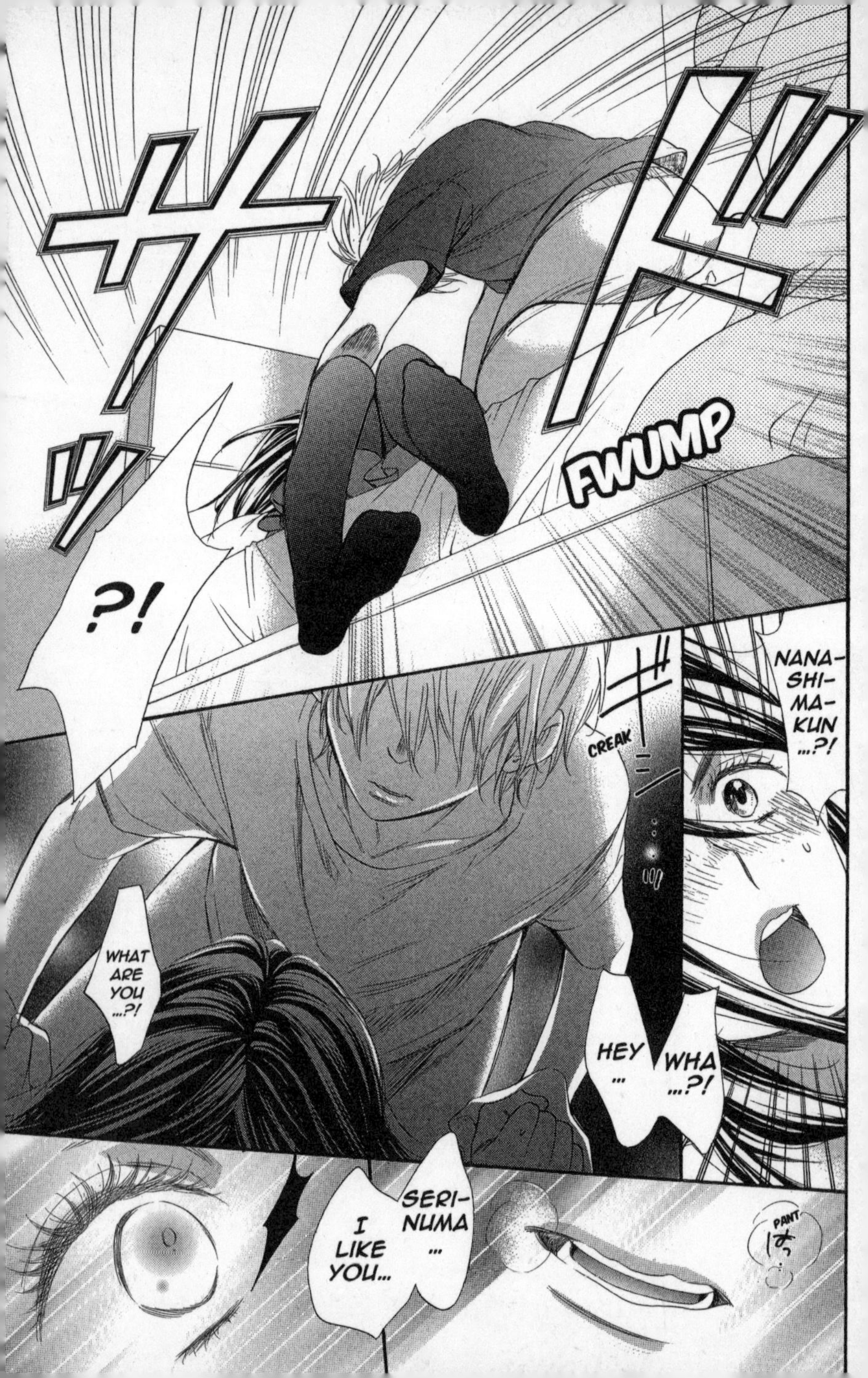
FWUMP
?!
NANA-SHIMA-KUN ...?!
CREAK
WHA ...?!
HEY ...
WHAT ARE YOU ...?!
PANT
SERI-NUMA ...
I LIKE YOU...

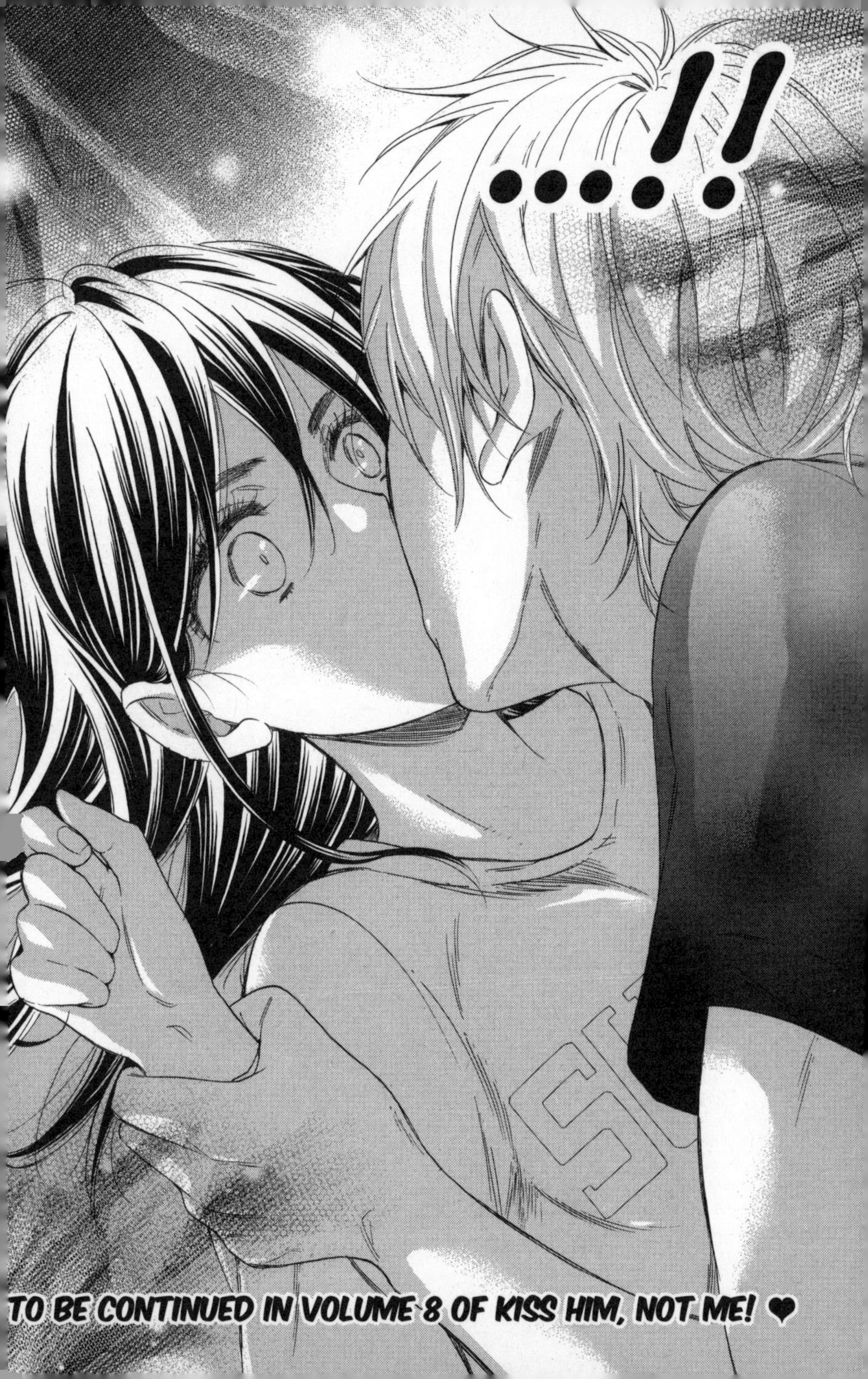
...!!
TO BE CONTINUED IN VOLUME 8 OF KISS HIM, NOT ME! ❤

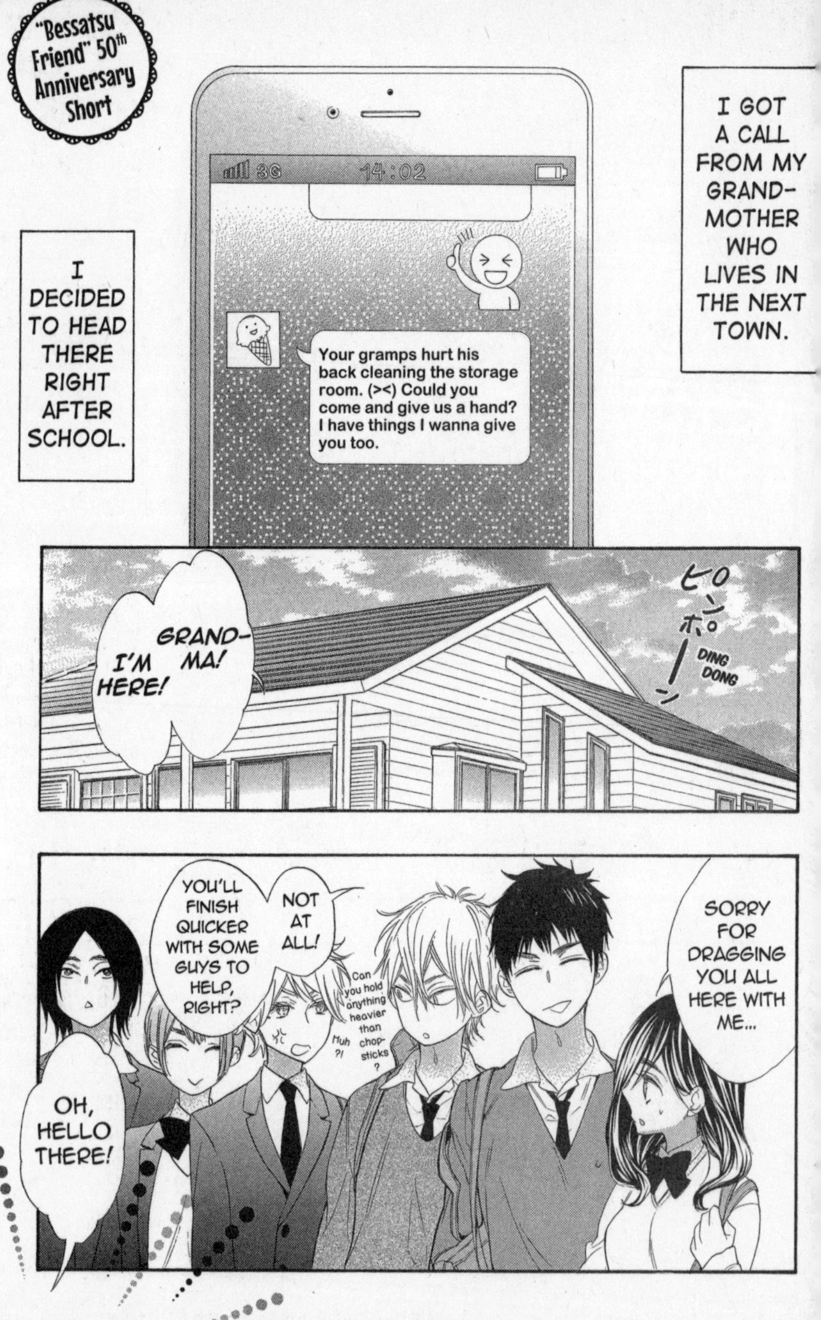
"Bessatsu Friend" 50th Anniversary Short
I GOT A CALL FROM MY GRAND-MOTHER WHO LIVES IN THE NEXT TOWN.
3G 14:02
Your gramps hurt his back cleaning the storage room. (><) Could you come and give us a hand? I have things I wanna give you too.
I DECIDED TO HEAD THERE RIGHT AFTER SCHOOL.
ピンポーン
DING DONG
GRAND-MA! I'M HERE!
SORRY FOR DRAGGING YOU ALL HERE WITH ME...
Can you hold anything heavier than chop-sticks?
Huh ?!
NOT AT ALL!
YOU'LL FINISH QUICKER WITH SOME GUYS TO HELP, RIGHT?
OH, HELLO THERE!

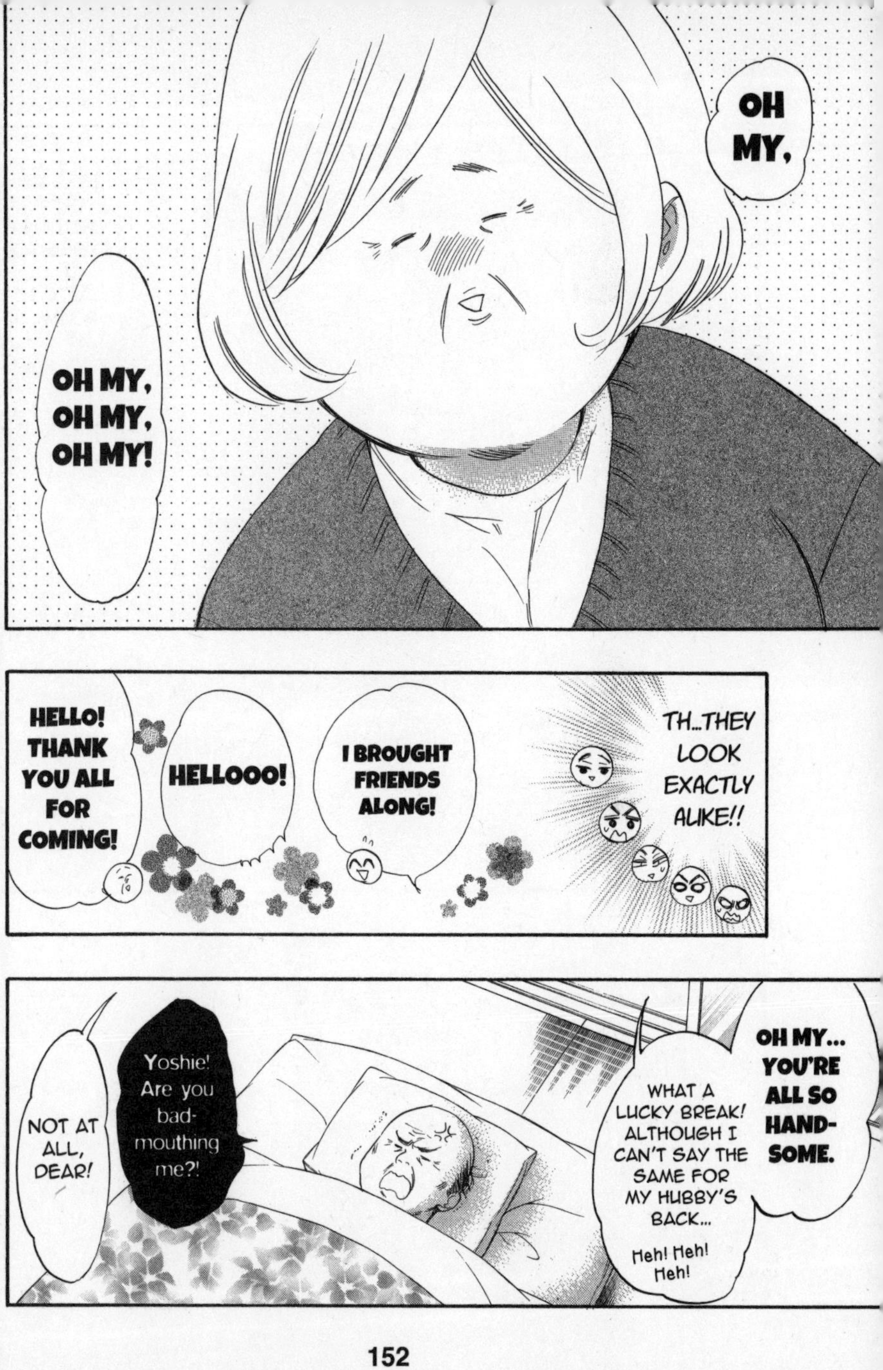
OH MY,
OH MY, OH MY, OH MY!
TH...THEY LOOK EXACTLY ALIKE!!
I BROUGHT FRIENDS ALONG!
HELLOOO!
HELLO! THANK YOU ALL FOR COMING!
OH MY... YOU'RE ALL SO HANDSOME.
WHAT A LUCKY BREAK! ALTHOUGH I CAN'T SAY THE SAME FOR MY HUBBY'S BACK...
Heh! Heh! Heh!
Yoshie! Are you bad-mouthing me?!
NOT AT ALL, DEAR!

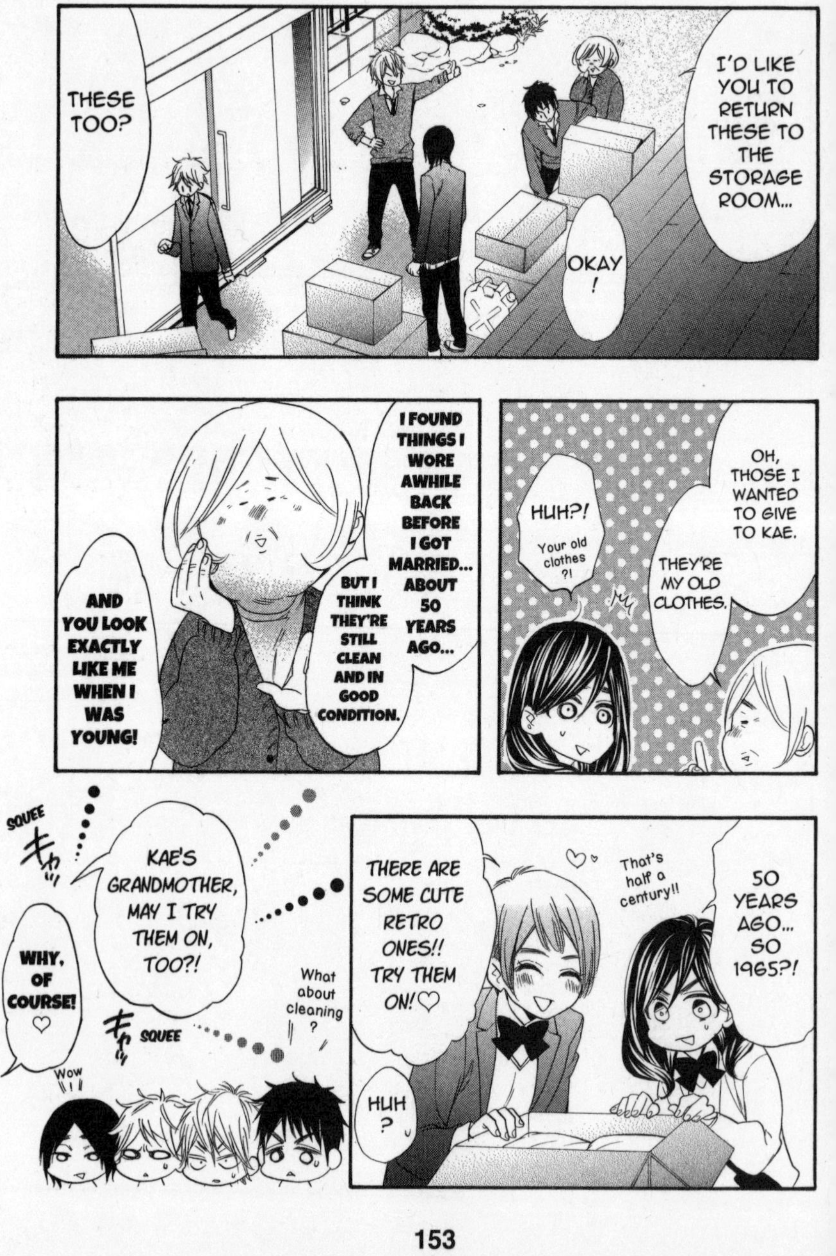
I'D LIKE YOU TO RETURN THESE TO THE STORAGE ROOM...
OKAY!
THESE TOO?
OH, THOSE I WANTED TO GIVE TO KAE.
THEY'RE MY OLD CLOTHES.
HUH?!
Your old clothes ?!
I FOUND THINGS I WORE AWHILE BACK BEFORE I GOT MARRIED... ABOUT 50 YEARS AGO...
BUT I THINK THEY'RE STILL CLEAN AND IN GOOD CONDITION.
AND YOU LOOK EXACTLY LIKE ME WHEN I WAS YOUNG!
50 YEARS AGO... SO 1965?!
That's half a century!!
THERE ARE SOME CUTE RETRO ONES!! TRY THEM ON!♡
HUH?
KAE'S GRANDMOTHER, MAY I TRY THEM ON, TOO?!
SQUEE
SQUEE
WHY, OF COURSE! ♡
What about cleaning?
Wow

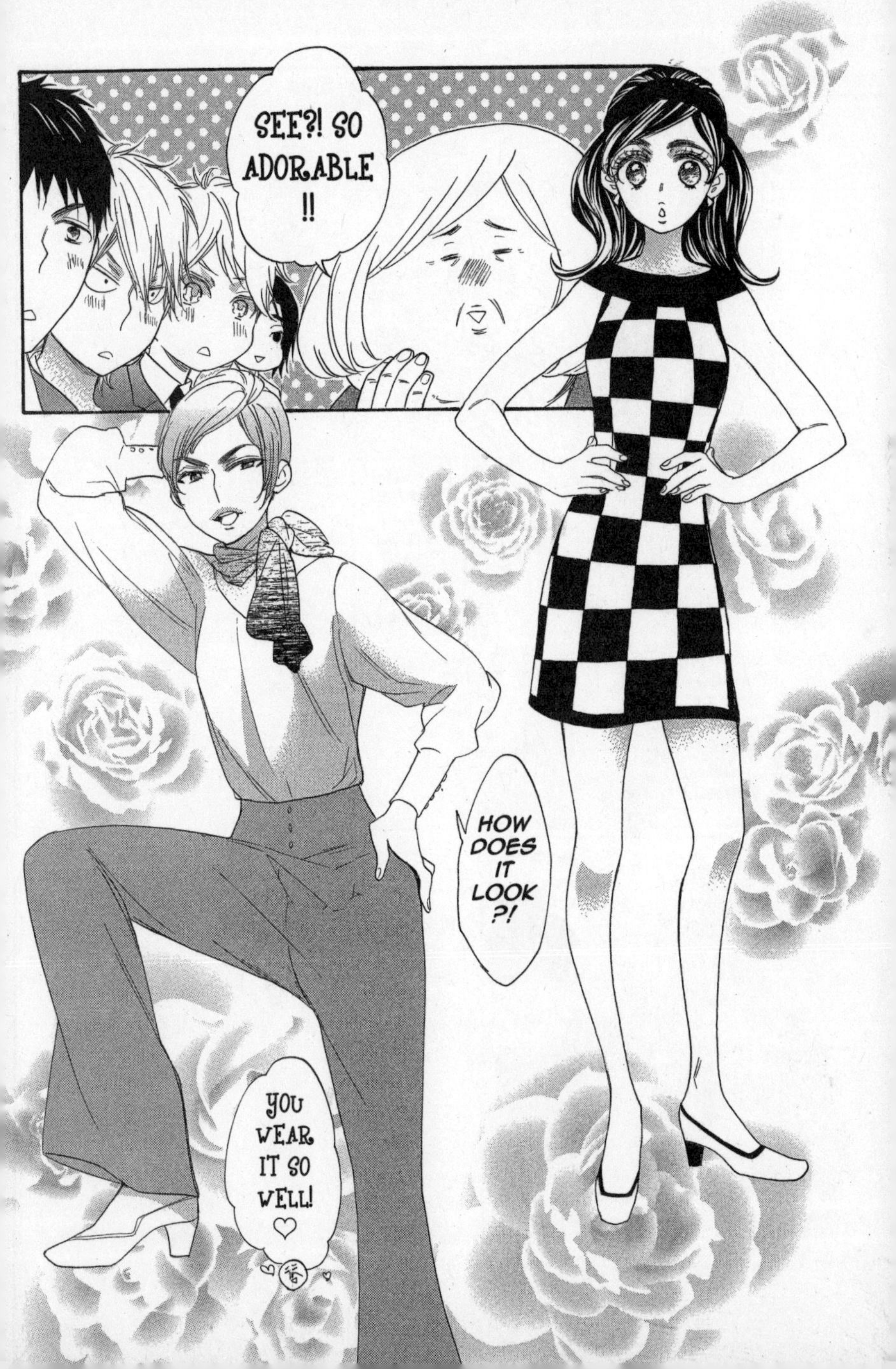
SEE?! SO ADORABLE!!
HOW DOES IT LOOK?!
YOU WEAR IT SO WELL! ♡

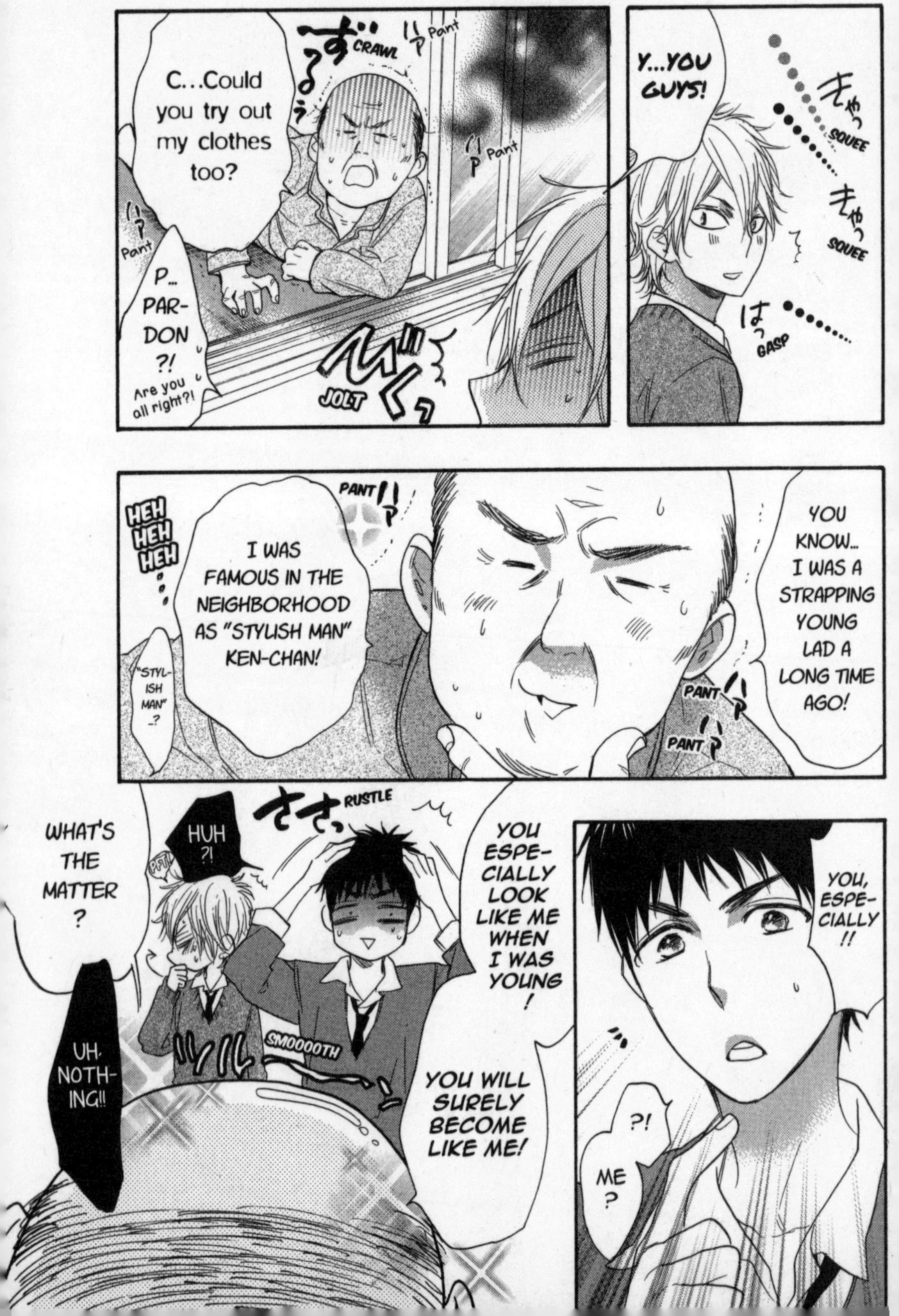
Y...YOU GUYS!
SQUEE
SQUEE
GASP
C...Could you try out my clothes too?
CRAWL
Pant
Pant
Pant
P... PAR-DON ?!
Are you all right?!
JOLT
YOU KNOW... I WAS A STRAPPING YOUNG LAD A LONG TIME AGO!
PANT
PANT
PANT
I WAS FAMOUS IN THE NEIGHBORHOOD AS "STYLISH MAN" KEN-CHAN!
HEH HEH HEH
"STYL-ISH MAN" ..?
YOU, ESPE-CIALLY !!
?!
ME ?
YOU ESPE-CIALLY LOOK LIKE ME WHEN I WAS YOUNG !
YOU WILL SURELY BECOME LIKE ME!
RUSTLE
SMOOOOTH
HUH ?!
WHAT'S THE MATTER ?
UH, NOTHING-ING!!

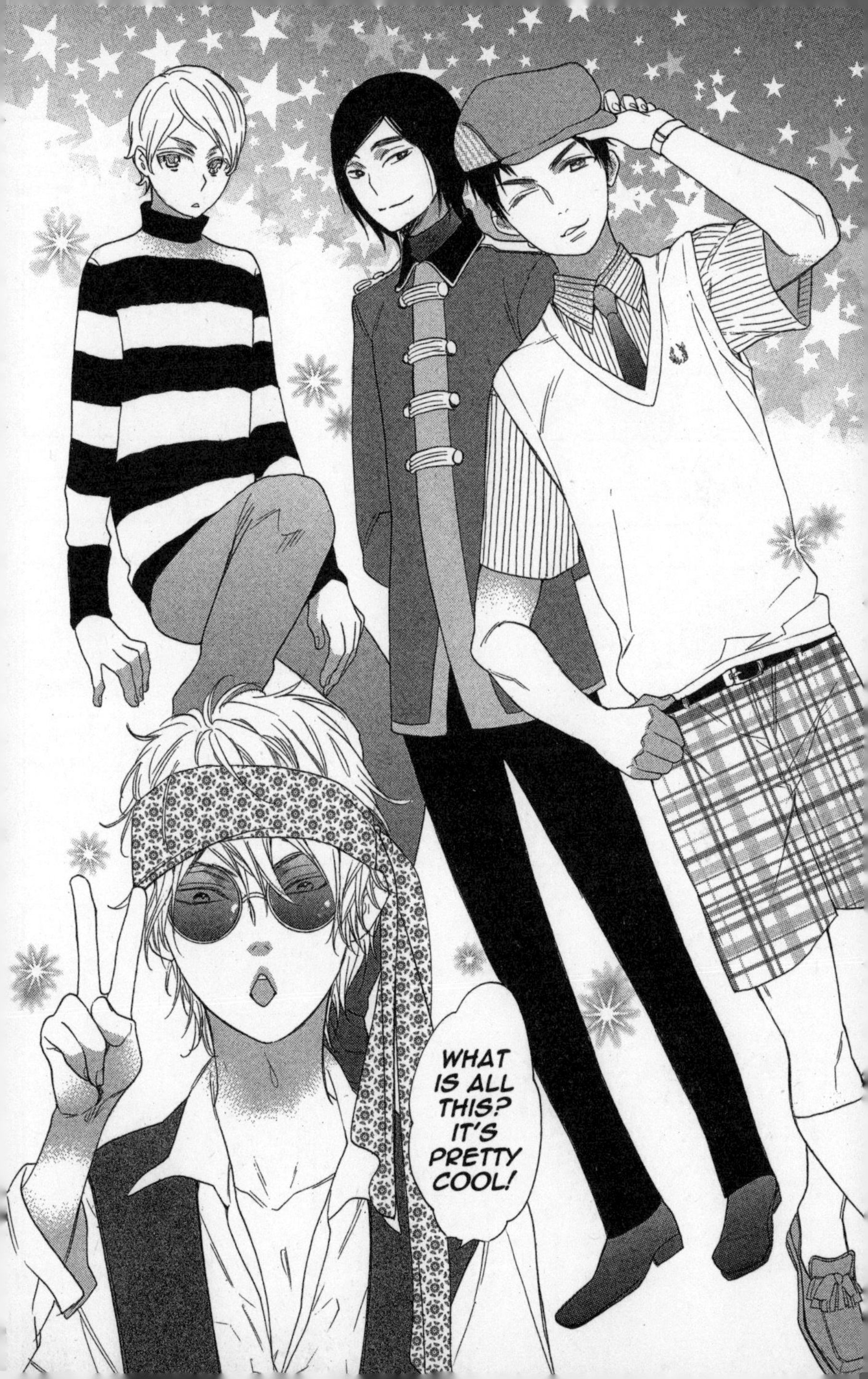
WHAT IS ALL THIS? IT'S PRETTY COOL!

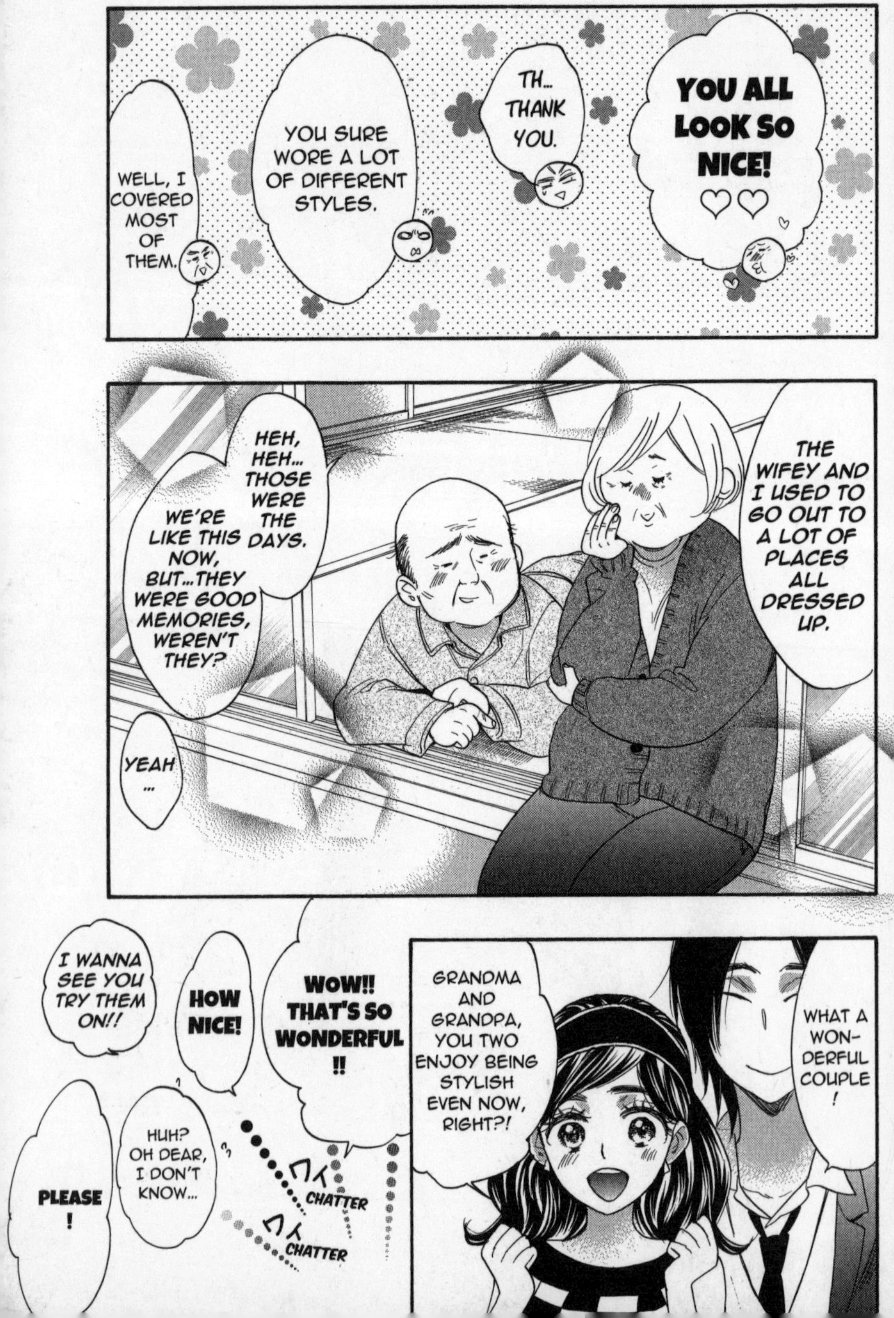
YOU ALL LOOK SO NICE! ♡♡
TH... THANK YOU.
YOU SURE WORE A LOT OF DIFFERENT STYLES.
WELL, I COVERED MOST OF THEM.
THE WIFEY AND I USED TO GO OUT TO A LOT OF PLACES ALL DRESSED UP.
HEH, HEH... THOSE WERE THE DAYS.
WE'RE LIKE THIS NOW, BUT...THEY WERE GOOD MEMORIES, WEREN'T THEY?
YEAH...
WHAT A WON-DERFUL COUPLE!
GRANDMA AND GRANDPA, YOU TWO ENJOY BEING STYLISH EVEN NOW, RIGHT?!
WOW!! THAT'S SO WONDERFUL!!
HOW NICE!
I WANNA SEE YOU TRY THEM ON!!
CHATTER
CHATTER
HUH? OH DEAR, I DON'T KNOW...
PLEASE!

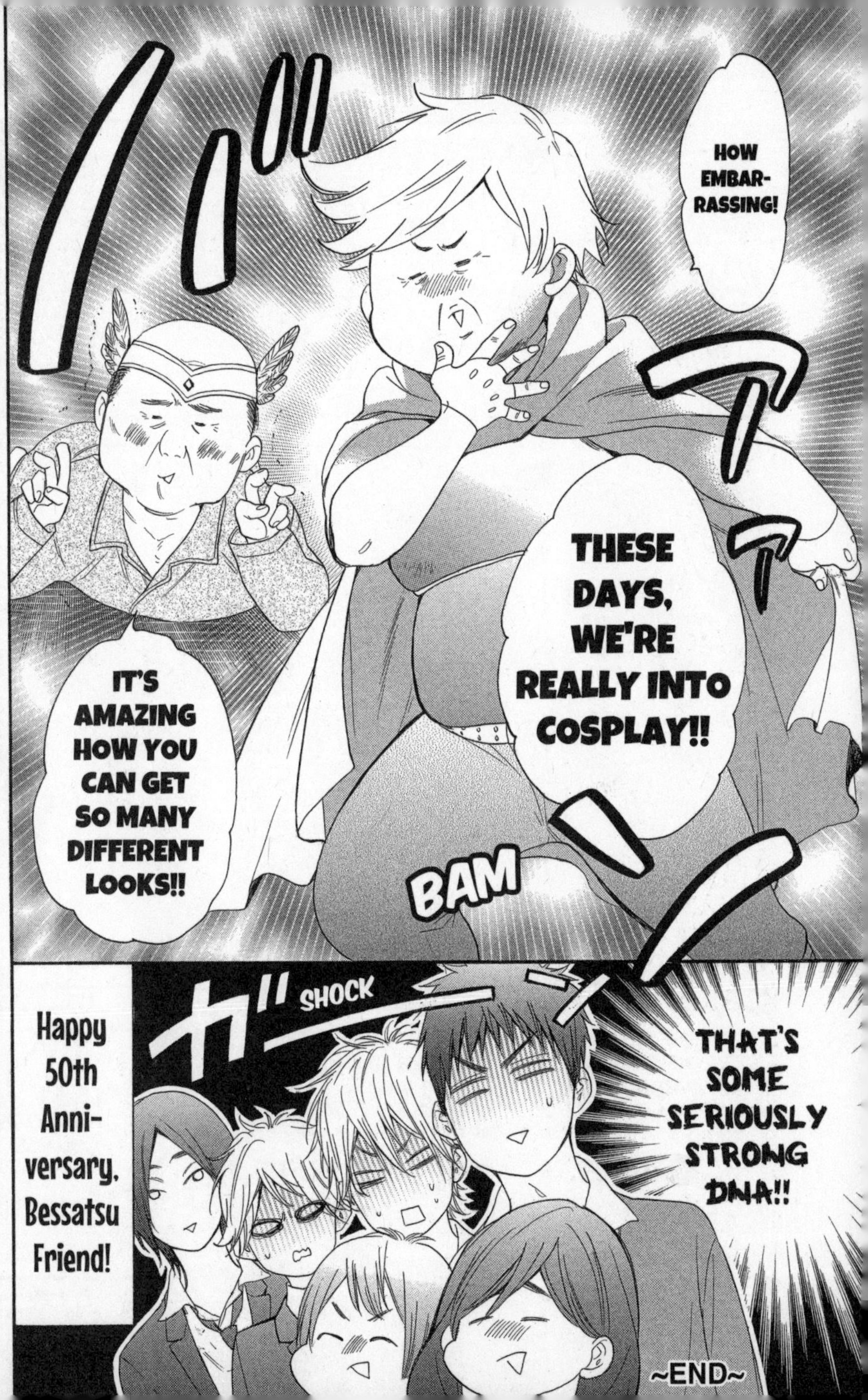
HOW EMBARRASSING!
THESE DAYS, WE'RE REALLY INTO COSPLAY!!
IT'S AMAZING HOW YOU CAN GET SO MANY DIFFERENT LOOKS!!
BAM
THAT'S SOME SERIOUSLY STRONG DNA!!
SHOCK
Happy 50th Anniversary, Bessatsu Friend!
~END~

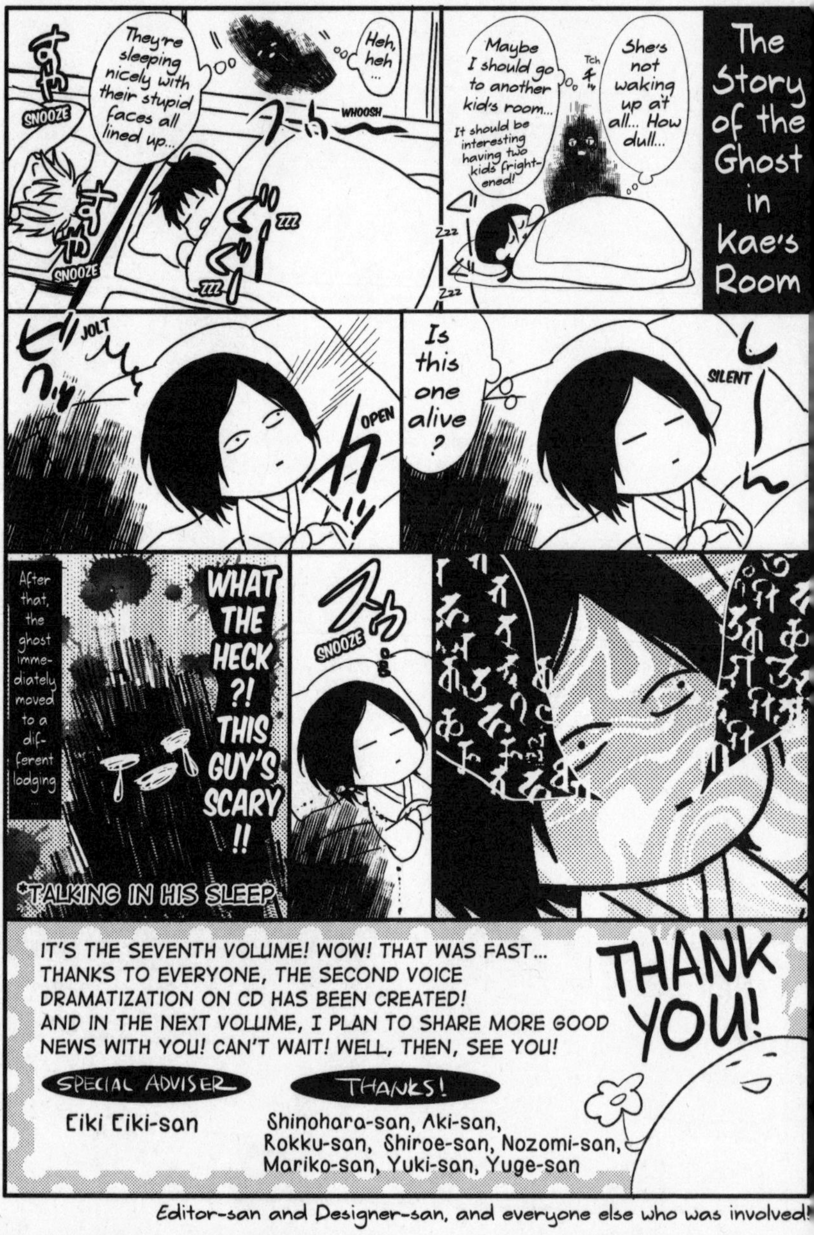
The Story of the Ghost in Kae's Room
She's not waking up at all... How dull...
Tch
Maybe I should go to another kid's room...
It should be interesting having two kids frightened!
Zzz
Zzz
Heh, heh...
WHOOSH
They're sleeping nicely with their stupid faces all lined up...
SNOOZE
zzz
zzz
SNOOZE
SILENT
Is this one alive?
OPEN
JOLT
SNOOZE
WHAT THE HECK?! THIS GUY'S SCARY!!
After that, the ghost immediately moved to a different lodging...
*TALKING IN HIS SLEEP

IT'S THE SEVENTH VOLUME! WOW! THAT WAS FAST... THANKS TO EVERYONE, THE SECOND VOICE DRAMATIZATION ON CD HAS BEEN CREATED! AND IN THE NEXT VOLUME, I PLAN TO SHARE MORE GOOD NEWS WITH YOU! CAN'T WAIT! WELL, THEN, SEE YOU!

THANK YOU!

SPECIAL ADVISER

Eiki Eiki-san

THANKS!

Shinohara-san, Aki-san, Rokku-san, Shiroe-san, Nozomi-san, Mariko-san, Yuki-san, Yuge-san

Editor-san and Designer-san, and everyone else who was involved!

AUTHOR'S NOTE

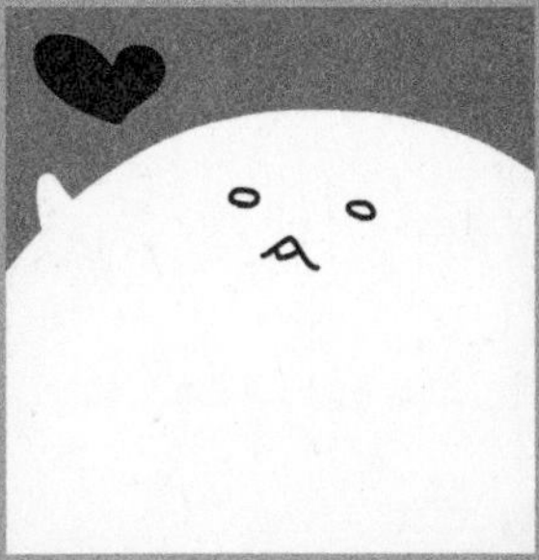

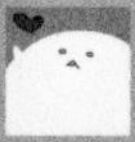

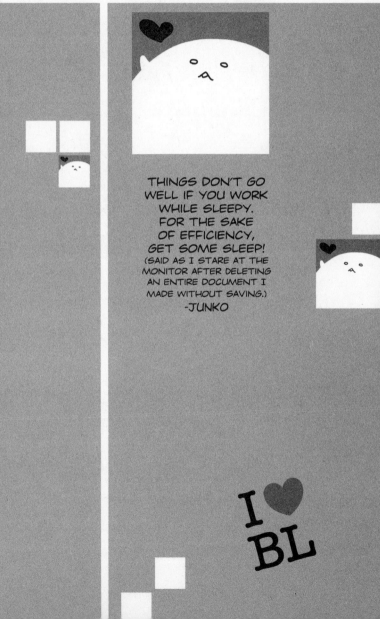

THINGS DON'T GO
WELL IF YOU WORK
WHILE SLEEPY.
FOR THE SAKE
OF EFFICIENCY,
GET SOME SLEEP!
(SAID AS I STARE AT THE
MONITOR AFTER DELETING
AN ENTIRE DOCUMENT I
MADE WITHOUT SAVING.)
-JUNKO

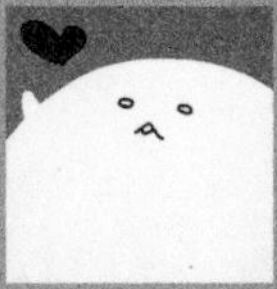

I ♥ BL

Translation Notes

School trips, page 12

In Japan, it's fairly common for students to have a big school trip with classmates in the same year. In many cases, the destinations are to places of cultural and historical significance, like Kyoto and Nara.

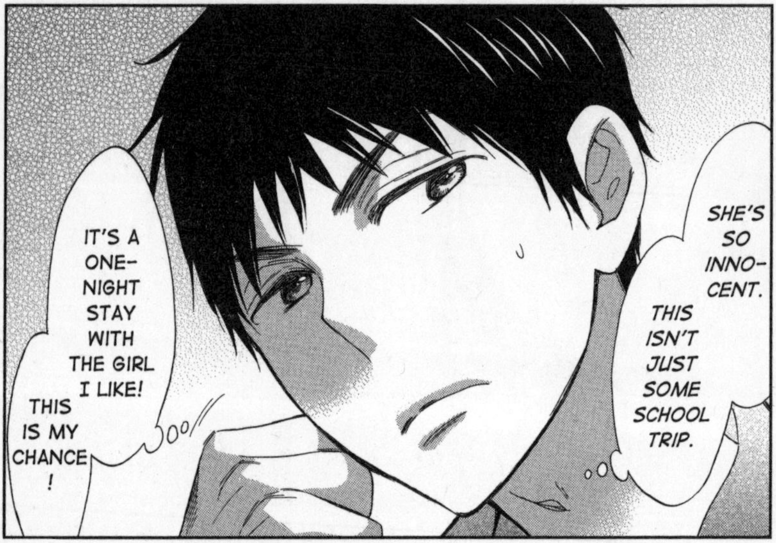
SHE'S SO INNO-CENT.
THIS ISN'T JUST SOME SCHOOL TRIP.
IT'S A ONE-NIGHT STAY WITH THE GIRL I LIKE!
THIS IS MY CHANCE!

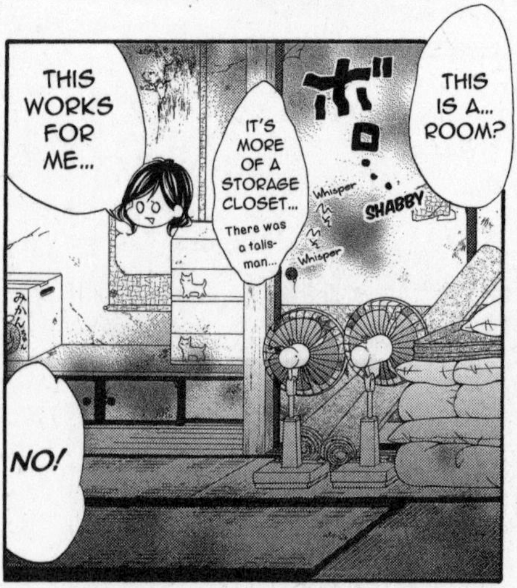
THIS IS A... ROOM?
ボロ
SHABBY
IT'S MORE OF A STORAGE CLOSET...
Whisper
Whisper
There was a talis-man...
THIS WORKS FOR ME...
NO!

There was a talisman, page 17

Someone seems to be indicating that there was a talisman (JP: *ofuda*) posted on the door to this room, which further supports the idea that the room is supposed to be a closet. Though the exact talisman that was posted is not clear, it may be some sort of talisman to ward off evil. Such talismans were typically posted in places where people don't usually pass through, which likely means the "extra room" was not originally meant for habitation.

Shirataki, page 18

Shirataki (lit. white waterfalls) are noodles made from the konjac or devil's tongue yam (JP: *konnyaku*). They typically have more in the way of texture (slightly rubbery) than flavor and can often be found in clay-pot dishes (*donabe*), cooked with a mix of meat and vegetables in soup stock.

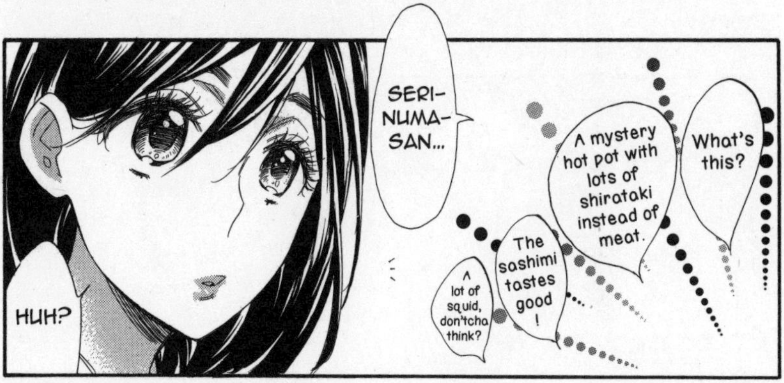
What's this?
A mystery hot pot with lots of shirataki instead of meat.
The sashimi tastes good!
A lot of squid, don'tcha think?
SERI-NUMA-SAN...
HUH?

Bath etiquette, page 21

Nanashima is breaking two cardinal rules for bathing in Japanese hot springs and communal baths: not washing with hot water beforehand, and jumping into the bath. The typical process for entering a communal bath is to first wash yourself (JP: *kakeyu*) and then to slowly ease into the bath. Doing otherwise might get your fellow bathers angry and annoyed.

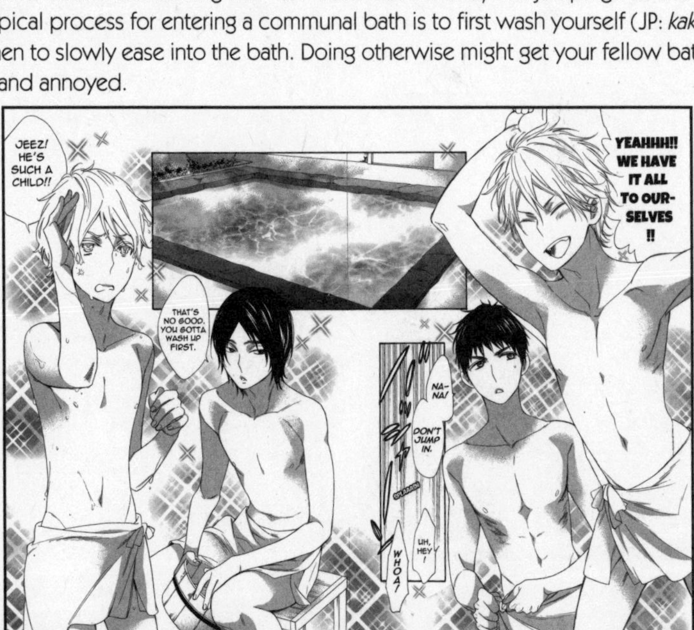
YEAHHH!! WE HAVE IT ALL TO OUR-SELVES!!
NANA!
DON'T JUMP IN.
UH, HEY!
WHOA!
THAT'S NO GOOD. YOU GOTTA WASH UP FIRST.
JEEZ! HE'S SUCH A CHILD!!

Shishi-odoshi (ka-plunk), page 22

A *shishi-odoshi* (literally "deer scarer") is a contraption that uses sound to scare off wildlife that would otherwise eat or damage one's crops. A famous type of shishi-odoshi that has become synonymous with Japanese gardens is one in which a bamboo tube fills with water until pushed beyond the center of gravity of its pivot, causing the tube to hit a rock or other hard object to produce a distinct "ka-pon" sound (ka-plunk in this translation).

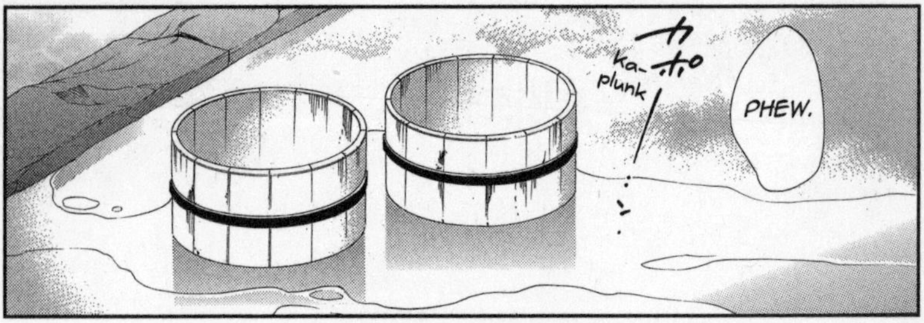
ka-plunk
PHEW.

Pwaaa, page 44

This is the sound of a very specific Japanese instrument called the *hichiriki*. The *hichiriki* is a double-reed flute used in Japanese classical music, and it emits a high-pitched, almost siren-like sound when played. Outside of a particular style of classical music (*gagaku*), the hichiriki can also be heard at Shinto ceremonies such as Shinto-style weddings, and in the case of *Kiss Him, Not Me*, a memorial service for the repose of a soul.

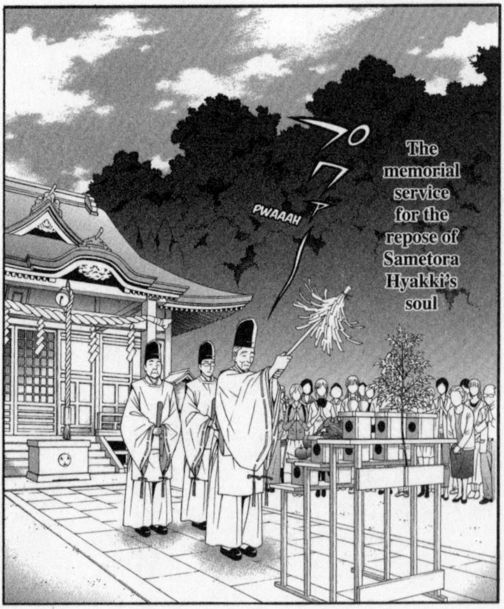
The memorial service for the repose of Sametora Hyakki's soul
PWAAAH

NHK period dramas, page 45

Japanese television network, NHK (similar to the American PBS), is well known for its long-running series of period dramas called *Taiga Dorama*. Different series have been running on the network at 8 p.m. on Sunday since 1963. The series change each year, but since they are period dramas, most of them take place in one of the eras of classical Japanese history, such as the Heian, Sengoku, or Edo periods.

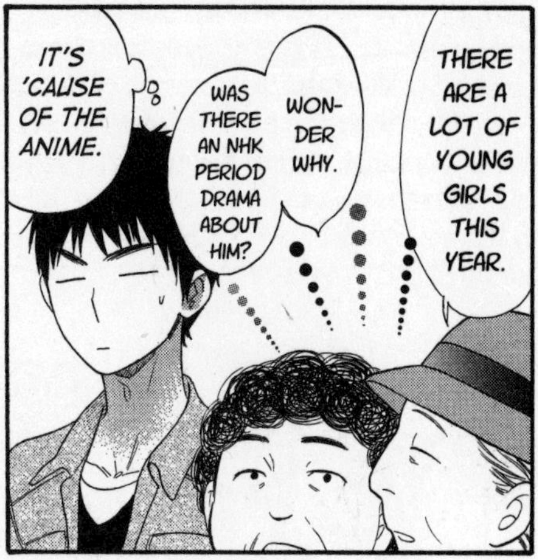
THERE ARE A LOT OF YOUNG GIRLS THIS YEAR.
WON-DER WHY.
WAS THERE AN NHK PERIOD DRAMA ABOUT HIM?
IT'S 'CAUSE OF THE ANIME.

Ema, page 46

Ema are pentagonal wooden plaques that are most often found and sold at Shinto shrines. Shinto worshippers write their wishes on these plaques so that they may be received by the gods. Originally, horses were given to shrines to evoke good favor, but this practice eventually changed to wooden plaques with drawings of horses on them, which is where the name *ema* (literally a combination of the kanji for "picture" and "horse") came from.

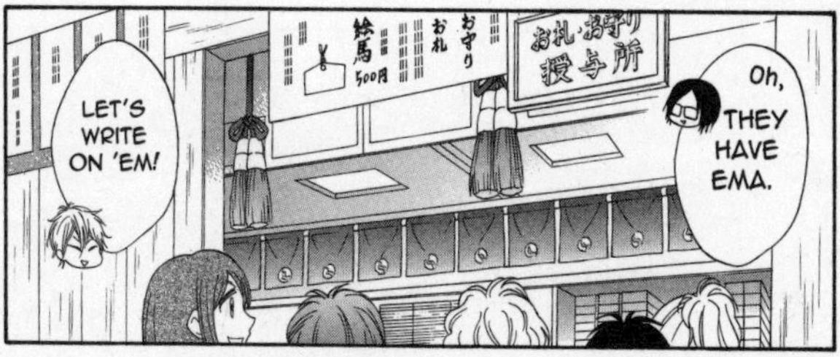
お札・お守り授与所
おまもり
お札
絵馬 500円
Oh, THEY HAVE EMA.
LET'S WRITE ON 'EM!

Placard = I want a PS4. —Nozumu Nanashima

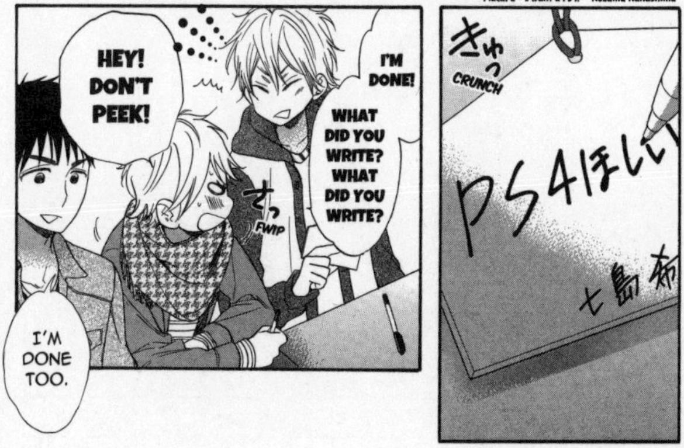
きゅっ
CRUNCH
PS4ほしい
I'M DONE!
WHAT DID YOU WRITE? WHAT DID YOU WRITE?
HEY! DON'T PEEK!
すっ
FWIP
I'M DONE TOO.

Cringeworthy, page 49

Shinomiya is actually calling the *ema* "*ita-ema.*" The "*ita*" here comes from the word for pain/painful ("*itai*") and it refers to a particular type of cringeworthy that comes from plastering manga and anime drawings all over an object. The *ita-* prefix is mostly used for *ita-sha*, which are cars that have been covered in garish anime/manga-based art by their otaku owners. However, the prefix has gone on to be used for other items, including *ita-baggu* (otaku-decorated bags) and even *ita-suutsu* (suits with anime/manga on the lining of the jacket).

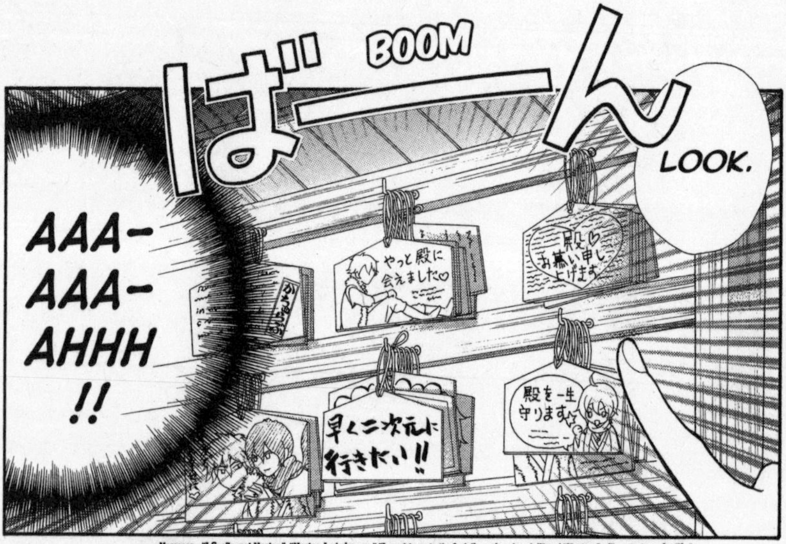
LOOK.
ばーん
BOOM
殿♡お慕い申し上げます
やっと殿に会えました♡
殿を一生守ります☆
早く二次元に行きたい!!
AAA-AAA-AHHH!!

Messages = "I finally met Master," "Master, I admire you," "I want to go to the 2nd dimension already!!" and "Master, I will protect you for life."

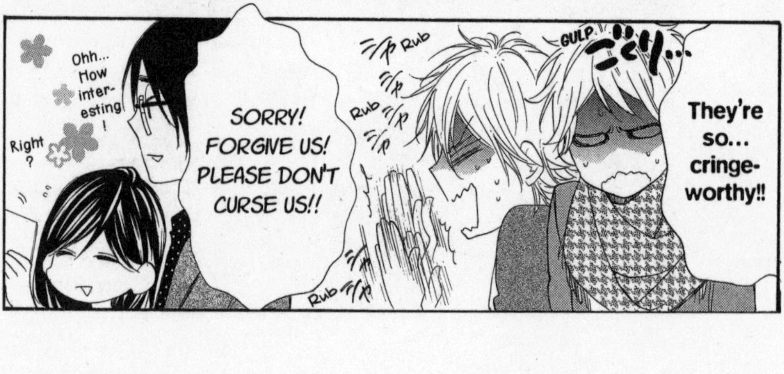
ごくり…
GULP
They're so... cringe-worthy!!
Rub
Rub
Rub
SORRY! FORGIVE US! PLEASE DON'T CURSE US!!
Ohh... How inter-esting!
Right?

Akane/vermillion, page 50

In Japanese, there can be dozens of readings for a single Chinese character, especially when it comes to names. The word for the color vermillion (*aka*, *ake*, or *shu*), can also be read as the name Akane. And because Akane is the personification of the Master's vermillion-lacquered armor, it's only natural that his name would turn out this way.

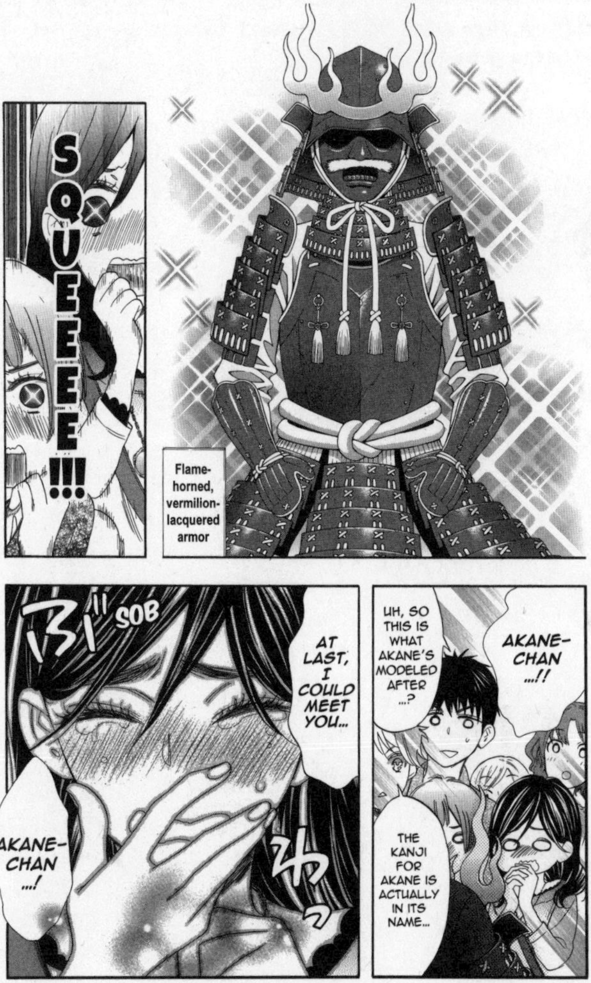
Flame-horned, vermilion-lacquered armor
SQUEEEE!!!
AKANE-CHAN ...!!
UH, SO THIS IS WHAT AKANE'S MODELED AFTER ...?
THE KANJI FOR AKANE IS ACTUALLY IN ITS NAME...
AT LAST, I COULD MEET YOU...
SOB
AKANE-CHAN ...!

I'm tired, Patrasche, page 54

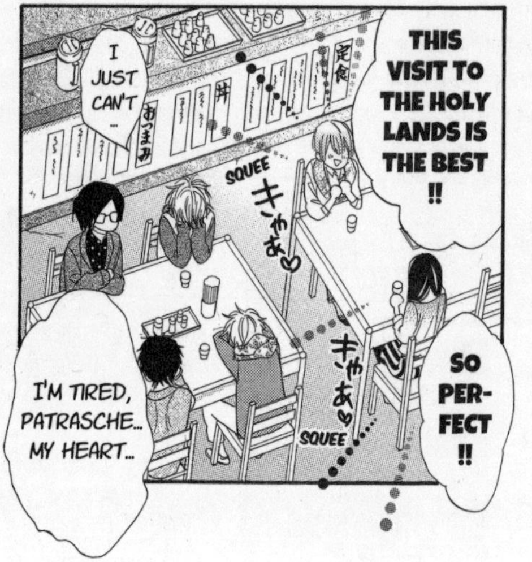
THIS VISIT TO THE HOLY LANDS IS THE BEST !!
I JUST CAN'T ...
SQUEE
SO PER-FECT !!
SQUEE
I'M TIRED, PATRASCHE... MY HEART...

This line comes from the 1975 Japanese animated tv series, A Dog of Flanders (JP: *Furandaasu no Inu*), which is based on the novel by Ouida. The series follows the tragic life of a boy named Nello and his dog Patrasche in Antwerp, Belgium. The famous line being used here in *Kiss Him, Not Me*, is from one of the last scenes of the series, where Nello and Patrasche go to see the artist Rubens' *The Elevation of the Cross* at Antwerp Cathedral. Unable to afford entry to view the exhibit, they are able to sneak in on the night of Christmas Eve, but exhausted and cold, Nello and Patrasche start to rest on the floor and Nello says his famous line before eventually freezing to death.

This series and that last line is well-known in Japan, and those words have since transformed to be used in a situation when someone wants to give up. In *Kiss Him, Not Me*, Nanashima is so tired and exhausted from the trip that he says this famous line.

Balls of fire, page 104

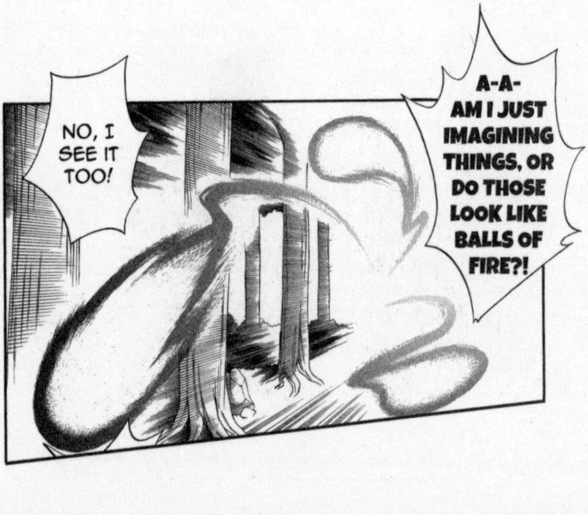
A-A-AM I JUST IMAGINING THINGS, OR DO THOSE LOOK LIKE BALLS OF FIRE?!
NO, I SEE IT TOO!

In Japanese ghost stories, disembodied spirits are often represented as balls of fire. In this case, they were literally called balls of fire, but *hitodama* (literally human souls) are essentially the same thing, though they are often depicted as blue balls of fire that appear at night.

Kuji, page 107

The nine-character incantation that Kae uses here is known as *kuji* (literally nine syllables/characters). This specific *kuji* originates from a Taoist text, and from the original Chinese, translates to "may all those who preside over warriors be my vanguard." Each syllable also comes with a specific mudra (hand posture) and the one Kae is doing is for the eigth syllable, *zai*. In Japan, kuji can be associated with a particular style of esoteric cosmology called *onmyoudo* and their practitioners, who often act as exorcists, called *onmyoji*. *Onmyoji* have been popular in anime/manga in recent years, so this and other related customs are likely to be familiar to otaku.

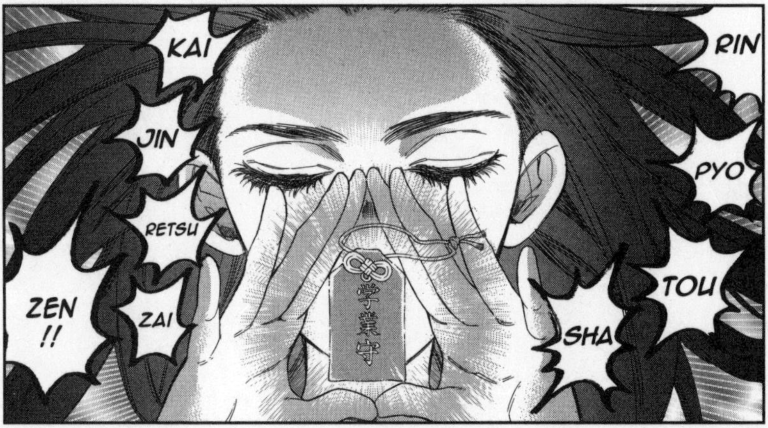
RIN
PYO
TOU
SHA
KAI
JIN
RETSU
ZAI
ZEN !!

Seimei-sama, page 107

Abe no Seimei (921-1005) is perhaps one of the most famous *onmyoji* in Japanese history and folklore. He is usually depicted as a wise, old man in priestly garb. However, in more recent media, he is often portrayed as a handsome man, which is another reason why he is popular with fujoshi like Kae.

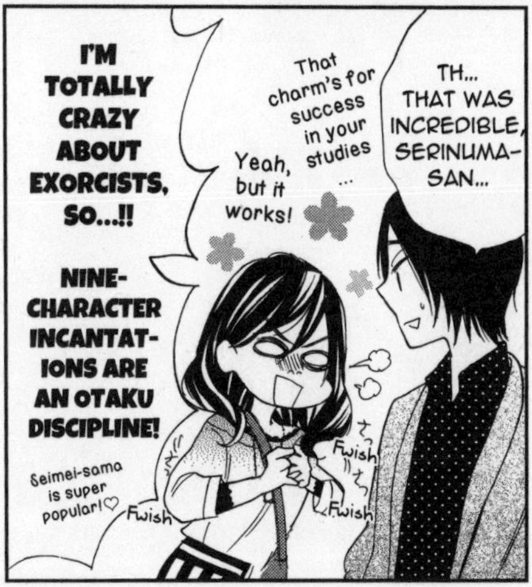
TH... THAT WAS INCREDIBLE, SERINUMA-SAN...
That charm's for success in your studies ...
Yeah, but it works!
I'M TOTALLY CRAZY ABOUT EXORCISTS, SO...!!
NINE-CHARACTER INCANTAT-IONS ARE AN OTAKU DISCIPLINE!
Fwish
Fwish
Seimei-sama is super popular!♡
Fwish

The Land of Peach Blossoms, page 113

The old man here is actually referring to Tougenkyo, the mythical land from the Chinese fable Táohua Yuán (EN: Record of the Source of the Peach Blossoms). Tougenkyo is sometimes translated as Paradise or Shangri-La and has similarities to the latter as a hidden utopia.

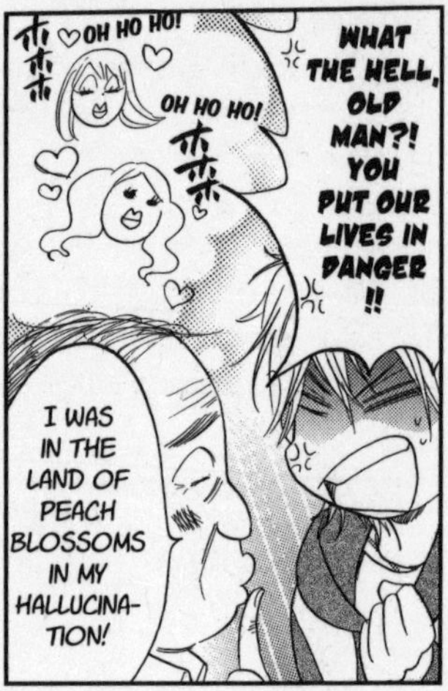
WHAT THE HELL, OLD MAN?! YOU PUT OUR LIVES IN DANGER !!
OH HO HO!
OH HO HO!
I WAS IN THE LAND OF PEACH BLOSSOMS IN MY HALLUCINATION!

My Little Monster

OPPOSITES ATTRACT...MAYBE?

Haru Yoshida is feared as an unstable and violent "monster." Mizutani Shizuku is a grade-obsessed student with no friends. Fate brings these two together to form the most unlikely pair. Haru firmly believes he's in love with Mizutani and she firmly believes he's insane.

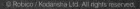

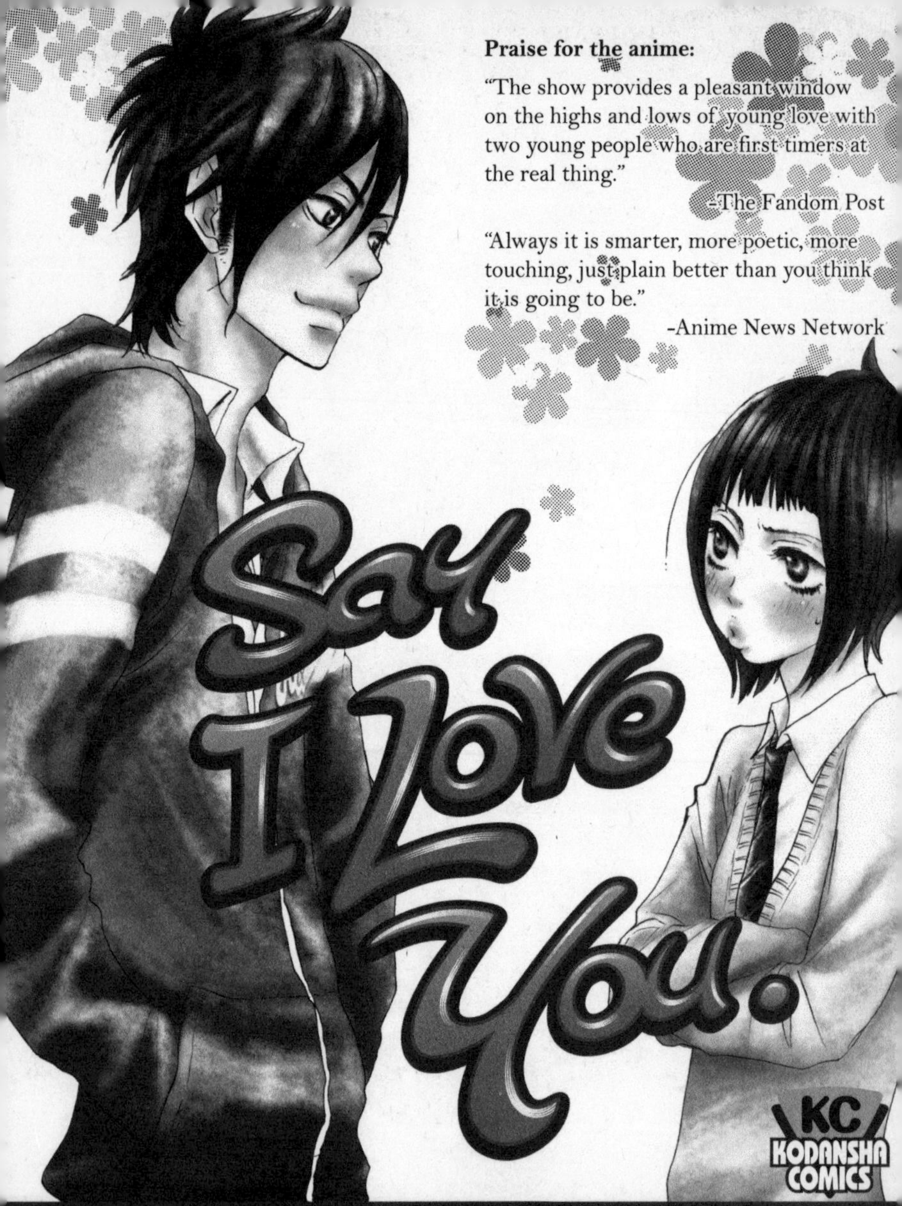

SAY I LOVE YOU.

KC
KODANSHA
COMICS

Mei Tachibana has no friends — and says she doesn't need them!

But everything changes when she accidentally roundhouse kicks the most popular boy in school! However, Yamato Kurosawa isn't angry in the slightest— in fact, he thinks his ordinary life could use an unusual girl like Mei. But winning Mei's trust will be a tough task. How long will she refuse to say, "I love you"?

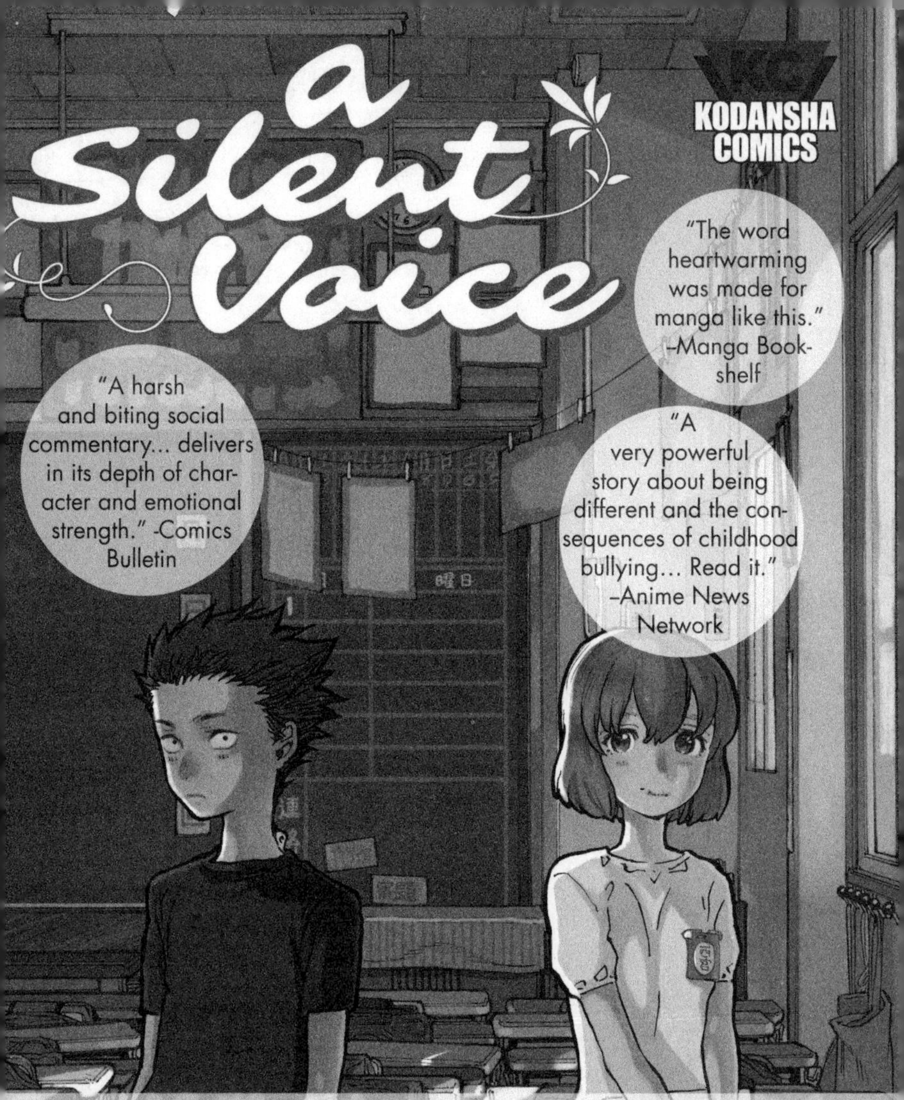

a Silent Voice

KC KODANSHA COMICS

"The word heartwarming was made for manga like this." –Manga Bookshelf

"A harsh and biting social commentary... delivers in its depth of character and emotional strength." -Comics Bulletin

"A very powerful story about being different and the consequences of childhood bullying... Read it." –Anime News Network

Shoya is a bully. When Shoko, a girl who can't hear, enters his elementary school class, she becomes their favorite target, and Shoya and his friends goad each other into devising new tortures for her. But the children's cruelty goes too far. Shoko is forced to leave the school, and Shoya ends up shouldering all the blame. Six years later, the two meet again. Can Shoya make up for his past mistakes, or is it too late?

Available now in print and digitally!

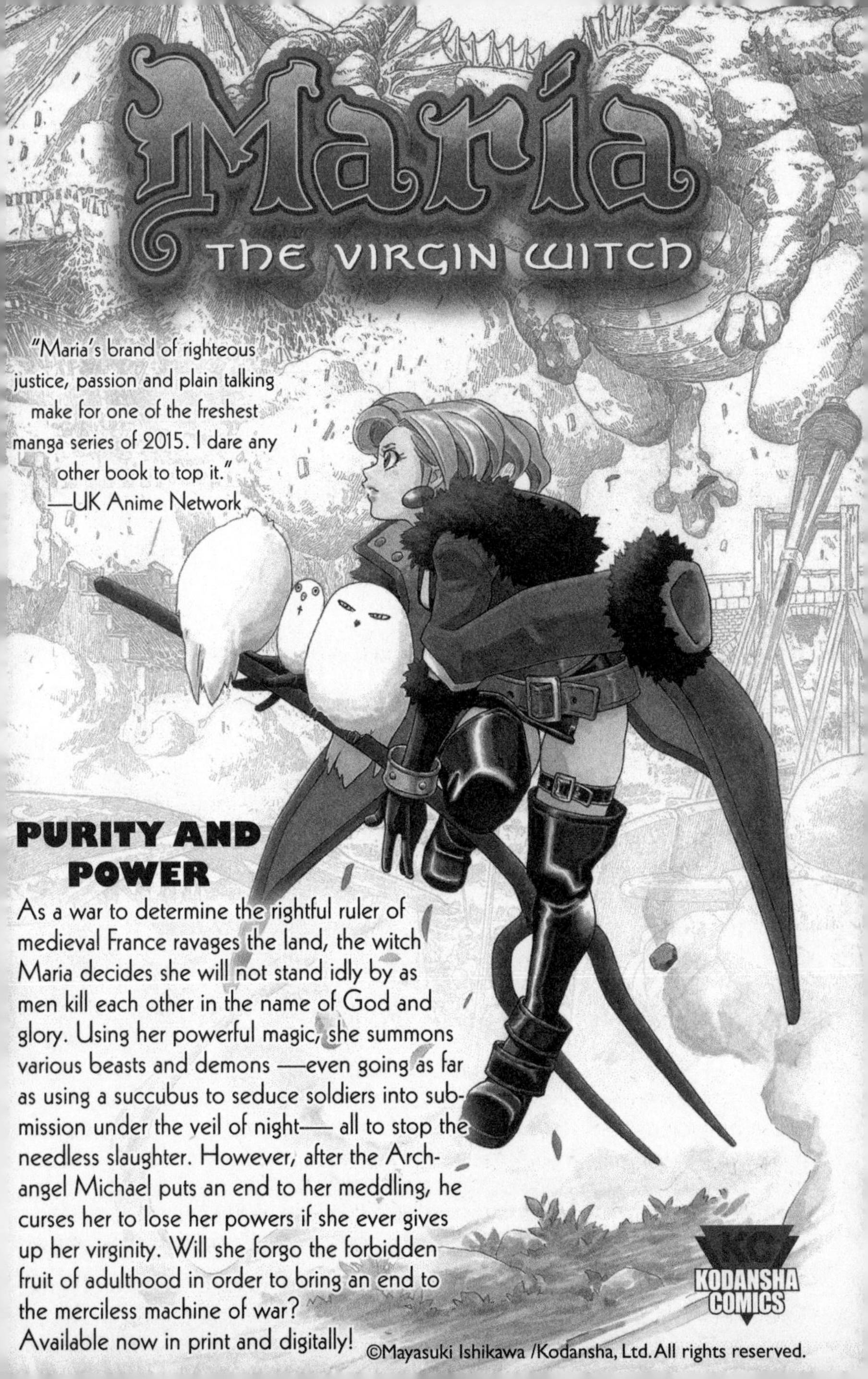
Maria
THE VIRGIN WITCH
"Maria's brand of righteous justice, passion and plain talking make for one of the freshest manga series of 2015. I dare any other book to top it."
—UK Anime Network
PURITY AND POWER
As a war to determine the rightful ruler of medieval France ravages the land, the witch Maria decides she will not stand idly by as men kill each other in the name of God and glory. Using her powerful magic, she summons various beasts and demons —even going as far as using a succubus to seduce soldiers into submission under the veil of night— all to stop the needless slaughter. However, after the Archangel Michael puts an end to her meddling, he curses her to lose her powers if she ever gives up her virginity. Will she forgo the forbidden fruit of adulthood in order to bring an end to the merciless machine of war?
Available now in print and digitally!
KODANSHA COMICS
©Mayasuki Ishikawa /Kodansha, Ltd. All rights reserved.

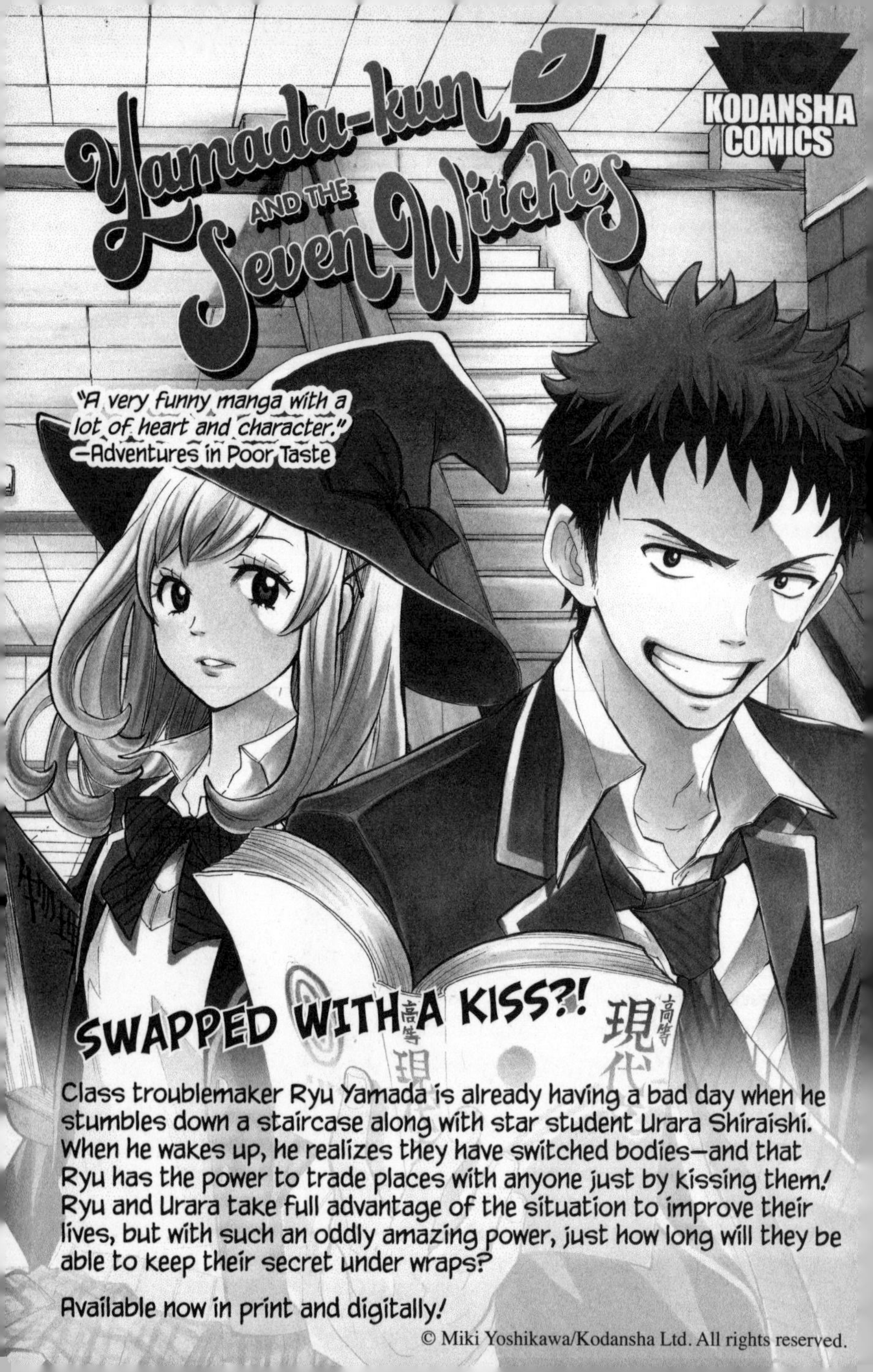
KODANSHA COMICS
Yamada-kun AND THE Seven Witches
"A very funny manga with a lot of heart and character."
—Adventures in Poor Taste
SWAPPED WITH A KISS?!
Class troublemaker Ryu Yamada is already having a bad day when he stumbles down a staircase along with star student Urara Shiraishi. When he wakes up, he realizes they have switched bodies—and that Ryu has the power to trade places with anyone just by kissing them! Ryu and Urara take full advantage of the situation to improve their lives, but with such an oddly amazing power, just how long will they be able to keep their secret under wraps?
Available now in print and digitally!
© Miki Yoshikawa/Kodansha Ltd. All rights reserved.

Kiss Him, Not Me volume 7 is a work of fiction. Names, characters, places, and incidents are the products of the author's imagination or are used fictitiously. Any resemblance to actual events, locales, or persons, living or dead, is entirely coincidental.

A Kodansha Comics Trade Paperback Original.

Kiss Him, Not Me volume 7 copyright © 2015 Junko
English translation copyright © 2016 Junko

Published in the United States by Kodansha Comics,
an imprint of Kodansha USA Publishing, LLC, New York.

Publication rights for this English edition arranged through Kodansha Ltd.,
Tokyo.

First published in Japan in 2015 by Kodansha Ltd., Tokyo, as *Watashi Ga Motete Dousunda* volume 7.

ISBN 978-1-63236-298-8

Printed in the United States of America.

www.kodanshacomics.com

9 8 7 6 5 4 3 2 1

Translation: David Rhie
Lettering: Hiroko Mizuno
Editing: Ajani Oloye
Kodansha Comics edition cover design: Phil Balsman